Helicopter Heroine

Helicopter Heroine

Valérie André—Surgeon, Pioneer Rescue Pilot,
and Her Courage Under Fire

Charles Morgan Evans

STACKPOLE
BOOKS

Essex, Connecticut
Blue Ridge Summit, Pennsylvania

STACKPOLE BOOKS

An imprint of Globe Pequot, the trade division of The Rowman & Littlefield
Publishing Group, Inc.
4501 Forbes Blvd., Ste. 200
Lanham, MD 20706
www.rowman.com

Distributed by NATIONAL BOOK NETWORK

British Library Cataloguing in Publication Information available

Library of Congress Cataloging-in-Publication Data

Names: Evans, Charles M., 1963– author.
Title: Helicopter heroine : Valérie André—surgeon, pioneer rescue pilot, and her courage
   under fire / Charles Morgan Evans.
Other titles: Valérie André—surgeon, pioneer rescue pilot, and her courage under fire.
Description: Essex, Connecticut : Stackpole Books, [2022] | Includes bibliographical
   references and index.
Identifiers: LCCN 2022029246 (print) | LCCN 2022029247 (ebook) |
   ISBN 9780811771924 (cloth) | ISBN 9780811771979 (ebook)
Subjects: LCSH: André, Valérie, 1922– | France. Armée de l'air—Biography. | France.
   Armée de l'air—Transport of sick and wounded. | Indochinese War, 1946–1954—
   Medical care—France. | Air pilots—France—Biography. | Women air pilots—
   France—Biography. | Physicians—France—Biography. | Generals—France—
   Biography. | Women generals—France—Biography.
Classification: LCC UH347.A53 E93 2022 (print) | LCC UH347.A53 (ebook) |
   DDC 355.345092 [B]—dc23/eng/20220622
LC record available at https://lccn.loc.gov/2022029246
LC ebook record available at https://lccn.loc.gov/2022029247

♾™ The paper used in this publication meets the minimum requirements of American
National Standard for Information Sciences—Permanence of Paper for Printed Library
Materials, ANSI/NISO Z39.48-1992.

Contents

Acknowledgments

This book is the culmination of a long journey that started when I was the curator of the Hiller Aircraft Museum in California. It was there where I first learned of Valérie André's story from photos in the museum's collection. I studied the photos of the woman with the helicopter and wondered who she was. My curiosity eventually led me to France, where I met this remarkable woman who I came to admire very much.

Many kind people helped me along this journey. I am forever indebted to General Michel Fleurence and his wife Giselle Giovanngélli Fleurence. General Fleurence wrote the exhaustively researched three volumes of *Rotors dans le ciel d'Indochine*, and I was able to find technical information that allowed me to better understand and write about helicopter rescue operations in Vietnam during the Indochina conflict.

I also thank Catherine Maunoury, president of the Aeroclub de France and former director of the National Air and Space Museum of France. Her friendship and support made it possible for me to get to the finish line.

Likewise, my thanks go out to Antoine Santini, son of Colonel Alexis Santini, who also encouraged me along the way.

My thanks also to the late Marcel Poirée, Hiller enthusiast who carried out the restoration of the Hiller H-23B on display at the National Air and Space Museum of France. Laurent Rabier, the manager of aircraft and aircraft fabrics at the National Air and Space Museum of France, was also instrumental in providing help and support for this project.

I am also very grateful to the Association hélicoptères air and Patrick Marbach, president, and Gérard Finaltéri, *conseiller* (adviser), for allowing me to use photos from the Robert Genay collection. Genay was a veteran of the Indochina war and served as a helicopter mechanic, who captured some incredible moments with his camera.

Other people I would like to acknowledge are Marie Yvonne Bartier, widow of Commander Henri Bartier, and her granddaughter Anne-Gaelle Breton; Daphne Desrosiers, author and pilot; and journalist Florent Bonnefoi for their help in completing this book.

My family also played a large role in supporting me in what sometimes seemed like an endless quest. I thank my brother, Casey James Evans, and my mother, Clara Stagi Evans, for their help and support of this project and for also for taking care of my dogs, Bobby, Chikali, and Fred, while I was away on numerous trips to France and Vietnam while researching this work.

I also thank my friend Nguyen Thibach Cuc, who allowed me to stay with her family in Vietnam during that phase of my research.

I also need to express my thanks to several people who read chapters from my book as they were completed, and lent their experience and expertise to my work: Gina Louise Freeman, for her unwavering friendship and professional help in editing this book for submission; Lt. Colonel Sam Dehne, U.S. Air Force, Air Force Academy graduate, and veteran bomber and reconnaissance pilot during the Vietnam War era; Colonel Terry Rowe, U.S. Army, and veteran of three tours of duty in Vietnam during the Vietnam War, serving as an advisor/officer with a ARVN batallion and as District Senior Advisor; and Nancy Syrett, editor and researcher at Stackpole Books, for her invaluable help in the final edit of this work.

I would also like to thank my agent Rita Rosenkranz, along with Dave Reisch, Stephanie Otto, and Hannah Fisher at Stackpole Books, for their patience in allowing me to see this project through to its completion.

But I reserve my greatest thanks to Général Valérie André, whose grace, kindness, and generosity I will never forget.

Charles Morgan Evans
July 1, 2022

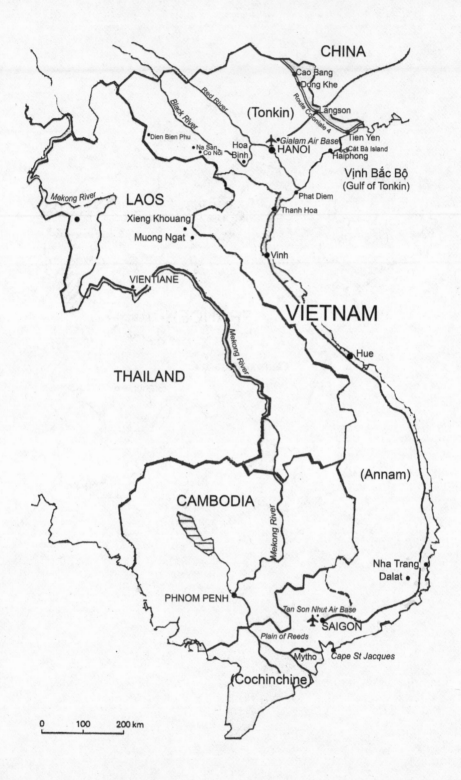

CHINA

Cao Bang
Dong Khe

(Tonkin)

Route Coloniale 4

Langson

Red River

Black River

Dien Bien Phu

Na San
Co Noi

Hoa
Binh

Gialam Air Base

HANOI

Tien Yen

Cát Bà Island

Haiphong

Vịnh Bắc Bộ
(Gulf of Tonkin)

Mekong River

LAOS

Xieng Khouang

Muong Ngat

Phat Diem

Thanh Hoa

Vinh

VIENTIANE

Mekong River

VIETNAM

THAILAND

Hue

(Annam)

CAMBODIA

Mekong River

Nha Trang

Dalat

PHNOM PENH

Tan Son Nhut Air Base

SAIGON

Plain of Reeds

Mytho

Cape St Jacques

(Cochinchine)

0   100   200 km

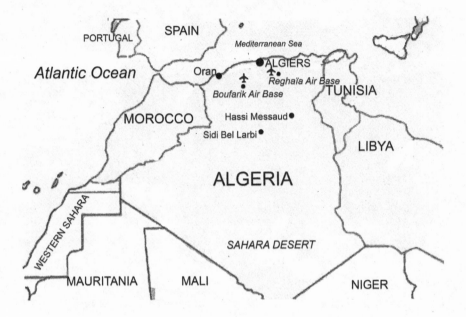

Chapter 1

No Place for a Woman

Near Nam Dinh, Northern Vietnam, November 16, 1952

The heat inside the fishbowl cockpit was unbearable, but the pilot—her left hand firmly grasping an overhead control stick—paid little attention to it. Her focus was on her mission and keeping her cantankerous helicopter airborne. And hopefully not drawing any gunfire from below.

The nimble little aircraft didn't always like to fly in the heavy atmosphere, but she knew how to coax it with finesse (and occasionally a few stern words) to a reasonably safe altitude when necessary.

Her destination was one of the small French army outposts that were concentrated along the Red River just past Nam Dinh. A young Vietnamese soldier with a critical head wound needed immediate transport back to Hanoi.

The journey from Hanoi on this day was uneventful, and the weather was calm. Following the winding Red River, the pilot took in the scenic panorama. The sensation of flight and the beauty of the countryside never failed to lift her spirits—even at the tail end of a grueling day.

With minutes to go before landing, she radioed in to air traffic control in Hanoi to report her position. She noted that her fighter escorts had not yet made contact.

At least the Viet Minh haven't any antiaircraft guns, she thought to herself.

The sky over Tonkin was clear and blue, giving little clue to the war taking place two thousand feet below. But on the ground, the pilot and her machine were vulnerable targets, and she fully realized the danger she was flying into. Her pulse quickened as she spotted her landmark by the river. The outpost was just ahead.

1

The French had built a series of blockhouses in northern Vietnam to station troops engaging with the enemy Viet Minh. Constantly under siege, the army experienced numerous casualties. Even when confronted with the large perimeters and land mines surrounding these forts, the Viet Minh always seemed to infiltrate and inflict heavy damage. The fort near Nam Dinh was no exception.

Long days and dangerous missions were not new experiences for this pilot. She had been in Vietnam for five years, serving as a surgeon in military hospitals. She had been airdropped into remote outposts to set up temporary medical facilities on the battlefield. And when the first helicopters came to Vietnam for medical evacuation, she immediately and enthusiastically volunteered to pilot them. Not only was aviation her lifelong passion, but she also reckoned that with her petite size and jockey-like weight that she could take on more wounded with the helicopter's limited payload.

Her Hiller helicopter was extremely vulnerable whenever it approached a landing zone. Its slender, insect-like fuselage provided no outward protection, and the large red crosses painted on the bottom and both sides of the machine did not deter the enemy. The Viet Minh would train their fire on it all the same.

For five years, the pilot's survival had depended on constant vigilance, quick reflexes, intelligence—and luck. She did not wish to push that luck and looked again for her escorts. To her relief, the fighter pilots arrived and performed a flyby past her slower-moving helicopter. She admired the fighter pilots and envied the speed of their aircraft.

If only the Hiller could go as fast. We could save so many more.

She could always count on the Viet Minh hiding in the thick vegetation to follow every move she made and to fire on her whenever they could. The helicopter could be struck and brought down even by light gunfire erupting from the brush. That was why the fighter planes were called into action and sent into the area before the unarmed helicopter would land.

The escorting fighter pilots knew what she expected of them. They came in at high speed and low altitude, laying down a merciless pattern of machine-gun fire that struck deep into the thick vegetation surrounding the outpost. Today it was only a strafing run. On other missions, it might be necessary to drop napalm—a flaming jellied gasoline concoction that instantly ignited anything it came in contact with, including human flesh. Their barrage only lasted a minute or so, but it was enough to keep the enemy at bay.

With their work finished, the fighters split off to head back to Hanoi. Only the helicopter remained as the pilot sucked in her breath, guiding her machine toward the outpost for a landing. She had already transported four other wounded men to Hanoi that day, and fatigue was setting in. Below was the landing zone, crudely marked out with linen sheets and scraps of wood secured by stakes and stones to the ground.

She wasted no time. Evacuations at remote outposts were always carried out quickly to avoid cutting power to the engine. It wasn't always a sure bet that the Hiller's engine would start again after a complete shutdown.

One thing was sure, however. The Viet Minh would soon regroup.

The helicopter's rotor blades slowed as the engine wound down to an idle. The men from the outpost knew not to move until the aircraft was on the ground. The pilot stepped out from the cockpit as a field medic and two other soldiers approached in a crouching run bearing the wounded man on a stretcher.

"Bullet in the head," the medic shouted to her above the din of the engine and still swishing rotors. "He's in a coma and been stuffed with Sedol."

The wounded man's face was ashen. The medics had wrapped the top of his head in linen gauze. The bandage was already blood soaked, and his wound continued to seep.

She looked the patient over carefully. He was probably not even twenty, she surmised. He was one of many Vietnamese now fighting alongside the French against other Vietnamese. This soldier was smaller than a typical Frenchman but somewhat stocky with broad shoulders.

"Could you tie up his hands?" she asked. "I would prefer it."

The pilot knew all too well from experience never to underestimate what could happen while moving a wounded patient by air—even one as severely injured as this young Vietnamese soldier. The medic nodded to one of the men bearing the stretcher, and he produced a small length of cord. With the comatose soldier's hands now secured, they began moving the patient toward one of the side-mounted stretchers attached to the helicopter.

The extra seconds spent tying the patient's hands further exposed the pilot and soldiers to unseen threats on the ground. No one could shake the sense that enemy eyes and weapons were trained on them. They were all targets and the threat of weapons fire erupting at any moment was very real.

Once the soldiers had positioned the patient beneath the Plexiglas faring enclosing the helicopter's stretcher, the pilot twisted the throttle to rev the helicopter's engine for liftoff. Hanoi was less than a half hour away at full power, but the helicopter's engine always labored in the sweltering tropical atmosphere. It seemed an eternity as they climbed sluggishly.

Finally, the Hiller achieved a relatively safe altitude and pushed along at its normal cruising speed of seventy miles per hour. She retraced her flight along the banks of the Red River leading back to Hanoi. The pilot exhaled deeply, flexed her hands, and stretched a bit to release the tension in her neck and shoulders.

But her relief was short-lived. She glanced back at her patient and saw to her horror that he was regaining consciousness.

Merde, she thought. *Not enough Sedol!*

The soldier awoke in wild spasms, terrified at finding himself in the air. Looking down, the pilot could see the primal fear in his eyes. Alarmed, she watched as the man clenched his jaw and fought his restraints, summoning almost supernatural strength to retake his freedom despite being more than a thousand feet above the ground.

She could see that the patient had slipped free of his restraints and that he was struggling to reach into the cockpit. His desperate hands thrust inside the cabin, grabbing at the helicopter's floor-mounted foot controls. The pilot's attempts to calm the soldier went unheard as he clutched and clawed at her feet. The aircraft pitched wildly, perilously out of control, as she fought the crazed soldier and wrestled with the Hiller.

It was a nightmare scenario. There was no one she could call out to for help and no way to reason with the wounded soldier. Many would have panicked, but not this pilot. She coolly reviewed her choices as she fought for her life and his. She could have immobilized him with a kick, but that would probably have killed him. Not an option for a doctor who had taken the Hippocratic oath.

And so she desperately battled with her feet, trying to push the frantic soldier away from the controls and back into his litter. His clutching at the foot controls could easily have caused the Hiller to spin, disorienting the pilot and leading to a lethal crash. Had he succeeded in jarring her arm and triggering a "mast bump," a loss of control, the helicopter would likely have plummeted. And so she fought for time, for the minutes it would take to get them to safety.

Her efforts paid off. As suddenly as the man had risen from his catatonic state, his face froze, his body stiffened, and he went limp. He fell back into his coma and mercifully into a deep sleep.

Breathing heavily and with great effort, she brought the helicopter back under control. Her body, jolted by adrenaline, vibrated like a tuning fork. Minutes later, they made it to the outskirts of Hanoi, not far from the landing zone at Lannesan Hospital.[1]

Gently placing the helicopter onto the immaculately groomed hospital landing zone, the pilot was met by medics who offloaded the young Vietnamese soldier and rushed him inside for surgery. She would later learn that the young man had survived.

With her mission complete, she was able to shut the helicopter down. Her khaki coveralls were drenched in sweat, and she noticed that the soldier had undone her bootlaces.

Leaning against the side of her helicopter, she slowly lowered herself to the ground while pulling a cigarette and a lighter from her pockets. She stared blankly ahead as she dragged deeply and exhaled a long stream of smoke. For a short moment, she could relax. It had been a punishing day.

Medical rescue helicopters were an innovation on the battlefield, and a female pilot even more so. Many in Indochina had heard of the pretty young woman who rescued gravely injured soldiers from the battlefield, but few knew much about her. To some, she was something of a legend.

But others mistrusted her presence.

Was she qualified? Should she be allowed to fly? Why was she doing the work of a man? Some of her comrades whispered their opinions behind her back but others spoke them aloud and in no uncertain terms.

The pilot knew what the men said about her. It was impossible not to. Even with her skill, endurance, and commitment to duty, the same thing would be pronounced over and over again:

This was no place for a woman.

Chapter 2

Dreams and Destiny

Strasbourg, Alsace-Lorraine, France, 1922–1939

Her future ambition first revealed itself in nightly dreams.

While there were variations, the theme was the same. First, a feeling of floating in midair, then sudden acceleration and dizzying heights. Whizzing through the atmosphere, propelled by an unknown force, untethered by gravity. The journey was unknown and the destination always nebulous, but never frightening. Only the endless domain of space existed. It was a feeling of boundless exhilaration sustained by a confidence that no harm would come.[1]

These were the dreams of a young French girl named Valérie André.

Valérie Edmée André was born in Strasbourg, France, on April 21, 1922, to Philibert and Valérie Collin André. She was the sixth of nine children in her family.

It would be easy to assume that in such a large family of relatively modest means that the hopes and dreams of a young girl would get little attention. But norms and conventions of the day did not apply to this young girl or her family.

Valérie's father, Philibert André, was a music teacher at the Lycée Fustel-de-Coulanges, a high school for boys in Strasbourg. He was described as a man of immense stature, cultivated and domineering to his students and his family. He regarded his children as "exceptional beings" who he would prepare to become the best individuals that they could be.

No less an influence, Valérie's mother also pressed her children on to greater things. Distinctly ahead of her time, she passionately believed that her four daughters should have the same access to higher education as her five sons.

"I would prefer that my daughters have a solid diploma, rather than to merely give them a dowry to just marry them off," Valérie's mother would say to her daughters.[2]

"My parents regarded their nine children as exceptional individuals and dedicated themselves to aiding each one to become a brilliant success," Valérie would later recall.[3]

But the path to success would not be easy.

The city of Strasbourg was part of Alsace-Lorraine, a region squarely in the middle of Europe's political divide. In the aftermath of World War I, Alsace was now part of France, which was a cause for rejoicing among the French population. But tensions with the ethnic German population in the area remained. Control had passed back and forth between France and Germany since 1870. Nonetheless, the status of Alsace remained a bitter issue for many in the wake of Germany's defeat in 1918.

Nationalism aside, however, the Alsatians developed a unique identity among Europeans, which was backed up by an appetite for hard work and independent thought. The André family exemplified this. Young Valérie prided herself on a thirst for knowledge and questioning the rule of the day. In school, her teachers would speak of the universal right to vote that was extended to men, which was seen as a progressive step in a country that had adopted *liberté, égalité, et fraternité* as its national motto.

"At school I was astonished that our professors could speak to us about universal suffrage,[4] while women remained excluded," Valérie would note to herself. "I challenged them, without hesitation, that this was inherently false."[5]

In the schoolyard, it was often the same. Valérie took an indignant view of boys who taunted other boys saying things like, "he cries like a girl." To Valérie, such expressions only reinforced the image of "courage wrongly reserved for boys only."[6]

Even with a heightened awareness of the inequities that she constantly encountered, Valérie also believed that she could overcome any obstacles in her way. Her philosophy would serve her well in the future.

"I considered that each woman possesses the possibility of choosing her own life, even if that choice required more tenacity than that of a man."[7]

While social change in the 1920s and 1930s moved slowly, the rapid pace of technological change would open up another world for Valérie. The Strasbourg aerodrome announced a special guest attraction: the French *aviatrice* Maryse Hilsz was to make an appearance there.

Maryse Hilsz had made headlines in 1931 by establishing a record-breaking long-distance flight from Paris to the city of Saigon in the far-flung French colony of Indochina and back again. Only thirty-one years of age, and extremely photogenic, Hilsz embarked on a publicity tour following her flight and was to stop by the Polygon aerodrome in Strasbourg in March 1932.

The visit stirred ten-year-old Valérie André's imagination.

Hilsz was a woman unconstrained by the conventions of her time. She had flown nearly thirteen thousand miles in a fragile Gypsy Moth biplane, aptly named *Paris-Saigon*, and accomplished what had previously been declared as "impossible for a woman." Valérie begged her mother to take her to the airfield to see Hilsz.

That event would change many things in Valérie's life.

Clutching a small bouquet that she had picked out herself for the acclaimed pilot, Valérie waited among a throng gathered at the aerodrome of both ardent supporters and doubters who were curious to see the female aviator up close. As they all waited, someone in the crowd shouted:

"It's her. She's coming!"

Sure enough, a small dot in the sky steadily grew larger as Hilsz's monoplane came into view. Police had to hold the crowd back as the plane landed and taxied to a stop. Valérie was enthralled as the young pilot extricated herself from the cockpit.

"I rushed to her. I had possibly imagined only a small compliment from her, as I tightly grasped a bunch of flowers and presented them to this superb young woman in her smart uniform. She presented a splendid image of female dignity. I asked her for her autograph and she agreed with a large heart."[8]

The impression that Hilsz made on the young girl was immeasurable. To Valérie, Maryse Hilsz embodied what could be possible, not just a dream. On that day she vowed to herself that someday she, too, would become an aviator.

The passion for aviation became deeply planted in Valérie. She devoted her small allowances to buying monthly aviation magazines from newsstands. She devoured the exploits of famed aviators like the American Amelia Earhart, or the pioneer French *aviatrices* Marie Marvingt and

Maryse Bastié. When Amelia Earhart made the first solo transatlantic flight by a woman, also in 1932, Valérie followed every minute detail of the journey from Newfoundland to Ireland.

The stories of pilots were not Valérie's only interest. The technical features of aircraft, such as the latest machines to roll out the doors of French builders Morane-Saulnier, Potaz, Farman, and others, fascinated her equally.

But it was the audacious accomplishments of women aviators that prompted Valérie to pose a question to herself:

"Why did aeronautics always attract women?"[9]

As Valérie André blossomed from a young girl into a teenager, she began preparing for her adult future. While never abandoning her passion for aviation, she remained grounded in her education. As an outgrowth of her interest in flying, however, general science became a cornerstone of her studies. It was natural for a mind that was always questioning to relate to a discipline that was at its root a method to establish solutions. While science studies were not encouraged for girls of Valérie's era, it mattered little to her. The field of medicine struck Valérie as the perfect vocation, and as she progressed at her *lycée* toward her *baccalauréat*, she devoted herself to the prospect of one day becoming a doctor.

The dream of aviation still continued to pull at her. She spent her few, precious moments of free time at Polygon aerodrome, where she watched airplanes take off and land, and sometimes conversed with pilots and mechanics at work in the various hangars. Many of the pilots came to know the precocious teen well and often invited her to engage with their own dreams they had for flight.

Valérie longed to fly. Her first opportunity came when her older sister's husband, who had recently received his pilot's license, offered to take her up for a short flight.

"It was a Caudron Firefly, with an open cockpit, where the pilot and passenger were open to the free air. At an altitude of five or six hundred meters, we began to make our way back to the ground. But it was some minutes of extraordinary happiness. It was almost the conquest of the sky for an enthusiastic teenager, such as myself. This first exposure confirmed my resolution to become an aviator, although I was well aware of the obstacles a girl would face to get there."[10]

One such obstacle was the cost of obtaining flight instruction. During the 1930s, the French government had initiated Aviation populaire, a program that encouraged young men, like Valérie André's brother-in-law, to learn the basics of piloting, providing flight instruction at no cost. But the program was only open to men. A young woman desiring flight lessons would have to find a way to pay for flight lessons. The cost was roughly three thousand francs, a small fortune back then.[11]

"I resolved to tutor lessons in French and arithmetic and to add that to the small personal savings I had," recalled Valérie. "My family, by no means, sought to oppose my ambition. However, they initially saw it only as the whim of a child. But I believe that my tenacity was something daunting to them. The road that I had mapped out for myself was clear and straight, and I was determined to follow it, regardless of the obstacles along the way."[12]

But other obstacles emerged on the eastern horizon of Strasbourg. Germany's remilitarization of the Rhineland in 1936 and the rise of Adolf Hitler and the Nazi Party began to menace France and Belgium, but neither country directly challenged Hitler's actions. From there, Germany annexed Austria and sent occupation troops into the Sudetenland in 1938. Following the disastrous Munich Agreement concluded by Germany, Italy, the United Kingdom, and France, the German war machine marched into Czechoslovakia in March 1939. By summer 1939, all of Europe was a case of dynamite with the fuse already lit.

During this uncertain summer, the inhabitants of Alsace-Lorraine felt particularly vulnerable. The region shared a border with Germany's western frontier, and many Germans who lived in Alsace believed that Germany held a rightful claim to the region. The growing threat affected everyone, including Valérie André.

"Nazism horrified me. The Nazis wanted to dominate the world. I had a passion for order and freedom, and in my eyes no power could be tolerated that condemned freedom. And no power should be based on the submission of others."[13]

The German threat was not Valérie's only concern. Life was also changing in fundamental ways for her now that she had turned seventeen. Graduation from her *lycée* was fast approaching, and she had set her sights on attending the University of Strasbourg and its prestigious school of medicine. Little did she know at that time that this decision would place her on an even more arduous path.

As war clouds increasingly darkened the summer sky, there was one brief moment when the skies opened up for Valérie.

"I finally earned enough money to register with the flying club. I would finally learn how to fly," she triumphantly recollected.

"The first lesson captivated me. It was marvelous, this feeling to control the aircraft and become one with it. We still lived in an age where to take off from the ground astonished us every time. I had so wanted, so waited for this moment. . . . I promised to quickly become the youngest French pilot."[14]

She described the experience of flight as an "intoxication." Her instructor was Edouard Pinot, a World War I veteran nicknamed "the Owl." Pinot was regarded as an extraordinary pilot and instructor with the flying club that operated out of the Polygon.[15]

Throughout July and August, Valérie's lessons progressed well. She waited eagerly to take her first solo flight scheduled for the latter part of August; however, fate would dictate otherwise.

"My father regularly tuned into the radio every day and we religiously listened to the news," said Valérie. As each day went by, the news only became worse. The Germans were amassing men and armor on Poland's border. Fear and panic among many in Strasbourg were palpable. With Germany on a war footing, it was only a matter of time before it would attempt to retake Strasbourg.

Valérie's father had anticipated the worst for months. Philibert André had applied and was accepted for a position at a college in Thann in Haut Rhin, some one hundred kilometers from Strasbourg. The family had an ancestral home at Bourbach-le-Haut, where Philibert was born.

"On the day before my solo flight my father ordered me to prepare a suitcase," Valérie said. "I was to leave Strasbourg immediately. The declaration of war was imminent."

Valérie André implored her father to allow her to stay in Strasbourg for just one more day to complete her flight training, but the situation in his eyes was dire. In no uncertain terms, Philibert demanded Valérie was to leave with the rest of the family immediately.

"What a disillusion!" recalled Valérie. "It seemed impossible for me to give up my pilot's license when I was so close. I swore to myself that I would obtain my license at my first opportunity, despite the war. Whatever the costs."[16]

Chapter 3

War Comes to France

When Germany declared war on Poland on September 1, 1939, France and Great Britain followed suit, declaring war on Germany on September 3. With France sharing its eastern border with Germany, fear and uncertainty began to take hold, especially in Strasbourg. For Valérie André, the changes affected every aspect of her life.

Bourbach-le-Haut was far from the cultured and diverse city of Strasbourg. Its pastoral landscape was beautiful, but it felt like a prison to Valérie. Her life was no longer hers to plan. The University of Strasbourg—where Valérie had hoped to begin her medical studies the following year—had closed its campus and moved its faculty and students to Clermont-Ferrand, some 470 kilometers away to the southwest of France. The thought of completing her pilot's training was now just a dream—to be deferred in the best of circumstances, forgotten in the worst.

In Alsace-Lorraine, fear of invasion ran high. Many fled to the interior of France if they could. Others stayed, resigned to what they felt was inevitable. There was, of course, the Maginot Line, France's impressive network of artillery defenses and tunnels that ran along its eastern border with Germany. Many millions of francs had been spent on the Maginot Line in the 1930s to prepare for a war that seemed unavoidable once again. France had hoped to deter Germany from invading from the east as they had in World War I.

But the residents of Strasbourg would see no benefit from the Maginot Line. It ran to the west of Strasbourg, leaving the city and surrounding areas vulnerable to German attack.

Valérie was absorbed with newspapers and radio accounts of Germany's relentless advance into Poland, just like everyone else in Europe. And every day brought more grim news. The Poles fought valiantly and alone, suffering great losses. France and Great Britain could not bring an expeditionary force together soon enough to be of any use to Poland. Emboldened by their recent nonaggression pact with Germany, the Soviet Union invaded Poland from the east on September 17. Poland would surrender to both forces in October and would exist as a divided country thereafter.

With the war in the east at an end, it was only a matter of time before France met its own fate.

These were dark times for Valérie André. Fully grown, she was a very petite woman, slightly more than five feet tall and very slender. Undaunted by circumstances, she pressed on with her studies. She enrolled at the *lycée* in the nearby village of Thann and prepared to take her *baccalauréat* in advanced math and science—courses that girls were discouraged from taking, but necessary for a medical career. Valérie was to learn that the provincial attitudes of Thann would not always make life easy for her.

"In my math course, I was the only girl in a class of eleven boys," Valérie recalled. "I was by no means intimidated by that—I actually preferred the company of boys."[1]

But her math instructor had different thoughts on the matter.

"You can't sit next to another boy in class," he told her bluntly on her first day. "It's not proper."

Valérie was somewhat taken aback by this, though she complied.

"He complained that I wore socks that revealed too much skin below my skirt and compelled me to cover myself with an incredibly long skirt to disguise my shape. I was also seated at my own personal desk at the head of the class separate from the boys. This was done to stress my exceptional, if not scandalous presence in class."[2]

The division between boys and girls even extended to the schoolyard, where boys and girls were separated by a chalk line drawn on the ground. To Valérie, it was as if boys and girls were to regard each other as "foreigners or adversaries." It was all the more ridiculous, given that Valérie and her classmates were on the cusp of adulthood and that outside the *lycée* their code of conduct was markedly different.

"My male friends were *très sympathique* and intelligent and our complicity was only strengthened. We played pinochle in cafés and I smoked cigarettes with them. Oh, the sacrilege! A woman should not smoke!

However, smoking was not out of any desire to offend, but just for the fun and challenge."[3]

As for the outside world, things were disturbingly quiet in the aftermath of Poland's defeat. The next German offensive, which was anxiously anticipated after France declared war on Germany, failed to materialize. Indeed, these uneasy months would become known as the period of the "Phony War," in which the threat of war would never fully subside, but actual shooting failed to commence.

Yet, in the absence of an all-out war, this uncomfortable period of lull created an atmosphere of rampant suspicions and mistrust. Because a large portion of the inhabitants of Alsace-Lorraine was of German ancestry, neighbors began to suspect other neighbors of being Nazi spies. This dark cloud of distrust hung heavily over the streets, the shops and cafés creating their own oppressive and somber mood felt by almost everyone.

"It was as if a real psychosis had seized a small city like Thann," Valérie recalled. "I remember adults were obsessed by fifth column activity that they thought they saw everywhere. People reported their suspicions to the authorities. One could not disentangle truth from falsehood."[4]

Aside from a brief skirmish on the Rhine River region near Strasbourg, the French military virtually refrained from any offensive actions until spring 1940. For the most part, the French made preparations for a defensive war that would make use of the Maginot Line.

As France bided its time with Germany, Valérie managed to continue with her studies in math and science. But that was not all. Having given up her goal of obtaining her pilot's license the previous summer, Valérie set her sights on something more terrestrial.

"I decided to get my driving license."

Her simple decision set off the first of a series of major disagreements she would have with her father.

"From the start, my father opposed it. I was not of majority age yet. But it was easy for me to circumvent my father's refusal since the legal age for a driver's license was lowered to seventeen in time of war.

"In great secrecy I arranged to go to Mulhouse to register for one or two lessons, informing the authorities there that I had great need for a license in order to help my family. I obtained my license on my first attempt. When I returned home I placed the license on the dining table with great obviousness and without a word. My father was stunned."[5]

The war with Germany meant that every aspect of life in France was subject to change. When the boys in Valérie's class were subject to military draft, it meant that exams for the *baccalauréat* were to be moved up by a few months. In early spring 1940, Valérie graduated with her *baccalauréat* in math and science.

On April 9, 1940, the Phony War came to an end when the Germans marched into Norway and Denmark. This was just a prelude, however, to a much larger operation launched on May 10, 1940, when the German Wehrmacht struck again. The Germans were fully aware of the heavily fortified Maginot Line so they instead opted to deploy their armed forces to the countries north of France—Luxembourg, the Netherlands, and Belgium. The defenses of these countries crumbled in a matter of a few short days.

Then on May 14, the Germans crossed over the Meuse River from Belgium into northern France. Their objective was to invade France through the densely wooded Ardennes Forest that the French thought was impenetrable. The Germans bypassed the mighty Maginot Line without a single shot being fired at them.

With the anticipated invasion now a reality, panic gripped France. Even in Paris, a sense of defeatism quickly set in. By May 16, the government began planning an evacuation of the capital.

"Already on the roads of France entire families were fleeing the invader," said Valérie, recalling the terror that began to spread throughout the nation. "How would it be possible to live under the yoke of the enemy?"

Estimates suggest that as many as twelve million refugees took to the roads of France, fleeing from the advancing German army.

"My father's position was very clear. He had already decided that he was too old to leave. He had decided that it would be better to remain where he was at and defend our family's property and the spirit of France."[6]

Valérie would have none of it, however. There was already rampant speculation as to what to expect from the Germans if they were to occupy Alsace-Lorraine.

"It seemed rather impossible to think of a future where we would be deprived of our freedom and treated as the vanquished."

Valérie knew that the prospects for any young person left behind would be odious. Despite oppressing forces that were quickly bearing down, Valérie was resolved to find a way to escape Alsace. At the same time, however, she knew that her decision to leave would again place her in direct conflict with her father.

"I knew that my father would refuse me his permission to go. I was eighteen years old, a young woman barely of majority age, and as such I was still heavily dependent on the authority of my parents. To leave Alsace was to take considerable risks. I was aware of the risks but was by no means discouraged by them."

The inevitable confrontation came, and neither side would give in. Philibert's concern was for Valérie's safety. He had witnessed the oppressiveness of German rule during the last war and knew how cruel punishment could be meted to those who defied them.

But Valérie stood firm.

"You raised me as a French woman and I don't want to become German," she finally said to him. "I will not remain here."[7]

As fate would have it, an opportunity arose to leave Bourbach-le-Haut. One of Valérie's friends from school was preparing to leave with his mother by automobile to Clermont-Ferrand. Valérie's older sister was already attending the relocated University of Strasbourg in Clermont-Ferrand, which was Valérie's objective as well.

On the morning that she was to leave, Valérie's father made one last attempt to keep his daughter from going through with her plan.

"My father grabbed my suitcase from out of my hands."

He refused to give the suitcase back to Valérie, again demanding that she was not to leave. He told Valérie that he would lock her in her room if that's what it would take to keep her from leaving.

But her father's actions made no difference to Valérie. Valérie found herself forced to leave her family's home by way of stealth.

"I carried almost nothing with me. I would have to make do with what I had. Waiting for me was my friend's car, overflowing with bags, luggage, and various items."

The distance between Bourbach-le-Haut to Clermont-Ferrand was more than five hundred kilometers to the southwest. Roads were clogged, and vital supplies, such as gasoline, were limited.

"Our journey toward the south revealed to us the extent of the rout of the French military. There were thousands of refugees—many of them old men, women, and children—with their backs broken by weariness, trailing behind them all the possessions they had time to gather together. Carriages drawn by horses followed, overfilled with mattresses and pieces of furniture. The dreadful sadness engraved on their faces haunted me. Had I, up to this point, understood what the war meant in terms of horrors and miseries? One must live this close to the face of war to actually know."[8]

The world was collapsing all around her. Despite a few counteroffenses to Germany's seemingly invincible war machine, the end for an independent France was near. In Paris, France's prime minister, Paul Reynaud, resigned because he refused to agree to surrender to the Germans. His successor, Marshal Philippe Pétain, announced on June 25, 1940, that he would negotiate an armistice with Germany immediately.

Despite the armistice, not all military actions ceased. At Dunkirk, off the coast of Belgium, a massive evacuation of troops from the British Expeditionary Force and French army was taking place. Nearly 200,000 British and 140,000 French soldiers were rescued that week off the beach at Dunkirk by a flotilla of British navy craft and privately owned boats.

The invasion of France, however, had taken a heavy toll—68,111 troops of the British Expeditionary Force were either killed, wounded, or captured, and 360,000 French troops were either killed or wounded, with an additional 1.8 million troops captured.

The future of a free France would have to rely on those who would manage to escape and join the overseas Free French movement and also upon those who remained in France who never submitted to German rule. As Valérie André would declare:

"How could I lose hope? I was now eighteen years old. With all my might I pledged to finish my studies, to become a doctor, and to learn how to pilot. The war had done nothing to change my goals. On the contrary, it had galvanized me."[9]

Chapter 4

Occupation

France was defeated. The government was abolished and replaced with a puppet regime not based in Paris but in Vichy. Its population was either uprooted, in hiding, or in exile. More than 92,000 French soldiers were killed, and another 1.8 million were sent to German prison camps. Those who could escape to England or the colonies did so, and stories of a new "Free French" soon circulated. France's once proud military, however, was essentially defanged.

A new order was in effect, one that bowed to the symbol of the swastika. And more than one hundred thousand German soldiers were in France to back it up. France was now also a divided country, split into zones with their own regulations and penalties.

Alsace-Lorraine was reincorporated into German territory, becoming a Forbidden Zone for its citizens. No one was allowed to leave there without permission from the German authorities under penalty of imprisonment or worse.

Valérie André was now considered a criminal.

Having narrowly made her way out of Bourbach-le-Haut before France surrendered to the Germans, Valérie and her companions arrived at Clermont-Ferrand in the Free Zone.

"The city was flooded with refugees, many of whom were Alsatians . . . students, professors," Valérie recalled. "My sister had a somewhat suitable room in a boarding-house. As it was, all the hotels were overcrowded. We had to make do with a mattress in a room shared with several others."

Long lines for food and scarce necessities were the norm. Initially, the government provided a meager amount of funds from France's national relief program, but the Pétain regime stopped all payments.

"The misfortune of people of all ages—penned-in, uprooted, with all that they gave up now behind them—appeared crueler to me each day."

Valérie was among those displaced from their homes, carrying only a few personal possessions; however, she chose not to focus on her own plight. Many were worse off. At least she had a room.

Rumors and speculation filled hushed conversations more than anything else. The Germans officially cut off any legitimate news from the outside world. Listening to foreign radio broadcasts was especially forbidden and carried a heavy penalty. But word of a general who managed to escape France quickly spread.

"Conversations would often allude to a certain General de Gaulle. He had begun broadcasting from London, launching a call to continue our fight."[1]

Everything in France was in a state of flux. The relocated University of Strasbourg—sharing facilities with the University of Auvergne—was far from up and running. Like Valérie and her sister, students and even faculty members were all adjusting to their new lives. As weeks wore on, there were new worries besides the chronic food shortages. Rumors of reprisals, especially in Alsace, began to circulate.

Some of the rumors told of the Germans rounding up inhabitants of Alsace-Lorraine for forced factory labor or conscription in the German military. Both the young and old were subject to the new orders.

Valérie and her sister worried about their family. Valérie, in particular, felt tremendous guilt over the acrimony with her father when she decided to leave.

"We became worried about the fate of our parents, and we decided to set out for Bourbach-le-Haut by any makeshift manner. We knew that the risks were great. We also knew that it would be useless to obtain authorization given the regime we were living under. The only solution was audacity and *sang froid*."[2]

Fortunately for Valérie and her sister, the German occupation of Alsace-Lorraine was not totally in place by summer 1940. There were still holes in the checkpoints between zones. The two women were able to return to Bourbach-le-Haut and reunite with their father and mother.

But the reunion was edgy. While Philibert was relieved that no harm had come to Valérie, he still couldn't forgive his daughter for her defiance. He felt that she had acted impulsively. Even Valérie's decision to return from Clermont-Ferrand, with the heightened danger from German soldiers being everywhere, did little to change his opinion.

As it turned out, many of the rumors Valérie had heard about Alsace-Lorraine proved to be true. Mandatory conscription into the German army was ordered for all male inhabitants of Alsace-Lorraine of enlistment age. Food shortages had begun since much of the meat and produce was seized for consumption by the German military. Curfews were in effect, and no one was allowed out at night for any reason. French Jews were stripped of citizenship. Moreover, each and every civilian was subject to searches and detainment for any reason whatsoever.

Valérie also learned that the new regime intended to wipe out any French influence in the region thoroughly. This new policy included sending Alsatian students to study at the University of Heidelberg in Germany and establishing the Reich University of Strasbourg in place of the former University of Strasbourg.

"How would it be possible to agree to live and learn on enemy soil?" Valérie wondered. "This idea was confounding to me. It was now even forbidden to speak French in Alsace."

Everywhere Valérie went, she came face to face with the fear and submission that had gripped the inhabitants of the area. The presence of the invading army was felt in all quarters. The Germans commandeered entire buildings to house troops or to use as command and operations headquarters.

"An atmosphere of fear and icy silences weighed on the city and each house."

The gloom extended to the home of Valérie's family. Philibert resigned himself to believing that things were to remain as they were, and thoughts to the contrary were futile. Staying in Alsace meant a life constantly under the oppression of a harsh German authority with a bleak outlook for a young French woman. Valérie vowed to have no part of it.

"I would rather go to prison or die than to give up a free future."[3]

Although her father tried once more to talk her out of going, Valérie was determined to leave. The danger was much greater compared to earlier that summer, however. Leaving the region now required considerably more of a clandestine effort.

For a second time, Valérie found a willing accomplice who would take the risk to get through German checkpoints.

"Marc Hinky was a stocky, brown-haired boy, with a very resolved manner," Valérie said of her companion.

Hinky had also returned to the Alsace region to check on his family after having managed to leave earlier. "He was preparing to get to Paris by any means possible, where he also wished to carry out his studies in medicine."[4]

By the time Valérie and Marc were ready to leave Bourbach-le-Haut, it was late in the year. The weather had turned cold, and fresh snow had fallen just a day or so earlier. Valérie and Marc waited until evening to begin their exodus. For the first leg of the journey, the pair traveled from Thann to Mulhouse near the Swiss border.

"In order to avoid being stopped by the Germans, it was necessary to go to Montreux Vieux and then another fifteen kilometers to Belfort, and then from there to Petite Croix, all on foot," Valérie said, describing the circuitous path taken. "The crossing of this route was subject to intense German surveillance, but Marc Hinky knew the area perfectly well and knew where the sentry posts were."

Walking where fresh snow had fallen was dangerous because it revealed tracks that the Germans could trace back to them. But there would be no turning back. Valérie was also concerned that her dark coat could be easily spotted in the stark, white snow.

"With thousands of precautions, we threaded our way along a path that brought us very close to a sentry station. Once we were past this danger, we found shelter behind a little glen. We hoped that the guard inside the sentry station wouldn't venture outside as the sight of our tracks would have alerted him at once."[5]

Good fortune favored their journey as Valérie and Marc arrived at the train station at Petite Croix early the following day. There they boarded a train headed for Chalindrey, 145 kilometers to the west. When they arrived at Chalindrey, however, they were required to submit themselves to a German control checkpoint set up inside the train station.

"The German police officer studied my identity card and noted that I was born in Strasbourg. He began to question me, intrigued for the reasons of my travel," Valérie remembered. She quickly realized that the German's questions could lead to her immediate arrest for leaving Alsace without authorization. "I gave the officer my reasons in French without a trace of an Alsatian accent. I told him that my father had been a civil servant who was temporarily assigned to Strasbourg during the time of my birth. This fabrication seemed to convince him, as did my surname, which didn't arouse any further suspicion about my origin."[6]

Now safely past the German checkpoint at Chalindrey, Valérie and Marc found themselves on foot again walking a rough-hewn road to Langres. Fortunately, the pair encountered not a single soul during the entire eight-kilometer route.

"Finally, we reached the station at Langres. While we were sitting inside the station there, we were suddenly inundated by a wave of German soldiers who had been on leave and were returning to their base. Some were very rowdy, and others were drunk. We were the only French people, side to side of them on the bench, and several of the soldiers gave us strange looks and made offensive remarks. Marc and I both agreed to pretend not to understand German. But then the aggressive attitude of one soldier, then followed by several others, caused us to seek out their commanding officer. The situation threatened to escalate when a miracle of miracles occurred—the train that would soon liberate us arrived in the station with a deafening noise. Imperative whistles ordered all of us to gather on the platform for boarding. We were saved!"[7]

Not long after, Marc Hinky and Valérie found their compartment on the train, where Valérie settled into a long, exhausted sleep. Bound for Paris, the train entered the station at Gare d'est on December 31, 1940. The weather was freezing in the former capital, and the city's atmosphere was equally cold. Reminders of Germany's control over the city were evident, with garish swastikas emblazoned on public spaces. Hinky had made sure that Valérie had arrived safely in Paris but could do no more for her. But Valérie had a plan, even if it was somewhat vague. She knew a family in Paris who often shared holidays with her family in the mountains near Vosges. She would contact them.

"Guy Dauvé was one of my best friends. However, his family had not expected my arrival and showed great surprise by my appearance. It was difficult for them to take a risk in sheltering me, and I felt it. They advised me about a hotel that they considered secured."[8]

While Valérie stayed at the hotel, she received a surprise visit from her brother-in-law. Valérie's father sent him, and he had located Valérie through the Dauvé family.

"He told me that I could live near my sister in Laval. I liked my brother-in-law and allowed him to convince me to leave, especially since the hotel I was staying at didn't seem so secure anymore."[9]

Valérie André spent the next few months in Laval, where she was able to continue her studies. But for Valérie, to remain long term in Laval was out of the question. Valérie still intended to enroll at the University of Strasbourg in Clermont-Ferrand; however, Laval was in the Occupied Zone, and to leave would require another round of covert maneuvers.

Once again, fortune rested on Valérie's side. Her brother-in-law was connected to the Resistance movement and could arrange safe, though circuitous travel. The first leg of her journey started in Laval, where Valérie took a train to Bergerac, more than five hundred kilometers to the south. After leaving the train station, Valérie was to rendezvous with a taxi driver who would be responsible for transporting her to other "handlers."

"We left the station, but I was unaware of our destination," Valérie recalled. "I seemed to detect a certain reservation and a lack of enthusiasm on the part of the driver. He dropped me off at a small inn outside the city."[10]

Once she arrived at the inn, the proprietor warmly received Valérie, where she was shown her room and warned to maintain silence during her stay. She would cross into the Free Zone in the morning.

Valérie's night in the small inn was not a pleasant one. Within no time at all, she could hear the sound of German soldiers who stopped by the pub downstairs to drink.

"I could hear their conversation through the walls," Valérie remembered. The clarity of voices was such that she could almost sense their intense glares piercing the walls and floorboards.

Presently, the Germans left, and the landlord knocked softly on her door.

"He had come by to reassure me. After he left, I remained stretched out on the bed, ready to react to the least provocation. I would not close my eyes that night."[11]

At the first light of dawn, the landlord returned to Valérie's door, accompanied by her new handler.

"We left on foot, with my guide leading me towards a deserted road. I had a small bag in my hand. We advanced in silence, but he told me after a while, 'It's all right. You won't have much further to walk before you will be on the other side.'"

Believing his work was done, the guide left Valérie to continue the journey on her own.

But not long after Valérie parted ways with her guide, the barking of German police dogs erupted in front of her.

"Very quickly two German soldiers stopped me and demanded that I follow them. They led me to a sentry station."

Although Valérie could understand German, she never let on to her interrogators, believing that she could better answer their questions if she could hear what they said to themselves in their own language.

"I explained to them that I was returning to visit a relative who was ill and whose condition was such that I was likely to stay a month or two." Fortunately for Valérie, the German soldiers didn't find a reason to believe she posed any real threat. But had the sentries chosen to search her belongings, the outcome may not have been as favorable.

"My brother-in-law was convinced as to the safety of his plan and had packed the bottom of my bag with anti-Hitler leaflets. The Germans let me pass, but not without recommending that I bring tobacco to them when I returned!"[12]

When she finally arrived at Clermont-Ferrand, Valérie found the registrar for the university. She explained her escape from Alsace-Lorraine and the secretive route that had brought her there. The story was a familiar one, unfortunately. Many of her classmates were forced into similar situations to continue their education. Valérie André was accepted for enrollment at the University of Strasbourg at Clermont-Ferrand in fall 1941.

"At Clermont-Ferrand the lecture halls were filled to nearly bursting. . . . Our unquenchable thirst for work and study and our outbursts of occasional joy were probably our way of drowning out the somber reality."[13]

Virtually everyone deeply felt the heavy burden of France's defeat and occupation. As Valérie reflected:

"Our vision of the defeat was not the same as that of the older generation. Above everything, this was because the failure was not ours."[14]

There was some truth to that sentiment that also echoed throughout France. France's prewar defenses—particularly its reliance on the Maginot Line—resulted from a much older generation deciding France's destiny. France's poorly executed military response to Germany's attack was widely blamed on General Maurice Gamelin. Gamelin, who was sixty-seven years old at the time, had failed to launch a coordinated counteroffensive. Gamelin's successor, seventy-three-year-old General Maxine Weygand, fared even worse in the public view by surrendering France's army to the Germans. And eighty-four-year-old Marshal Philippe Pétain solidified the failure of the older generation by first agreeing to an armistice with Germany and later becoming a Nazi collaborator as head of the Vichy government.

If there was any hope of redemption for France's future and its restoration of independence and pride, it would reside in a younger generation.

General Charles de Gaulle was among those who would lead that fight, even if it was from abroad. De Gaulle refused to agree to the surrender negotiated by Pétain and attempted to organize an officers' revolt against the new regime. De Gaulle, however, was faced with overwhelming adversity and fled to England, where he began organizing a Free French movement that would include those who had also fled France or were already residing in France's far-flung colonies in Africa, the Caribbean, and Southeast Asia. Using the services of the British Broadcasting Company's strong radio signal, de Gaulle became the voice that would inspire a nation to break the bonds of submission.

The long shadows of Nazi oppression brought darkness to France and the European continent. But even in the shadows, light could not be entirely extinguished.

Chapter 5

Escaping the Gestapo

It was France's darkest hour. A time when the best and the worst of what humanity was capable of stood in stark contrast. While many treated the German occupation of France as something that had to be endured—or at worst, profited from—others resisted and were determined to bring about the day when liberation would be at hand. For these individuals, liberation would only be achieved by undermining and destroying the German invaders.

The Resistance movement took root in France almost at the same instant as the occupation. The region of Puy-de-Dome, Auvergne, and Clermont-Ferrand was no exception. Throughout the region, clandestine groups organized to resist the Germans. While it was in the so-called Unoccupied Zone, Clermont-Ferrand was particularly strategic to the Germans because of the Michelin tire factory. As a result, there was a sizeable Wehrmacht presence in the area at all times. Many of the Resistance fighters—known as *maquis*—began committing acts of sabotage, especially at the tire factory, or simply killing Germans outright. As time wore on, German retaliation against the civilian population also increased.

Valérie André, now a student at the relocated University of Strasbourg, was well aware of the danger present. Many of the students and faculty were using forged identity cards. They knew that they would be subject to deportation to factories deep inside Germany as slave labor if they were discovered. Worse yet, the Pétain government issued new laws, *statuts des juifs*, that stripped French Jewish citizens of their rights. More decrees followed,

targeting other groups such as communists and freemasons, who were declared enemies of the state.

The only bright spot during this dismal period was when Germany de-
clared war on the United States in the aftermath of the Japanese attack on
Pearl Harbor in December 1941. Many felt that Germany had made a grave
mistake in supporting the action of its Axis partner and that the United States
would make not only the Japanese pay but also the Germans and Italians.
But it would be years before the Americans would land in France, and the
Germans were resolved to keep France under its jackboot in the meantime.
An uneasy feeling rapidly spread, especially among the university students.

"Some of my friends at the university were engaged in the Resistance,"
Valérie recalled. The Resistance movement was the only dim light in a dark
tunnel. "We all had a hope that was deeply rooted in our souls that prodded
us to work harder."[1]

For Valérie, it was a period of intense apprehension. Alsace-Lorraine was
now a part of Germany, not France, and Valérie lived in constant fear of arrest. Avoiding contact with anyone who seemed official, whether it was the
Germans, or worse, the French Milice, became a survival tactic. Her studies
at the university were sometimes the only thing that saved her from giving
in to deep despair.

"My first year in college presented a difficult challenge, but I managed
to make a success of it. I would begin my first year at medical school in the
autumn of 1942."[2]

After having had to make do with cramped living quarters near the university, Valérie was eventually able to find better accommodations.

"I had a large room with a bathroom. It was an unimaginable refuge that
the editor of a local newspaper and his wife rented to me for a moderate
price."

It was the home of Henri and Renée Prat. Henri Prat was the editor of
both *Le Montagne* and the pro-Vichy *L'Avenir du plateau central*. Prat was
also a member of the *maquis* in Clermont-Ferrand. Prat was initially going to
resign from his job but stayed to pass on valuable information to his fellow
Resistance fighters, especially news censored by the Vichy government.
Prat's role in the Resistance, however, was unknown to Valérie, who was
occupied with her studies.

Valérie continued to endure the hardships brought on by the occupation.
Movement was still restricted within France's so-called Unoccupied Zone.
Nerves were becoming increasingly frayed as Germans reacted harshly to

maquis partisan attacks and sabotage. One incident involving the shooting of more than a dozen soldiers on the way to a cinema resulted in massive arrests of civilians and blocks of houses and businesses burned down in Clermont-Ferrand in retaliation. In this climate, Valérie found it necessary to have allies who could prove helpful if her situation turned worse.

"I made friends with four boys from the region—four giants—the smallest of whom measured 1.85 meters (6'1") tall. They were the Chardon brothers."

The Chardon brothers were from a farming family. The eldest of the brothers wasn't of draft age in 1940, which allowed him to escape the fate of more than 1.8 million French soldiers held in prisoner of war camps. The Chardons knew the region of Puy-de-Dome and Clermont-Ferrand well and were accustomed to living off the land. The resourceful brothers had even managed to convert their family motorcar to run on a wood-burning gas generator, circumventing France's chronic gasoline and diesel shortages with fuel supplies commandeered by the Germans.

"The brothers treated me like a little sister," Valérie said of the young men who would not only be her friends but also her protectors.[3]

Valérie spent much of her free time with the four brothers touring nearby Cantal and Puy-de-Dome, known for its long-dormant volcano. The lumpy basalt hills leading up to the volcano overlooked the small farms and towns below. From that view, things almost looked normal again. It was easy to forget the occupation, if only for a little while.

The diversion from studies proved to be a beneficial thing for Valérie, as the rigors of medical school proved to be an exacting trial, especially for a young woman. Women were not numerous among the student body, or the faculty, so Valérie became something of a target from some of her less progressive classmates.

"There were hazings and 'anatomical' jokes that were not always of good taste, especially during the dissection sessions."

One can only imagine the heights—or depths—reached in terms of mischief in the classroom. Yet even the less-than-professional behavior of Valérie's fellow students only served to encourage her to rise above the situation presented to her.

"Student life was an opportunity for me to harden my character. I was cut off from my family, and I had to defend myself alone without anyone to act as an intermediary. I didn't like to be protected too much or to feel even less responsible for my well-being. However, I would soon be facing new tests even more serious than adapting to student life."[4]

The Gestapo—the German secret police—was very active in the Clermont-Ferrand region, collecting data on subversive individuals and activity detrimental to the German war effort. They inflicted unimaginable horror on anyone caught in their web. Their authority was unquestionable, and their ranks often included those who embodied the most venal elements of racism, sadism, and terror.

The Resistance movement was the prime target of Gestapo operatives. The Gestapo was also in charge of the arrest and deportation of Jews and political prisoners to concentration camps. As in Germany and other occupied countries in Europe, the Gestapo relied heavily on informants, who often traded malicious gossip and unfounded information in exchange for preferential treatment from agents.

It was well known that the University of Auvergne had allowed the University of Strasbourg to merge with their campus, and the Gestapo was aware of this. They knew that many of the students and faculty were in Clermont-Ferrand illegally from Alsace-Lorraine. There were also many informants inside the university. The campus chapter of the pro-German/anticommunist Doriot Association posed a threat, but at least its intentions were publicly known. The campus leader of the Doriot was dealt with by a homemade bomb cooked up in the school's chemistry lab before he could do too much damage.[5]

An even bigger traitor, however, was a twenty-year-old prelaw student named Georges Mathieu, a member of a clandestine campus group associated with the Resistance, Combat universitaire. Mathieu was seduced by a female German operative named Ursula Brandt, known as "The Panther" because of a panther-skinned coat she always wore. He became a willing accomplice for the Gestapo, identifying a number of students and faculty members with forged identity papers or others who "escaped" from Alsace-Lorraine, including Valérie André.[6]

The crackdown came on November 25, 1943. The Gestapo, backed by a company of nearly two hundred German infantry soldiers, dropped a human net around the university. By sheer chance, Valérie had left the campus on the afternoon of the raid to shop for a winter coat. On her way back from shopping, she stopped by her lodgings to have lunch with her landlords, Henri and Renée Prat.

"I had finished lunch . . . when the doorbell at the entryway was rung with a frenzy."

Renée Prat rushed to answer the door. At the door was a man who had witnessed the raid.

"Quickly," the man whispered in hushed urgency. "Mademoiselle André must leave now. The Germans are at the university. Students and teachers are being lined up in the courtyard, along the walls, with their arms in the air."

Impulsively and against better judgment, Valérie decided to hurry back to the university to see for herself what had happened.

"I thought that there was something that could perhaps be done."

Once she arrived at the university, however, the truth of the situation turned out to be shockingly real.

"The students were searched brutally."

Valérie watched in horror from a discreet vantage point, trying to avoid the attention of the Germans. "The soldiers inspected and were shouting orders. I left without excessive haste and went home to the Prats."[7]

The full extent of the raid was a horrific spectacle beyond imagination. The Gestapo was ruthlessly thorough in their operation. Separate actions were conducted on Avenue Carnot, the Rectory, and the student center known as "Gallia." There were roughly twelve hundred students, faculty, and staff at the university, and each person present was interrogated. The first casualty of the raid was Paul Collomp, a professor of ancient Greek studies who tried to prevent Gestapo agents from accessing student records. He was shot and killed on the spot.[8] A young male student was shot and killed as he tried to escape through a window. With Germans pointing automatic weapons, the faculty, staff, and students were forced to keep their hands raised in the air or suffer the same fate.

Of the twelve hundred people questioned that day, nearly eight hundred would be taken to a German prison set up at a former French military base near Clermont-Ferrand. They were accused of being part of the Resistance, having Jewish- or foreign-sounding names, or being from Alsace-Lorraine. Ultimately, two dozen professors and eighty-nine students were permanently detained.[9]

Valérie knew she was also in danger because of her Alsatian origins. The Prats also worried because of Henri's connection to the Resistance. They assumed that their house would be the Gestapo's next.

"I had to leave town quickly. I packed a suitcase in a hurry. The eldest Chardon brother was contacted to come to the Prat's house. He accompanied me to the train station and agreed with my decision to go to Paris, where it would be easier to hide."[10]

The pair traveled to the train station at nearby Auvergne, where Émile Chardon informed Valérie that he had heard that the Gestapo had already released most of the students and faculty, except those who had come from Alsace-Lorraine. Valérie would later learn that a large number of her Alsatian colleagues were deported to Germany. Some were sent to German factories to serve as slave labor. Others—because they were Jewish or were charged with committing subversive acts—were sent to concentration camps at Auschwitz and Buchenwald.

As for Henri and Renée Prat, they were safe for a while after the raid. The Gestapo never came to their house. But Henri increased his activity with the *maquis*, passing on information he obtained from his position at the newspaper that made its way to London. A year later, Henri Prat was arrested by the Gestapo. He was brought to the same army base where many of the University of Strasbourg students and faculty were sent.[11] Prat was tortured and suffered from advanced tuberculosis during his captivity, but he never revealed his connections in the Resistance. Georges Mathieu was a witness to Henri Prat's execution by firing squad in February 1944, attesting to this before his own execution following his trial for treason ten months later.

Life in France was now more treacherous than any time since the beginning of the occupation.

Valérie André's life submerged back into the shadows.

Chapter 6

The City of Light in Shadows

When Émile Chardon and Valérie André arrived at the train station in Auvergne, they were relieved to see that there didn't seem to be any heightened security present. Émile wasn't taking any chances. He told Valérie to wait across the street from the station while he bought the ticket for her. Fortunately, no one had ordered an interruption to the trains. It was still business as usual.

Émile wanted to hide Valérie with a family in Auvergne, but she refused. She told him that she knew people in Paris and would blend into the metropolis once she was there. It was a big gamble on her part. The area around Paris was tightly locked down. There were many security checks to go through before her final stop at Gare de Lyon. It was to be a dangerous journey and one that Valérie had not thought out well.

The pair waited for the last train heading in the direction of Paris. They both decided it wouldn't be a good idea to stay on the platform until it arrived, so they remained outside of the station until the train neared. Time slowly ticked away. Both of them imagined that a truckload of soldiers would turn up at the station any minute. More time went by. It was dark now.

After what seemed like minutes passing for hours, Valérie and Émile finally heard a train whistle in the distance. The Paris-bound train was arriving. Valérie reached up to hug the giant Émile Chardon, thanking him for getting her this far. The rest of the journey would be up to her.

Grabbing her valise, she quickly made her way through the station and onto the platform as the train came to a stop. As she walked, Valérie looked straight ahead and made eye contact with no one. She was expecting a German agent to order her to stop, and in the periphery of her eyes, she kept a lookout. She was not about to stop from boarding the train unless she was forced.

The locomotive chuffed out plumes of steam as it sat idling. The conductor paid no attention to Valérie as she stepped into one of the second-class cars. Finding her seat, she put her valise in the compartment above and sat down, waiting for the train to start again. It seemed like an eternity until the conductor blew his whistle for the last boarding.

Valérie breathed easier as the train moved slowly past the station, gradually picking up some speed. She noticed that the second-class rail car was rather shabby, and the upholstered bench seat was torn. No one bothered to repair such minor damage. But at least she felt some relief that it was dark inside the coach. The thought of being identified made her feel anxious.

It wasn't long after the train had left the station that the conductor came by asking Valérie for her ticket. He gave it a cursory glance, clipped it, then handed it back to her.

The train made steady progress but was running much slower than it would have before the war. The Germans took the better French coal for their own industrial needs, leaving the French railway system with dirty, low-grade coal to run their steam engines. The train's route would run through Vichy and then on to Moulins-sur-Ailler. Moulins-sur-Ailler was the last stop before entering the Occupied Zone that included Paris, although all of France was essentially now an occupied zone.

As the train slowed down and entered the station, Valérie noticed a small assembly of inspectors ready to board. Once inside the coach, Valérie waited for them to reach her. She handed her official identification to them, believing that showing them anything less would lead to trouble.

"As usual, my birthplace intrigued them, but I disarmed any suspicion by answering in a natural manner."

Valérie told the inspector the same story about how her father worked for the government and was temporarily assigned to Alsace-Lorraine at the time of her birth. The German, somewhat bored with his job and wishing to be finished for the day, accepted her story and handed her identification back to her, going on to the next traveler. Valérie was quite pleased.

"The confidence that I had in myself had raced to a new high once more."[1]

The train chugged on northward for another three hundred kilometers. Valérie, however, did not sleep for the entire journey, remaining bolt upright in her seat, vigilant at every stop. The train finally arrived at Gare de Lyon the next morning.

The oppressive atmosphere of the former capital was readily apparent the moment Valérie stepped out of the station. The red, white, and black swastika banners were everywhere, reminding everyone who was in charge. The early morning autumn sky was dense, cold, and overcast. That atmosphere extended to the people she encountered, who wore somber apprehension and weariness. The vibrancy and usual joie de vivre of Parisian life were visibly absent. Day-to-day living for most people throughout every quarter of the city was now just the toil of survival while at the same time staying clear of German authority.

Very little else mattered.

"Paris had changed a lot in only two years," Valérie observed. "People had sad and resigned expressions on their faces. The streets were full of Germans who patrolled day and night. It was an atmosphere of darkness, mistrust, fear that permeated everything like a rotting dampness."[2]

Once more, Valérie found herself with only a few options that could be played out. She knew that she was evading German authority and was subject to immediate arrest and likely deportation to Germany as a slave factory worker or worse. More than twelve million foreign workers, including prisoners of war, would be sent to Germany as labor, working primarily in production to support the German war effort.[3] Many would perish from the appalling working conditions.

In Paris, Valérie once again turned to her friend Guy Dauvé to help her find a place to stay.

"It had become less and less easy to find a shelter where I could safely stay," Valérie recalled.

Dauvé proved to be resourceful and found a room for Valérie at a dilapidated hotel in the eighteenth arrondissement on rue des Abbesses, one of the seediest districts of Paris.

"I took possession of an absolutely abysmal room that was without comfort or heating," Valérie said.

The room more accurately resembled a jail cell than a place to live. It was only about twelve feet long by ten feet wide and illuminated by a single light fixture strung by a cord to the ceiling. The small steam radiator in the corner never came on during the harsh winter. The paint was dingy and peeling from the walls. The bare wooden floors reeked of a stench that was a mélange of tobacco, alcohol, and just simply decades of human existence.

There was a primitive bath and toilet Valérie shared with the other tenants on her floor. The bed was a worn-out mattress that was hardly suitable for a dog to sleep on. The only luxury was a single balcony window that managed to let in some light and offset the ongoing psychological darkness that continually shrouded the city.

Despite its misery, however, the hotel had one redeeming aspect.

"Guy assured me that police checks were rare and that he knew the manager well and that she would look after me."[4]

Valérie's living conditions drew a clear picture of the isolated world she lived in. She was separated from both friends and family and allowed no other choice but to live in the shadows.

Living life as a Parisian during the occupation, one would witness many instances that would provoke reactions of utter shock and revulsion. From a scene on the Paris metro system, Valérie vividly recalled the sight of two young Frenchmen dressed in German uniforms seated together in one of the subway cars.

"Their accents suggested that they were from the countryside. One of them was playing around with his weapon and it fired off a bullet that ricocheted into the ankle of a passenger. A German officer in the same subway car addressed them furiously. I got out at the nearest stop, indignant, disgusted."[5]

The spectacle of French nationals dressed in the uniform of the occupying enemy was unfortunately not an altogether uncommon sight. Significant numbers of French escaped the occupation to serve as part of Charles de Gaulle's Free French with the Allies. And others remained in France who carried out acts of sabotage and guerilla warfare against the Germans within the *maquis* resistance. But it was also evident that there were many French who collaborated with the German authority and served in the German military cause.

Another menace was the Milice, or militia, created by Pétain's Vichy government in January 1943 as an auxiliary unit to the German occupation force. Their express purpose was to hunt down those active in the Resistance movement. At the height of its activity, the Milice numbered more than thirty-five thousand.

The Germans also created a French unit of the dreaded Schutzstaffel (SS) with the formation of the Eighth Sturmbrigade SS Frankreich and the Thirty-Third Waffen Grenadier of the SS, Charlemagne Division. The latter unit had the dubious distinction of being among the final defenders of Berlin when the Soviets entered the German capital in April 1945.

France was not the only country to offer up its men into the service of the German war machine. The brutal pattern of German alliances and occupations played out in multiple instances where non-German nationals fought in a cause that wasn't their own to begin with. In a country such as France, however—where the heroic actions of the *maquis* and Free French have justifiably celebrated with a national pride second to none—the more sinister aspect of France's collaboration with its enemy during the war marked a low point.

For Valérie, her quest to continue her interrupted studies was equal to her own need for survival. Although much of France's educational system was largely in disarray and now subject to Nazi doctrine, parts of the system remained more or less intact. Despite the hardship brought on by France's defeat, Paris's acclaimed Sorbonne continued its well-regarded medical program. It would become the obvious place for Valérie to continue her studies except for one important issue that needed to be resolved.

"Because of the haste in which I left Auvergne, I didn't have any evidence of my academic record with the faculty of Clermont-Ferrand," Valérie soon realized. "Fortunately, I met a student who was also originally from Strasbourg, who guided me toward other friends who also managed to leave Auvergne. The thread of my existence was resumed."[6]

Within her clandestine circle of associates, Valérie learned of a graduate student at the Sorbonne who was designated to deal with students in distress. Valérie resolved to seek him out to plot her next course of action.

As winter approached in Paris, a bitter chill descended on the city. With most of the city lacking coal to fuel furnaces, the cold nights became hard to endure. At the old *pensione* hotel where Valérie was staying, the lack of amenities was especially insufferable.

"I politely asked the woman managing the hotel if she could perhaps provide another blanket for the night," Valérie said.

The woman's response was typical of the period, as she looked incredulously at Valérie and remarked: "How can you be cold at your age? It's necessary to take in a lover!"

"I smiled as she seemed to be sincere and went back to my room. Shortly after, she brought me three blankets and two fried eggs prepared for me. Her hospitality was very touching."[7]

But nothing remained stable in Valérie's world. Little did Valérie realize that her presence as a single woman in the hotel was beginning to stir suspicion. Guy Dauvé arrived at her door in the middle of the night, informing Valérie that it was no longer safe to remain where she was.

"Is there any other place you can go?" Dauvé asked her.

While Valérie had some distant relatives living in Paris, asking them for lodging was impossible.

"I only began to notice how much my presence would be undesirable here or there," she realized. "It was every person for his or herself in this difficult situation. The lesson was rather cruel and disappointing, but it strengthened my character even more."[8]

Valérie checked into a small hotel near the Gare de l'Est train station with little money and few other choices. She knew that one of her brothers-in-law used the hotel when he had business that brought him to Paris, and she hoped that it would be a safe haven. Not long after, however, there was one night that brought the terror that she had long dreaded.

"In the middle of the third night I awoke with a start. Shouts reverberated as I quickly got dressed without turning on any lights. It was a search being carried out by the Gestapo. Obviously, they were seeking someone."

Valérie immediately believed that she was the subject of the search. Indeed, Valérie later learned that a woman came to the home of the Prats in Clermont inquiring about her whereabouts. Could someone have tipped off the Gestapo as to Valérie's whereabouts? The possibility of arrest was unthinkable. Valérie knew that the punishment for an Alsatian found in Paris would be severe.

"Very anxiously, I waited my turn. They arrived on my floor, and they began pounding on one door at a time demanding to be let in." One after another, doors opened to the jackbooted thugs. Through the thin walls, Valérie could hear the commander in charge of the squad demanding identity papers and answers to anything he deemed questionable.

"They were now knocking at the door of my neighbors." Valérie's anxiety level was unimaginable. The Gestapo officer's presence was felt as his sinister force filled the hotel. It was a feeling of overwhelming malevolence.

Yet the pattern changed when he reached a door near Valérie's room.

"It was a different scenario. I discerned through the walls a few snatches of conversation. It was a mixture of English and German, though I couldn't really understand what was said. Perhaps they were Dutch, I thought."

Valérie could hear the anguish of a woman, pleading with the Gestapo agent as her husband was forced to subject himself to the officer's interrogation. But no argument could sway the unyielding officer, and the faceless menace that could only be sensed through the opaqueness of the walls only served to heighten Valérie's anxiety.

"They were taken away without any consideration, despite the sobs and cries of the woman," Valérie later recalled. "Afterwards, a deathly silence fell. I could not sleep for the rest of the night."[9]

The following morning Valérie had an appointment with the graduate student who could hopefully help her resume her studies.

"From the start, he was very inquisitive with me," Valérie said. "He wanted to know all of my affiliations and my political opinions before committing himself to help me."

The student's line of questioning was understandable, given the highly charged atmosphere of suspicion that permeated every quarter of Paris. The German authority was highly suspicious of subversive activity among students that smoldered even in universities within Germany, let alone countries that it occupied. There had already been a sizeable student rebellion viciously quelled by German police at the University of Munich in January 1943. Infiltration into the French university system by agents and informants answering directly to the Gestapo was a possibility, as evidenced by the actions of Georges Mathieu in Clermont-Ferrand.

A few days later, Valérie arranged an interview with a representative from the University of Paris.

"I will never forget his noble and imposing stature," Valérie said. "He had a beautifully framed face offset with white hair, enlightened by a luminous gaze of intelligence and kindness. He presented me with a letter to take to the Secretary-General of the Faculty of Medicine."

Valérie immediately ran the letter over to the School of Medicine. Once there, however, she learned that there would be other obstacles in her path for admission.

"The Secretary-General was encouraging and sympathetic towards me. But he assured me that without transcripts from the university at Clermont-Ferrand, he couldn't do anything for me."[10]

Valérie's solution to resolve her lacking official school records left her with really only one choice—to return to Clermont-Ferrand.

"One might think that it was unnecessary to take a new risk to return to Auvergne to get my academic record," Valérie thought to herself.

But she weighed her options.

"In order not to lose another year of study, I was exposing myself to my own loss of life. I didn't doubt what my fate would be if the Germans were to stop me."[11]

Valérie knew that the decision to return to Auvergne was hers and hers alone. She knew that it would serve no purpose if she sought anyone's counsel. Quite logically, she likely would have been advised to abandon the idea.

Ultimately she chose to take the risk.

The state-run train system, SNCF (Societé nationale des chemins de fer français), had deteriorated to a deplorable state of condition. It was worn down by the demands of the Germans as well as by acts of sabotage and deliberately deferred maintenance by rail workers. When some travel restrictions eased between zones encompassing Vichy and the German-occupied territory, a tremendous crush of people flocked to the trains in attempts to reunite with long-separated relatives and friends.

"The travelers piled up in the trains like sardines, standing upright even in the corridors," Valérie related. "The toilets on the train were of no use, and even access to them was impossible. As a result, many were forced to abandon all or most of their human dignity."[12]

At Moulins, Valérie discovered that while the Germans still maintained a security checkpoint between the two zones, the inspection process was less rigorous than with her previous crossing.

"Probably because of the nauseating odors and general uncleanliness of the crowd of pilgrims arriving at the station at Moulins, the document inspection imposed by the Germans was at least reduced."

When Valérie finally reached Clermont-Ferrand, she contacted her friends, the Chardon brothers. They were both surprised to see her and, at the same time, fearful for her safety. The Chardons warned Valérie not to call upon the Prats, her former landlords. They knew that the couple had been contacted by agents who had inquired about Valérie after she left Clermont-Ferrand.

"The Gestapo had gone through all of the student records at the university and had visited my former home several times," Valérie later found out.

Despite the risks, Valérie called on the dean of the university's faculty to make an appointment to see him. The dean's secretary informed Valérie that under no circumstances would he meet with her in his office, but only on the street.

"I didn't understand such a casual attitude," said Valérie. "But when the hour of our appointment came, I could see that the dean was a man who was quite agitated."

"What are you doing here?" the man demanded. He was beside himself with fear and apprehension, worried that anyone could be watching or listening to them. "You should never have come back; it is far too dangerous. You must walk away from me immediately!"

Valérie had traveled too far and under conditions too hazardous to her own life to be overly concerned with the dean's fears.

"He refused to entrust my files to me but promised instead that they would be forwarded to Paris as soon as possible."

The dean's method for transmitting the transcripts was less than reassuring, but Valérie was in no position to press the matter further. But ultimately, the dean kept his word.

"My file was classified with a score of students with similar cases and was held in a secret place at the University of Paris," Valérie later learned. "In the event of a raid by the Germans, they would have been destroyed at once."[13]

Not long after she returned to Paris, Valérie was finally able to enroll at the University of Paris to continue her studies. While the austerity and deprivation of the occupation were still amply evident everywhere one looked in the city, Paris at the beginning of 1944 was slowly beginning to show a different tenor. While news continued to be heavily censored by the Germans, word was nonetheless beginning to filter down to inhabitants of occupied countries in western Europe that Hitler's war, especially in the Soviet Union, was going badly. In southern Europe, the Allied forces were beginning to move northward through Italy. Moreover, Joseph Stalin had been pressuring since 1942 for the British and American allies to open a western front against the Germans to relieve the pressure from the Soviet Union.

By late spring 1944, the yoke of the German oppression was about to be broken wide open. On June 6, 1944, D-Day, the largest military offensive ever staged, took to the air and sea from England to the beaches at Normandy.

"The months between the invasion of Normandy and the liberation of Paris in August seemed long and interminable to us. The daily expectation was loaded with a growing nervousness," Valérie recalled.[14]

But it wasn't just Valérie André who felt that way. All of France was nervous. The day of liberation may have been close at hand, but the potential for scorched earth and mass destruction was a distinct possibility. The entire population of France held its collective breath as the battle for liberation began.

Chapter 7

Paris Broken, Paris Outraged, Paris Liberated

Paris, June–August 1944

Paris in 1944 was a city on the verge of collapse. Food was in short supply, and other essentials were unavailable. Blackouts were common due to a perpetual shortage of coal for the city's power stations. Frequent Allied air raids that targeted the industrial sections of the city also injured and killed many civilian Parisians.

Through it all, the Germans maintained their daily twelve o'clock parade down the Champs-Élysées that spring. The troops making this show of authority were smaller in numbers and visibly older. Younger, more elite Wehrmacht regiments were sent to combat the Allied invasion force from the west following the D-Day invasion in Normandy or to the eastern front, where Russian troops steadily advanced on Germany.

But a destructive force remained, nonetheless. Executions and deportations by rail to concentration camps and prisons were ongoing. Rumors were rampant that the Germans had wired the entire city of Paris for scorched-earth demolition if they were forced to retreat. There were still twenty thousand fully armed Wehrmacht troops, along with thousands of Milice present in the city. The threat of mass extermination to the civilian population was very real.

Valérie André, along with the rest of Paris, was poised on the knife's edge of uncertainty during spring and summer 1944.

After beginning her medical studies, Valérie had managed to find an apartment in the Latin Quarter not far from the University of Paris. Although her medical studies were now finally underway, she was still forced to live

43

covertly. Day-to-day life in Paris was an exercise in existence and survival. Stark reminders of the occupation were everywhere. Food shops were mostly empty, and Valérie suffered the effects of the shortages acutely, dropping several kilograms off her already petite figure.

There were also many parts of the city that Valérie avoided. The nearby Jardin de Luxembourg was commandeered as a headquarters for the Luftwaffe. Bunkers were dug under the gardens to house personnel. Herman Goering was known to stay at Luxembourg palace during his many raids on French art museums while in Paris. The Wehrmacht took over the area near the mostly emptied Louvre museum on rue Rivoli. And everyone avoided avenue Foch, where many high ranking German officers took over expensive apartments abandoned by well-to-do Parisians who had fled the city. For this reason, it became known as "avenue Boch" during the occupation. The Gestapo also operated an interrogation center at 84, avenue Foch, where many Resistance fighters were kept and tortured.

Danger permeated every quarter of the city.

"My neighbors on the same floor as I was on were the Legrands, also refugees from Alsace-Lorraine. They took in the news of the military engagements and passed it on to me."

Monsieur Legrand monitored the BBC from a radio he concealed in his apartment. He was also a member of the Resistance and not only relayed information to Valérie but also coded messages transmitted by the BBC to his fellow *maquis*.

"Monsieur Legrand divided his time between Joigny and Paris for the Resistance. It was he who announced that the Allies were approaching Paris, for which we celebrated with the greatest joy."[1]

The Allies had originally intended to bypass Paris, expecting heavy resistance from the Germans still stationed there. Unknown to all but a few, Hitler ordered the commander of German troops in the city, General Dietrich von Choltitz, to destroy the great landmarks of Paris if forced to retreat. Von Choltitz mulled the order.

General de Gaulle, however, insisted that Paris was to be liberated. In Paris, the Resistance, led by Henri "Colonel Rol" Tanguy, was already moving against the Germans. Their objective was to retake the city.

"Paris is worth 200,000 dead, so long as the city frees itself before the Free French armies arrive," Tanguy declared.[2] Tanguy ordered all *maquis* to take to the streets with any weapons at their disposal, with or without the support of the Allies.

The city was shutting down everywhere one looked. The metro and bus service, the *gendarmerie*, and even the postal workers went on strike, bringing Paris to a halt. Barricades made of any scrap material that could be scrounged and strung with barbed wire appeared in many quarters of the cities.

With reports that the situation in Paris was reaching a breaking point, de Gaulle presented his argument to General Dwight Eisenhower, the commander in chief of the Allied invasion force, that the liberation of the city was crucial. Eisenhower was initially reluctant to send troops to Paris, but de Gaulle convinced him to dispatch General Philippe Leclerc, commander of the Free French Second Armored Division, to take the lead. Leclerc's division was composed of 14,000 men, including 3,350 from French colonies, plus more than 300 tanks, 216 halftracks, 400 jeeps, and 2,000 trucks carrying troops and supplies.

"We followed the progress of Allied troops with feverish impatience," Valérie André recalled. "As their approach to Paris was reported, the atmosphere in the Latin Quarter became very tense."

Small arms fire erupted in all neighborhoods. Bullets would rain down from the upper floors of apartment buildings, oftentimes seeming to be randomly fired. Blood stained many of the sidewalks of Paris. It was a free-for-all of violence.

"Invisible snipers, hidden in the buildings, were targeting pedestrians. While I tried to meet friends on *Rue des Bernadins*, a bullet rang out, ricocheting off a wall near me. Then there was a second bullet. I only had time to roll into a doorway. I remained huddled there for some time before running to my apartment. The surrounding streets were deserted. I learned later in the day about the death of one of my friends. He was killed by a bullet in the forehead when he left his home."[3]

Street fighting in Paris was out of control by the third week of August. The Resistance fighters were equal in number to the Germans in Paris, but they were poorly armed. Between 800 to 1,000 *maquis* lost their lives to the Germans, while another 1,500 were left wounded. As the fighting raged on, Swedish consul general Raoul Nordling approached General von Choltitz to broker a cease-fire with the *maquis*. Von Choltitz initially agreed, but the *maquis* maintained their hit-and-run tactics against the Germans.

On the morning of August 25, Free French general Philippe Leclerc's Second Armored Division entered the western section of Paris, sweeping through the Arc de Triomphe and the Champs-Élysées while simultaneously the U.S. Army's Fourth Infantry Division mopped up the eastern part. The celebratory outpouring was something unimaginable just a short time before.

"It was in choking heat, the 25th of August, but a virtual human tidal wave swept through Rue Saint-Jacques when the first tanks arrived."

Valérie marveled as the long nightmare of France's bondage began to come to an end.

"Hordes of men, women, and children swarmed the Allied tanks, clinging to their sides, offering flowers and wine, and hugging every soldier in sight. There were civilians out on the street as far as one could see."[4]

Even amid jubilation, danger in the city still existed.

"Suddenly, a popping sound burst out. Its origin was difficult to detect. I saw soldiers on the tanks pointing their weapons toward the roof of the Sorbonne. There was a rumor that the Japanese had found refuge there."[5] As improbable as that rumor may have been, the sniper fire caused the celebrating crowd to break up in a panic. As more French and American soldiers flowed into the city, however, the calm returned.

"The dust had settled, and our liberators continued their procession to a cheering, laughing, and tearful crowd."[6]

Throughout the day on August 25, Free French and American forces clashed with the remaining Germans. By day's end, 71 Allied soldiers were killed and 225 wounded. The bulk of the German force left in Paris—more than 14,000—surrendered, including General von Choltitz. More than 3,200 Germans were killed. The rest had either deserted or fled the city to rejoin German divisions that were now in a full fallback position.

General von Choltitz ultimately chose not to follow Hitler's personal order to destroy Paris. The explosives that were rigged to obliterate the city's most prominent landmarks and bridges were never detonated. Whether the reason for von Choltitz to defy his orders was to take a stand against a madman or to acknowledge the inevitable defeat of Germany, the general would ultimately be spared condemnation in a postwar world.

On the following day, August 26, General Charles de Gaulle arrived in Paris.

"I attended the spectacle on August 26 at Notre Dame cathedral, gathered at the time to celebrate the arrival of General de Gaulle," Valérie recalled. "It was pure jubilation among the population, but shots rang out from the rooftops causing the crowd to disappear underground."[7]

The danger was real. Automatic weapons fire came from the rooftops of apartment buildings near the cathedral. It was also thought that there were assassins in the bell towers of Notre Dame itself. The last remnants of French fascist sympathizers, Milice, and collaborators were bound by their fanaticism to kill de Gaulle, the symbol of a new France. Casualties, both civilian and military, were severe, as both American and French motorized artillery countered the attack by firing back into the top floors. All the while, de Gaulle remained calm, smoking a cigarette as his tall, imposing frame stood out. He never ducked for cover, nor did he seek shelter from the barrage. He remained steadfast with his Free French forces in defiance of fascism's last stand in Paris.

Most of the terrorists were killed. The ones who were pulled alive from their assassin's roosts were beaten to death by the angry crowd.

Despite the danger, de Gaulle addressed the massive crowd gathered on the plaza and streets surrounding Notre Dame, where he proclaimed, in the powerful voice that France came to know so well:

> Paris!
> Paris outraged!
> Paris broken!
> Paris martyred!
> But Paris liberated!

The danger was still clear and present, as it had been throughout the long four years since France's ordeal under oppression began. But on this day—a day that many had not lived long enough to see—Valérie André, along with thousands of her fellow French citizens, had at long last witnessed the beginnings of the rebirth of a free France.

Chapter 8

In the Company of Modern Knights

France, 1945

The liberation of Paris and eventually the whole of France became moments quintessentially frozen in time for many who lived to see the rule of tyranny end. Valérie André summed up the feeling of many of her compatriots:

"It was as if the world itself began to breathe again."[1]

Even after a long and often brutal four years of occupation, people in France indeed began to breathe once again. But serious issues hung over the postwar nation.

Old scores were not forgotten. First and foremost in the minds of many was how to mete out punishment to those who collaborated with the Germans during the occupation.

The Vichy government was an obvious target. When the Germans retreated from France, Marshal Pétain and his right-hand henchmen, Prime Minister Pierre Laval, were taken back to Germany and kept at a castle near Sigmaringen. Following Germany's defeat in May 1945, Pétain and Laval would be extradited to France to stand trial. Because of his military service during the Battle of Verdun in World War I and his advanced age, Pétain was sentenced to life in prison. He died at the age of ninety-one in 1951. Pierre Laval—who mercilessly persecuted Jews, Communists, and the *maquis*, and sent French citizens to Germany as slave labor—received a death sentence and was executed in October 1945.[2]

A bloodbath was unleashed in France with many wishing nothing more than revenge against anyone either known to or, in some cases, merely

49

suspected of aiding or profiting from the Germans or receiving preferential treatment from them during the occupation. More than three hundred thousand formal accusations of collaborations were issued when Charles de Gaulle's provisional government took over in autumn 1944. And more than twenty thousand people—some belonging to the Vichy government, but the majority being civilians—were killed in the immediate aftermath of the liberation, with most executed outside any court of law.[3]

The dreaded Milice, the Vichy political militia that relentlessly hunted down the *maquis* and others who resisted Fascist rule, were themselves hunted down following the liberation. The Milice had in many ways become an extension of Hitler's SS, and many joined in French units of the Waffen SS beginning in 1943. In that year, it was estimated that more than thirty-five thousand *miliciens* were operating for the Vichy government. While many *miliciens* would be killed in these German units as the Allies advanced on Germany, another fifteen hundred would be killed by French citizens who especially came to despise the cruelty they had inflicted.[4]

As for the two young Frenchmen dressed in German uniform who Valérie André witnessed on the Paris subway during the occupation, their fate, and the fate of many like them, was likely of equal oblivion. If the two young men had not already been killed when they were thrown into battle on Germany's eastern front—especially at Stalingrad—then they were likely reorganized along with more than sixty-five hundred French into the Sturmbrigade SS Frankreich division that engaged the Soviets as they advanced toward Pomerania in northeastern Germany. Fewer than one hundred survived capture by the Soviets or outright death. Those who did survive were purportedly sent to defend the Reich Chancellery during Hitler's futile and devastatingly destructive last stand in Berlin. If any survived after the declaration of the war's end on May 8, 1945, they were sent back to France to be tried for treason and either imprisoned or executed.[5]

While government and military traitors and those who collaborated for economic gain were obvious targets for retribution, French women accused of *collaboration horizontale* with the Germans were an even more vivid reminder of the outrage and hysteria expressed by the French. Charged with having sexual relations or bearing the children of German occupation soldiers, countless numbers of women were shaved of their hair and paraded through the streets in many cities in France.

The impact of the Holocaust also played its role in the aftermath of France's liberation. Deportations to German concentration camps had continued up until summer 1944, and it's estimated that more than 42,500 were sent eastward, most never to return. In all, approximately one-quarter of France's prewar Jewish population perished during the war.

The German and Allied bombing of France during the war also took its toll on the civilian population. By the end of the war, more than sixty thousand French were among the dead from bombings alone.[6]

Indeed, the world began to breathe once again, and from the ashes of war, there would arise anew. As Charles de Gaulle said:

"France is a country that is carrying on; it is not a country that is beginning."[7]

The city of Paris emerged relatively unscathed from physical destruction during the war. Still, a return to normal life was slow in arriving. Valérie André endured the deprivations of many Parisians in the aftermath of the liberation—desperate poverty and chronic material shortages. The second year of studies at the Faculty of Medicine in Paris completely absorbed her, however. Valérie's dedication was also recognized by members of the senior faculty at the school.

"My financial situation began to improve somewhat, thanks to the care I lavished on patients who were entrusted to me by my supervising professors outside of my regular courses," Valérie recalled. Small gratuities would be arranged from patients with means who were under the care of physicians who served on the university's faculty. The students, who provided extra care to these patients at a time when doctors and medical personnel were scarce in Paris, were essentially nurse's aides. And because financial need was dire in postwar France, students were grateful for any form of financial assistance.

"A number of students during these difficult months benefited from the protection of our eminent instructors who were fully aware of our precarious resources."[8]

During this time, Valérie André formed a strong bond with Dr. Leon Binet, the chair of the Physiology Department. In June 1945, Binet brought news of a unique project to include his most gifted students.

"Professor Binet . . . received an invitation from General de Lattre to visit the French zone of occupation in Germany with a delegation of students and professors. He proposed that I be among the group. I accepted the invitation, especially as an Alsatian, with the journey representing a kind of revenge."[9]

By summer 1945, defeated Germany was divided into four sectors and occupied by France, the United States, Great Britain, and the Soviet Union. Initially, France was not given an occupation zone in postwar Germany.

A proposal made to General de Gaulle's provisional government recommended that French industrial capacity should be rebuilt using the coal and steel resources from Germany's Saar Valley. In a showing of postwar unity, Great Britain and the United States agreed to carve out and cede a zone to the French. The economic devastation from four years of occupation was enormous, but a fine line was necessary not to repeat the mistake following World War I of exacting excessively harsh reparations from Germany.

The First French Army, the liberators of Valérie André's Strasbourg, totaled more than 135,000 soldiers, many of whom were former *maquis*.[10] The bulk of the troops were stationed at the headquarters of the French occupation zone in Baden-Baden, Germany.

Valérie André would not have missed the opportunity to aid and assist her country's soldiers for anything. Venturing into the lair of France's former occupiers in the company of her liberators also brought some closure to her five years of personal hardship.

Unknown to Valérie at the time, the towering figure of General Jean de Lattre would feature prominently in her future; however, for his actions in Alsace, de Lattre's reputation as the "Liberator of Strasbourg" was enough to cement the importance of his image in Valérie's consciousness.

Along with her fellow students, Valérie André's first impression of de Lattre was of a hero who stood larger than life. With a determined face dominated by a bold, aquiline Roman nose, the general had the aura of a natural-born leader. When de Lattre spoke, his words were precisely chosen and inspired both confidence and respect. It was an impression shared by many.

"The great lord, de Lattre, welcomed us with regard and flourish," Valérie observed. "His imperial style struck me."[11]

The men of de Lattre's army were held in equally high esteem. They were an amalgamation of those who escaped France before or after the occupation, former Resistance fighters, and soldiers drawn from French colonies, particularly from Africa. The soldiers were almost universally young, and their youth represented hope for a new era of leadership and direction for all of France.

The elevated place of the military in postwar France approached the status of near knighthood, and this perception embodied the most chivalrous aspects of knighthood in the eyes of most French. And Valérie André was hardly an exception.

"We were received with extreme kindness by men of all ranks who enjoyed an immense prestige in our eyes, and they knew it," Valérie recalled.

"Many of them were soldiers who took part in the landing in Provence and all the battles of the Liberation. Some were also former students who joined the Free French."[12]

The soldiers asked the medical students about how things were in Paris, many of them eager to see the city once more. One of the young men who struck up a friendship with Valérie André was a twenty-five-year-old aspiring writer named Jean Pierre Lucien Osty. Osty was typical of the many soldiers that Valérie encountered. Of humble origins, he later wrote that his family was "of poor mountain peasants whose names were found inscribed on war memorials, but not in history books."[13] After the German occupation, Osty escaped to Spain and, from there, joined de Gaulle's Free French, where he fought in Italy, France, and Germany. And like many of his comrades, he received numerous decorations including two Croix de guerre medals and the prestigious Legion of Honour award.

After mustering out of the army in 1946, Osty changed his name to the nom de plume Jean Lartéguy. As Jean Lartéguy, the former soldier would become one of France's most prolific war correspondents and would score a literary success with the publication of *The Centurions* in 1963. Although they both could scarcely realize it at the time, Valérie and the future author were destined to cross paths several times throughout their lifetimes.

Lartéguy was one of many soldiers who made an impression on Valérie. Many of the soldiers who were still convalescing from serious wounds were a constant reminder of the sacrifice that was made for the liberation of France. The tales of courage and fellowship in the face of unimaginable adversity filled the young woman's mind. Moreover, the soldiers also exhibited an exuberant sense of optimism for the future, now that they felt they had played a part in vanquishing Fascist evil from the world.

"I was comfortable in this atmosphere of chivalry," Valérie fondly remembered. "Most of the soldiers were of our age. They were our idols. They were intoxicated by victory, their thirst for hope, their courage. How I loved them."[14]

The medical group from Paris remained with the soldiers in Baden-Baden for ten days, but the experience would last a lifetime for Valérie.

"My first encounter with the army was to remain unforgettable to me."[15]

Upon her return to France, Valérie devoted herself to her studies once again with a renewed enthusiasm. The seed had been planted of the possibilities of how she could make her contribution when her time came.

"From heart and soul, I was on the side of the army, the elite of men dedicated to serving the motherland and the noblest of causes," Valérie declared. "To join them one day, perhaps, but in the meantime I 'slaved away,' focusing on my exams and progressing towards the goals I had set for myself."[16]

One thing that changed for Valérie was a renewed acquaintance with her first passion: aviation.

"The barriers that I suffered, like everyone else during the war, prevented me from flying for five years," recalled Valérie. "Upon my return from Germany, I discovered a flying club had been created for glider training at Beynes near Mantes-la-Jolie. I returned to aviation with the passion I had for flying that had not left me for a second."[17]

The aerodrome at Beynes was located about an hour west of Paris. Club aéronautique universitaire was one of the first aeronautic clubs and was established in France in 1928. Beynes was the center of glider plane activity in France before the war and recommenced training following the liberation in 1944. Caudron C-800 Epervier or "Hawk" tandem gliders were typical of the aircraft used by the club to train students in the postwar years. The Caudron C-800 was a modern design with a smooth, high-winged fuselage where the pilot and student were seated side by side. It was manufactured by Caudron in Issy-les-Moulineaux, a suburb of Paris. The Aeronautic Club allowed students to learn how to become pilots for a nominal fee. It was the continuation of baptism by air for Valérie André.

Beynes also had an instructor certified to teach skydiving. The prospect of jumping from a plane was something that harkened back to her childhood dream of zooming through the infinity of space. When she completed her first jump, she felt that she had come full circle with a vision that held close to her heart. In time, she would become a certified parachutist.

By the end of 1948, Valérie André's studies at the University of Paris were drawing to a close. Her date of graduation was November 17, 1948, with a degree as a doctor of medicine, with a specialty in aeronautic medicine. Aeronautic medicine is a study devoted to monitoring the biological and psychological stresses and anomalies that pilots, aircrews, and even aircraft passengers are subjected to in the course of air travel. Valérie's choice to specialize in aeronautic medicine could hardly be viewed as a surprise. It was a prescient career move given the burgeoning role commercial aviation would play in the postwar world. In this same year, Valérie André would also publish her graduate dissertation, "The Pathology of Skydiving."[18] Her experience at Beynes played a major part in researching the work.

There had been long years of desperation and deprivation, not just for Valérie, but for virtually everyone in France. Valérie's journey reflected the journey that a nation had endured during a relatively brief but still onerous dark age. And just like many others, she longed to make a positive difference, not only for France but also for the world in general.

"It was Professor Leon Binet who told me of the need for doctors in the Expeditionary Corps in Indochina to strengthen the staffing of health services there," Valérie later recalled.[19]

The Corps expéditionnaire français en Extrême-Orient, or Far Eastern Expeditionary Corps, was a volunteer military force sent by France to reestablish control over the country's former colonies in Southeast Asia of Laos, Cambodia, and Vietnam. The area collectively was known as Indochina.

Indochina was vital to France's postwar economic rebuilding process; however, the colonial system that France had mapped out before World War II would not be easy to re-implement in a world that had seen the rise and fall of rabidly mega-colonizers in the forms of Nazi Germany, Fascist Italy, and Imperial Japan. By 1947, an anti-French colonial faction was already engaged with the French military in Indochina to end France's colonial rule. It was a conflict that was already shaping up to be bloody on both sides.

While Binet encouraged Valérie to enlist, Valérie's father, Philibert André, once again disapproved of her decision.

"My father tried to dissuade me, worried about the dangers of such a mission. But he knew from experience that in the end, I would not yield to any other will than mine. The spirit of adventure burned in me and the prospect of belonging to a surgical field hospital convinced me to make a commitment to Indochina."

Valérie André would not be dissuaded.

"I left for Indochina at the end of 1948."[20]

Chapter 9

Into the Cauldron

The Port of Marseilles was still rebuilding after the devastation wrought by the Germans and Allied bombing. There was still ample evidence of the destruction, but the cranes were back at work loading and unloading cargo ships at the docks. The port had returned to a sense of normalcy as ship traffic grew month by month in the years following the war. Marseilles was also the main disembarkation point for France's military as it focused attention on a new dilemma in the post–World War II world: Indochina. This is where Valérie André found herself in December 1948, as she prepared to board the steamship *Champollion* bound for Saigon, Vietnam.

The anticipation of something new and something exotic was palpable for Valérie. Plunging into the unknown was something familiar to her by now, but Indochina was to present its own set of challenges. The struggle in Indochina for French troops was daily news in the French press, but many people in France wondered why their country was even involved in a war in another part of the world, especially so soon after the war in Europe was over. Shouldn't France be more concerned with rebuilding itself after World War II than be involved in the affairs of a remote, Southeast Asian colony?

The answer to that question was complicated.

France established its first connections to the countries forming French Indochina—Vietnam, Laos, and Cambodia—beginning in the 1600s when French Catholic missionaries arrived in Vietnam. Vietnam, Laos, and Cambodia were then separate kingdoms ruled by their respective emperors. The entire region became collectively known to the West as Indochina because it marked a midpoint between the vast nations of India and China.

At first, the foreigners were welcomed. French Catholic missionaries were among the first to arrive. While their religious influence brought suspicion from the ruling class, the missionaries also brought culture and technical skills from Europe. One missionary, Alexandre de Rhodes, took it upon himself to create a dictionary of the written Vietnamese language. The Vietnamese language was originally based on complex classical Chinese characters, but de Rhodes built his interpretation of the language on the Roman alphabet. The "Romanized" Vietnamese language was used exclusively by Catholics in Vietnam at first; however, by the early twentieth century, it was universally adopted throughout the country.

The next batch of foreigners to arrive were French merchants. The merchants traded Western goods for exotic far eastern tea, coffee, silk, and spices. They also brought modern weapons to Indochina. At first, the ruling classes in Vietnam, Laos, and Cambodia were more than happy to trade with French merchants. The French made sure that the emperors' armies were well armed to maintain control over their respective kingdoms. But as more merchants arrived in Indochina, weapons deals were struck with rival factions to these kingdoms, particularly in Vietnam. The weapons trade undermined the existing power structure. Merchants often supplied their favored warlords with weapons to defeat their foes in exchange for control over territories possessing valuable resources for export back to France. This became such an established pattern by the nineteenth century that a third batch of foreigners came to Indochina.

The French military.

By the mid-nineteenth century, the Nguyen dynasty had grown distrustful of Catholic missionaries and foreign influence in Vietnam. Vietnamese emperor Tu Duc closed his country off to foreigners and instituted a repressive policy toward Catholics. The French emperor Napoleon III retaliated by sending an armada of fourteen warships and 3,300 men that attacked Saigon on February 17, 1859. The French were outnumbered by the Vietnamese and suffered various maladies from the tropical and foreign climate, but they were better armed. By the end of 1859, the French had defeated Tu Duc forces and negotiated a treaty that established France as colonial masters of Vietnam. Tu Duc would curse the French to his dying day.

From that point onward, more foreigners arrived in Indochina, and France continued to exert more power and influence over the whole region, essentially becoming the hedgehog in the tortoiseshell. As the nineteenth century progressed into the twentieth, thousands of French nationals flocked to

Indochina to seek their fortunes. The French transformed the large cities of Saigon and Hanoi into smaller replicas of Paris in terms of architecture and amenities. France also brought modernization to Indochina in the form of roads, bridges, railways, electrification, and more. But it all came at a price.

As France pumped more money into Indochina, colonial administrators began to demand a sizable return on that investment. The Vietnamese, in particular, bore the brunt of the bounty exacted by their new mother country. Heavy taxes were levied on the Vietnamese people, which resulted in many losing their property to the new arrivals. New resources were exported—coal, zinc, and tin—and widely used in domestic French industry. Rubber was especially prized, and the Michelin tire company acquired vast tracts of lands in Vietnam to meet the growing demands for its products. Rice—which was never exported outside of Vietnam before the French—was now sold by French exporters around the world. While production of exportable commodities grew in Vietnam, poverty increased as well. Many Vietnamese employed in plantation or mining work were barely paid living wages and often suffered from malnutrition and disease.

Also, taking a page out of the drug pusher's playbook, one French governor-general, Paul Doumer, legalized the use of opium throughout Vietnam. Once a sizable portion of the population was hooked, Doumer imposed a tax on the drug that contributed one-third of France's revenue necessary to govern Indochina.[1]

Meanwhile, French colonists maintained a comfortable lifestyle evidenced by exclusive hotels and resorts, private parks, and lavish villas. And French exporters grew rich.

It was an inequitable situation doomed to failure in the long run.

One visionary who saw the inequity of French rule was Ho Chi Minh. Born Nguyen Sinh Cung in the village of Hoàng Trù in 1890, the young man who would grow up to lead a revolution witnessed the disparity in his country firsthand. In his mind, French colonial rule only served to make foreign invaders rich while impoverishing the Vietnamese people. Uprisings against French rule were frequent and dealt with harshly. Brutal imprisonment and death sentences by guillotine were often the results in many cases.

But Ho Chi Minh was to take a different path. In 1911, at the age of twenty-one, Ho left the port of Saigon and would not return to Vietnam for the next thirty years. His travels would take him to the United States, Great Britain, and eventually France. It was while he was in France that Ho discovered his political awakening.

While living in Paris during World War I, Ho took an interest in democracy and representative government, but not necessarily the government in France. He was enamored with the United States and its role in the world as an up-and-coming power. He studied the U.S. Declaration of Independence and the Constitution and found them worthy models for his own ideas regarding Vietnam's independence.

But Ho was also influenced by the rise of the Communist Bolsheviks in Russia. Their revolution against the imperial Russian monarchy became a symbol for overthrowing the status quo worldwide. Ho joined the French Socialist Party, which morphed into the French Communist Party following the Russian Revolution in 1917. But Ho also formed a Vietnamese nationalist society while in Paris. Although Ho saw parallels with the Russian Revolution and Vietnam, he didn't entirely give up on the ideals of democracy altogether.

At the end of World War I, the Allied powers met with Germany and the Central powers to hash out peace terms at the Versailles Peace Conference. In the aftermath of a devastating war, along with the revolution occurring in Russia, many felt a new age was dawning. Ho Chi Minh was among those who felt this optimism. He was inspired by U.S. president Woodrow Wilson's "14 points" speech, which spelled out the steps necessary to avoid a second world war. Wilson's fifth point, "a free, open-minded, and absolutely impartial adjustment of all colonial claims," especially appealed to Ho.

With Wilson's words providing the inspiration, Ho attempted to push for Vietnamese independence from French rule at Versailles. But his petition to speak at the conference was predictably ignored. It would not be the last time a U.S. president's words would let him down.

Following his inevitable disappointment at Versailles, Ho Chi Minh left Paris for Moscow in 1923. He immersed himself in the study of communism and spreading revolution. Ho was frequently sent to Asia by Communist agents throughout the 1920s and 1930s to help foment revolution. He was nearly fluent in several languages, including English, which was an incredible asset. The experience he gained in those years in terms of organization and recruitment of a revolutionary movement proved invaluable. When Ho Chi Minh returned to Vietnam in 1941, France would take notice.

The year 1941 was a pivotal one for Ho Chi Minh. He founded Viet Nam Doc Lap Dong Minh (League for Vietnam's Independence), or Viet Minh for short. He also appointed Vo Nguyen Giap, a former schoolteacher and history student, as one of his closest advisers. And with France defeated by Germany, Ho Chi Minh saw this as the ideal time to begin his quest anew for Vietnamese independence.

There were obstacles along the way, however. With France defeated, Germany's axis ally, Japan, stepped in to fill the power vacuum left in Vietnam. The Japanese proved to be even crueler than the French, exacting more resources and labor to support their war effort against the United States in the Pacific. Ho was still an ardent admirer of the United States. He may have even taken Franklin Roosevelt at his word when the U.S. president said:

"I can't believe that we can fight a war against fascist slavery, and at the same time, not work to free people all over the world from a backward colonial policy."[2]

Ho Chi Minh and the Viet Minh also played a significant role on the side of the allies during World War II. The Viet Minh rescued a downed U.S. pilot and provided reconnaissance on Japanese movements in Vietnam for the U.S. Office of Strategic Services (OSS). The OSS was a clandestine paramilitary organization that eventually became the Central Intelligence Agency in the United States. The OSS would infiltrate enemy-occupied areas and work with local partisans. The Viet Minh established a strong bond with the OSS officers in Vietnam. The Americans went so far as to train Ho's men to fight against the Japanese using American-made weapons. However, the war ended with Japan's defeat in August 1945, ending plans for a joint U.S.–Viet Minh commando force.

With Japan's defeat came another power vacuum. France was still in political chaos in mid-1945. Ho Chi Minh seized on this opportunity, and the Viet Minh marched into the capital city of Hanoi and declared Vietnam's independence under the banner of the Democratic Republic of Vietnam, or DRV. Through the head of the OSS mission in Vietnam, Archimedes Patti, Ho sent Franklin Roosevelt's successor, Harry Truman, a personal letter outlining Vietnam's separation from France.

For Ho Chi Minh, the moment was ripe. Ho rationalized that if Germany, Italy, and Japan were examples of unbridled and rabid colonization with their empire-building conquests during World War II, then the world had to condemn colonialism in any form it took. Even Charles de Gaulle was said to have remarked that "France would be open to eventual independence for the colonies."[3]

Additionally, Ho Chi Minh had spent the past four years organizing the Viet Minh into a national movement with the backing of a substantial number of Vietnamese people, especially in the north. When Ho and his cadres moved into Hanoi's seat of power in August 1945, there was massive support for Vietnam's independence.

Ho hoped that Truman would embrace Roosevelt's words and end colonial rule not only in Vietnam but also the world over. But Ho Chi Minh never received a reply from Truman.

From that point on, the relationship between the Democratic Republic of Vietnam and the Western world quickly deteriorated. In deference to the wartime allies of the United States, Truman raised no objection to France and Great Britain's resumption of colonial rule. In September 1945, the British peacekeeping force in Hanoi even began aiding the French to reestablish their control over Indochina. The British did not act out of any sense of generosity toward France but rather out of reactionary fear that if the French lost their colonial empire, so would Britain.

There was also an economic necessity for Great Britain's and France's need to reaffirm their power over the colonies. Both countries were economically devastated following the war and desperately needed the resources and revenue from their colonies to rebuild. Britain and France believed that, without the colonies, the domestic economies of both countries would likely collapse.

Charles de Gaulle, who was now the head of France's postwar provisional government, sent Philippe Leclerc and a large contingent of French soldiers to Saigon in March 1946. De Gaulle also sent Admiral Thierry d'Argenlieu to serve as high commissioner of the colonies. Leclerc and d'Argenlieu detested each other. Leclerc didn't see the situation in Vietnam as a military conflict but more of a diplomatic mission. D'Argenlieu, however, preferred antagonizing Ho Chi Minh and the Viet Minh movement. Leclerc didn't remain in Vietnam for long. General Jean Étienne Valluy replaced Leclerc in July 1946.

The combination of d'Argenlieu and Valluy created the perfect storm in Vietnam. Both men were staunchly pro-colonial and had no use for Ho Chi Minh, the Viet Minh, or independence for Vietnam. The DRV was still the de facto government in Hanoi. The French government in Paris expressed interest in negotiating with Ho Chi Minh. Ho had reached a tentative agreement with a French emissary named Jean Sainteny that might have provided the solution that Leclerc believed was possible. To that end, Ho and a delegation of Viet Minh were invited to a conference held at Fontainebleau castle just outside of Paris to discuss the future of Vietnam.

With Ho out of the country, d'Argenlieu declared southern Vietnam—the part the French called "Cochinchine" that included Saigon—an "autonomous republic." Cochinchine was anything but autonomous under the French, but the move outraged Ho. The declaration of autonomy was a sham. D'Argenlieu never intended for Cochinchine to act independently from France. The ploy was to undermine Viet Minh support in the south and weaken Ho's grip on Vietnam.

The Fontainebleau conference was also a bust for Ho and the Vietnamese independence movement. Elections in France in 1946 had brought a conservative government to power, and the mid-level politicians and diplomats who met with Ho and his delegation conceded nothing. When Ho returned to Hanoi, he found the French more entrenched in power in Vietnam than ever before, with more French soldiers arriving in his country every day.

The second incident that directly triggered the war between the Viet Minh and the French happened in November 1946. A French naval patrol boat boarded a Chinese transport in Haiphong harbor off the north coast and demanded that an import tax on their cargo be paid to the French colonial administration. The DRV protested the move—they had been collecting tax since taking power in 1945. The Viet Minh retaliated, seizing the French patrol boat and arresting its crew.

Chaos erupted in Haiphong. The French escalated the war of retaliation. General Valluy deployed close to ten thousand French troops in a door-to-door search-and-destroy operation in Haiphong, killing Viet Minh operatives on sight. He then ordered an aerial bombardment of the city as a follow-up. The death count of both civilians and Viet Minh in Haiphong was estimated to be as many as twenty thousand.

Valluy then turned his military force to the nearby capital in Hanoi. Ho Chi Minh and the Viet Minh attempted to fight back, but they were no match to the superior weaponry of the French. Ho and his followers were forced to flee the capital. They retreated to the mountainous area of Viet Bac near the Chinese border.

From this point onward, there would be no turning back. The war between France and Ho Chi Minh's Viet Minh nationalists had begun.

Flash forward two years later, Valérie André was commissioned as a captain with the Corps de liaison administrative pour l'Extrême-Orient (CLAEO),[4] following her graduation from the Sorbonne. Valérie had been encouraged to enlist for military service by her professor, Leon Binet, but she had an additional reason for volunteering.

"I learned that there was also the prospect of belonging to a parachute surgical unit. The spirit of adventure burned inside of me."[5]

CLAEO was an organization within France's military that included the Service de santé, the medical support service. Valérie was among the more than seven hundred women assigned to Indochina by this time, with most serving in various support roles from medical specialists and nurses to ambulance drivers.[6] Her tour of duty was to last two years.

As the *Champollion* sailed out of Marseilles, Valérie André's thoughts were filled with anticipation.

"Was I well informed about the war in Indochina at that time?" Valérie reflectively asked years later. "In honesty, no.

"At that time, France was ashamed of this conflict. Moreover, it was only involved in the conflict through an army of volunteers. The bulk of the army never took part. However, I had the feeling that to fight there was to serve one's country and the influence of France. There was no ambiguity in my eyes. No hesitation possible."[7]

Universal military conscription was mandatory in France for all male citizens reaching the age of eighteen. Yet because the war in Indochina was unpopular with a great majority of the French, service in the Far East was voluntary. As Valérie would see firsthand, many fighting on the French side in Indochina came from the Foreign Legion, France's North African colonies, and Indochina itself.

Between her CLAEO indoctrination and the scraps of information she could pick up from military personnel and colonists returning to Indochina aboard the *Champollion*, Valérie had some inkling of the situation she was to encounter.

"At the end of 1948, the expeditionary force in Indochina was comprised of 70,000 men, which even then was an inadequate number to control the region. In the south, they were facing *Viet Minh* guerrillas and terrorist attacks. Across an immense, inextricable country, made up of forests, rice fields, jungles, and isolated villages, French troops fought a difficult battle without much means, several thousand kilometers from the motherland and increasingly cut off from the world. It was a war of remote outposts that attempted pacification. However, villages that were won by day, were lost by night.

"Thousands of French soldiers were already killed. The enemy hid but infiltrated everywhere, disappearing to strike more effectively. Patrols searched the jungles for *Viet Minh* camps, but the vegetation, the climate, and the terrain always favored the enemy."[8]

The French learned the hard way not to underestimate the Viet Minh. Ho Chi Minh appointed Vo Nguyen Giap as the commander of the Viet Minh infantry forces. The former schoolteacher and student of history would prove to be a formidable opponent. When General Valluy launched Operation Lea in October 1947, the French intended to crush the Viet Minh once and for all. At first, the French seemed to have the upper hand. Valluy first sent in eleven hundred paratroopers to begin securing the mountainous area, and then he deployed fifteen thousand ground troops as reinforcement. While the French possessed aircraft and firepower, they moved slowly through the treacherous terrain, often ambushed by Viet Minh guerillas. The French nearly captured Ho and Giap near the village of Bac Kan, but in the end, they only managed to kill an adviser to the Viet Minh instead. In revenge, Giap unleashed forty thousand of his Viet Minh troops against the French. They were poorly armed and poorly trained, but they believed in the cause of Vietnam's independence. Yet, losses for the Viet Minh were enormous. The French claimed that they killed or wounded more than nine thousand Viet Minh. But Valluy's army suffered six thousand dead and injured by the time Operation Lea wound down in November. It was not the total victory that Valluy had promised.

When Valérie André arrived at the port of Saigon on New Year's Eve 1948, the war in Vietnam was becoming one of attrition.

Chapter 10

Sang Froid

"You'll see more of the damage the bullet caused when we peel back the dura mater and shattered skull fragments. Once we cut away the damaged part of the skull, we cut a flap into the dura mater."

Dr. Carayon was meticulous as he sliced away the part of the filmy membrane covering the soldier's brain still intact. The doctor moved his right hand deftly and methodically so that Valérie André could observe his every action.

"We might be lucky with this one," the doctor continued, in a quiet, even voice. He motioned with a slight gesture of his hand for Valérie to apply suction to some of the disconnected brain matter surrounding the area of the bullet's impact. "The bullet is not buried deep, and he was still responsive when he was brought in. He might recover well, but it's hard to say. Bullets and shell fragments never leave a man the same."

Carayon had a workman's way of explaining the intricacies of neurosurgery. For Carayon, it had become rote, almost as if he was a mechanic explaining truck repair. It was easy to be inured to seeing so many wounded men day in and day out. Still, Carayon never accepted compromise when it came to the wounded. He had been assigned at Coste Hospital for more than a year.

Yet, it was a reality that some of the men who came to Coste with severe head wounds could be saved, but others simply could not. The degree of recovery also varied. For the uninitiated, the staggering number of wounded could be heartbreaking. Being emotional, however, would not serve the wounded. For Carayon, it all was a matter of maintaining *sang froid*—staying composed when the situation was intolerable. Carayon hoped that

67

his new protégé would learn that lesson as well. From what he knew of her, he thought she would.

"Now we're ready to extract the bullet," Carayon said, gently using his forceps to probe through the damaged brain matter. "We're also looking for shattered bone fragments."

He stopped and handed the forceps over to Valérie.

"Here, André, let's see how you do."

Before Valérie set foot at Coste, Carayon had reviewed her file extensively. He had no use for a flight surgeon; however, her records from Paris looked good, and the recommendation from Leon Binet meant that she had strong possibilities as a candidate for neurosurgery. Doctors were in short supply in Saigon, and he had to take what was available. But at least she was fresh and seemed eager to learn.

Valérie had dissected many cadavers, but the man on the table was still alive and breathing. When she took the forceps from Carayon, it meant that his life was now in her hands. At least the bullet was visible and accessible, so it wasn't a particular challenge. But simple wounds would rarely be the norm.

"Very good," Carayon said to her as she dropped the bullet in a tray on the operating table. He thought to himself that Valérie's small, delicate hands would work to her advantage as a surgeon. He knew that Valérie had signed up for *antenne chirurgicale parachutiste*—the frontline mobile surgical team. Carayon wondered if this young doctor could hold up to the physical and psychological rigors of the seemingly endless chain of casualties that constantly flowed into Coste.

"Now you have to clean up some more of the damaged tissue. Fortunately, there's not too much damage. We will be able to suture most of the dura mater back in place. In other cases, you'll see how we make a graft when there is too much damage. We'll create a plate to close up the missing part of the skull after we know there will be no swelling.

"Miss Botto will help from here," Carayon said as his nurse stepped in to assist Valérie.

The operation was a success. The wounded man recovered and would be sent back to France. But not all would be so fortunate. There was also a ward reserved for the wounded brought to Coste alive but stood no chance of being saved. They were the living dead. These men were kept isolated from the rest, given their last rites, and allowed to quietly die, alone.

When Robert Carayon requested Valérie André to work at Coste Hospital, she jumped at the chance. The hospital was overwhelmed by the sheer number of severely wounded men brought to them, and there weren't enough specialists in Indochina to treat head and spinal cord wounds. It may have been somewhat unorthodox to train a doctor to perform the intricacies of neurosurgery in a military hospital in time of war, but not unheard of. Carayon saw it simply as an extension of Valérie's internship.

"Carayon was well known in Indochina, and I accepted working with him on the spot," Valérie said. "Coste Hospital is where I first saw the reality of the war in all its daily horror."[1]

Valérie André had been in Vietnam ten months by now, but not all of those ten months had gone smoothly for her. When she first arrived in Saigon, Valérie met with Inspector General André Robert, head of Service de santé (health services) in Vietnam. Robert realized the need to improve the medical aid available to troops in Vietnam. But the resources he had on hand were stretched very thin and, in many places, were simply nonexistent.

Much of this was because of the shortage of qualified medical personnel and the geography of fighting a war far from urban centers. Roads were often impassable, especially in the monsoon season when torrential rain would pour down, turning unpaved routes into virtual rivers. Service de santé started using fixed-wing aircraft to hasten the transport of the most severely wounded early in the war. But it was an imperfect solution. Even though the Criquets were short takeoff and landing aircraft, they still required a runway.

Robert was intrigued that the young doctor from Paris wanted to be part of *antenne chirurgicale parachutiste* (ACP) units, but he had his reservations. It was a unit that demanded much of its volunteers. The French ACP could be best described as the equivalent to the Mobile Army Surgical Hospital, or MASH units, established by the United States in Korea. Instead of transporting personnel and equipment by trucks to a location *near* the front line, ACP personnel and equipment were airdropped by parachute into the many remote French outposts in Vietnam. ACP personnel had to be exceptionally fit both emotionally and physically to withstand the rigors of paratrooper training. Anything less would not be adequate.

Valérie was undeterred. She had written her graduate thesis on the pathology of parachuting[2] and understood both the training and stresses paratroopers experienced. Valérie had practiced jumps at Beynes. While she was well aware of the difference between airdrops in France and airdrops into enemy zones in Vietnam, Valérie was still determined to join the elite group.

General Robert had his misgivings. It was hard not to notice Valérie's slight build and wonder if she would have the strength and stamina to endure

the rigors of hospital life in Indochina, let alone the deadly hazards out in
the field. He had already seen far too many in Indochina who were either too
eager or thought they were well prepared for the harsh life they would encounter. The cemeteries didn't need any more French idealists. Nonetheless,
Robert told Valérie that her application to ACP would be passed on, and he
would not voice an objection if she were accepted.

As Valérie waited for approval to join the airborne service, she was assigned to a small military hospital in My Tho, seventy kilometers southwest
of Saigon. Situated on Route Coloniale 1, the main road leading out of
Saigon, My Tho was a backwater town near the front line and considered a
strategic area by the French. The city bordered an expanse of the Mekong
Delta and was linked to Saigon by Route Colonial 1.

The military hospital in My Tho was small and somewhat primitive compared to facilities found in Saigon. As part of Inspector General Robert's plan,
the French military was establishing feeder medical facilities in Cochichine
to stabilize wounded frontline soldiers before sending them on to Saigon.

Like all military medical facilities in Vietnam, the hospital at My Tho was
understaffed. Any qualified addition to the staff should have been welcome;
however, Valérie soon learned to what extent sexism existed in the ranks of
the male-dominated military.

"I immediately encountered the hostility of a captain who was responsible
for securing my lodging," Valérie recalled. "He couldn't conceive of the notion that a woman could be a doctor and admitted as much that it was even
more difficult to believe that a woman could be a soldier with the rank of
officer. He told me flat out that there was no housing available for me. The
last of the accommodations was intended for officers and their wives!"[3]

It was a situation that wouldn't have happened if Valérie was a man.
Sexism was rampant and institutionalized in the French military. Even
though she was equal in rank to the officer, he showed no respect to her.
Valérie had to resort to finding a superior officer to force the captain to find
her housing on the base. The captain reluctantly complied and then led her
to a building in the back of the hospital.

"Here," he sneered at her. "This is the best I can do."

The officer's best effort was underwhelming, to say the least.

"I was marooned in a cramped and tiny room, furnished with a mattress
on the ground and with a mosquito net attached to the ceiling with a string,"
Valérie said of her quarters. "There was not one piece of furniture. And the
shower was outside, on the other side of the building."[4]

Valérie was not resentful because the accommodations were so spartan but because the officer had demonstrated such spiteful behavior. Yet she remained calm, determined to make the best of her plight.

"Without batting an eyelid, I placed my footlocker against the wall and used it for the chair and table that were denied to me. I adapted as well as possible to my temporary quarters."[5]

Fortunately for Valérie, her inconvenient situation would prove to be temporary. As luck would have it, Dr. Leon Binet—Valérie's medical professor from Paris—had traveled from France to check on the progress of the medical personnel who volunteered to serve with the military in the Far East due to his urging. Along with Binet was Inspector General André Robert from Saigon. During lunch in the officers' mess, Binet asked how Valérie was getting on and how she liked her quarters at the hospital base. Valérie had no intention of complaining, but before she could answer, another officer seated at the table cut her off, answering for her.

"Dr. André is on standby housing. We're working on a solution."[6]

"What exactly is standby housing?" Binet inquired. "And how long does it take to find a solution?"

The officer who answered for Valérie was at a loss for words.

"I would like to see where Dr. André is being kept," Binet demanded.

A great "consternation" that bordered on the comical ensued, according to Valérie.

Both Binet and Inspector General Robert visited the cell-like billet assigned to Valérie. Binet was outraged and took the insult to his former student personally. Binet demanded to see the male captain who placed Valérie in the barebones room.

"This is unacceptable," Binet said, demanding that the captain find better accommodations for Valérie.[7] Inspector General Robert agreed. The captain tried to make excuses for Valérie's treatment but was verbally dressed down by General Robert for his lack of courtesy to a fellow officer. It was a harsh lesson in civility.

Through Binet's intervention, Valérie did receive better quarters. But her triumph over the petty captain was only temporary. Valérie was transferred to Hospital 415 in Saigon less than a month later.

Hospital 415—also known as the "Flemish Hospital"—was the older of the two military hospitals in Saigon. Hospital 415 was in the Cholon district of Saigon near the large marketplace of Binh Tay, which was also home to a large ethnic Chinese population. Hospital 415 was *une infirmerie-hôpital* where the less severely wounded were sent. Valérie interned in war surgery and received a comprehensive overview of the various wounds troops experienced on the battlefield. It was an introduction to the more advanced hell she would later face at Coste Hospital.

Valérie's assignment at Hospital 415 was also her first encounter with Vietnam's largest city. Saigon from that period was a city of myriad thrills and diversions mixed in with a large dose of danger.

Many parts of Saigon had a distinctly French flair, so much so that some referred to the city as the "Paris of Southeast Asia." Beautiful parks bordered grand boulevards. Saigon's downtown area had impressive hotels and popular nightclubs. The architecture of many of the buildings constructed at the turn of the twentieth century could easily fit within Paris's cityscape. For example, the municipal opera house was modeled after the Petite Palais in Paris. And while the Vietnamese people would never embrace the nuance of French cheese, the fusion of other French and native Vietnamese dishes created a cornucopia of tastes and sensations to explore.

But there were also many contrasts where Western culture and Eastern culture collided. The gothic twin spires of Saigon's Notre Dame cathedral seemed odd and out of place with the numerous Buddhist and Confucian temples. While wealthy colonials lived in ornate villas, the poverty of many Vietnamese was also quite apparent. Once one got past the beautifully paved promenades of central Saigon, there were the dirt roads where crudely built houses were crammed together side by side. During the typhoon and monsoon seasons, families sometimes found it necessary to literally hold down the tin roofs of their crude houses to keep them from flying away in the wind and heavy downpours.

Open sewers and drainage ditches often attracted rats and mosquitos, and along with them came pestilence. Dengue fever, typhoid fever, malaria, tuberculosis, and a host of other infectious diseases were rampant.

Throughout each day, Vietnamese women streamed up and down the dirt roads, wearing their conical *non las* atop their heads and carrying yoke baskets with food and other goods. Food was a major preoccupation with the Vietnamese. There never seemed to be enough food with many staples, such as rice and sugar cane, earmarked for export. Still, many of the more enterprising women either sold what goods they could acquire at the communal markets like Binh Tay or Ben Thanh or set up small, makeshift eateries on the streets outside their homes.

As Valérie André observed, the French and Vietnamese maintained a strained coexistence. There was a bureaucratic class that employed many

Vietnamese as part of the colonial administration. Still, there were also many Vietnamese who served in menial and servant occupations to the French. Racial and class segregation was quite apparent. A particular example of this was Cercle Sportif, a popular gathering spot for colonials in Saigon. It was a large sporting complex—nearly twelve acres—built on the grounds of the municipal gardens. Among its features were a swimming pool, multiple tennis courts, and a football field with stands that could hold twelve thousand spectators. The club catered to the upper levels of colonial society. But the Cercle Sportif was off limits to most Vietnamese unless they worked there as laborers.

Gambling, cheap saloons, prostitution, and opium parlors were also part of Saigon's seedier side. They were attractions to French soldiers, and as Valérie would find out, many men ended up at Hospital 415 either with venereal disease symptoms after dalliances with Vietnamese prostitutes or stab wounds from bar fights and run-ins with Saigon's crime lords.

Saigon was also teeming with Viet Minh operatives.. While Ho Chi Minh was immensely more influential in the north, he intended to spread the revolutionary call to all of Vietnam. Saigon was essential to that mission. Many Viet Minh were deep undercover. Some were even embedded in the colonial bureaucracy, gathering information on the French that could be passed on to a network of cells that worked its way up to Ho Chi Minh's jungle headquarters in Viet Bac. But others worked more proactively. Terrorist attacks in Saigon were not as frequent as one might have imagined at that time. The Viet Minh was careful not to scare off noncommitted Vietnamese away from the movement. Instead, Viet Minh operatives resorted to other maneuvers, such as when they wrung 340,000 piastres from the Chinese-operated Le Grande Monde casino in Cholon in exchange for protection.[8] Money raised, extorted, or stolen would go to buy weapons and other supplies to be used against the French military.[9] A clandestine trade route thrived between Vietnam and China. Many of the Viet Minh's supplies, including weapons, were coming from China by 1949.

Valérie André was not oblivious to this environment—it was impossible not to take note. But her tenure at Hospital 415 in those first months took up much of her time. Her presence in the mostly male-dominated institution, however, stirred up prejudice. The doctor in charge was displeased that a woman was added to his staff. Women were adequate as nurses but not as equals to doctors. For Valérie, it wasn't always a conducive work environment.

"I devoted myself to war surgery with a passion that the sarcasm of my training supervisor, Dr. Michard, could not dampen," Valérie said, looking back on those early days. "Besides, I couldn't hold any grudge against him, and I was rather grateful for the knowledge and the know-how he brought me."[10]

Each day created new learning experiences for Valérie. It was hard to quantify, but she was certain that each week she spent treating the sick and wounded in Saigon was equal to months of study in Paris. She also found that improvising treatments were often necessary as there was always something missing in the hospital's storehouse of supplies. It was a challenge that she met with enthusiasm in these early months but would later find frustrating and limiting as her time in Vietnam wore on.

While Valérie served her days and nights at Hospital 415, she regularly checked on her status with the ACP.

"I reminded *Service de Santé* from time to time that I was still a certified paratrooper."[11]

Her persistence eventually paid off. Valérie received orders to report to Tan Son Nhut airfield with the Third Colonial Battalion of Parachute Commandos (3eBCCP).

"It was with great joy when I received my orders signed by Squadron Leader Decorse, dated May 27, 1949."

Valérie would make her practice jump with the 3eBCCP over the ominously named Plaine de Tombeaux, or "field of tombs," in Saigon District 10, an immense underground burial site dating back more than two hundred years.

"The jump would be under the same conditions as the surgical antennas."[12]

The test airdrop's purpose was not only to gauge the abilities of the medical team to land near the designated DZ, or "drop zone," but also to serve as a trial run to drop the crates of equipment and supplies the team would need to recover and set up once they arrived at an actual French army outpost. It was all too easy to let valuable supplies fall too wide of their target and fall into the hands of the Viet Minh. Precision for both the medical team and their stores was crucial. Valérie would soon find out if *sang froid* was enough to see her through these next series of challenges.

Chapter 11

Trial under Fire

"Tell me, *mademoiselle*, aren't you a little uncomfortable at this place when you're wearing a parachute?"

The commanding officer of the paratrooper unit looked at Valérie André with a sidelong glance as he spoke. To further illustrate his point, he drew a line with his finger across the parachute harness straps bound tightly to Valérie's chest.

"I am less uncomfortable than you might be a little lower, with the parachute harness straps wrapped around your . . . ," Valérie shot back, but stopped herself, looking down at the officer's lower torso. Her remark brought out a roar of laughter from the other men. It was an honest observation.

"The men saluted my insolence . . . and deservedly so. I only noted an obvious fact—wasn't it indeed true that a man's use of a parachute would *encumber* him the most, not a woman?"[1]

The C-47 Dakota transport plane was warming up on the tarmac as the paratroopers readied themselves for another practice jump. Valérie was in the middle of a "stick," the slang used for a group of paratroopers who jumped in rapid succession once they were over their drop zone (DZ). For some of the men, Valérie's presence seemed out of place.

"The truth was that my presence surprised this still stunned officer," Valérie said of the incident. "Yes, a young woman in the middle of a *stick* ready to embark. The officer in charge of the jumps was quick to justify this unusual situation. If I was skydiving as part of the boy's military preparation, it was because the reserve doctor in charge of medical supervision had asked me to replace him from time to time. In any case, regulations stated that a jumping session could only be carried out in the presence of a doctor. In exchange, I would be allowed to make a jump at the end of the session."[2]

Valérie was learning that bartering her professional services often resulted in making personal gains that would otherwise be denied to her. There was a reluctance on the part of the paratroopers to include her on practice missions; however, in her role as flight surgeon she was indispensable to their operations. As much as the commanding officer disliked allocating resources to a female, he was left with no option.

Still, some of the men firmly believed that Valérie would be a danger to herself and potentially to them, as well, and refused to take her seriously. Because of her slight build, many were certain that she would be blown far off from the DZ. What they didn't consider was that her lightweight figure also made it less likely for her to sustain injury when she landed. Ankle and leg injuries were common among paratroopers.

Whether male or female, medical personnel attached to the *antenne chirurgicale parachutiste* (ACP) were often at a disadvantage to their counterparts trained for combat as far as their own instruction was concerned. While the French military maintained formal training for combat paratroopers, both in France and Indochina, training for medical personnel, like Valérie, was distinctly low priority. The military side of operations argued for better-trained medics who could be dropped into combat zones. But medics could only go so far in helping to stabilize the wounded.

The ACP also produced a far different form of paratrooper than the airborne commandos trained to go into a battle zone to reinforce troops already on the ground or to form a beach-head to confront the enemy. In contrast, the ACP's airdroppable surgical units were a highly unusual experiment that brought much of the necessary personnel and equipment to areas where it was desperately needed. These areas were typically remote outposts that had been under siege but were relatively secure once again.

Back on the tarmac at Tan Son Nhut, the drone of the twin radial engines of the Dakota increased as the plane made its way down the runway, building speed for takeoff. Its relatively long wingspan in relation to its slender fuselage allowed the craft to make short use of the runway, despite carrying a full load of paratroopers. The plane lumbered into the air and began its climb upward toward roughly 600 meters (1,950 feet). Any higher altitude could cause a parachutist to drift too far away from the DZ.

For Valérie, the climb was both exhilarating and one more step into that familiar feeling of joining with the infinite realm of space that she carried deep inside her psyche. Her parachute was attached to the static line running fore and aft of the Dakota's cabin. When the squad commander gave the word, the plane began to empty. Man after man made the leap out the Dakota's side door. When it came for Valérie's turn, the young doctor felt a slight tug from the static line connected to her chute. Instantly the wind caught the chute as it unfurled and billowed in the sky. The initial pull upward as the parachute filled with air was a jolt, taking Valérie's breath away. At less than five hundred meters now, the ground was rapidly approaching. There was little time to consider anything other than to prepare for landfall. Despite the misgivings of some of her comrades, she lined up well with the designated drop zone. Contact with the ground was seconds away. She had the points of a safe landing ingrained in her memory. She landed on the balls of her feet, with her knees slightly bent, chin tucked in, then falling over sideways to distribute the shock of landing to the side of her body.

It was another successful jump, but would it be enough for her to be allowed on a real mission? That was a question that couldn't be answered yet.

Valérie's continued internship under Dr. Carayon at Coste Hospital meant that her time spent preparing for the ACP was limited. When she was not needed for medical supervision of paratrooper operations at Tan Son Nhut, her priority was with the hospital.

Dr. Carayon was something of an enigma. He had a studious composure. It was the nature of his profession. Only those who truly showed skill and commitment were worthy of any consideration. To be an instructor was also a commitment on his part. It was not an endeavor he undertook lightly. With a quiet demeanor that demanded perfection, Carayon's expectations were immense.

Under the watchful eye of Dr. Carayon, Valérie performed numerous assists in her abbreviated apprenticeship. Carayon's opinion of her abilities increased as her command of the operating room grew.

"Carayon was my guide," Valérie would later recall. "He assessed my progress, balancing my competence before allowing me to progress to more difficult interventions . . . and eventually to perform alone, or in other words, become a responsible surgeon and team leader."[3]

Valérie's first experience as lead surgeon came with the admittance of a critically wounded soldier. With the soldier anesthetized and his head firmly held steady in a three-point fixture device resembling an oversized c-clamp, the procedure began.

"It was a deep skull wound caused by a mortar shell fragment," Valérie recalled of her first solo procedure. The skin had already been cut away to expose the scalp. "To extract this, I had to open a 'flap.'"[4]

A "flap" was the first step in exploring the extent of the wound by removing a portion of the skull bone to expose the membrane known as dura mater covering the brain. While an entry wound was already present, it was often necessary to enlarge the area surrounding the punctured skull by using a bone saw or drill. The outer flesh surrounding the wound would be peeled back beyond the border of the bone flap, usually held in place by clamps called retractors. Once the bone flap was cut away it would be removed from the rest of the skull.

Any exposure to the brain from a torn membrane could result in a deadly infection. In an era long before advanced imaging machinery was available, extracting the minute particles of shrapnel left from a mortar explosion required both critical eyesight and a deft hand. A high-precision magnifying loupe worn over the eyes aided in the search for tiny fragments. Some slivers of metal were virtually invisible to the naked eye. A combination of extraction tools and gentle suction had to be used to find particles. Any fragments left behind had the potential of inhibiting the healing of the brain and causing a potentially fatal infection.

Often there were many hours, even a day or more, between the time a soldier was wounded and his wound was dressed in the field and the time that the soldier would arrive at a hospital. Debridement, or removal and cleaning of the dead, necrotic tissue, was another step in the process of stabilizing an extensive wound.

The details in a surgical procedure couldn't be overlooked, and there were never any shortcuts. Critical observation was *de rigueur* for a surgeon. Without breaking her concentration, Valérie knew she was also under critical observation, too.

"I was so absorbed in my work that I did not hear the door open and close again. Carayon came closer, took a peek, then looked at me," Valérie recalled. "I read approval in his eyes."[5]

No words between them were exchanged or even expected. Carayon was satisfied that his protégé had the situation under control and left as quietly as he had entered.

Completing the procedure required an attempt to repair the damaged dura mater membrane, to seal off the brain's tissue, and to seal in cerebral spinal fluid. The dura mater was not capable of regenerating itself so a fascial graft to patch the missing area of dura mater was necessary. Valérie extracted an adequate portion of *fascia-lata* after she made an incision into the soldier's upper thigh. It was important for her to connect the tissue graft with closely spaced sutures in order to make an impermeable seal.[6]

Because of the damage made by the mortar fragment shattering the skull, a replacement plate substituting the soldier's natural skull would have to be fashioned in the patient's post-operative recovery to entirely complete the procedure. With success found in acrylic polymers toward the end of World War II, a synthetic patch made of methyl-methacrylate could be formed to replace the damaged piece. The plate would be permanently attached to the soldier with fine titanium screws and attaching plates securing the cranial patch directly to the skull.[7]

But the more immediate issue facing a recovering patient was swelling, or edema, in the brain. The first twenty-four hours following surgery would be the most critical; however, even with the success of a soldier surviving such traumatic surgery, the prognosis for recovery would not be known for several weeks or even months. Yet even in the best of cases, some degree of permanent impairment would be likely because of the initial damage caused by the wound.

For Valérie, her initiation into the maelstrom of medicine in a war zone was complete. Her gender might still be an issue for some, but surgical skill and endurance for the nonstop onslaught of mangled bodies were the only factors that mattered, even in an environment that took on an almost assembly line aspect in the repair of human bodies. Her skill had to equal or surpass the skills of her colleagues. Dr. Carayon accepted no less. Valérie's place on Carayon's surgical staff was not a position given to her for any reason other than her resourcefulness and tenacity—words that would be often used to describe her from here on. But there was no respite for one to lay back on laurels.

"Work at Coste Hospital was a night and day ordeal," Valérie observed.[8]

The flood of wounded pouring into military hospitals grew in proportion with French offensives taken against the Viet Minh as the war dragged on from 1948 to 1949. The year 1949 also marked a turning point in the war because of developments occurring north of Vietnam's border. The Communists in China led by Mao Zedong had waged a war against the regime of Chiang Kai-shek since 1946. Despite initially being overwhelmed by Chiang's nationalist forces, Mao's ultimate victory in October 1949 signified a new power to be reckoned with in Asia. Additionally, Ho Chi

Minh and his Viet Minh cadres now had a Communist ally on Vietnam's northern frontier.

"It was no coincidence that the *Viet Minh* mounted an offensive in the Upper Tonkin in February 1949," Valérie noted of the war's progression. "The *Viet Minh* captured the outpost at Pho Lu, on the Red River. An ambush surprised a convoy out of Tien Yen. There were marauding gangs from China throughout the area. Vo Nguyen Giap, the *Viet Minh*'s strategist, aimed to capture the harvest of opium which would allow them to purchase weapons.

"Their attacks soon spread in every direction, along Route Colonial 4, a vital thoroughfare on the edge of the border. An outpost fell into the hands of the enemy for the first time. RC 4 would now never cease to be threatened. The entire region was plunged into permanent insecurity."[9]

The resulting casualties were grueling in the north, and French military hospitals in Hanoi were especially hard-pressed to keep up with the flow of wounded; however, military offensives in the south also increased. The Viet Minh had finally sent a substantial military force to the south under the command of General Nguyen Binh. Binh reversed the earlier Viet Minh policy of excluding civilians and merchants from their conflict with the French.

Beginning in May 1949, Binh ordered his troops to burn all markets operating in French-controlled territory. Merchants who supplied the French with bricks to build the blockhouses used in remote outposts were especially targeted. Vietnamese merchants that dealt with the French were labeled as "traitors."[10] The new military threat prompted the French force in the south to take action.

"At the end of May 1949, the presence of four to five *Viet Minh* battalions in the Plain of Reeds in Cochinchine convinced General de Latour to 'clean up' the sector," Valérie recalled of the situation. General Pierre Boyer de Latour was regional commander of French forces in South Vietnam. "Operation Jonquille [Daffodil] mobilized 4,000 men who combed an area filled with booby traps for several days. Confronting the *Viet Minh* was difficult and bore witness to the fighting spirit of the enemy."[11]

Battle conditions for areas like the Plain of Reeds were especially difficult for the French. The plain, located to the west of Saigon, was massive, encompassing some thirteen thousand square kilometers. During the monsoon season, from July to December, the Plain of Reeds would swell into a massive shallow lake, yet with a depth of some ten to twenty feet in places. In May, when the Viet Minh offensive began, the Plain of Reeds was reasonably dry, but still difficult to tread through with its maze of vegetation and soggy soil. In the aftermath of the rainy season, the remnants of swamps of turgid water contributed to the plague of mosquitoes spreading dengue fever and malaria. Despite the nominal success of forcing the Viet Minh to recede, French casualties remained high.

"On the French side, the toll paid out was heavy. Whole ranks of young officers were destroyed," Valérie said of the campaign, which translated into the nightmarish workload arriving at Coste Hospital. "We operated without relief, overwhelmed at times by the massive arrivals of injured coming from any of the fronts in Indochina."[12]

For medical personnel, the workload seemed never ending.

"The physicians and surgeons took 'watch' one night out of every three days," Valérie said of the arduous hours. "There was little time in between to recover from the exhaustion. Extractions of bullets and shell fragments, suturing nerves, opening cranial flaps. Despite the skill involved to repair the damage wreaked by the battlefield, the procedures almost blurred together into a seemingly endless chain."[13]

During the height of the Operation Jonquille offensive, Valérie André performed more than 150 surgical procedures in one month.[14]

The war in Vietnam only became worse from that point on. Even when the French high command gave up on the massive offensive operations, casualties still poured into the major military hospitals of Vietnam. With a weapons trade route now open with China, the situation in Vietnam was only poised to become much worse.

Even though her time was limited, Valérie continued her training with the ACP. It was during one of her visits to Tan Son Nhut that she learned of a revolutionary new type of aircraft to be unveiled at the airfield. The first helicopter was about to make its debut in Vietnam.

Chapter 12

The Helicopter and How
It Came to Vietnam

Tan Son Nhut Airfield, January 12, 1950

The news of the helicopter demonstration at Tan Son Nhut spread quickly and turned out to be a major event not only for the military aviation community but also for the medical personnel based in Saigon. Many were just curious to see a helicopter in action for the first time. Valérie André was also there among the curious. Up to now, helicopters were only things she had read about in magazines. But she would be one of the few who could readily see the unique potential the aircraft had in medical rescue—a function that was touted by the helicopter's pilot and promoter, an Englishman named Alan Bristow.

The helicopter was parked in front of the hangars of the 2/30 Normandie-Niemen fighter squadron where Bristow and one of the fighter plane mechanics spent the past few days assembling and tuning the aircraft after it arrived in crates in Saigon from the United States. It was a Hiller UH-12/360 built in East Palo Alto, California, near San Francisco.

Alan Bristow's story was rather involved and complicated. He went to work for Helicop-Air, the Hiller distributor in France, after punching out a sales executive during an argument at helicopter builder Westlands in the United Kingdom while working there as a test pilot. Helicop-Air needed an experienced test pilot, and Bristow—despite the Westlands incident—had practical experience dating back to when he was a pilot in Canada test flying Sikorsky R-4s. Helicop-Air hoped to convince the French air force to buy a fleet of Hiller helicopters, and they needed a demonstrator. The small, unarmed, and lightweight helicopter was completely unsuited for use as an offensive weapon, but it was extremely maneuverable. Its ability to land within its own footprint meant that runways would not be necessary, allowing the Hiller to land at even the most remote military outposts in Indochina. Helicop-Air sent Bristow to Vietnam to demonstrate the Hiller's unique characteristics and arranged for a helicopter to be sent from the Hiller factory in California to Saigon.

Bristow began his presentation at Tan Son Nhut by reeling off the Hiller's strong points. It had a fuel range of 340 kilometers (210 miles), and its pay-load capacity was 360 kilograms (800 pounds). It could fly at speeds of more than 144 kilometers per hour (90 miles per hour) and had a service ceiling of 4,000 meters (13,000 feet). But he downplayed the Hiller's 178 horsepower engine, which struggled to perform adequately in the tropical environment.

Bristow ordered a Stokes litter kit from the factory that fitted stretchers on each side of the aircraft. The stretcher kit included Plexiglas bubbles built into the doors and covers over the Stokes litters to minimize wind buffeting to a patient while in transit. Equipped with the Stokes litter kit the Hiller UH-12 could carry two wounded individuals plus the pilot to a fully equipped hospital faster than any ground-based vehicle ever could. The Hiller could fly in a virtual straight line rather than meander dangerous jungle roads.

Bristow offered demonstration flights after his presentation. He was eager to make a commission by selling the helicopter to the French military.

"The news that the Hiller was available for demonstration flights spread quickly among the senior army and air force officers and they queued up for the opportunity to fly," Bristow recalled. "Despite their enthusiasm, it seemed to me that I was not doing something right because I could not extract the promise of an order even after I made detailed presentations on operations and costs."[1]

The cost of a Hiller UH-12/360 was around US$20,000 at the time. It was a sizable financial commitment considering that a full complement of spare parts would cost roughly the same amount. There was also the issue of training pilots how to fly a helicopter that required a vastly different skill set from fixed-wing piloting. Training mechanics on how to service the Hiller was also an issue. The French were interested in the machine, to be sure, but they tempered their interest in a machine that up to this time did not have a proven track record.

But all of that was about to change. Despite Bristow's somewhat merce-nary stance that he was in Vietnam to simply sell the helicopter in a war-torn country, he found himself directly drawn into the conflict. As he explained:

"One morning at the airfield I had just completed a routine ground run on the Hiller when the commanding officer of the Normandy Squadron came running out in a state of agitation."

As it turned out, a battle was raging sixty miles away between the French and Viet Minh. Several soldiers were gravely wounded, and time was of the essence to transport them to a hospital. The French commanding officer implored Bristow to use the Hiller for the rescue.

"Listen, I am really only here to sell a helicopter," he said to the French officer. "I already fought in a war and this is not my business."

The French officer would not take no for answer.

"Monsieur, I was a Spitfire pilot with the Free French and flew out of England during the war," he said. "I helped your country when it needed help, now I ask you to do the same for mine."[2]

Bristow didn't want to take on a rescue mission. He knew the risks of taking the aircraft into a combat zone, even though he was touting the Hiller's advantages as an aerial ambulance.

The French officer made one final plea.

"I'll give you an escort of two *Bearcats*, there and back."[3]

Bristow was hard-pressed to refuse the officer. In the back of his mind, he knew that if he was successful with this mission he could make the case for the Hiller's usefulness in retrieving the wounded. Success could mean a sale, but the risks were enormous. Despite his reservations, Bristow relented and followed the officer into the briefing room to study a map to the outpost.

"The battle was going on in the middle of a peninsula five miles long and a mile and a half wide, with the *Viet Minh* entrenched on the mainland side."

Since the battle was taking place near one of the tributaries of the massive Mekong Delta system, Bristow's first question was if it was possible to send in a Dinassaut, one of the heavily armed French naval assault vessels that patrolled the rivers of Indochina.

"No," the officer replied, shaking his head. He had already looked into that possibility. "It will take more than twelve hours to get there. They'll be dead by then."[4]

Despite his reservations, Bristow realized that he was the only option for the survival of these wounded men.

Beyond the promise of fighter plane escort to and from the landing zone, Bristow and the Hiller would only be equipped with the barest of defenses. As the helicopter was being fueled, the commanding officer of the Normandy squadron armed Bristow with six hand grenades, a commando knife, a 9 mm pistol, and a parachute that would be useless in an emergency involving a helicopter. Given the haste the mission was assembled, even Bristow's attire was sparse—a white cotton shirt, white shorts, and white socks. Bristow looked more like a British tourist in the tropics than a man mounting a rescue mission.

Once he was airborne, the flight itself took less than sixty minutes, and Bristow kept the helicopter at an altitude of four thousand feet, well out of range of the Viet Minh. The Bearcat fighter escorts had to constantly double back to Bristow's position because of their considerably faster cruising speed. Presently the helicopter neared its location, and Bristow was able to make out a large white cross set out by the soldiers to mark out a landing zone.

Before putting the Hiller down, however, the pilots in the two fighter escort planes blew past the helicopter to lay down a pattern of machine-gun fire on the Viet Minh position. In the chaos of gunfire, Bristow took that as his cue to land the Hiller.

"I became keenly aware of the amount of small arms fire that was being directed at my way by the *Viet Minh*," Bristow said. "So I put the Hiller into a steep, near-vertical spin, trying to make it look like the helicopter had been shot down. To avoid gunfire I landed about 150 meters from where the white cross had been left out for me, which was a stroke of luck because before I left an incoming mortar shell blew the white markers to pieces."[5]

Bristow had shut down the engine and was letting the main rotors slow to a stop as a junior officer and sergeant ran up to the helicopter. They were with the Seventh Parachute Brigade—paratroopers who had been trained to enter into combat zones in support of troops stationed at remote outposts. They explained to Bristow that eight wounded men needed to be taken to a hospital at once.

Bristow knew the limitations of the little Hiller helicopter. In the best of circumstances, it was only ideal to load the two side stretchers with wounded and fly back to base. The weight of human occupants, plus fuel, and other miscellaneous additions to weight had to be reckoned with against the Hiller's eight hundred pounds of payload capacity. And even that payload was best achievable only in ideal climate conditions. The hot and humid tropical climate of southern Vietnam had a decidedly detrimental effect on the helicopter's performance. As soon as he left the cockpit of the Hiller, Bristow began making observations of the situation he had landed into.

"The men of the 7th Parachute Brigade were some of the hardest I have met in my life—thin and spare, they were built like barbed wire. They were seemingly oblivious to the mortar bombs falling in the jungle all around. They had developed a fine instinct for survival."[6]

That survival instinct most likely saved Bristow's own life when a sergeant grabbed him by the arm and pulled him into a boggy trench dug into the earth. His white attire was now coated in wet mud. The direction of enemy mortar had shifted toward their direction. Fortunately, a lull in the battle occurred that provided an opportunity to regroup and prepare the wounded for evacuation. Crawling out of the trench, Bristow saw that the most severely injured were already being loaded into the Hiller.

"I saw that four wounded men were being placed in the helicopter," said Bristow. "Two were laid out on the Stokes litters, the stretchers on the outside of the helicopter. The other two were classified as walking wounded, although neither could walk without help."

The two "walking wounded" were placed on the bench seat inside the helicopter's cockpit.

"I can't take all these men with me," Bristow told the lieutenant colonel in command of the unit. "My ship can't carry the weight of this many."

The lieutenant colonel pleaded with Bristow to take all four men. Bristow, however, estimated that the four wounded men weighed in the area of 150 pounds each. A quick calculation, including his own weight and the weight of the remaining fuel on board, meant that the Hiller would be more than 200 pounds past its payload limit.

"I must have switched off mentally. . . . It was a serious error of judgment on my part. I agreed to take them, but in all likelihood the helicopter would fail to get airborne, and if it did it would probably crash, killing us all."[7]

Once the wounded were loaded and everything was made secure, Bristow started the Hiller's engine and began its rotor run-up. When the Hiller's main rotor blade reached its full idle speed, Bristow was as ready as he would ever be for takeoff. With his eyes focused on the tachometer reporting engine revolutions in the instrument panel, Bristow began twisting the throttle grip housed in the collective control stick, bringing the engine up to its maximum operating speed and wringing out its full 178 horsepower. The tachometer had a redline indicating just how far he could push the engine. Any further than that redline and the engine could easily have a catastrophic meltdown.

"I raised the collective and barely got the machine light on its wheels," said Bristow. "The ground in front of the helicopter was more or less level for about 150 meters (492 feet) before trees sprung up to a height of more than sixty feet. I nudged forward the cyclic control to try and get enough transitional lift—the additional lift you get from forward movement—to clear the trees."

The trees started to loom up too quickly, and Bristow knew his maneuver wouldn't work.

"After a few meters it was clear that I wasn't going to make it, so I ran the machine onto a slope and stopped."

Being in the middle of a combat zone didn't allow for much time to consider another tactic for takeoff.

"For my second attempt, I again revved the engine to the maximum."

Bristow cursed under his breath, trying to transfer his will to the collective stick to raise the helicopter.

"I pushed the [cyclic] stick will forward and headed straight for the trees, waiting as the airspeed climbed agonizingly slowly to shift every ounce of power from the tail rotor to the main rotor to give me more lift."

Applying pitch to the tail rotor added to the thrust provided by the main rotor blades, but it also put the helicopter into a steep bank to the right side.

"I scraped through the treetops, and no matter how I played with the collective pitch and engine revs I was unable to gain height. . . . The two men on either side of me . . . looked too far gone to care. I don't suppose they knew that they'd probably be better off on the ground, having it out with the *Viet Minh*.

"Many times I brushed the treetops in the jungle that seemed unbroken all the way to Saigon. It took the best part of an hour, but slowly the trees began to thin out on the outskirts of the city."[8]

With Saigon now in sight, Bristow was sorely tempted to put the overloaded Hiller down at the first opportunity. But he pressed on to Tan Son Nhut airport.

"Finally Tan Son Nhut slid beneath the helicopter and I made a running landing on a taxiway, where two ambulances and a group of doctors and nurses waited to take my passengers to hospital."

"I had walked about fifty meters clear of the helicopter, sat down on the grass, and lit up a cigar," Bristow said of the aftermath of his mission. "I was absolutely exhausted. My only comfort was a sad-looking Montecristo cigar, the last one in a leather case that normally held four. But then a young woman in a white coat came up and she explained she was a neurosurgeon. She had come to collect a man with a bullet lodged in his forehead."

The woman was Valérie André.

Bristow was captivated by the young French doctor. He later learned that Valérie had trained with members of the Seventh Parachutist Brigade in preparation for her own airdrops into outposts as a member of the emergency medical parachutists.

"She thanked me profusely in a mixture of French and English for saving this chap's life. She told me that he surely would have died had medical help been further delayed. I accepted her thanks with good grace."[9]

Bristow furthered his observation of the woman, adding:

"Valérie André was very pretty."[10]

Bristow's fascination with Valérie was interrupted by a soldier who drove up in a jeep informing Bristow that the situation had improved at the battle zone and that it would not be necessary for him to return with the helicopter to transport the additional wounded. An ambulance truck would bring them out.

"I was not sorry about having to go back. The Hiller had been cruelly mistreated, but it was a brand new engine and, in fact, it never gave me any trouble despite the torture I had put it through."[11]

Putting both the rescue and the Hiller out of his mind, Alan Bristow returned his attention to Valérie, who was tending to her patient and preparing for the ambulance ride back to Coste Hospital. Before the Englishman could say anything, Valérie invited Bristow to come back to the hospital with her and her patient so that he could witness the bullet extraction firsthand.

"As I rather fancied her I agreed to go."

Once they reached the hospital, Valérie oversaw preparation for surgery on the young paratrooper, while Bristow—who was still dressed in his soiled whites—was told to wear a cap, a mask, and a green rubber apron.

"I was told to put out my cigar by a nursing orderly," Bristow said. "I followed Valérie into an operating theater where my right-seat passenger was lying with a triangular frame over his head.

"The tripod had been fitted with a vertical ring, graduated in degrees, into which was set a metal collar to hold an electric drill. As far as I was concerned it looked just like a Black & Decker drill in my toolkit."[12]

What startled Bristow was that the patient was aware of what was taking place.

"Amazingly, the poor patient was awake—the operation was to take place under a local anesthetic."

As Valérie began the operation, Bristow began to feel uncomfortable about being there.

"Calmly and precisely, Valérie began drilling a ring of small holes around the area occupied by the bullet. I felt a wave of exhaustion come over me as two tiny rubber suckers were placed on the patient's forehead, apparently to remove the bone and get to the bullet. I know no more, for I crashed to the floor in a dead faint and had to be dragged out of the operating theatre and laid on a bench in the passageway."

Later, when Bristow came to, the first person he saw was Valérie.

"Captain André told me that she'd removed the bullet and that there was a good chance that the man would be restored to full health in a few weeks," recalled Bristow. "I listened intently as she explained how fortunate the patient was that the bullet had lodged in what was known as the shield or buffer zone of the brain. I was happy to feign interest because Valérie had ravishing dark hair and very big brown eyes."[13]

According to Bristow, Valérie referred to him as "*L'Ange Blanc*" or "the White Angel," because of his heroism in the rescue of the four men.[14] Bristow was amazed to learn that Valérie was also an avid aviation enthusiast and had seen the demonstration of the Hiller at Tan Son Nhut. In every way she was convinced that the helicopter was an essential tool for the French medical corps.

"In the days that followed she arranged a private meeting with the officer commanding the medical corps, *Medicin General* André Robert. I had told her the story of how I'd tried to sell the Hiller to the *Armée de l'Air* but had been unable to arrange meetings with the most senior officers who made the decisions."

According to Bristow, Valérie André would prove to be instrumental in championing the cause of the helicopter.

"Over lunch at General Robert's private residence, however, she made a passionate case for medical evacuation helicopters and managed to convince the General so completely that he began talking of having a squadron of twelve Hillers under his command."

With the hope of collecting a commission on the sale of multiple Hillers, Bristow described his rescue of the four wounded men and drove home the point that they wouldn't have survived out in the field without a helicopter landing at their base. No other aircraft, and certainly no ground-based transportation, could have pulled off this feat.

"I may have overplayed my hand, but having read his mind I felt sure he was convinced of the urgent need for helicopter field rescue services."

Later that same day, Bristow met with Valérie at the Continental Hotel in Saigon. Over drinks, Bristow wanted to know General Robert's thoughts after their meeting. She admonished the Englishman for being rather forceful in his approach with the general but added that might not have necessarily been such a bad move. According to Valérie André, General Robert was going to contact the commander in charge of the French air force in Indochina to recommend the purchase of additional helicopters.

The news was quite welcomed by Alan Bristow.

"Seizing the opportunity, I wrote a letter to General Robert suggesting that facilities should be made available at the airport where pilots could be trained on my Hiller until the medical corps had helicopters of their own."[15]

Bristow had briefly entertained the idea of remaining in Vietnam to offer his services to the French as a pilot instructor but reconsidered that plan. The situation had deteriorated significantly in Saigon since his arrival. Bristow narrowly escaped being killed by a bomb detonated near his room at the Continental Hotel. Not long thereafter, Bristow left Indochina to seek fame and fortune in other parts of the world, eventually establishing his own helicopter firm in Britain to service offshore oil platforms beginning in the 1960s.

With the decision made to create France's first military helicopter rescue fleet, the only question that remained was who would be selected as France's first military helicopter rescue pilot.

Chapter 13

The Corsican Pilot

Valérie André and other medical personnel from the large urban hospitals were not the only people to witness the increasing number of wounded flowing from battlefronts in Vietnam. There were many in support roles, such as medics and ambulance drivers, who operated under hazardous conditions to provide aid and transport for the wounded. There were also dedicated bush pilots who flew small aircraft, like the Morane-Saulnier Criquet, to crudely cut out airfields in remote areas to retrieve the most severely wounded. One such pilot was Alexis Santini.

Alexis Santini was a ruggedly built man, suited from birth to live a life under demanding conditions. He was born in 1914 in Ota on the island of Corsica.[1] Ota was an area known for sheepherding, and people there learned to live with the limited resources they had. It was a hard life that taught Santini the value of hard work and self-reliance. But he was not destined to become a sheepherder. In 1935, he left Corsica to join the French air force.

Santini was assigned to the Second Battalion of the French air force at l'Air d'Istres, near Bouches-du-Rhône. The young man dedicated himself to a military life. Designated a soldier first class on August 21, 1936, Santini rose quickly thereafter to the rank of corporal and then sergeant by June 1937.

There was an understated air to the young soldier, who was described as handsome in youth with auburn hair and steel blue eyes, with a compact, muscular body. His round face often wore a serious look. Santini well understood the growing threat that was facing France from across its borders. When his first tour of duty ended in 1937, he signed up for another two years of service. This was followed by yet another tour beginning in 1939.

93

Santini began his career in aviation during the latter part of the 1930s, first by enrolling in a flight-crew training program for noncommissioned officers. In November 1938, the young sergeant was sent to Nîmes-Courbessac, again in the south of France, to begin pilot training. By May 1939, Alexis Santini was commissioned as a pilot in the French air force and returned to l'Air d'Istres air base where he was trained in the flight operation of twin-engine aircraft.

Proving to be an exceptional pilot, Santini was transferred to the air corps's center for reconnaissance instruction in May 1940, where he was to pilot France's most advanced bomber/reconnaissance aircraft, the Bloch 174. But the training sessions were cut short, as France's war effort began crumbling in June from the onslaught of the Nazi advance. When it became inevitable that France would fall to the Germans, a decision was made to transfer much of France's military aircraft inventory to its colonies in North Africa.

With aircraft in short supply, on June 11 Santini was ordered to sail on a troop carrier from Bordeaux to Oran, Algeria. In Algeria, Sergeant Santini joined Reconnaissance Group 2/36, which was soon placed under the authority of Marshal Pétain's Vichy government.

Contrary to many misconceptions, the Vichy government maintained a provisional "armistice army" following France's capitulation to the Germans. There was a certain logic for the Germans to allow France to maintain a small contingency force, although none of the more than 1.8 million French soldiers imprisoned in German prisoner of war camps would be allowed to join. Hitler and his generals reasoned that a small, collaborationist Vichy army of fewer than one hundred thousand men—directly controlled by the German Wehrmacht—would continue to monitor France's internal security.

With his country's military power essentially neutered, Alexis Santini would soon learn that Reconnaissance Group 2/36 would also be disbanded. In August 1940, Santini was ordered to return to France and to report to Uzes, near Nîmes, where he was to be retrained for duty in Indochina, although that overseas transfer was placed on indefinite hold.

There was probably little pride in Santini's promotion to lieutenant in April 1942, with the state of the French military as it was. Santini remained marginally attached to air groups such as Fighter Squadron 1/13 based at Nîmes, although the operational effectiveness of these units was nil under France's Nazi overseers. By the end of 1942, Santini was demobilized from military service, save for a brief period where he was recalled to control tower duty at the airfield at Drôme.

When Santini's military service with Vichy's armistice army ended in early 1944, he was approached by operatives with the *maquis* of Nîmes to join the Resistance. Santini's decision to join the Resistance was simple. Those who truly wanted to see the overthrow of Nazi occupation in France were left with little choice, join the Resistance or sit on the sidelines of history. Within weeks of his formal inclusion in the *maquis*, Alexis Santini created a separate Resistance group in Crupies.

Santini had connections through the *maquis* to the intelligence-gathering network that passed on information to the Allied war effort in Britain. Before his discharge, Santini had been assigned to security work at military airfields in Crupies and Montélimar, then used by the Germans. Santini was able to report on the number of German aircraft, their type, and their movements— information that was vital in planning the Allied invasion of Europe.

With the D-Day invasion in June 1944, the work of the Resistance shifted, as General de Gaulle called on *maquis* cells in France to take up arms against the Germans. The *maquis* cells became FFI, French Forces of the Interior, and fought alongside de Gaulle's Free French as auxiliary infantry units. With the name change came better weapons, enabling the former Resistance fighters to take on more audacious raids. On August 22, 1944, Alexis Santini led such a raid on a German position in Péage de Vizille, near Grenoble. With American tanks providing fire support, Santini and his men went house to house until they found a company of entrenched Germans. A firefight ensued, and there were casualties on both sides. When the Germans finally surrendered, Santini's team captured seventy-five prisoners. After Péage de Vizille, they joined up with an American unit in the liberation of Grenoble afterward. Santini and his men were awarded the Croix de guerre with palm for their heroic action.[2]

As the liberation of France eventually wound down, Alexis Santini once again reenlisted in the air force. He flew aerial reconnaissance missions during the battle of Autun, and encountered heavy flak from German cannons, but he managed to survive unscathed. Santini rode out the remainder of the war assigned to routine reconnaissance duty over the Alpes-Maritimes on France's southeastern frontier.

Following the end of World War II, Santini remained in the air force and was among the first to volunteer for service in Indochina, the posting that he missed out going to in 1940. He had accumulated more than six hundred hours of flight time by 1946, despite the interruption to his service during the occupation years. But Santini suffered a bad reaction to vaccinations he received before being shipped out and, while en route to Indochina, required hospitalization in Alexandria, Egypt. Nevertheless, he arrived in Indochina in May 1946.

Santini was given command of the Second Artillery Observation Aviation Group (2e GAOA)[3] based at Tan Son Nhut airfield in Saigon. His immediate predecessor, Captain Chesnais, was shot down by the Viet Minh only the month before. Even though the Viet Minh didn't possess sophisticated weapons early on in the war, low altitude flying and a lucky shot could bring down the small, lightweight, and unarmed observation planes.

The original mission of the 2e GAOA was to observe French artillery positions and to help direct them from the air via radio to increase their effectiveness, but these types of missions quickly gave way to reconnaissance flights. Only a month after arriving in Saigon, Santini was flying a mission over U Minh in southwestern Vietnam along the Mekong Delta. Suddenly, machine-gun fire ripped through the fuselage of his plane. He assessed the damage and found that he wasn't injured, nor did any of the shots damage anything vital to the aircraft. Santini was able to continue his flight over the enemy area that resulted in the capture of weapons once ground forces were sent in. Unlike Captain Chesnais, Santini was able to return to base at Tan Son Nhut. The citation entered into Santini's record made particular note of his *sang froid*—cool-headedness—that allowed him to complete his mission.[4]

As the war dragged on, transporting the wounded became more of an occupation for Santini and other pilots like him. In 1949 Alexis Santini, now promoted to captain, was reassigned to command Escadrille de liaisons aériennes 52 (ELA 52). ELA 52 was more focused on the rescue of wounded soldiers in remote areas. The group's Morane-Saulnier SM 500 Criquets were modified to include a stretcher carrier built into the fuselage behind the pilot's seat. The most severely wounded could be driven by truck, jeep, or ambulance to a dirt airstrip out in remote parts of Vietnam where the small aircraft could land. The most severely wounded then stood a chance of surviving if they could be flown back to a fully equipped hospital in time. Flying under these conditions could be just as dangerous as low altitude reconnaissance, however. The aircraft required runways in areas that made them extremely vulnerable during takeoffs and landings, and the small Criquets could only carry one patient at a time. Larger and heavier aircraft, like the C-47 Dakotas, could carry much more but were not suited for landing on crudely built airstrips.

There were limitations to the work that ELA 52 could accomplish. If one of the blockhouse outposts was too remote or still engaged with fighting the Viet Minh, it would be nearly impossible to send the wounded out by ground transportation to rendezvous with a medical Criquet. Many soldiers were being lost simply because they couldn't be treated for survivable injuries. But an extraordinary change in battlefield rescues was coming.

Alexis Santini was among those who witnessed Alan Bristow's helicopter demonstration at Tan Son Nhut in January 1950. Santini was fascinated with the Hiller. Its long, slender insect-like fuselage and cockpit enclosed in a bubble of Plexiglas seemed like something out of the future. There was very little protection for a pilot inside the Hiller, and it was slow. But Santini thought that the same thing could be said about the Morane-Saulnier Criquet, too.

Not long after the demonstration flights, Santini heard of Alan Bristow's rescue of four severely wounded soldiers out on the delta. It was an astounding feat that had demanded much from both the pilot and the lithe aircraft. Bristow did not reveal how harrowing the flight actually was in the severely overloaded aircraft, and that he and the wounded barely got back to Saigon safely. In the end, the mission was successful and proved that the little helicopter was a practical tool for rescue.

Orders were handed down from the French air force that two Hiller UH-12/360s were to be purchased and would be assigned to ELA 52 at Tan Son Nhut. Alexis Santini was chosen to become France's first military helicopter pilot. With more than 1,000 fixed-wing aircraft flight hours, and 315 hours of flight time in combat zones, Santini was the logical choice for this new era in rescue flights.[5] In early March 1950, he was ordered to return to France to train at Helicop-Air's facility at Cormeilles-en-Vexin just outside Paris.

When Santini arrived at the airfield at Cormeilles-en-Vexin, he met with Helicop-Air's owner, Henri Boris. Boris had been a pilot with the Free French during World War II. His life revolved around aviation, and he was a major proponent of the helicopter. He had jumped at the chance to sign on as the exclusive distributor of Hiller products in France. He envisioned helicopters in such diverse fields as agriculture and construction, aerial photography, tourism, and even in advertising and entertainment. His overall philosophy when it came to introducing the helicopter to the public was "to be able to train pilots and mechanics of helicopters to be as proficient and almost as ubiquitous as the drivers and mechanics of trucks."[6] Boris was certain that establishing the helicopter with the French air force would go a long way toward his goal of making the helicopter a universally accepted form of transportation.

Santini underwent several weeks of intensive training in the Hiller at Cormeilles-en-Vexin. A basic civilian helicopter pilot's license in France only required twenty hours of flight training; however, a military pilot was expected to go through much more rigorous training. Crop dusting was one of the tasks that the Hiller was suited to perform, and Boris often made extra revenue by renting his helicopters out for these services. More advanced novice pilots, like Santini, gained valuable experience in learning to control the helicopter under different load and handling conditions when the aircraft was outfitted with spray equipment.

When Santini completed his training at Helicop-Air, he was awarded the twenty-third civilian helicopter pilot's license by the Aero-Club of France. Alexis Santini was now ready to return to Indochina and assemble a team that would effectively become the first operational military helicopter rescue service in Southeast Asia.

Chapter 14

Évasan

When Alexis Santini returned to Saigon in early May 1950, he found two Hiller UH-12/360s inside ELA 52's hangar at Tan Son Nhut. The helicopters were under the command of both the French air force and Service de santé, the French health service corps in Vietnam. The air force was to provide the pilots and the maintenance of the helicopters, and Service de santé was to direct their use as rescue aircraft. They were the first medical rescue helicopters to enter service in an active combat zone in all of southeast Asia.[1]

The operations of the helicopters in the service of transporting the wounded from remote locations to proper medical facilities and hospitals also necessitated the coining of a new acronym. In French, the medical role of the Hiller became known as *évasan*, or *évacuation sanitaire*, meaning "medical evacuation." The English language equivalent to *évasan* would become *medevac*, essentially carrying the same meaning.

The new rescue helicopters had not arrived for the French too soon. The expanded rescue services of ELA 52 were needed more than ever. By 1950, it was obvious to many that France's war in Vietnam was going poorly. Jean Étienne Valluy—the general who ordered the bombing of Haiphong and attack on Hanoi in 1946, and who had vowed to crush the Viet Minh in a short military action—had failed to find a way out of the deep hole that he dug for his one hundred thousand French all-volunteer force in Indochina. In the course of a few short years, the army of the Viet Minh—now also known as the People's Army of Vietnam (PAVN)—had grown from disorganized and poorly equipped bands of guerilla fighters into a disciplined and highly regimented force under the leadership of Vo Nguyen Giap.

Thanks to Valluy's insistence that the French military show its presence in the form of many small blockhouses and some larger fortifications in even the most remote parts of Vietnam, Laos, and Cambodia, much of the French army and French Foreign Legion's ground force were now stretched extremely thin. The outposts, constructed of concrete blocks with walls up to thirty to forty centimeters (three feet) thick and standing some six to eight meters (nineteen to twenty-six feet) high, were often placed at one kilometer from each other to give the illusion of military strength. But in reality, these small blockhouse outposts were often defended by garrisons of as few as a dozen or so men.

The Viet Minh, however, were attracting new members to their ranks on a daily basis. By some estimates, their numbers grew to more than 250,000 by 1950.[2] The PAVN learned to be resourceful, making do with outdated or improvised weapons and living off the land or finding support in villages for food and other supplies. But the fortunes of the Viet Minh radically changed for the better in 1949, when the Communists took over China. Beginning in January 1950, both China and the Soviet Union formally recognized Ho Chi Minh and the Democratic Republic of Vietnam as the legitimate government of Vietnam. As a result, the Viet Minh began receiving even more weapons and supplies sent across the Chinese border from both countries.

After Valluy's offensives in 1947 and 1948 failed to score the knockout blow against the Viet Minh that he promised, the conflict in Vietnam began to stagnate into a war of attrition. As Ho Chi Minh presciently said to an interviewer at the onset of the war:

"It is the fight between tiger and elephant. If the tiger stands his ground, the elephant will crush him with its mass. But, if he conserves his mobility, he will finally vanquish the elephant, who bleeds from a multitude of cuts."[3]

It was quite apparent that the French were bleeding heavily from "a multiple of cuts" by 1950. Valluy left Indochina at the end of 1949 and was replaced by General Marcel Carpentier.

Meanwhile, back at Tan Son Nhut, Alexis Santini had his work cut out for him. Santini was Indochina's only helicopter pilot. He had a list of men as potential candidates to fly the other Hiller, but they would require the same amount of training, certification, and experience that Santini had undergone. Santini realized that, for now, he alone would be called upon to perform the most difficult rescues.

Not long after his return to Saigon, Alexis Santini was dispatched on his first mission. On May 16, 1950, a call came late in the afternoon that two wounded soldiers would need to be airlifted to Saigon. The wounded soldiers, along with their unit, were in a forest clearing near the village of Tân Uyên, fifty kilometers northwest of Saigon. Because the call for an airlift came late in the day, part of the one-hour roundtrip flight would involve flying at night.

Santini needed all of his experience to pull off his first rescue by helicopter. Four years of flying fixed-wing aircraft in Vietnam at least made the terrain familiar, but flying at night would still be very dangerous. The sun was beginning to recede in the west when Santini lifted off from Tan Son Nhut. Less than a half hour later, he came to a forest clearing where he found the men waiting for him with the wounded.

Even as the sun sank into the horizon, the oppressive heat in South Vietnam contributed negatively to the helicopter's performance. Tropical weather performance was not the helicopter's strong suit. Getting used to how the Hiller flew in Vietnam compared to how Helicop-Air's Hillers flew in France would take some adjustment. Santini made a mental note to discuss that with Sergeant Petit, the Hiller's mechanic at Tan Son Nhut.

The soldiers at Tân Uyên were instructed to lay out a marker to designate the landing zone. Santini spotted it from the air and prepared to make his landing. The helicopter had large red crosses painted on its sides and under its fuselage, but Santini knew that the Viet Minh would open fire on him all the same as soon as he came into range. He hoped that the men had established a wide enough perimeter to avoid that from happening.

Men who served in the remote areas of Vietnam were often referred to as "*les soldats de la boue*," the "mud soldiers," because they operated under the most primitive and deprived conditions. Supplies would mostly come from transport planes that would drop food, munitions, and other materiel by parachute. Sometimes trucks were used, but traveling the primitive dirt roads of Vietnam was dangerous enough during daylight and suicidal at night. Ambushes and firefights were expected at all hours of the day but were most heavily concentrated at night.

Valérie André treated many of the wounded soldiers from these remote outposts and knew how they felt.

"Mud soldiers always feared that they could not be treated in time and operated on in case of serious injury."[4] Most expected to die if they were seriously wounded.

But on that day, the soldiers at Tân Uyên saw Santini's landing as something of a miracle. Two of their own might make it back to safety tonight. They also marveled at the Hiller. It looked like no other aircraft they had ever seen. As soon as he landed and secured the still running helicopter, Santini quickly stepped out of the cockpit and instructed the soldiers how to load the men onto the Hiller's built-in litters. He had to tell them to stay down low and out of the way of the still spinning main and tail rotor blades. In the growing darkness, the rotors were nearly invisible, and contact with them could be fatal. With darkness came another danger. The Viet Minh would soon begin their nightly harassment of the outpost.

When the two wounded were finally loaded onto the aircraft's side litters, Santini ordered the other men to stay back as he increased the rotor speed for liftoff. It was now completely dark. Only the faint backlight of the instrument panel provided any kind of illumination. A quick read of the instruments showed that the engine temperature and oil pressure were in range, and Santini only needed his compass to set his course back to Tan Son Nhut. When the Hiller finally climbed to three thousand feet (nine hundred meters), he was confident that he was out of range of any gunfire and ultimately relieved when he saw the lights of Saigon. As he flew over Saigon, he radioed that he was on approach, and soon he was in sight of the landing lights marking the runway at Tan Son Nhut.

An ambulance was waiting for the two wounded men near ELA 52's hangar. As the two wounded were driven away to Coste Hospital, Sergeant Petit walked up to Santini and asked how the mission went.

"No problems," he tersely told Petit. "It's good, but try to wring a little more power out of it."

Rescue operations were complete for that night, but Santini would return to Tân Uyên over the next two days transporting more wounded back to Saigon. With this workload, he knew that other pilots would have to be checked out on the Hiller, and the sooner, the better.

The French air force also realized that Santini could not continue as a solo act for very long, but a lieutenant sent to Helicop-Air's training facility experienced a fatal accident at Cormeilles-en-Vexin. Each pilot trainee was required to perform an emergency autorotation landing of the helicopter in case of an engine failure. Something went wrong when the lieutenant attempted a power-off landing and was killed when his helicopter came down too quickly. The postmortem found that the lieutenant had been drinking before his fatal flight. Unfortunately for Santini, it meant that another candidate would have to be found to take the lieutenant's place.

Back in France, Sergeant Raymond Fumat learned of the accident involving the lieutenant through a mechanic friend training to service Hillers at Helicop-Air. Fumat had been in the air force since 1939. Unlike Santini, Fumat escaped from France in 1940 to join de Gaulle's Free French in North Africa, where he enlisted in ground-based operations. Fumat was part of General Leclerc's Second Armored Division that liberated Paris in August 1944.[5] Fumat reenlisted in the air force in 1947 as an instructor for fixed-wing pilots, but he was intrigued by what the mechanic had to say about helicopters. With authorization from his superiors, Fumat enrolled at Helicop-Air and, in July 1950, arrived in Saigon with his certification as a helicopter pilot.

Fumat was welcomed by Santini, who was keen on expanding the rescue operations further. It was not only the lack of pilots Santini was concerned with, however. Keeping the two Hillers flight ready at all times also presented its own set of challenges. Fortunately, the two aircraft came with crates of spare parts. But adapting the helicopters to fly in Vietnam's tropical climate required constant adjustment and fine-tuning. Additionally, rescue missions with the Hiller presented new learning experiences for Santini, as he worked out procedures to make each flight more efficient and safer than the last. He had already found issues with landing zones on many of his missions and knew that improvement had to be made to secure his and the helicopter's safety. With Sergeant Petit's mechanical assistance, Santini managed to get through nine missions, rescuing fifteen men before Fumat came aboard as helicopter pilot number two.[6]

Although it was his first time in Indochina, Sergeant Fumat settled in a routine with the crew of ELA 52. He lent his particular character and personality to hangar life as well, when the helicopters were in between missions. He was an adept mandolin player who could be counted on to liven up morale with a song that handily went with wine and food during the crew's off-duty hours.

Fumat was eased into his role as rescue pilot for the first few months. Teething problems with the new service continued to be worked out, and a brief lull in hostilities during the summer relieved some pressure. But in fall 1950, Vo Nguyen Giap launched a new offensive in northern Vietnam. The Viet Minh were now equipped with better weapons and tactical support from China and had targeted French positions at Cao Bang and Dong Khe in the north near the Chinese border. The casualties were heavy, and there was fear that the Viet Minh would make a push toward the capital in Hanoi.

Logistically, the helicopters were not ready to support the number of casualties expected from the battle in the north. Their specialized maintenance meant that they could not as easily be serviced in field operations near a battlefront at that time, but that day would also come. For the time being, they remained at Tan Son Nhut. Even so, they were hardly idle.

On October 13, outposts at Thủ Dầu Một, Tra Vinh, and Ben Suc—all near Saigon—came under attack. The assaults were intended to keep the French off balance in the south. Santini and Fumat both engaged in nonstop rescues throughout the day, with six wounded transported by Santini and fourteen by Fumat. It was exhausting work. No sooner would they touch down at Tan Son Nhut than they would be back up in the air and back out to the battlefield.

Ben Suc was the bloodiest of the three destinations. It was under fire most of the day, making it hazardous to land at any time. On one of Fumat's missions, the enemy surrounding the outpost began their harassment with heavy fire trained on the soldiers stretchering two wounded men to the helicopter. The air was ringing with bullets, and it was impossible to load one of the men onto the litter that was exposed to enemy fire. Having no choice but to load one man on the right-side litter, Fumat climbed into the center seat of the cockpit and told the men to help the other man into the right seat of the cockpit. It was an ill-advised decision. Loading both of the men on the right side of the aircraft created a severe imbalance, but Fumat saw no alternative. With everyone strapped in, Fumat lifted off.

Once in flight, Fumat discovered a flaw in the helicopter's control design. The Hiller lacked hydraulic assist in the cyclic control that affected the pitch of the main rotor. With the unbalanced load, the overhead stick became unwieldy and difficult to control. Fumat fought the stick constantly all the way back to the airfield in Saigon. While Fumat was able to land safely once he was in Saigon, his arm was wracked in pain for the next two weeks as a result of the poorly designed control.

Another noteworthy mission that Fumat undertook was also one that established a new facet in helicopter rescue. Lieutenant Maurice Jacquesson of the Normandie-Niemen fighter/bomber squadron was forced to ditch his Bearcat over an area known as the Plain of Reeds (Plaine des Joncs). Jacquesson's squadron had been ordered to bomb and strafe enemy targets just southwest from Saigon, not far from My Tho. After dropping their bomb load, the squadron turned their way back toward Saigon. That's when Jacquesson knew his plane had engine trouble.

Jacquesson's Bearcat was flying at low altitude when its engine stalled, making an emergency bailout by parachute impossible. With only moments to spare, Jacquesson had no choice but to make a forced landing.[7]

Fortunately for Jacquesson, the marshy Plain of Reeds allowed for a relatively soft landing of his plane. When the Bearcat made contact with the earth, it managed to stay intact as it slid along the surface of the swampy plain; however, a fire broke out from a leaky fuel line. At first, Jacquesson thought that he was going to be engulfed in flames as the smell of raw gasoline and smoke began to seep into the cockpit. He barely made it out of the wreck alive. The impact caused the canopy release to jam, so Jacquesson was forced to kick out the Plexiglas canopy to escape the burning aircraft.

Jacquesson's comrades from the Normandie-Niemen squadron initially thought there was no way that the downed pilot had survived. The Bearcat was on fire, and the smoke from the wreckage was dense. Even with low-flying passes, the pilots were unable to catch a glimpse of Jacquesson. They radioed their report of the downed pilot and returned to Tan Son Nhut.

A search of the area was immediately launched from Hanoi. One low-flying search plane was struck by a Viet Minh sniper, piercing the cockpit and the knee of the copilot. None of the search planes turned up a trace of Jacquesson. They didn't realize that Jacquesson, knowing the crash would attract the Viet Minh, had managed to get almost a kilometer away from his plane.

The next morning more rescue planes were sent to the area. Jacquesson heard one of the planes approaching and pulled out a signal mirror from his survival kit. Catching the rays off the early morning sun, he managed to create flashes. Would it be enough to attract any attention from the air, or would it signal the Viet Minh?

The Siebel made a circular pattern for the search. At first, Jacquesson was certain his efforts were not yielding any results. But soon he noticed the Siebel concentrating more on the area he was in. At last, the crew in the Siebel saw him, and Jacquesson knew it. They waved their wings at the downed pilot. The crew radioed a message back to Saigon:

"Jacquesson is alive!"

The only question to be answered now was how to get him out. A plan was quickly improvised to use one of the helicopters. Raymond Fumat volunteered to go. With coordinates furnished by the search crew, Fumat charted Jacquesson's position. Less than an hour after the pilot's discovery was radioed in, Fumat lifted off. He would be accompanied by fighters from the Normandie-Niemen squadron, who would strafe the area if they saw Viet Minh closing in.

Fumat had little idea of what to expect. It wasn't known if Jacquesson was badly injured. To top it off, the downed pilot was likely waist-deep in a swampy marsh, making it impossible for Fumat to land the helicopter.

When Fumat finally arrived at Jacquesson's location, a search plane was still circling. Fumat was hovering low and proceeding slowly when he finally caught sight of him, as Jacquesson frantically waved at the helicopter. Fumat could see that Jacquesson seemed to be mostly uninjured, which was a good thing. Fumat's only plan for the rescue was to hover low over the marsh so that Jacquesson could climb up on the landing gear of the helicopter.

As Jacquesson later described his rescue:

"There was no ladder, no hoist. Getting to the cabin floor [of the helicopter] was up to me. With Fumat hovering as low as he could, he shouted at me to pull myself up by seizing the frame and climbing into the empty seat next to him.

"I raised my right leg to rest on the cockpit floor. It was impossible, my leg felt stiff and it slipped away from the cabin. . . . But I wasn't going to give up. I grabbed ahold of anything that seemed solid with my arms and pulled. With a struggle, I was soon chest flat on the floor of the cockpit."[8]

Wasting no time, Fumat made sure that Jacquesson had strapped himself into a seat. He then put the Hiller into a climb and headed back to Saigon. It may have not been the smoothest of rescues, but Lieutenant Maurice Jacquesson was soon safe again at Tan Son Nhut. And Sergeant Raymond Fumat made history by becoming the first person to successfully rescue a downed pilot by helicopter.

Fumat's time in the hero's spotlight would ultimately be cut short. Not long after Jacquesson's rescue, he was involved in a rollover accident in a jeep and suffered a severe spinal cord injury. Fumat was repatriated back to France where he eventually recovered, but his military career was over.

The loss of Fumat meant that another pilot was needed to fill the second position at ELA 52 after Alexis Santini. Few would have predicted that a female neurosurgeon would become France's next helicopter rescue pilot.

Chapter 15

The Woman and the Dragonfly

Valérie André was mesmerized by the helicopters. Any time she was at Tan Son Nhut to train with or medically supervise paratroop operations, she would also visit ELA 52's hangar where the Hillers were kept. The stories she heard about helicopter rescues fascinated her, and her admiration for the men who flew the aircraft into dangerous war zones was enormous. But there was a question that Valérie rolled over in her imagination:

Was there more that could be done?

The work of Santini and Fumat was heroic; of that there was no doubt. Although they were exemplary pilots who had proven themselves, they lacked the specialized knowledge that a doctor would have to stabilize a patient before transport. There were field medics, to be sure, but their knowledge only went so far. Valérie knew about the problems the pilots were having with the Hillers when they were overloaded. There had to be cases when a doctor would be necessary to stabilize a wounded patient, but bringing a doctor along with the Hiller's limited payload was out of the question.

But what if the pilot and the doctor were one and the same?

This is the solution that came to Valérie's mind when she first witnessed Alan Bristow's demonstration of the helicopter and its potential in saving lives. A doctor/pilot could see to a patient's wound being properly pre-treated and that he was correctly sedated prior to transport. Stabilizing a severely wounded soldier in the field would increase his chances for survival manyfold. Moreover, in Valérie André's case, a doctor/pilot who weighed a

107

breath under forty-five kilograms (one hundred pounds) could potentially transport three wounded soldiers given the compromised payload in the Hiller. With this reasoning, Valérie presented herself to General André Robert as a candidate for medical helicopter flight training.

While Valérie knew the benefits of the helicopters in providing relief to soldiers assigned to Indochina, she also knew the budgetary limitations that France was imposing on continuing the war effort.

"The budget was so restricted that the politicians were careful not to weigh down France with the cost of the war. The helicopters could almost be considered a luxury," she observed.[1]

But the regular missions by Captain Santini and Sergeant Fumat served as an inspiration to the young surgeon.

"It was a veritable thunderbolt that struck me about this magical machine," Valérie said, with no lack of awe in her admiration of the helicopter's abilities. "What could it be compared with? Perhaps a dragonfly, most certainly—a fabulous kind of mechanical dragonfly that had to be learned how to be controlled . . . and to be mastered as a test of all of one's resources."[2]

"The possibilities of this new machine dazzled me," she continued. "To me, it seemed to lend itself as a wonder in the medical field, with the daily adventure of rescuing casualties from remote outposts."[3]

Based on her lifelong passion for aviation it was without hesitation that Valérie submitted her request for helicopter flight training. Her request was not overwhelmingly received.

To begin with, as a woman who was already serving as a surgeon in a military hospital Valérie André was something of an unusual commodity. While she faced prejudice upon her arrival, that initial skepticism of a woman commanding a team in a surgical theater had already faded to a great degree. She had been able to prove her capabilities in a grinding environment.

Also, with a shortage of qualified medical personnel in Indochina, a person of her skills was someone who could ill afford to be lost in a program that relied on a flying machine that many still branded as highly experimental.

But several factors worked in Valérie André's favor when it came to advancing her cause. The jeep accident that ended Sergeant Fumat's service in Indochina in April 1951 pointed out the need for other pilots. Even before Fumat's accident, losing a pilot limited the effectiveness of the helicopter program when a replacement or standby pilot was not available. And it would also leave a helicopter idle, an issue Valérie knew weighed heavily with General Robert. From that perspective she saw a possible opening.

"I presented my candidacy and total availability to General Robert, and backed up my qualifications by presenting my hours piloting light planes and sailplanes, plus my parachute jumps."[4]

Valérie was hopeful that she had struck a receptive chord with the general.

"General Robert was very encouraging toward me and had no prejudice," Valérie said. "He was a decision-maker who was very much ahead of his time. . . . He only wanted to assure himself of my capability to fulfill missions."[5]

But General Robert was not the only person that Valérie had to convince. The air force had definite ideas of who should pilot helicopters, and Valérie didn't match their vision. But the helicopters were more under the purview of Service de santé than the air force, so the ultimate decision was General Robert's; however, the support of Dr. Robert Carayon, her immediate superior and mentor at Coste Hospital, was also crucial. The loss of a valuable member to his medical team would deal a serious blow in treating the ever streaming scores of wounded. Without Dr. Carayon's acceptance, Valérie would not become a pilot.

"The professional requirement was initially a concern," Valérie said. "With my commanding doctor, Carayon, at his side, General Robert asked how many surgical operations I took part in or carried out personally. I answered, '150 per month.'

"This number underscored the need for my presence in the neurosurgery service. In the event of my departure for flight training to pilot helicopters, it would be essential to envision my replacement."[6]

The odds of her being accepted for flight training were not in her favor. Military aviation, especially when it involved flying into combat areas, was still very much considered a man's occupation. There was no precedent for her request. Still, Valérie felt that she had made a compelling case. When she finally learned of Robert's and Carayon's decision, she was nonetheless stunned by it.

"It was a miracle: my candidacy was accepted."[7]

Her written orders were confirmed on May 26, 1950. Her training would coincide with a leave of absence from her post at Coste. Valérie André was to leave Saigon and return to France on May 31 to begin training with Helicop-Air at Cormeilles-en-Vexin.

When the day finally came for her to leave for France, Valérie boarded a C54 Skymaster medical transport plane. There was a grim reminder of the war inside the plane loaded with wounded soldiers. They were the fortunate ones, however. They were going home.

"I was solicited many times to lavish care on the numerous casualties being transported [back to France]."[8]

It had been nearly three years since Valérie André left France to serve in Indochina. France was still in its postwar rebuilding stage, but there were signs of economic recovery. It was the beginning of what would become known as *les trente glorieuses*, the thirty glorious years of economic expansion for France.

Part of the economic recovery could be seen at Cormeilles-en-Vexin, where civil aviation mixed with military flight training in the helicopter program at Helicop-Air. The airfield buzzed with activity. The helicopter was still a novelty in France, and the hangars of Helicop-Air possessed an almost magical aura and mystique.

The environment that Valérie André found at Helicop-Air was not highly encouraging. In a class with five other male student pilots, she wasn't taken very seriously at first.

Why was a woman being trained to fly a helicopter for the military?

For some, it was hard to comprehend, especially since military service in Indochina was not compulsory in France. When it was found out that she was being trained to fly into combat zones, the disbelief only increased.

Her instructor was André Onde. Onde had been a test pilot for a highly experimental helicopter program at the French aviation firm of Nord, before working for Helicop-Air. During a test flight, Onde miraculously escaped severe injury when the aircraft touched the ground in a turning maneuver and flipped over.[9] The Nord helicopter program series was canceled, and Onde found instructional work at Helicop-Air as a somewhat safer way to continue to indulge in his passion for flight.

Onde stressed safety in his instruction, but a large part of flight training also involved helicopter care and basic maintenance. Valérie didn't shirk from any activity involving the helicopters. In a story about Valérie written for *France illustration* reported in the journalistic vernacular of the day:

"She never takes advantage of being a woman to cut corners. Like everyone else, she pushes the helicopters back to the hangars at night and helps to get them out in the morning. She fills up [their fuel tanks] and polishes and cleans the aircraft."[10]

Flight training at Helicop-Air was a serious matter, and company owner Henri Boris had laid out a very specific regimen of instruction that all novice pilots were to follow. As Commandant Boris wrote in an article from 1953:

"For the pilots, the program is divided into four phases. First of all is the elementary stage, composing of thirty hours of flight. . . . It is around fifteen hours that the release takes place, that is to say, the first flight of the student alone on board."[11]

Valérie André followed an extremely regimented training procedure with the Hiller. Flight simulators did not exist for helicopters in 1950. Outside of classroom instruction—where training manuals and 16 mm films were the primary training aids—actual hands-on experience with the aircraft was the only way to learn.

All Hiller helicopters were set up with dual controls from the factory, making it possible for instructors to teach new pilots with side-by-side training. There was a collective control mounted in the center, where the pilot normally sat, and another collective control mounted on the left side of the cockpit, where the instructor would sit. On early model Hillers, the cyclic stick that controlled the pitch of the main rotor was overhead in the center of the cockpit with a handle sprouting out on each side for both instructor and student. And two sets of foot pedal controls, which affected the pitch of the tail rotor for axis turning maneuvers, were mounted both in the center and left side of the cockpit. The instrument pedestal that monitored the helicopter's vital functions was located in the center of the cockpit.

Onde instructed Valérie to become thoroughly familiar with inspecting her aircraft even before entering inside. Preflight inspection of a Hiller was especially crucial. While it was the responsibility of certified aircraft mechanics to keep the helicopters maintained and flight ready, it was also necessary for the pilot to know the ship almost as well as a mechanic did. There was often little recourse when a mechanical failure occurred in midair, other than the possibility of an autorotation landing. Everything from the marker lights to the teetering of the main rotor blade to the condition and balance of the driveshafts connecting the tail rotor to the main transmission had to be given the once over visually before entering the cockpit.

Once inside, Onde had Valérie go over every item on the Hiller's preflight checklist. Everything from the engine's oil pressure and temperature to the condition of the battery and charging system had to be in a set range. If any significant difference turned up while the aircraft was still on the ground, the flight would be over before it had even begun.

The excitement for Valérie André was palpable the first time she brought a Hiller to life at Cormeilles-en-Vexin. With several cranks of the starter

motor, the Franklin motor sputtered to life as each of its six cylinders belted
out a raspy exhaust note. It was important to start off with a steady idle and
not to bring up the engine's RPMs too quickly, or else the clutch that connected the transmission to the main rotor could be blown out. The clutch
used mercury as a viscous coupling, and the main rotor would slowly start
turning whenever the engine started. As the engine began its gradual run-up
to operating speed, the rotation of the main rotor also increased, adding the
distinctive "whoosh-whoosh" to the cacophony of sounds.

Flight training would start with Onde in total control of the helicopter
while Valérie would mimic Onde's movement of hands and feet, but not
interfere with his control. Onde had enough hours as a pilot to instinctively
know the precise moment to pull up the collective control to concentrate the
downward force of the main rotor blade that pushed the aircraft away from
the ground. He knew that his student had her hand on the center collective
stick following his movements so she could duplicate them on her own. A
tentative pull upward and then back down was to make sure that the collective was operating correctly. The sudden upward thrust made it feel as if
gravity no longer mattered.

With the pull of the collective, the aircraft was off the ground for the first
time with Valérie in control. She felt an incomparable exhilaration, a feeling
of doing something incredible. Emotions and sensations flowed through her.
For her, this was the miracle of flight.

"I felt, as did my fellow students, with all the passion of a pioneer,"
Valérie said of her first flight.[12]

Her skills consistently improved on the Hiller. The intricacies of hand
and foot coordination came to her readily. Although sessions with the Hiller
would often be delayed that summer due to both mechanical problems with
the helicopters or unfavorable weather conditions, by mid-summer Valérie
André was ready to graduate to the next level in instruction.

Whenever Valérie was able to get "stick time" in a Hiller, she put the
practice to good use. A look at her flight logs from that summer revealed
both the number of hours and number of flights she undertook as she gained
experience with the aircraft:

June 1950: 2 hours flight time; 6 missions
July 1950: 7 hours flight time; 12 missions
August 1950: 7.5 hours flight time; 8 missions
Total: 16.5 hours; 26 missions

"On August 11 my training was judged ready enough to allow my release [to solo]."[13]

It would be no other than Commandant Henri Boris, who would be present at Cormeilles-en-Vexin to witness Valérie's solo flight. As Boris was later quoted saying:

"She did well! What a master!" He added, in what is perhaps one of the highest compliments a Frenchman can bestow on anyone, "This girl has marvelous *sang froid*!"[14]

Valérie was ecstatic. She proved herself to be equal among her peers and had earned her wings.

"I received my private pilot's license twelve days later," she said, in triumph.

This, however, was only the beginning of Valérie's training. In phase two of Boris's instruction, Valérie would perform commercial services for Helicop-Air, gaining more experience with the Hiller. Further practice was something that Valérie relished. Even with a newly minted license from the Aero-Club of France, she knew she was far from ready to see service in Indochina.

"It would be ridiculous to quantify my claim to carry out medical evacuations when I returned to Indochina," she said, fully realizing that the experience from the minimum number of flight hours to secure a private pilot's license was insufficient to prepare her for the rigors of *évasan* service. "I knew the risks and had no doubt about the experience I was expecting. I arranged to have some additional flight time in the south of France, and became involved in an advertising campaign for *Stemm* stockings."[15]

The Stemm ad campaign was curious for its high concept approach to advertising. In one full-color magazine ad, Valérie is shown hovering the Hiller over an almost empty yard in front of a factory, with a lone young boy standing below. From the helicopter, a long ribbon of nylon stocking is unfurled and grasped by the boy. The significance of the imagery, while dramatic, seems to have no other significance than to use the novelty of the helicopter for visual impact.

Valérie shared flight time with the Hiller with another classmate from Helicop-Air, who, she said, "cut into my hours." But the little helicopter must have performed admirably during the ad campaign's tour through the regions of Aix-en-Provence, Valence, and Avignon. In fact, Valérie found a new meaning to the traditional French children's song, "The Bridge at Avignon," where "everyone danced on top of the bridge.

"We had fallen in love with this miraculous little machine, which enabled us to fly *under* the bridge at Avignon, contrary to the song!"[16]

While she was at Helicop-Air, André Onde related a story to a journalist that illustrated the compassionate nature of Valérie André. It was a hot summer day in August, and they were in a car together. A construction crew was paving the road they were on, and the asphalt was still soft. A raven had landed on the road and became firmly stuck to the pavement.

Valérie told Onde to stop their car. Nearby she saw the group of workmen laughing at the poor bird, as it struggled to pull itself free. Valérie saw nothing funny about it. She told Onde to wrap the crow in a towel she grabbed from the backseat of their car to keep the bird's wings from thrashing them. Ever so gently she freed the bird from the sticky tar. But the process of freeing the raven had caused serious injury to the bird's talons—it had torn three of its claws. But Valérie was undaunted. She grabbed her medical kit, which she always kept with her. She dressed the raven's wounds, as Onde held on. Once she was satisfied that the raven was patched up well enough to take care of itself again, they set it free.[17]

Before Valérie left France to return to Saigon, she stopped by Henri Boris's office in Paris to say goodbye. While in his office, Boris introduced Valérie to Helicop-Air's most illustrious student to date, Alexis Santini. Santini had returned to France to update his flight training on the SCAN 30 amphibian fixed-wing plane, one of France's newer aircraft entering military service, and stopped by Helicop-Air to visit with Boris. He knew that Valérie had been assigned to ELA 52 and wasn't completely happy about the decision. The assignment was made without any input from him, and he had reservations about someone who was such a novice at flying in combat areas in Vietnam.

"[Of course] the name of the man responsible for the two Hiller helicopters in Saigon was already familiar to me," Valérie said. "However, I was totally unaware of the man I met in Henri Boris's office. He was of average size but with a muscular body, an honest face with extremely lively hazel eyes."

It seems incredible that Valérie had not yet met Alexis Santini, given that she had spent considerable time at Tan Son Nhut air base where the helicopters were stationed. She had only seen Santini piloting the Hillers from the air base from a distance.

Having already experienced discrimination from many males in the military, Valérie was wary of her first contact with the man who was now her commander.

"First of all, I knew I wouldn't have any dealings with an adversary," Valérie declared. "But just as much, would I be able to count on [Santini's] help?"[18]

The meeting was cordial, but not very conclusive. Santini looked the young doctor over, trying to size up her abilities, her dedication, her resourcefulness. She would need all of that and more to survive the kind of missions he had already completed. Yes, he had heard of Valérie's reputation as a neurosurgeon at Coste Hospital, and he also knew she was training with paratroopers as part of ACP. But that meant little to him when it came to her usefulness as a pilot now that she was headed back to Indochina.

Would she be an asset or a detriment to his unit?

The answer to that question was the only thing that mattered to Alexis Santini.

Santini congratulated Valérie on obtaining her pilot's license.

"However," he added. "In order to continue your training, you will have to wait until I return to Saigon."[19]

Valérie continued to assess her new commander.

"[He was] even-handed, but somewhat dry. His sentence hung in the air between us. Such was Santini's style—direct, assured, energetic, and without concession and nothing would change the course of his direction."

But it was obvious that Valérie admired Santini for what he had already accomplished as a pilot.

For both Alexis Santini and Valérie André, there was much they were to learn about each other. But of that meeting that day with Santini, Valérie concluded with some amount of understatement:

"While at the point of packing my luggage for Saigon, I was still unaware of the exceptional importance that would be in store for me with this comrade. . . . But I knew instinctively that Santini would count in my life."[20]

Chapter 16

The Prestige of Men

While Valérie André was in France in summer and fall 1950, the French position in Indochina was rapidly deteriorating. Reports of France's losses to the Viet Minh in northern Vietnam were especially ominous. Valérie followed reports out of Indochina with growing apprehension:

"The news that came to us from Indochina was incredibly catastrophic. On September 16, 1950, the *Viet Minh* attacked a massive [French] outpost on RC 4 at Dong Khe.

"The French commanders readied an evacuation from Cao Bang, which was considered to be very threatened. This truly fortified base was on the edge of the Chinese border, and was also at the mercy of an attack."[1]

Route Coloniale 4, or RC 4, was the northernmost part of Vietnam's main road network. RC 4, like all of the major roads in Vietnam, was primitive, unpaved, and heavily rutted, swirling in dust in the dry season and abysmally flooded in deep mud during monsoons. The roads were the lifeline to the French in these remote outposts and forts. Dong Khe and Cao Bang were considered key to the French in maintaining their control in the north.

The Viet Minh attack on the French on RC 4 was also General Vo Nguyen Giap's attempt to flex the muscles of his ever-increasing army. The nationalist movement continued to attract increasing numbers to its ranks. When Giap finally struck back in 1950, his forces outnumbered the French by a considerable margin. It's estimated that thirty thousand Viet Minh rained down on less than ten thousand French and allied Vietnamese troops defending French forts on RC 4. Overland travel on RC 4 to Cao Bang and Dong Khe had become so treacherous that it was now only possible to resupply the fort by airdropping men and materiel.[2]

Back in Paris, Valérie was annoyed as she made her final preparations for the long journey back to Asia. She had waited until the last minute to finish packing her suitcases, and now time was running short before her departure to Orly.

"I had little time for thoughts of other things than the temperamental locks on my suitcases."[3]

Her brief meeting with Alexis Santini had been encouraging but, at the same time, noncommittal on Santini's part. Valérie knew she was months away from becoming operational as a rescue helicopter pilot in Vietnam. Before she left Henri Boris's office, Santini told her he wasn't sure when he would finish his training on the SCAN 30. Santini was adamant that Valérie's training on the Hiller would not continue until he returned to Saigon.[4] Nonetheless, she sensed something positive about Santini, even though she knew very little about him. As she reflected on their first meeting:

"At that time, I was unaware of the exceptional valor of the man who shall become for me a comrade, a leader, and a friend, but he had already gained my trust and I wished to see him again."[5]

Aside from the stubborn locks on her valise, Valérie's thoughts were also focused on other matters. The past few months in Paris and at Helicop-Air's flight training school at Cormeilles-en-Vexin had been intoxicating. Her dream of taking to the air in controlled flight had finally been realized. Touring France in Helicop-Air's Hiller as part of Henri Boris's sponsored promotions also introduced Valérie André as a pilot and role model to a new generation of aviation enthusiasts, who flocked in large numbers any time she appeared. Throngs of young boys and girls were fascinated by her ability to pilot such a strange new aircraft. She had the same inspiring effect as Maryse Hilsz had on her at the Strasbourg aerodrome when she was a little girl.

On the evening of October 30, Vietnam still was thousands of miles away. For Valérie André, however, it started to feel closer as every moment went by.

"Friends were calling at my door, it was high time for me to get to the TAI [Transports aériens intercontinentaux] offices on the Rue de la Paix, where the passenger bus for Orly was parked," Valérie said. When she opened the door for her friends, they were staggered by the amount she was taking with her.

"The appearance of my luggage generated some surprised looks among my male friends," she said. "Who will volunteer to carry the heaviest of my suitcases down to the car, the one in which I have crammed my books, especially several textbooks dealing with operating techniques?"[6]

After her friends dropped her off at the bus stop, Valérie had her luggage weighed.

"Sixty-three kilograms, Madame," the clerk informed her. "You're thirty-three kilos over the allowance. I'll have to charge you for them."

The surprise, which almost shouldn't have been a surprise, was somewhat unpleasant to Valérie.

"Did I seem upset?" She felt that she must have brought some attention to herself as she discussed the overweight bags with the clerk. "In any event, a tall blond man emerged from the group of passengers readying to board the bus."

"I have no luggage," the man said to Valérie. "I can take your surplus on my ticket."[7]

Valérie could tell he was a veteran returning to Indochina.

"I examined this pleasant stranger," she later recalled. "His martial bearing and his face seemed to show the marks of one or more stays in the Far East. He was undoubtedly an officer!"[8]

The young officer's gesture provided some relief to her and left her with one less thing to worry about. As the bus for Orly was about to take off, Valérie's friends, who remained to see her off, gave her their last farewells.

"My friends handed me a bunch of violets and my new acquaintance stepped aside to allow me to climb onto the bus. Soon, we were on our way along Highway 7, leaving behind the lighted avenues of Paris."[9]

After arriving at Orly, Valérie was fascinated with the bustling activity of the airport.

After checking with the TAI ticket counter, Valérie and the other passengers were ushered into a departure area that was separated by a large glass door.

"The closing of the door created a barrier between those who were departing from those who remained," she noted metaphorically. "It pushed us far away from our family and friends whose faces reflected sadness. But the separation has left us—whether we wanted to or not—to our selfish pleasure of yielding to the attraction of a long journey."[10]

Most of the passengers were bound for Vietnam as their final destination. "Our wait seemed long to us—the departure of a plane was always likely to be delayed."

To pass the time, Valérie played a game in her head where she studied the faces of her fellow travelers and, in some cases, attempted to ascertain their backstories through a deduction of their appearance and movements. It was a skill she had picked up during the occupation when it was necessary to figure out who you could trust and who you should avoid.

"I began to observe the others [who were also waiting] . . . it was certain that our small group represented a microcosm of Saigon during this period: I presumed the young woman smoking a cigarette—she had some wrinkling at the corners of her eyes and dry skin—she nervously asked about the time of departure, and once she is told, sinks into a weariness, overwhelmed by her own fatigue.[11]

"Farther over, a man—a young person still—seems to be wrapped up in his thoughts. Was this seasoned soldier thinking about his preceding campaigns or his future assignments?

"There is also a delightful, beautiful, and gracious woman, half Vietnamese and half European, with her two children.

"And yet another group, this time three messieurs of a ripe age—one obese, the other thin, and the third one short—surveyed the room stiffly with an absolute immobility. It was as if they were stuck. However, with the same methodical gesture, they looked at their watches just like businessmen. Saigon was calling to them. Anxious and worried about their impending journey, they exuded opulence and their clothes were nothing like those of the military officers disguised in civilian clothes."

A voice on the loudspeaker system announced that Valérie's flight was now ready to board.

"We followed a charming stewardess who opened the door to the aircraft's cabin," Valérie said. "Now sure that we were finally leaving, we settled into the plane. The engines come to life, one by one. The plane taxied to the end of the runway, rolls, gathers speed, and to our greatest satisfaction, takes off."[12]

Although Valérie herself was now a pilot, it was obvious that all of the nuances of any flight possessed a deep fascination to her.

The flight to Saigon would entail several stops in the age when nonstop flights were practically nonexistent. From Paris, the plane flew to Tunisia, with a short stopover there before continuing to Cairo, Egypt. The passengers bound for Saigon would spend the next twenty hours in layover there.

Because of the long flight, the airline included booking of the passengers at the same hotel.

"An employee of TAI gave us the name of the hotel we were to stay at," Valérie said. "Once there, a swarm of small Egyptian boys awaited us and then trailed and pursued us. Each one of the scamps had trinkets for sale and advice to give us, which was often useful, especially when we needed to exchange our currency."[13]

Interestingly, some sightseeing opportunities in Egypt were offered.

"There was the inevitable walk around the pyramids and the sphinx, and our group didn't split up," Valérie said. "Without any knowledge of the area, we really couldn't separate. However, the time we spent together didn't reveal much; my companions remained unknown to me."[14]

Later that day, when Valérie returned to her hotel, she took note of a new assembly of arrivals there.

"In front of the terrace at the hotel, I noticed a rather curious group. These men seemed to be almost floating in their clothing and had a nervous look to them and quite haggard. They were hardly able to carry their steps."[15]

It turned out that the men were wounded soldiers being repatriated from Vietnam back to France.

"I immediately sprang toward them," she said. In the five months that Valérie had been away from Vietnam, she closely followed the reversals suffered by the French there. Now she was face to face with the actual devastation.

"Do any of you come from Coste Hospital?" she asked of the men. "Do any of you know Mademoiselle Botto?" Ms. Botto was Valérie's faithful operating nurse, an individual whom she described as a "stand-out woman always ready to give of herself."

"She's still over there," one of the men replied.

Valérie then asked the men, "What is the name of the doctor who is with you?"

The answer came back from several of the men:

"Carayon."

Almost at that exact moment that Valérie heard that name, she heard a somewhat sardonic voice come from behind her.

"So, André, how is it possible that you have accepted a return to Indochina?"

She spun around and was face to face with the man who had formed and mentored her skills as a neurosurgeon, Dr. Robert Carayon.

"His voice was moderate, a bit caustic, but affectionate at the same time," Valérie said. "He looked me over with a probing glance, just like the day he first entrusted to me my first serious operation."[16]

So much of Carayon's demeanor was transmitted with his eyes.

Carayon moved across the hotel lobby toward Valérie.

"As he approached, he looked at me deeply." Valérie felt as if she was being studied. "I read approval in his glance. These silent dialogs, so often repeated at Coste Hospital, did not save me from his ever-present sense of irony. I believed that his particular turn of mind was a part of his mysterious charm."[17]

"So," Carayon began in his usual probing manner. "Will you be flying helicopters or performing surgery?"

"Aren't both compatible?" Valérie answered without hesitation.

The doctor cast a doubtful eye.

"Compatible? I don't think so," he evenly replied.

Even though Carayon went along with General Robert's decision to allow Valérie to train for the helicopter service, the current course of the war meant that hospitals were operating under their heaviest workloads yet. To Carayon's way of thinking, losing the full-time services of an experienced surgeon to an experimental rescue program might not be worth the trade-off.

Valérie countered that she had volunteered for the helicopter medical rescue service primarily for the reason that she believed that a soldier's chances for survival would increase dramatically if a surgeon could be brought in by air to the battlefield.

Carayon was not convinced, and his doubts were not completely unfounded. A helicopter pilot required much of the same amount of concentration, skill, and precision as a surgeon. But in the application of those skill sets, both fields of practice were completely unrelated. It would take an exceptional individual not only to be adept at the two vocations but also to be their masters. Dr. Carayon knew that Valérie possessed a considerable reserve of ability and resolve as a surgeon. But would those character traits be successfully carried over to her ability to become a helicopter pilot? In Valérie's case, only time would tell.

Even Valérie reflected upon some of Carayon's reservations.

"I would later realize that piloting a helicopter, just like surgery, would require an intensive inner drive if one wanted to obtain exceptional results."[18]

For the remainder of their meeting, Valérie and Carayon mostly discussed events taking place in Vietnam since she had left for France. Carayon could not add much to what Valérie already knew about the new northern offensive. But the heavy toll from the war was starkly evident, etched into the face of every man in the hotel going home with Carayon.

As the evening drew to a close, Valérie André exchanged farewells with Carayon. They would be leaving for opposite destinations in the morning.

Before leaving for her room that night, however, Valérie could not resist one last look at the men being repatriated home. For all they had gone through and for all they had suffered, she noted that the thought of returning home had at least placed a somewhat more relaxed expression on their faces.

From Cairo the plane traveled to Bahrain and then to Karachi, Pakistan. From there it was onto Delhi and then Calcutta before flying the last leg of the journey across Burma and the Gulf of Siam.

"We recognized the forests of Kampuchea and Cochinchine, the rice plantations along the Mekong," Valérie recalled, intently enthralled with all of the geography spread before her from the safe altitude of the airliner. Not long after, the familiar cityscape of Saigon appeared as the airliner prepared to make its landing at Tan Son Nhut airport.

It was nightfall in Saigon.

During the time that Valérie was in France, significant changes had taken place. General André Robert, the medical director for all health services in Indochina and the man who had approved Valérie's candidacy as a rescue helicopter pilot, was now on leave in France. But Robert's replacement offered no obstacles to Valérie's return to military life once again.

"He granted all of my requests," Valérie said. "I was reinstated to the neurosurgical unit at Coste Hospital once again. . . . I was to meet up with many of my same colleagues there and to resume those practices that were important to me."[19]

Although months had gone by since her leave in France, the routine of life in wartime Saigon quickly came back to her.

"I was housed at the Annam Hotel not far from the bustling market square in Cholon. Every day at dawn I went to Coste. My work at the hospital, just as before, absorbed almost all of my days. Night watch duty returned for me every fourth night, as well."

Valérie's work schedule was relentless, as Coste was one of the better-equipped and well-staffed military hospitals in all of Vietnam. Its capacity of 540 beds was often stretched to the breaking point and then some. As Valérie explained:

"Coste Hospital could perform most of the specialized surgeries, and for that reason received casualties from all over Indochina. It was rare when all of the beds were not full."[20]

In addition to her duties at Coste, Valérie was also keen to restart her training exercises with the airborne forward surgical unit. Always on call to the hospital, she was only afforded a few hours on Monday and Thursday afternoons to pursue aviation-related activities at Tan Son Nhut. But when an airdrop exercise was scheduled for November 24, a Friday, Valérie was able to take part and dutifully reported for her assignment.

"I was ready on that day at 06:00 hours," she said. "A truck took us down from Coste to the airfield. I had hoped to be back at the start of my duty schedule for that day. At Tan Son Nhut, I donned my parachute equipment with quite a bit of elation."[21]

There were sixteen who were scheduled to make practice jumps that morning. As usual, a C-47 Dakota was used as the jump plane.

"The airfield was quiet at that time in the morning," said Valérie. "Some twenty minutes later the aircraft was on its way and at 1,000 feet of altitude. The DZ was going to be near the Phu Tho horseracing track in the Cholon district, not far from Coste Hospital."

The racetrack was built by the French in the 1930s but had a notorious reputation for horse doping, although it maintained a huge following among the ethnic Chinese living in Cholon.

Once over the drop zone the parachutists prepared for their exit from the plane.

"My haste to get back to Coste on time naturally prompted me to volunteer to jump as the '*seekee*,'" Valérie said. A "seekee" or "pathfinder," is the first of a group of parachutists to touch the ground and to set up a base for the rest to follow.

"The descent of a lone jumper also allows the pilot and jumpmaster to check the wind velocity. As I was more than light, I was assigned a companion, who was the biggest and heaviest medic. By watching our jumps, the men in the aircraft were able to get an average figure."[22]

The jumpmaster bellowed the command—"Go!"—and Valérie once again dropped into the sky. It was her seventeenth successful jump, and one she simply described afterward as "uneventful."[23]

Valérie's "uneventful" jump, however, did indeed have its own set of consequences. Not long after, as she resumed work back at the hospital, Valérie learned that she was the subject of a report that was circulating through the offices of the Directorate of Health Services. It turned out that a significant number of male military personnel were upset that a woman was allowed to take part in training exercises deemed only suitable for elite paratroopers.

"I was being severely criticized simply for damaging masculine prestige," Valérie said, after reviewing the contents of the report. "That a woman could jump by parachute, that was the rub! Alluding to other rather petty reasons, the report disapproved of any further jumps."[24]

Valérie was not about to accept this arbitrary verdict without countering it.

"The following day I paid a visit to the Airborne Troops Headquarters," she said. "I was determined to make my point of view known. Wasn't jumping from an aircraft within the capabilities of everyone, including women? True, once on the ground combatants are assigned tasks which only elite men can accomplish.

"But a doctor, and more so a woman, can comfort and tend to the wounded. Such was the theory I defended with great energy, and which my male detractors finally condescended to accept."[25]

But if a female among the ranks of paratroopers caused some male egos to become ruffled, her next foray would raise even more eyebrows, although many in Saigon were already aware of the new skill she had attained while in France.

"One day, I learned that Captain Santini was due back in Saigon at any time," Valérie noted. "I would then resume my helicopter training. Santini had only two Hiller helicopters which, for the last few days, I was gaping at with envy."[26]

Santini returned to Saigon in November 1950. Good to his word, he agreed to meet with Valérie at Tan Son Nhut and observe her abilities.

"This opened up a new phase in my flight training," Valérie said of the new undertaking. "Right away Santini gave me dual instruction in the Hiller. During my first session, however, I didn't exactly shine. I was used to easy flights on the aircraft without any medical evacuation equipment, and thus lighter."

The addition of stretchers on the side of the Hiller, along with the extra Plexiglas farings built into the cockpit doors to protect the wounded, took away from the total payload the diminutive helicopter could handle.

"Furthermore, in a tropical atmosphere the lift provided by the air was not as effective."

That was also very true when it came to the Hiller's performance. Environmental operating conditions such as higher altitudes and air densities in certain regions could affect the helicopter's flight characteristics dramatically. While Saigon was at sea level, the limited high altitude performance of the aircraft's Franklin engine was not a factor, but Vietnam's tropical climate conditions most definitely were. In an area of high humidity—where water vapor was added to the air—the density of the air itself is decreased. The rotor blades of a helicopter perform optimally in conditions where the air is at its highest density.

For Valérie, however, other potential limitations of the Hiller in Vietnam were not as striking, such as its fishbowl cockpit canopy.

"I was not bothered by the extreme brightness of the light. Dark glasses provided good protection for the eyes, and in no way altered the exceptional beauty of the landscape."[27]

Despite some of the shortcomings she exhibited in her first outing as a pilot operating in Vietnam, the impression she made upon Alexis Santini could not have been all that bad.

"Upon landing, Santini took me aside," Valérie recalled of that day. "He made a few comments but also issued a few encouragements, too. But most importantly, he made an appointment for a future flight training session."[28]

Despite the misgivings of her first performance, there was no doubt that Alexis Santini saw the promise in the young doctor's ability and drive to succeed as a pilot. For now, he would accept Valérie André.

Chapter 17

Roi Jean

The French position in northern Vietnam veered from bad to worse in October and November 1950. Étienne Valluy's successor, General Marcel Carpentier, proved to be just as hapless against the latest Viet Minh offensive as his predecessor. The small outposts held by the French along Route Coloniale 4 (RC 4) were abandoned to shore up defenses at the major fortifications at Cao Bang and Dong Khe, but the situation at both places was soon untenable. Evacuation orders for Cao Bang and Dong Khe were issued. Valérie André followed the ever-evolving military situation as did everyone else in Indochina that autumn.

"The evacuation maneuver that ensued seemed risky," Valérie said. "[For its success] it would have to make use of the RC4 which was infested with *Viet Minh*—true cut-throats for convoys."[1]

An aerial evacuation was considered, but it was feared that units left to guard the landing strip for transport planes would have to be sacrificed. But the ground evacuation via RC 4 was further complicated by the need to clear out civilians—primarily the wives and children of the White Thai ethnic minority fighting along with the French—who may well have been slaughtered if left behind.

The evacuation of Dong Khe and Cao Bang courted disaster almost from the beginning. The weather played havoc against the French, with heavy monsoon rains drenching RC 4 and turning it into a river of mud. The evacuation of Cao Bang turned out to be especially problematic. The thick cloud coverage over the area made protection from the French air force impossible, and the evacuation soon became a chaotic rout. Women and children, even grandparents, trudged behind the long line of weighted-down trucks clogging the sodden route. While it had been hoped that the evacuations of Dong Khe and Cao Bang could be accomplished quickly, the slow-moving convoys were wide open for a major attack. At one point, the commander of the force from Cao Bang decided to abandon much of the heavy artillery pieces his convoy was transporting to speed up progress along the route.

The hopelessness of the situation was soon amplified when another French commander of some seven thousand men vastly underestimated the strength of the enemy Viet Minh. The French force consisted of both the Foreign Legion and a large contingent of Moroccans who had been airdropped into Dong Khe in the weeks leading up to the battle.

While the Moroccans and Foreign Legionnaires were considered among the fiercest fighting units in Indochina, the ensuing battle underscored how French commanding officers dismissed the capabilities of the Viet Minh. The French force was lured into a setup by the Viet Minh, who forced them to leave RC 4 on foot and cut paths through dense jungles with machetes and whatever else was at their disposal. Unable to hold their ground, the French found themselves in one fallback position after another, with safe escape routes cut off to them. Soon they were pushed back to the cliffs of a limestone quarry near the Coc Xa gorge. What was left of the original force of more than seven thousand men soon found themselves up against an unstoppable foe.

The results were devastating as the French were badly outnumbered. During the ten-day battle, several thousand were either killed or wounded, and the wounded were left to die. The survivors who were still able to walk were taken prisoner when the French finally surrendered. Of those who surrendered, none survived captivity with the Viet Minh to ever see the day of their release. The only true survivors—twenty-three of the original seven thousand battle force—managed to escape by scaling down the limestone cliffs and were able to get back to French lines. As Valérie André described the debacle in its aftermath:

"Under fire from the enemy, the troops could only manage an unorganized resistance and were cut up on the spot. They were destroyed, when they were caught in a terrifying ambush on October 6. In a period of eight days, we lost 7,000 men, 450 vehicles, three armored groups, and 8,500 rifles. Hundreds of prisoners were forced to march to *Viet Minh* prison camps."[2]

With the loss of two important outposts in the northern extremity of Vietnam, the morale of the French military plunged to new depths. Lang Son was the next major military fortification on RC 4 to come under attack. It was only 158 kilometers (98 miles) from Hanoi. Once again, Valérie André offered her own take of the latest setback for the French:

"Panic set in at Lang Son, which was in turn evacuated. Hanoi was plunged into defeatism. Back in Paris, the imminent fall of [Hanoi] was announced. All of Indochina was dumbstruck, as was France. It would be the first major military defeat of a great power in the free world, all with support from Moscow [and Beijing]."[3]

The evacuation of Lang Son was a particularly bitter pill for the French military to swallow. By leaving their position at Lang Son, the French were essentially conceding their inability to maintain their control over the north. General Vo Nguyen Giap had succeeded in his aim not only of handing a defeat to the French but also demonstrating the supremacy of his home-grown army that he had nurtured along in only a few short years, albeit with Chinese assistance.

The French abandoned Lang Son on October 17 and left the bulk of their munitions and materiel in their hasty retreat, a blunder that would have consequences for years to come. As French journalist Lucien Bodard wrote after the withdrawal, "Much of what the *Viets* fired at the French in the years after came from Lang Son: there were 1,100 tons of ammunition, including some 10,000 75-mm shells (and the *Viets* had 75-mm guns); there were 4,000 new submachine guns; hundreds of gallons of gasoline—an incalculable treasure of military stores."[4]

The devastating news from Indochina sent shockwaves throughout France. The war was already labeled there as *la guerre sale*, or "the dirty war." The French Communist Party fanned the flames of public dissent by "developing a widespread feeling of guilt through its propaganda and largely contributed to making the conflict in Indochina a war of shame."[5]

The sentiment in France against the war was such that the French government had passed legislation that allowed men conscripted for compulsory military service to opt out of combat in Indochina. The upshot of that decision meant that by 1950 the war in Indochina was fought by only those in France who volunteered for Indochina combat service, the Foreign Legion, and volunteers recruited from French colonies. It should also be noted that many who fought with the French were also Vietnamese.

While many in France would have preferred to abandon the colony in Indochina, the area was a source of economic wealth for the mother country. Vietnamese rubber plantations kept Michelin tire factories humming, and an abundance of other relatively cheap natural resources and labor were helping to propel France's postwar economic boom. It was felt that to withdraw from Indochina completely would jeopardize France's prosperity.

On the international scene, there were now bigger implications as well. The conflict had grown into becoming a major component of the Cold War by 1950. When the Soviet Union and China recognized Ho Chi Minh and the Viet Minh over the French-backed regimes in Vietnam, the United States stepped up its interest in the region. The United States began bankrolling the French with massive amounts of American military aid, while fully immersed in its own conflict on the Korean peninsula against Communist forces. In what would later be called the "domino theory," Indochina, Korea, Latin America, and even Europe were all seen as individual pieces that would topple one after another to Soviet and Chinese influence unless it was stopped by Western powers.

In the short run, the French military suffered from a lack of decisive leadership in Indochina, and the reversals at Dong Khe, Cao Bang, and Lang Son illustrated that fact all too clearly. Although there was widespread fear that Hanoi would be the next target in the Viet Minh onslaught, General Giap was content to restrain his army for the moment and to plan for a new offensive at a later date.

The French could not afford the luxury of complacency, however. If France's control of its colonial interest in the whole of Indochina was to continue, many believed it would only be possible through the ultimate destruction of Giap's army. To that end, in December 1950 General Jean de Lattre de Tassigny was appointed to become not only the supreme commander of the French Far East Expeditionary Corps but also high commissioner for all of Indochina.

De Lattre's appointment was an inspired choice. As commander of the Free French First Army during the second Allied invasion of Europe in World War II, de Lattre proved himself as an extremely capable and charismatic leader. He was arguably the second most respected military figure in France after Charles de Gaulle.

De Lattre was very much an extroverted perfectionist who demanded the most that his army had to deliver. To that end, de Lattre earned the sobriquet, *Roi Jean*, or "King John," for his rather imperialistic persona. It was a persona that brought results if history was to judge. He believed in France, he believed in the mission assigned to the French army, and he believed in his men.

De Lattre had hardly been idle in the years following World War II. Following his stint as commander of the French sector in occupied Germany—where Valérie André encountered the general and his army for the first time—de Lattre was appointed as vice president of France's Superior War Council, while simultaneously serving as inspector general for all of France's armed forces. From October 1948 to December 1950, along with British field marshal Bernard Montgomery, de Lattre was the first commander in chief of ground forces in western Europe, the precursor to NATO armed forces.

But the appointment to Indochina harbored numerous pitfalls. François Mitterrand, who was at the time France's overseas minister and would later become France's president in 1981, advised de Lattre of the risks involved in accepting a command position in the Far East, despite having the dual role of commander of the military and high commissioner.

"You will never have a free hand to do as you see fit in Indochina," Mitterrand told de Lattre at a private dinner. "A year or two ago was something else. Today everything is too defined and fixed, the page is no longer white."[6]

De Lattre responded to Mitterrand's advice, simply stating that he "could not turn down an opportunity to command and serve for both the glory and honor in the name of France's soldiers."[7]

One soldier, in particular, had already convinced de Lattre of the importance of the Indochina mission—his only son, Bernard de Lattre. Bernard had served as the youngest combatant in de Lattre's French First Army during Operation Dragoon in 1944, and was wounded at the Battle of Autun. Bernard remained in the army after the war and shipped out to Indochina in 1949 where he served as a lieutenant and commander of a motorized platoon. Bernard was only twenty-two years old, but he was already battle hardened and an astute observer of the French military's successes and failures in Vietnam, as he often related to his father in letters home:

"What we need is a leader who leads," Bernard wrote in one letter. "Fresh blood, fresh machinery, and no more niggling with small-time warfare; and then, with the morale that we still have despite it all, we could save everything."[8]

To "save everything" would have been a considerable undertaking in the most favorable of circumstances, and General de Lattre undoubtedly knew that. December 1950 marked the lowest point in the war for the French since its outbreak four years earlier. But the news of Jean de Lattre's appointment as commander in chief and high commissioner struck Vietnam like a lightning bolt. He wasted no time in overhauling Indochina's situation when he arrived in Hanoi on December 17, 1950. The city was still on edge for fear of being overrun by the Viet Minh at any moment. De Lattre immediately took steps to defend the Vietnamese capital. He armed and mobilized French civilians to take over guard duty in the city. And as heartless as it may have seemed, de Lattre also forbade the evacuation of French women and children back to France. As he was quoted as saying, "As long as the women and children are here, the men won't dare to let go."[9]

Borrowing a page from the script he used in Algeria when he took over the Free French Army destined to become the second invasion force in the liberation of Europe, de Lattre staged a huge military parade in Hanoi to demonstrate that France still had the determination to face its enemy.

Even Vo Nguyen Giap took notice of the regime change. An ardent student of history, Giap was familiar with de Lattre's reputation and reportedly said of his new foe, "finally an adversary worthy of his steel."[10]

As one observer summed up the arrival of General de Lattre in Vietnam at the end of 1950, "'Roi Jean' had found his kingdom."[11] But the kingdom was far from secure.

Chapter 18

First Flight

The feeling of impending disaster that spread throughout Vietnam at the end of 1950 began to give way to the hope of at least some stability with the arrival of Jean de Lattre. While anxiety still ran high in Hanoi, it was no overstatement to say that de Lattre inspired a renewed fighting spirit and morale that had been sorely lacking.

"Our hopes were truly raised by the arrival of General de Lattre," Valérie said. "He was the only one of France's great military leaders to take on this formidable mission."[1]

It was true. Other French generals had been offered the post to command in Indochina, as it was a voluntary service even for a high-ranking officer. But only de Lattre had accepted the challenge. It would take a leader of his prestige and his aggressive stance against any enemy to summon the reserve necessary to keep the Viet Minh at bay. Even Valérie André was swept up in the renewed enthusiasm the French military had for their mission.

"It was obvious since Cao Bang, that the need of a true leader had become indispensable," she said. "The vigor of his command had obviously upset the most ingrained habits of inertia."[2]

Indeed, both inertia and dueling personalities among the French high command had led to the disastrous losses in the north and ceding a major victory to Vo Nguyen Giap and the Viet Minh army. General de Lattre was determined not to repeat the mistakes and failures of his predecessors.

It was obvious that Valérie's admiration for de Lattre came from her contact with the general and his army when they were stationed in the French occupation zone in Germany after World War II. It was de Lattre who commanded the army that liberated her home city of Strasbourg, after all. But it could also be said that Valérie André's esteem was mirrored by many who saw de Lattre as France's best chance to end the war in Indochina with some semblance of honor.

"He had a sense of grandeur and gesture, and was a conqueror to his core," she said of de Lattre. "I came to greatly admire this man who possessed an almost regal air about him."[3]

By the end of 1950, there was a sense that the war in Vietnam had ground down to a war of attrition, where the Viet Minh would ultimately gain the upper hand unless decisive action was taken. But at the same time, the same confidence that had propelled the revitalized Viet Minh army to their successes in the fall also had its consequences. Without a doubt, General Vo Nguyen Giap had grown somewhat overconfident in the aftermath of the autumn offensive in which the Viet Minh had routed the French and now had unfettered access to materiel supply lines coming from the Communist Chinese. While it was true that the Viet Minh now dominated the more densely forested areas to the northern frontier, they were as yet an unproven force in the more densely populated areas. Moreover, General Giap also realized that control over Vietnam's river deltas, which also produced rice, was essential to keep his army fed.

Despite the obvious danger of taking the French head-on, Giap was a risk-taker at heart. He seemed all too willing to challenge the French where their strength was at their greatest—even if it meant throwing massive amounts of his human slaughter-bait into the war's meat grinder. Success would mean the end of French rule in Vietnam, and Giap confidently predicted that victory would be at hand by the *tet* lunar new year celebration for 1951.

Jean de Lattre was not without his resourcefulness but Mother France could not be counted on to send troop reinforcements or additional materiel for the foreseeable future. Time was of the essence to claw back territory and at least save face from a total and humiliating defeat. De Lattre was well aware of the military strength that he had at hand and had the utmost confidence and commitment to his fighting men. The French military in all of Indochina in late 1950 numbered a total of 190,000, including 10,000 serving in the air force and 5,000 serving in the navy. De Lattre may have wished that his numbers were greater, but he was confident that he could make the most with the hand he was dealt.

Giap opened his renewed assault on the French by first sending a division to attack a fifty-man outpost a few miles north of Vinh Yen on January 13. The attack was not a complete surprise, and de Lattre wasted no time in dispatching Mobile Group 3 to relieve the beleaguered outpost. But the lone mobile group, which numbered some three thousand, was not enough to hold back an entire division, which numbered more than ten thousand. With air support conducting bombing runs around the perimeter of the outpost, however, Mobile Group 3 and the remnants of the outpost managed to stage a retreat back to Vinh Yen.

Initially, the retreat almost seemed like a replay of French military failures from fall 1950. But then in a move typical of de Lattre's hard-driving character, the general insisted on being driven from Hanoi to Vinh Yen to personally oversee the movement of his troops. De Lattre also brought with him a fresh mobile group from Hanoi to reinforce his position in Vinh Yen.

When Giap became aware of the reinforcements that de Lattre sent to Vinh Yen, he committed yet another division to the battle and essentially sent a human wave to annihilate the French. This was the gambler mentality of Giap. Not content with the small gains of hit-and-run guerilla tactics, he was emboldened by the successes of the previous autumn. Giap intended to deal a death blow to his opponent.

But de Lattre had no intention of sacrificing his army. When it was apparent that the Viet Minh were ready to begin their assault on Vinh Yen, de Lattre ordered the French air force to take to the air in the war's largest aerial assault to date. Even at night, he ordered C-47 transport planes to drop aerial flares all around the area to prevent the Viet Minh from seeking shelter in the dark. But along with conventional bombing tactics, de Lattre also ordered a controversial new wrinkle to the style of warfare he intended to play out against Giap.

Napalm.

Before its use in Indochina, napalm had not been widely used on human targets but, instead, mainly on structures, which caused collateral damage. By the late 1940s, napalm dispersal devices and bombs had been adopted into the U.S. military arsenal and, as a result, became part of the military aid package delivered to Indochina to combat the Communist insurgency. The use of napalm on combatants was not outlawed by the Geneva Accords on the conduct of war, but its devastatingly injurious and lethal effects made its use controversial. Nonetheless, Jean de Lattre was determined to turn France's fortunes around in Indochina and to use any weapon at his disposal to do so.

Napalm didn't have the obliteration effect of saturation bombing, but its contact with human flesh was agonizing. Foliage was no longer the friend of the Viet Minh, where they could take refuge and become invisible from above. Entire forests and fields of elephant grass could be set ablaze to force the Viet Minh into the open.

The effect was devastating, as one Viet Minh soldier wrote:

"A plane swooped down behind us and again dropped a napalm bomb. The bomb falls closely behind us and I feel its fiery breath engulf my whole body. The men are fleeing in all directions and I cannot hold them back. . . . I stop at the platoon commander . . . his eyes were wide with terror. 'What is this, the atomic bomb?'"[4]

The battle at Vinh Yen was a decisive victory for the French, and the fear of a Viet Minh attack on Hanoi dissipated for the time being. Viet Minh losses were staggering in the wake of their recent fall campaign. In the battle of Vinh Yen, the Viet Minh suffered more than seven thousand casualties, including sixteen hundred killed and more than six thousand wounded.[5]

Vo Nguyen Giap had seen the folly of taking on too much all at once and in abandoning his strategy of bleeding the French elephant in short strikes. For the moment, Jean de Lattre held the upper hand. And for his raining flame from the sky, *King Jean* would earn a new nickname from the peasant Vietnamese people of the delta:

The *Fire General*.

With the threat of total submission to the Viet Minh somewhat in abeyance, French military life proceeded to return to normal, or at least what amounted to normal in Indochina. Skirmishes that unleashed both deadly and crippling blows still flared up in all parts of Vietnam. Although the larger battle had taken place in the north, Viet Minh cells continued to infiltrate everywhere. And the areas around Saigon were hardly immune to violence. The filled-to-capacity Coste Hospital could attest to that.

Despite her unrelenting workload at Coste, Valérie André seized every opportunity to be at ELA 52's hangar at Tan Son Nhut.

"Twice a week, depending upon my schedule, I would return to the field," Valérie said. "At the time, the trip from Cholon to Tan Son Nhut didn't represent any danger, particularly in the daytime."[6]

There were times when Valérie would convince one of her fellow surgeons to take over her watch at the hospital, just so she could join the helicopter crew at the airport. But despite her frequent visits, the two helicopters were rarely available for practice flights.

"My flights were rare," Valérie said. The problem of making practice flights wasn't just because of the demands on the ships for rescue. "The

Hiller turned out to be a rather fragile instrument. While its engine was mostly trouble-free and even more so the transmissions, the search for the causes of unexplained vibrations required frequent disassembly."[7]

Valérie would spend time with Chief Warrant Officer Petit, ELA 52's chief mechanic, when one of the two Hillers was in a state of disrepair. Petit would both curse and cajole the various parts of the Hiller to work in unison as if he were coaxing a living being. And in a sense, the members of ELA 52 considered the sometimes ornery aircraft as living creatures, worthy of praise when they operated efficiently, and condemned with a stream of blue language when they failed to perform.

The Hillers were a finicky breed of aircraft. Many of the maladies afflicting the aircraft could be traced to the dual driveshafts connecting the power takeoff from the transmission that ran to the rear-mounted tail rotor through a cardan joint connecting the two shafts at the stinger-like tailboom's midsection. Any imbalance in these components could shake a helicopter to pieces in a matter of seconds if left uncorrected.

"Most of the time, one of the two aircraft was down for maintenance," Valérie observed. "If by any chance both helicopters were on flight status, one remained on stand-by while the other performed constant medical evacuations."[8]

Raymond Fumat was still a part of ELA 52 at the time Valérie André joined the squadron. She would often encounter Fumat also waiting to put time into one of the two Hillers.

"[Fumat] was always on the lookout for an opportunity to fly," Valérie recalled, saying that oftentimes Fumat would console himself by playing his mandolin in the hangar to entertain himself and others. Except for the mechanic Petit, all of the men associated with ELA 52 were bachelors.

Valérie was well aware of Fumat's daring rescue of Lieutenant Jacquesson, the downed Bearcat fighter pilot who spent a nerve-wracking night in the delta marsh waiting to be rescued by helicopter. While Fumat's low hovering maneuvers over a shallow swamp resulted in Jacquesson—with considerable physical effort—being able to pull himself into the helicopter, it was felt afterward that there were many ways to improve procedures to facilitate a more effective rescue. Alexis Santini knew that a better method for rescue could be developed.

"Santini thought of crashed pilots who might be incapable of any physical effort," Valérie said. "From the helicopter, the rescue pilot would unfurl a rope several meters long, with a snap hook at its end. All of the fighter pilots carried a parachute. In this case, Jacquesson merely could have attached the snap hook to one of the rings of his parachute harness and been lifted to safety."

Santini wanted to test the idea, and with Valérie eager to make herself of use to the squadron, she volunteered as the guinea pig for the experiment.

"Santini shrugged his shoulders, and accepted my offer," said Valérie. "I solidly fastened my parachute harness to my body, and rather intrigued by what was to happen next, I sat on the ground and waited for the helicopter.

"With Santini at the controls, the helicopter approached and descended, hovering over me, and as planned I fastened the snap hook. As I was lifted into the air, my body started to spin rapidly. Although I spread out both arms and legs, nothing helped. I kept on spinning. A minute later, Santini lowered me back gently to the ground."[9]

It was a system that required further refinement but still represented an incremental improvement. Future developments for personnel rescue via tether line to a helicopter would be to base a rescue device on a parachute harness or even a sling. But rescue techniques by helicopter were still in their infancy, and it was necessary to write the rules as situations arose.

"For want of a better system at least this would serve to rescue a pilot wounded in a danger zone," Valérie concluded after the test. "Upon reaching a friendly outpost, the casualty could be placed into one of the two litter baskets on the helicopter. At that time, Santini also requested rope ladders for his aircraft."[10]

Skirmishes with Viet Minh cadres were still common all over the country, even in the aftermath of the Giap's defeat at Vinh Yen. On January 22, 1951, a radio message came into Saigon from Bien Hoa, some thirty-seven kilometers away. Several casualties required airlifting back to Saigon, and both Santini and Fumat were set to make several roundtrips with both Hillers taking part in the rescues. It was a grueling series of flights, but toward the end of the afternoon, only one soldier remained at Bien Hoa who required the services of one of the Hillers.

"I ventured to ask Santini for permission to accompany him on this mission," Valérie said. "I reminded him that I only weighed 45 kilos and I wouldn't cause any problems. It would be a great opportunity to fly!"

To her astonishment, Santini agreed to let her take the controls of the Hiller under his supervision and fly to Bien Hoa. This would be Valérie's opportunity to show that she was as capable of flying a rescue mission as any of her male counterparts, and she knew that any future opportunities would depend on the outcome.

"I had the map spread on my knees, and I took care not to make any error on our heading," she said, as she applied the collective and powered the helicopter upward.

"Where are we?" Santini would shout at various intervals along the route, testing her navigating abilities. Santini knew that a pilot could easily become disoriented and lost in an instant; however, Valérie would point to the exact location on the map, as she used the landmarks below to identify her position.

"My finger found the exact spot," she remarked. "As checkpoints, the rivers in Cochinchine are both precious and treacherous."[11]

The sky was perfectly clear that day, and the helicopter operated as close to normal as possible in the tropical atmosphere. But Valérie knew she was flying over territory where enemy Viet Minh could strike at any moment, especially in the event of a forced landing. But she was reassured by the presence of Alexis Santini, who maintained a steadfast vigilance over all operating aspects of the aircraft.

It took almost a half hour to finally reach the forest clearing where the soldiers waited with the last of that day's casualties. Up to this point, Valérie had been in control of the helicopter, but for the final approach Santini took hold of the stick.

"Without a word, Santini grabbed the controls and started a spiral descent," Valérie said. The men had their wounded comrade already stabilized on a stretcher as the helicopter landed nearby. "Bearded and shirtless, the men urged us to move quickly. They knew that the area was not perfectly secured."

The casualty was a Frenchman wounded in the foot. Valérie noted that the expression on the soldier's face was one of both fear and helplessness. His expression changed to one of wonderment, however, when he gazed into Valérie André's face looking down on him, hardly comprehending the presence of a woman in an obvious danger zone. Valérie smiled at him, a smile that she might have shown to a hundred people in the course of a day in her rounds at Coste Hospital. But in a battle zone, where fighting men had taken on the mantle of being the "soldiers of the mud," a smile from a woman was something almost unimaginable. The soldier thought back to France, to his mother, his sister, the girlfriend he left behind. For a moment—just one moment—his pain was eased to the degree that his mind continued to puzzle over the mystery of just why a woman was there.

With the help of the other soldiers, Valérie had the man moved into the left-side litter of the Hiller and securely strapped in. By necessity, everything was done swiftly and efficiently.

"It was getting late and the men who stood watch over the wounded were already disappearing under the trees," Valérie said. "They had to get back to their outfit before nightfall."

Back in the helicopter, Valérie let Santini take the center seat to control the aircraft while she took her seat on the right side up against the cockpit door to help compensate for the weight imbalance caused by the single soldier situated in the opposite litter. Once again, the incredibly humid atmosphere made every inch of altitude seem like a great effort, but Santini was used to the increased burden of the underpowered Hiller under these conditions.

"We rose inch by inch," Valérie recalled. "Suddenly, Santini shoved the helicopter forward, picked up airspeed, turned, and finally, in an impressive lurch, bounced over the trees. Once past the obstacles, I am handed back the controls."

It was a complex escape maneuver that Santini intended to demonstrate to Valérie and drive in the point that nothing was ever cut and dry on any rescue mission.

"So André, you saw that," he shouted to Valérie over the din of the helicopter's engine and rotor noises. "Could you do the same?"

With a sense of both confidence and some irony, Santini waited for Valérie's response, watching her from the corner of his eye.

"Certainly, of course!" came the equally confident answer from her with a characteristically confident grin on her face; however, despite the façade she presented to Santini she was not sure her answer convinced the seasoned pilot.

"You're awfully confident! You don't seem to doubt anything!" Santini shouted back to her. Then he grumbled, somewhat grudgingly, "You'll have to get more flight time. Afterward, we will see!"

The response was as close as Valérie would receive as validation, but at least she knew she would fly again. With little fanfare, Santini handed the controls over to Valérie, and she completed the flight back to Tan Son Nhut without incident.

"During this magnificent evening, as the last rays of light turn the clouds purple, I began thinking of future missions to be carried out alone."[12]

Chapter 19

The Exhilaration of War

The disaster at Lang Son that ceded a large supply of weapons and munitions to the Viet Minh that previous autumn was still fresh on almost every French soldier's mind in Indochina. But a possibility arose in early 1951 for at least some partial redemption.

Aerial reconnaissance had revealed a large weapons factory built in a cave on a sharp, mountainous slope near the Cambodian township of Kampot near the Vietnamese-Cambodian border. Viet Minh operatives working in the south took a page from the playbook of their northern counterparts by seeking refuge over the border to carry out clandestine affairs. Where the northern Viet Minh used sovereign Red China for their base of operations, however, Cambodia was part of the French Union of Indochina, and French forces could cross into Cambodia and put a stop to the activities of the southern Viet Minh cells.

And that's where Conan and his paratroopers came in. Lieutenant Colonel Pierre Chateau-Jobert, better known by his combat name Conan, was ordered to take the Second Colonial Parachute Commando Demi-Brigade into Cambodia and to raid the cave-based munitions factory. With some three hundred paratroopers making a landing near the cave where the illegal arms activity was taking place, heavy casualties were expected.

Conan was a veteran of numerous engagements, and as an experienced leader, he knew what to expect. But he also knew what his resources were. Conan knew what to ask for to minimize the risk his men were about to undertake. He asked for air support, a mobile medical unit on standby at the nearest airstrip, and one last important thing. Conan requested the presence of one of the new medical evacuation helicopters to also be on standby at the airstrip.

Valérie André was to take part in this operation.

"My mission was a modest one. It consisted of setting up an aid station at the airstrip. A medical Morane fixed-wing aircraft would establish the liaison with the hospital at Phnom Penh [the Cambodian capital].[1]

Preparations for the raid and its support took shape in Saigon, some 270 kilometers (170 miles) from Kampot, in early March 1951. While Valérie was to be part of the medical team waiting at the airfield, she traveled with the helicopter crew of ELA 52 to Cambodia.

"As much as I have never loved war, I constantly sought the intoxication of action," Valérie confessed, enthused with the prospect of flying a helicopter into a frontline battle area. "The extreme pleasure of flight—the same as sailors experienced in sailing—stirred an exaltation in me with the demands of flight."[2]

"Elated, I reached Tan Son Nhut on March 7 at 05:00 hours, and fly off with Santini and Chief Warrant Officer Petit."

While the helicopter was loaded to its capacity, a Siebel light observation airplane took some of the additional medical and rescue supplies for the mission. The first leg of the trio's journey would take them to Sa Dec, a provincial town situated on the Mekong Delta.

"I am pleased once more to see the Mekong," Valérie said, noting the intricacies of the vast waterway as she traveled above it. It was necessary to stop at Sa Dec and refuel the Hiller to continue their journey.

From Sa Dec the helicopter and its crew flew on to Kampong Trach in the Kampot region of Cambodia, another long leg of more than four hours. Kampong Trach was only a fifteen-minute flight from the final destination at the airfield near Pontuk.

"At Kampong Trach we were greeted by a lieutenant, with whom we shared a simple meal in his quarters. Nothing is nicer than such improvised meals, where all is offered so generously," Valérie remarked of their host's hospitality. Even though Kampong Trach was a fairly well-established colonial township, outposts located far away from the established cities of Saigon or Phnom Penh always meant supplies were at a premium. The largesse supplied by the young lieutenant exceeded all expectations.

But time was also at a premium, and it was necessary to move on to the airfield at Pontuk to set up the essential aid station for the raid to be carried out by Conan and his men.

"With the arrival of our helicopter, the small improvised air squadron is complete," Valérie observed. "It consisted of two Moranes—one in medical and the other in observation configuration—three Hellcats, and one Junker 52."[3]

The Hiller was to be used as a relay to the larger transport airplanes in the event a worst-case scenario occurred. The helicopter's role was to fly directly to the front line and transport the wounded back to the airfield so that they could then be transferred to either the Morane or the Junker and flown quickly to an airfield close to a well-equipped military hospital. The Hellcat fighter planes would act in a supporting role to clear the front by strafing or dropping napalm on enemy Viet Minh so that the helicopter would have a clear place to land with minimal risk from enemy fire. Supplementing the air units at Pontuk was an infantry company that had set up their tents near the runway to keep the aircraft protected.

As soon as Alexis Santini, Sergeant Petit, and Valérie André landed at Pontuk, they learned that Conan's raid was already underway.

"No sooner had we set foot on the ground we were informed of the development of the attack," Valérie recounted. "The morning's airdrop took the enemy by surprise and they didn't even use their weapons. The *Viet Minh* were on the run—some through rice paddies and some getting to sampans hidden at the mouth of the various river inlets to the area."

Conan had launched his assault close to the cave where the clandestine weapons factory was located. It was a classic example of the enemy's ability and ingenuity in using an overlooked and virtually inaccessible locale to construct an arsenal of mass destruction. The opening to the cave was just a mere slit cut into the face of the mountain, covered in thick vegetation. It would later be learned that gaining access to the cave would require one to nearly bend in half.

But strength came in numbers that day. When the first of several runs of Dakota C-47s began unloading the paratroopers to the ground for their assault, it was surmised that the drone of the radial engines caused a panic among the Viet Minh in charge of guarding the weapon's stash. Not a shot was fired. What Conan and his men found, however, was astonishing.

The cave was immense inside with several room-like chambers. There was a makeshift assembly line of landmines and other explosive devices in one section of the cave, with a sizable number of the devices already completed and awaiting distribution to various terrorist and sabotage cells within the Viet Minh network. There was also a radio transmitter/receiver that had kept this particular cell in regular communication with other cells.

According to Valérie, one surprising item found in the cave came curiously close to equaling all the weaponry that was discovered.

"Perhaps the most precious catch was a stock of pepper that was worth several million francs," she noted of the raid's results.

Cambodian Kampot pepper was much more of a trading commodity than one could have imagined. Only three thousand metric tons were produced in all of Cambodia in 1950, and it was highly prized as the "spice of choice" in French restaurants.[4] The pepper was so highly valued that it could easily be turned into hard currency to buy even more supplies for the manufacture of weapons.

While the seizure of the weapons cache paled in comparison to the loss that had occurred at the expense of the French at Lang Son the previous autumn, it helped restore some of the morale and prestige to France's military presence in Indochina.

The aftermath of the raid demonstrated that the intense planning that went into the mission resulted in relatively minor casualties, a welcome change to events in recent memory.

"Up until now, only one casualty was reported. Just a simple fracture of the fibula caused by an unfortunate landing in the crotch of a tree," Valérie noted with relief.

Alexis Santini fired up the Hiller to bring the wounded paratrooper back to Pontuk. It was just a routine pickup and would have been a routine handoff to the medical Morane airplane waiting on standby at the airfield. But the mission underscored the often cantankerous nature of the Hiller.

Santini made his way to the mountainside where Conan's men were waiting with their wounded comrade. Since there was no emergency present from either the wounded man's immediate medical condition or from enemy fire in the area, Santini opted to shut the Hiller's engine down for a few moments. When it came to restarting the Hiller, Santini discovered the twenty-four-volt battery failed to produce sufficient current to the starter to crank the Franklin engine back to life. It was likely that vibration had caused the lead plates in the battery to separate. Reluctantly, Santini radioed back to Pontuk that the Hiller required a fully charged battery to get back to the airfield.

It was a simple enough request, but it required somewhat difficult logistics to make it so.

"Santini wanted a new battery," Valérie recounted. "Such a spare is awkward to drop by parachute. I suggested, tongue in cheek, that Sgt. Petit jump holding the battery in his arms. He wouldn't hear of it."[5]

With no other viable solution, a request was sent to Saigon and onto Tan Son Nhut where Sergeant Raymond Fumat and the other Hiller were on standby. Fumat and another Hiller mechanic, Chief Warrant Officer Marcel Lambert, were to fly to Pontuk at their earliest opportunity. The request had come quite late in the day, and their departure would have to take place the following morning. That meant that Santini and the disabled Hiller would have to spend the night in a zone that wasn't entirely secure.

"Even though Santini and the helicopter were under heavy guard, I was worried about them," Valérie remarked, interestingly equating her concern for Santini with the aircraft.

It must have seemed like a long night, even though most everyone was convinced that the Viet Minh had vacated the area when Conan's assault force landed. But the enemy was both stealthy and resilient. It would not be unusual for the Viet Minh to stage a withdrawal and lull the French forces into a false sense of security before striking again at a most vulnerable point.

Much to everyone's relief, however, the distant din of the two flat-six motors and the whoosh of rotors gradually increased in the air at Pontuk.

"It was shortly after noon and the two Dragonflies appeared in the blue sky," Valérie said, emphasizing the Hiller's distinctive insect-like appearance.

"Happy to be with us, Fumat climbed out of the first aircraft to refuel the helicopter," Valérie said. "He had to take off again almost immediately; another operation launched in the vicinity of Sa Dec required his presence. Over there, he wouldn't be short of work."[6]

The casualty with the broken leg was strapped to a litter in Santini's helicopter, as he and Petit made their landing shortly after Fumat's.

"It turned out that he was, in fact, not too badly off," Valérie said, as she took charge of the patient when he was back on the ground. "We pampered him a bit—he was mostly hungry. Afterward, we loaded him in Lieutenant Quercy's Morane."[7]

The medical rescue team remained in the area for a few days before returning to Saigon. In a welcome turn of events, there were no emergencies to seriously engage the crew.

"Of course I remained on the ground," Valérie noted in her log. "There was nothing to report regarding helicopter activities. Time went by relatively rapidly, as there was no other doctor in Pontuk. I treated a few cases of dysentery, but that was all."[8]

She also noted that the infantry unit assigned to protect the aircraft and their personnel at Pontuk was not totally without amenities.

"I adapted perfectly well to the 'comfortable war,' and I much admired the camp set up by the *biffins*." *Biffins* is French slang for infantrymen. "The tents were roomy, and a real kitchen was in operation. And—the ultimate luxury in the heat—we even had ice!"[9]

Valérie could well have been experiencing the first of supplies beginning to trickle into service from the increased military aid and financial assistance provided by the United States at the time. While a "comfortable war" might seem to be a complete contradiction in terms, this reflected the continuation of a trend to decrease the abjectly stark and primitive conditions that had dogged soldiers in wars going back to the dawn of humankind.

As much as this one camp of *biffins* may have seemed to be living a some- what more comfortable situation, the appointments for other camps were not always comparable, however.

"I was well aware that many posts were lost in the forests and mountains that languished in desolation and loneliness," Valérie said.[10] And her experi- ence from eventually visiting some of these camps would bear that out all too well.

March 9 turned out to be a fairly quiet day, as mop-up operations with Conan's paratroopers continued at the mountainside munitions site. With the Viet Minh seemingly nowhere to be found, the main task at hand was to eliminate the ammunition and weaponry from the caves. As the unexpected lack of resistance on the part of the Viet Minh brought an unexpected lack of casualties, it also provided a welcome respite. Not far from Pontuk, the picturesque seaside village of Kep beckoned to the crew of ELA 51.

"We were transported by truck to Kep where a dinner awaited us," said Valérie. "Afterwards, bathing in the ocean relaxed us, and by moonlight, we returned to the bungalow near the ocean and our rooms. So much comfort in a remote corner of Indochina at war surprised me."

The inn where Valérie, Alexis Santini, and Sergeant Petit stayed also hosted a small saloon that attracted other French soldiers stationed in the surrounding area. With fraternization regulations strictly in effect, Valérie undoubtedly must have felt safe to be in the company of her two trusted male comrades. But the soldiers who frequented the bar had not recently encoun- tered much in the way of female companionship in their isolated posting.

"At the bar, until late at night, the owner—a lady way past her prime— resisted the unsolicited assaults of our fellow soldiers," Valérie observed further, noting at the same time that the barkeep was long experienced in successfully thwarting the advances of her more unruly customers.[11]

On the following day, the team found themselves back at Pontuk where they were informed of a very sick patient requiring an evacuation by airlift from X-Son, a nearby Cambodian village. The patient was reported to be in very serious condition, and Valérie and Santini set off in the Hiller for the rescue.

"We left immediately and flew at low altitude," Valérie recalled, once again thrilled to take part in a mission. Once they landed, she was able to assess the patient's condition.

"I examined my patient who showed symptoms of acute appendicitis and he required immediate transport to Phnom Penh," she noted. There was one problem, however. With low fuel onboard, Santini had been forced to shut down the Hiller's engine to refill its tanks with the spare jerry can of gasoline they had carried along with them. He had not expected a repeat of the battery issue and the helicopter's intermittent starting problems, but they resurfaced once again.

"When I returned to the aircraft I found that Santini was unable to start the engine up again. The captain was furious and I thought better of further irritating him with questions." Valérie simply went back to tending to her patient, confident in her feeling that a solution would be found.

And so it was. A nearby French naval detachment, operating a Dinossaut assault boat on the river delta shared between Vietnam and Cambodia, came to the rescue of the stricken aircraft.

"The Navy boys were of the greatest help," Valérie said with admiration. "They brought a battery in by boat up the X-Son inlet. It had belonged to a Marine commando unit's assault craft. We finally got the engine started and breathed a huge sigh of relief. We took off with the helicopter and made our return to Pontuk, where the patient was put on board the medical Morane for Phnom Penh."[12]

On March 11, all activities involving medical air transports had come to an end in Pontuk, and the various units began to prepare for a return to their respective bases.

"We received our orders to ship out," Valérie recalled. "Some of us were delighted to leave. I was not happy . . . not happy at all. I was so passionate about this life that I received the orders to go back to Saigon with some ir-ritation. With regret I watched the Hellcats, the Junker, the Moranes take off, each in turn."

Sergeant Petit had left in one of the Moranes back to Tan Son Nhut to re-lieve some of the weight inside the Hiller. Petit hoped that the Hiller would suffer no more mechanical issues.

"Bringing up the rear, we got airborne. Phnom Penh and its gilt roofs, the Quatre-Bras, the Mekong River all glide by, and now we come to Svay-Rieng. We gassed up there."

The exhilaration she initially felt for the mission at Pontuk and Kampot was now rapidly evaporating as the cold reality of returning to the progression of mangled bodies arriving at Coste Hospital began to set in. It wasn't as if there was no satisfaction in saving lives that entered the hospital, sometimes in hopeless condition. But as many first responders even today can attest, there is nothing quite like being on the front line. It can almost be likened to an addiction. As Valérie was to learn, however, there was no such thing as predictability while one lived and breathed in a war zone.

At Svay-Rieng a noncom messenger ran up to Valérie and Santini as the Hiller took on fuel. He addressed Santini.

"*Monsieur capitaine*, there is a wounded man at an outpost not far from here, and there is need for your machine to bring him to a hospital," the man exclaimed breathlessly. The young private told Valérie and Santini that the casualty had suffered a severe gunshot wound.

The outpost was at Ong-Tan, not from Svay-Rieng. Santini was uneasy about taking the Hiller off its course back to Saigon, given its recent mechanical issues. But hesitation was out of the question for Valérie, and she convinced Santini that they had to perform the rescue. Soon they were off to Ong-Tan.

"Half an hour later, we spotted the small square tower of the Ong-Tan outpost," said Valérie. "It was ringed by barbed wire and bamboo palisades. It stood guard over a flat countryside which appeared to be uninhabited."

It was fortunate that they could see that the area surrounding the fortification was barren and devoid of any presence of the enemy because they had to land the Hiller in the grass outside the fenced compound. But just because the enemy couldn't be seen didn't mean they weren't present. Santini's uneasiness concerning the Hiller's fickle starter circuit made it necessary to keep the helicopter's engine running at idle, which consumed precious fuel needed to return to Saigon. But shutting down the engine risked another starting failure.

The rotor blades of the helicopter slowed as Valérie and Santini waited. And waited. Almost fifteen minutes went by, an eternity in enemy territory, where the helicopter and its occupants were nakedly exposed.

"At last, they brought the man to us," Valérie said, as the stretcher-bearers emerged from the fort. "He was a Cambodian, and he had suffered a bullet wound to his abdomen. I estimated that the wound was already two hours old."[13]

Valérie had her medical supply kit with her and immediately began administering pressyl, syncortyl, and morphine, as the man was loaded to one of the litters of the Hiller. It was a serious wound and would have undoubtedly had fatal consequences had the helicopter not been nearby. Santini twisted the throttle grip on the Hiller, and the rotors increased their revolutions until he could apply collective for takeoff. He would waste no time in getting back to Saigon and to the first hospital to be reached by air coming from the west of the city.

"We reached the Flemish Hospital in Saigon-Cholon first and the wounded man got there within adequate time for an operation."[14]

The mission to Pontuk was now officially over. Valérie would return to her duties at Coste Hospital. But as she would learn, her return to Coste would not be without its consequences. As Valérie remarked, "in a war like this, one mission succeeds another at an often exhausting pace, without any time for breathing."[15]

And her comrades at Coste Hospital no doubt felt the same. The unrelenting pace at Coste would come in direct conflict with Valérie André's ambition to continue as a helicopter rescue pilot.

Chapter 20

True Believer

The French victories over the Viet Minh in early 1951 marked something of a turning point in the course of the war. The *de Lattre effect* had instilled a new sense of purpose and morale for the French. General de Lattre was seen as the only leader capable of standing up to the Viet Minh, and he had both the military and administrative authority to make significant policy changes in Indochina. And de Lattre took his role seriously, believing that an honorable end to the war was possible. As opposed to his predecessors, de Lattre listened to his enlisted men and junior officers who faced the war from its numerous battlefronts. His son Bernard—who could have landed a safe position on de Lattre's staff in Hanoi—remained a commander of a mobile group and regularly wrote to his father about his observations and opinions of the war while stationed in the rural mountain areas of central Vietnam.

It was a lull, to be sure, but as long as Mother France was reaping the benefit of "King" John's reign over the colony, Paris saw no need to interfere with de Lattre's success.

If Valerié André's view was any indication of the attitude that was changing in Indochina, then de Lattre already accomplished more than his predecessors had.

"The presence of a real leader . . . had become indispensable. There is no need to overstate the admiration I felt for this man of imperious and imaginative authority," Valerié declared.[1] For Valerié and others serving in Indochina, de Lattre put an end to France's losing streak in the war.

While some of the pressure had been relieved on the French after Vinh Yen, unrelenting casualties still poured into military hospitals as the Viet Minh returned to their tactic of hit-and-run warfare. Back in Saigon, Valerié found that her recent absence from Coste Hospital as part of the medical team supporting the weapons raid in Cambodia had not gone unnoticed. Casualties remained high, and the hospital's resources were critically limited.

"All of the staff was anxious and there weren't enough rooms to accommodate all of our patients. Extra beds were needed in the hallways. Every working day was set against a background of cosmopolitan rumors."[2]

"Cosmopolitan rumors" referred to the gossip and speculation about the war from the multinational and multiracial soldiers representing more than half of France's military force in Indochina. The casualties that filled Coste Hospital were representative of France's colonies the world over, in addition to foreign nationals volunteering with the French Foreign Legion. As Valérie described her patients:

"The wounded spoke Arabic, Annamese [Vietnamese], Cambodian, all the languages of Europe, as well as the most mysterious African dialects. The expeditionary corps was made up of all the volunteers of the French Empire, Tabors as well as Senegalese. Often, from one bed to another, a neighbor served as an interpreter with the doctor."[3]

There was concern that some of the soldiers who came from the colonies might also join up with insurrections in their own countries against France once they returned home. The erosion of French prestige and power was a clear threat to the empire that France had created and was now protecting.

Yet, de Lattre's successful strategy at Vinh Yen had abated some concerns. But the threat of an invasion of the Viet Minh—with active backing from Red China—always hung in the air.

"If Mao Tse Tung had unleashed his masses against us, the truth was that we would have been pulverized," Valérie fatefully observed.[4]

And the concern was more than justified. Only some 2,200 miles (3,600 kilometers) to the northeast, the United States, along with a large contingent of United Nations combatants, were engaged in their struggle against a Communist force backed by Mao Tse Tung and the Soviets in Korea. The combined force of the Chinese and North Koreans had managed to beat back the Americans and their allies to the southern tip of the Korean peninsula. Mao had committed an additional two hundred thousand Chinese troops to the more than two hundred thousand North Korean troops already fielded by Kim Il Sung. The Chinese threat was so immense that war correspondent Lucien Bodard wrote:

> Everyone thought . . . this was the end of whites in Asia. Henceforth China was a cauldron with six hundred million people in it, all at the highest pitch of emotion. . . . Outside the country this was the time when floods of men in greenish uniforms rushed into the inferno of American fire, confronting American strength and falling by thousands, by tens of thousands, beyond counting, but still advancing—men who could not be stopped. . . . Thus, after slumbering for hundreds of years the Chinese dragon had awakened—and woe to those who were . . . within its reach![5]

If there was a bright spot in the depressing news reaching Vietnam, it was that the Communist Chinese were too involved with their offensive against the Americans and their allies to be able to devote substantial assistance to General Vo Nguyen Giap and his Viet Minh army. As the winter of 1951 progressed into spring, it became apparent that the war in Indochina had reverted back to the Viet Minh's unpredictable guerilla tactics. Giap was methodical, however. In the absence of all-out offensives in the near term, he was devoting his efforts to honing the Viet Minh army into a highly organized fighting unit—a strategy that was seen as paying off in the long term.

But de Lattre was methodical as well. While the Chinese may well have been immersed militarily on the Korean peninsula, de Lattre knew that the Viet Minh could still find respite on the Chinese side of Vietnam's border, where they would rebuild and reorganize to strike again. In anticipation of a strike against French outposts in the remote area of Lai Chau, in April 1951, de Lattre ordered a large French force to defend Vietnam's northern frontier.

Lai Chau was, and remains, one of Vietnam's poorest regions. But as a strategic location, it was important. The White Thai ethnic minority[6] who made up a large part of Lai Chau's population had proved themselves loyal to the French cause. In support of the Lai Chau operation, one of the ACP (*antenne chirurgicale parachutiste*) medical units was activated. Valérie André was ordered to deploy with them.

"To our great pleasure, Field Hospital No. 4 was designated for the mission," Valérie said, with her unflagging sense of adventure. "But alas, we would not be airdropped over Lai Chau, but transported there by air and then by truck."[7]

On April 7, Valérie and the rest of the medical team reported to Tan Son Nhut airport in Saigon, where they boarded a Bristol transport plane bound for Hanoi. The normal complement for a field hospital unit typically included two doctors and three nurses, along with drivers for the trucks and ambulances used to move the wounded from the temporary hospital to the airfield for further transport to a more fully equipped hospital. Once the team reached Gialam airport in Hanoi, they transferred over to a C-47 Dakota for the final leg of the journey to Lai Chau.

The weather conditions between northern and southern Vietnam are a study in contrast. The south always seemed oppressively hot and humid, but in the north, it was somewhat cooler the closer one got to the Chinese border. Some of Vietnam's tallest peaks also were centered in this area, and dense cloud coverage was not uncommon.

"The weather was not too favorable," Valérie said as she studied the view from the window of the C-47. A heavy, murky layer obscured any familiar landmarks, and the pilot was forced to rely on navigation instruments. The danger to both the pilot and his complement was increased by the mountainous topography of the region. A steady eye on the altimeter made sure that the aircraft did not dip down below the highest peak.

The Dakota with the mobile surgical team was not the only aircraft in the air. A directive had been issued from Hanoi to establish an air bridge between the capital and the remote outpost. To supply the area, a transport plane was scheduled to arrive every fifteen minutes either bearing troops or supplies, but bottlenecks occurred when the airfield couldn't be located from above.

"Two more Dakotas were circling the sky waiting to find a hole in the clouds and have permission to land," Valérie noted, as the pilot maintained the Dakota's altitude above the dense layer.

Finally, an opening appeared, and the airfield was spotted.

"Suddenly, below us, stretched out in a fold of the Black River, the Lai Chau airport runway appeared," Valérie said, as the Dakota finally lined up its approach to preparing for landing. The river and its proximity to the airfield prompted Valérie to surmise, "It was beautiful, but unusable during the rainy season."[8]

Once on the ground, Valérie and the rest of the medical team were hurried off the transport.

"As soon as we landed, our equipment was thrown to the ground, a bit too roughly in my mind," Valérie noted. In order to keep a flow of supplies and personnel between Hanoi and Lai Chau, the flights were necessary. As Valérie said, "The Dakota had to take off again, at once."[9]

Along with all their equipment and supplies, they were transported by truck to a nearby trade school that was to serve as an improvised hospital.

"The buildings made available to us were not perfect, but the medics quickly cleaned them up and we settled in. That our installation . . . was precarious, didn't really surprise us," Valérie said of the group's accommodations. "Doctors are permanently confronted in the field with makeshift means. But, all the more reason for us to be exacting. Our daily battle was the safeguarding of hygiene."

Maintaining an environment where even the most basic surgical procedures could be carried out was often a serious challenge. The trade school at Lai Chau may have led a few to believe it was a substantial structure, but in reality, the rickety building barely boasted of a roof capable of keeping most of the elements out. At the very least, it was an available shelter that did meet the minimum needs for a makeshift hospital.

"We opened the baskets that contained our supplies." Valérie was by now well familiar with the particular requirements of a mobile surgical unit. "Soon the operating room, the resuscitation room, the wounded room were all equipped. The generator was working and the engineer [necessary to keep equipment like the generator operating] was at his post. In anticipation of running water outages, a huge tank was brought to us. We will be able to work."[10]

With the close proximity to the northern border, there was serious anxiety about the possibility of the Communist Chinese joining ranks with the Viet Minh and spilling over into Lai Chau.

"Is the Chinese invasion going to happen today?" Valérie fretted. It was the main subject on everyone's mind. News reports from Korea only served to heighten daily tensions. But as the days wore on, the feared devastating threat from the north failed to materialize, and as Valérie put it, "The nightmare had disappeared."

But as Valérie also added, "It would come back tomorrow."[11]

While the feared large-scale invasion didn't happen, skirmishes between the French and Viet Minh were frequent.

"Light wounded began to arrive," Valérie said. "There have only been skirmishes in the area of Tsin-Ho. The unit managed to thwart ambushes from the *Viet Minh*, but had wandered several days along trails, providing for their defense."

The soldiers had experienced General Vo Nguyen Giap's fallback strategy where the stealthy Viet Minh tiger shredded the back of the French elephant. If a full-scale invasion wasn't going to materialize, the tried and true ambush tactics of the Viet Minh would suffice. The attacks were serious, however, as Valérie related:

"The soldiers told us that their more seriously wounded comrades remained on the spot without any hope of evacuation."[12]

Despite the ambush on the platoon that had ventured into the mountainous highlands of Tsin-Ho, the border situation settled into routine operations, and casualties, thankfully, dwindled for a while.

"The field hospital activity slowed down," Valérie said of the temporary respite. "A few days of total inactivity gave us a chance to swim in the Black River and to stroll around. The weather was beautiful."

The temporary lull in the action soon came to an end, however.

"The engagement around Tsin-Ho was more severe than we thought," Valérie said, as the frequency of skirmishes began to increase. "Arrivals of casualties resumed at an irregular pace. If some of the wounded only traveled a few hours, others took several days to reach Lai Chau. Their wounds were deeply infected. They were operated on right then and there by Lieutenant Rit, or by myself, and then evacuated by ambulance aircraft to Hanoi."[13]

Additionally, water often became a scarce commodity for troops on patrol in remote mountainous areas.

"They were exhausted," Valérie noted. "Often, they rushed up to the first source of water they came upon at the risk of getting dysentery. We also knew that the most seriously wounded had to die on the trails, too much weakened to cross long and perilous distances. How to get to them and where to go? Lai Chau is located in a basin, surrounded by mountains where a lost soldier could wander to death without being able to signal his position."[14]

The border highlands of Vietnam would soon be a memory for the young doctor. On April 24, 1951, Valérie André received new orders.

"Colonel Costes, the commander of the Thai territories,[15] relayed a telegram to me from the Tonkin Health Services Directorate ordering my immediate departure for Hanoi. Captain Cazenave, the surgeon with Field Hospital 900, was unavailable for duty and I was to replace him."

Valérie was to go to Tien Yen, a location on the north coast of Vietnam not far from Halong Bay. Even in the harshness of war, Valérie could find beauty in the landscape of Vietnam.

"I had the pleasure of discovering the Bay of Halong I have dreamt so much about," she said as she watched transfixed through the window of a Morane medical transport airplane on its way to the airfield at Tien Yen. Halong had long been one of the most picturesque landscape marvels rarely seen by people outside of Vietnam. In the distance some of the many islands off the coast of Halong and into the Gulf of Tonkin could be seen.

"Flying in between very white cumulus clouds, we got an occasional glimpse of an astonishingly blue sea. What a spectacle, compared to the low, grey, dull coast of Cochinchine (southern Vietnam)."[16]

The airfield at Tien Yen was small, just a landing strip and little else. The Morane transport plane didn't have a radio, and the pilot was forced to find another means to communicate his intention to land.

"The pilot buzzed the colonel's command post several times," Valérie said. "The dipping of the wings of the airplane was understood, and after a rather acrobatic landing we found a jeep at our disposal."[17]

The colonel whose post the pilot "buzzed" was Colonel Maurice Redon, a career French army officer who had fought with the French Resistance and with General de Lattre's army of liberation during World War II. He had been among the first sent to Indochina after the war to reestablish control over the colony. At the time of Valérie's arrival in Tien Yen, Colonel Redon was commander of French forces for the entire north coast region of Vietnam.[18] From the airfield, Valérie and her equipment were transported by jeep to Redon's camp. It was there she met Redon for the first time.

"Colonel Redon greeted me at the mess hall," Valérie recalled. The colonel proceeded to fill her in on her new mission. He told her that she was to leave with him for Hongai, some eighty kilometers (fifty miles) by boat. Once in Hongai, she was to rendezvous with the 123rd Colonial Infantry Regiment that was returning to Tien Yen by motorized convoy, which the colonel himself was personally supervising. All Valérie was told was that the regiment needed a doctor.

"That same evening, I boarded a small boat," Valérie said. The journey was incredible to her, as she added, "By night the Bay of Halong is just as attractive as it is by day."[19]

But the beauty of Vietnam's scenery soon gave way once again to the drudgery and grim reality of wartime maneuvers. After reaching Hongai, Valérie learned that her mission was quite dangerous. The road that the convoy was going to take back to Tien Yen was known to be staked out by Viet Minh ambush units.

"On April 28 the convoy got underway very slowly," Valérie said. "We stopped many times."

The pace was exhausting. As with most of the roads in Vietnam, the conditions were primitive. Progress occurred in start-and-stop increments, with the sloppy condition of the road sometimes forcing the convoy to pause altogether when one of the heavy trucks got bogged down. Almost everyone felt sleep deprived, including Valérie.

"During one of the halts, slightly worn out by the lack of sleep, I hit upon the unfortunate idea of seeking shelter in a deep rut in the road," she recalled. "However, I was suddenly awakened by the loud screeching of brakes. I had indeed fallen asleep. Driving up to the head of the convoy, at a good clip, was Colonel Redon himself. He nearly ran me over."[20]

As the convoy progressed and the route changed from coastal ruggedness into an area with denser vegetation, tension mounted among the ranks.

"Intermittently, the men suddenly appeared to be very tense," Valérie noted. "They were ready to fight. Everyone was ready for a possible attack. There was no attack, and any *Viet Minh* remained quiet as we went by."[21]

Eighty kilometers with the slow-moving convoy must have seemed an eternity, however, the 123rd finally rolled into Tien Yen, where Valérie was dispatched to the mobile hospital she was assigned. Once again, the hospital was established in a local trade school, as it was the most viable structure in the surroundings.

"I was greeted by Chief Warrant Officer Le Coz, and I immediately got to work," said Valérie. "The equipment there was in good condition, although the building was again subpar. The operating room and the patient recovery room required improvements. With the help of Colonel Redon, I would be able to improve the operating room and the casualty ward."[22]

The colonel ordered some of his men to help carry out necessary repairs and improvements per Valérie's direction, albeit with scarce supplies available.

It wasn't very long before Valérie was deluged with more than her share of casualties.

"From April 30 to May 13, I performed twenty-eight surgeries," she stated matter-of-factly. "Soldiers, civilians, and even two *Viet Minh* prisoners."

It was the first time that Valérie had treated the enemy, but her dedication to saving lives saw no distinction.

"Why underline here the difference, since in my eyes there is none," Valérie stated pointedly. Her ethos was simply this:

"A doctor is at the service of all people, in time of peace as in time of war. Every wounded person is sacred, even if he is one of the enemy."[23]

The wounds to both of the Vietnamese men were serious. As Valérie detailed their respective conditions:

"One of them was shot in the chest by a sentry as he tried to escape from the detention camp. The intervention went well, and his healing will be fast, but the poor soul play-acts with me every time he sees me and pretends to be near death to stay with us as long as possible. As for the second, he was in a bad state on his arrival, with intestinal perforations complicated by typhoid."[24]

The second man required a laparotomy, a surgical procedure where an incision is made to the abdominal wall. The surgery was a dangerous proposition with a great chance for sepsis in such a crude medical facility. But confidence was hardly lacking in Valérie André, and she ably demonstrated her versatility and skill as a surgeon despite the primitive environment.

"I operated on him immediately, fearing a fatal outcome in the following hours," she said. "Constant monitoring was necessary. Streptomycin and penicillin, plasma and serum, and cardiotonic succeeded in saving him."[25]

Saving the two Viet Minh prisoners from their wounds was one matter, but saving the two men from the other wounded French and allied French soldiers who shared the same recovery room was another.

"These two were installed in a common room with the others who threw deadly glances at them. So, I took them under my protection," Valérie said of the two prisoners. "At the same time, I had to preserve them from the aggressive reactions of their roommates. I saw in their eyes all the confidence they had in their doctor."[26]

While her dedication as a doctor showed no bounds, Valérie also thought of the equation from the other side of the front line.

"I didn't have the right in front of them to ask if, on their side, a French prisoner would be treated with the same concern for equality and the same humanity. We know perfectly well today that it wasn't always the case."

It was true. The Viet Minh were not signatories to the Geneva Conventions that covered the humane treatment of prisoners of war. French soldiers captured in battle by the Viet Minh were subject to many atrocities, and the survival rate for them was extremely low. French soldiers with similar wounds suffered by Valérie's Viet Minh patients would have likely perished as prisoners.

"Had I known at the time the barbarism of the *Viet Minh* detention camps that would have, of course, changed nothing for my respect of a wounded person, no matter what his origin," Valérie said.[27]

Work continued around the clock, and the small mobile hospital needed to be ready to receive the wounded at any time of the day or night. Tien Yen was far from being a likely place for a large battle, but small skirmishes constantly took place and added to the total of wounded. Despite the shortcomings of housing a hospital in completely makeshift surroundings, Valérie found that many of the most needed supplies were at her disposal.

"The field hospital was very well supplied with medicines. The only shortage was chloromycetin. Despite my telegrams, Hanoi was unable to send me any, for at the time that special drug was very rare in Indochina."[28]

Even though the Viet Minh didn't adhere to the Geneva Conventions, the French did. As a result, representatives from the international Red Cross had arrived in Tien Yen to check on the treatment of the two Viet Minh prisoners kept in the recovery room at the small hospital. The representatives were two Swiss doctors.

"I showed our two visitors the wounded Vietnamese," Valérie said. As the two doctors examined the men, Valérie hit upon an idea. The chloromycetin that was vitally needed was nearly nonexistent through regular channels; however, Valérie knew that the Red Cross doctors had access to it.

"These colleagues did indeed have a supply of the precious medicine," Valérie discovered. "But they lent a deaf ear to my requests. The chloromycetin was intended only for the *Viet Minh*!"

Valérie was beside herself with anger at their denial of this potent antibiotic that had the potential to save many lives. She was later to learn that the Red Cross also played a role in prisoner exchanges and often had to trade the scarce antibiotic to secure the release of French soldiers captured by the Viet Minh.

"I left the doctors in vain, bursting with anger," Valérie said of the incident. "I lost a lot of my illusions about the Red Cross."[29]

On May 14, Captain Cazenave returned to duty in Tien Yen, and Valérie received orders to return to Hanoi. Her work at Tien Yen was over, but she reflected on both the good memories—where she played a vital role in saving men who might have otherwise died—and other memories where she could not be of help at all.

"One memory was particularly painful," Valérie said. "One night we were informed by radio of a mortar accident at a nearby outpost. I was waiting for the arrival of five casualties. Suddenly, the truck carrying the men stopped in front of the school. The driver jumped to the ground and opened the back of the vehicle. I approached to discover that all five had died during the journey."[30]

It was a hard and emotional blow to a woman who had already seen more than most could imagine. But Valérie knew that emotion couldn't rule her if she was to continue as a doctor.

"We would not succeed in doing this job by abandoning ourselves to too much emotion," she philosophized. "It was necessary to impose self-control without releasing one's self. It was necessary to maintain a balance while not being confused with coldness."[31]

"Neither that night nor the other days, was I insensitive to the sinister spectacle imposed on me. But tomorrow there will still be lives to save, wounds to heal, and sometimes miracles to perform."[32]

It was time for Valérie André to leave Tien Yen.

"Free to leave, I request a medical Morane to take me back to Hanoi," she said. "I was to leave with the *Viet Minh* prisoner upon whom I performed the laparotomy. My patient was to be operated on again by Colonel Delom at Lanessan Hospital, and then, after a prolonged convalescence, returned to his prison camp."[33]

Tien Yen had only been a mere few weeks in her life, but it had been exhausting and felt much longer. Very few could say that they had experienced the deprivations, the horrific scenes, and the terror of being that close to frontline operations. The experience reinforced Valérie's dedication. But those few weeks took their share of a physical and emotional toll, even though Valérie loathed showing it outwardly.

The flight from Tien Yen to Hanoi aboard the Morane ambulance plane was relatively short. As the plane made its landing at Gialam airport in Hanoi, Valérie's quickly scanning eyes caught the surprising sight of some very familiar aircraft.

"When I landed at Gialam, I was very surprised to find our two Hillers," she said, quite naturally excited. "I ran out to their hangar. The entire team was there. Santini informed me that the helicopters were to be loaded aboard a Bristol transport plane and transported to Hanoi. The helicopters were assigned to the Tonkin (northern Vietnam) region for an undetermined period of time."

But the reunion was to be brief. Valérie had orders to return to Saigon on one of the next transport planes leaving Hanoi.

"*I couldn't help but make a quick calculation,*" she thought to herself. "Interrupted already for two months, my helicopter training was not about to resume. This encounter made me regret that I was leaving Hanoi, although that town was less hospitable than Saigon. But I must indeed rejoin my post in Saigon."[34]

Chapter 21

The Woman Who Came from the Sky[1]

On May 30, 1951, a knight fell.

Lieutenant Bernard de Lattre, the only child of General Jean de Lattre, was killed during an attack on his mobile group's position on a karst bluff known as Heron Rock, near Ninh Binh on the Day River, ninety-four kilometers (fifty-eight miles) south of Hanoi. Bernard had been the general's eyes and ears of the regular soldier serving in the field in Vietnam. He could have easily served in a less dangerous position, but he chose to be a frontline soldier—just as when he was the youngest frontline soldier in his father's First Army during the liberation of France. It was Bernard de Lattre's fate.

It would not be the first time or the last time that a general's son would be killed in combat, but the death of Bernard de Lattre shook the very core of the men and women who served the French cause in Indochina. If a general's son could not survive the nightmare of Vietnam, what did that mean for everyone else?

Even many years later, when I asked Valérie André how Bernard de Lattre's death affected her and others in Indochina at that time, she became uncharacteristically emotional and wept without answering.[2]

The exhilaration of victory and the depths of sorrow were the two inextricably linked emotions describing the French experience in Indochina in 1951. The victories came from battles that the French high command claimed they had won over the Viet Minh. Yet victories came from the loss of many lives, in addition to Bernard de Lattre, and the depth of sorrow only grew deeper. The only element that could have provided solace between triumph and sorrow was hope. But hope remained elusive as long as the Viet Minh remained committed to making France bleed.

In France, sentiment toward the war had soured considerably. Fueled by France's Communist Party, the press continued to negatively view the ongoing conflict in Indochina as *la guerre sale*, the "dirty war." Enlisting volunteers for Indochina in a contentious political environment had become impossible. With the constant negative news emerging from the colony along with a serious lack of commitment by France's revolving-door governments, the attitude on the part of the home front was not supportive.

Even with the lackluster support from home, however, the commitment by France's volunteer army already serving in Indochina only seemed to grow deeper. It is difficult to know how every man and woman serving at the time felt, but there seemed no doubt concerning the mission in Vietnam on the part of Valérie André. She characterized this sentiment as "the faith of the volunteers."[3]

"We chose this commitment in Indochina," she said of her undertaking. "It was imposed on us by no one. We decided it freely and knowingly. Serving in the army imposed a spirit of dedication and a sense of constant solidarity, but also some detachment. We could not give in to long periods of reflections or moods, or to withdraw into ourselves without the risk of losing the taste of adventure."[4]

Adventure sustained Valérie. Her enthusiasm for the army remained as ardent as it had been in 1944 when she witnessed the liberation of Paris by the Free French. Her character was such that she enthusiastically looked forward to her next assignment. She still craved to take to the air, and her desire was partly fulfilled when she was able to get in a half hour of "stick time" in one of the Hillers at Tan Son Nhut on July 10, 1951. Little did she know that her brief time with the helicopter would be her last for quite a while. A new assignment was handed down to Valérie.

"Are you willing to be parachuted into a post in Upper Laos? A patient there is in serious condition." The question came directly from General André Robert. The soldier's condition required her to leave immediately. The mission was strictly voluntary and not connected to the mobile medical team she had trained with. She would have to go it alone. Not hesitating for a moment, Valérie agreed.

"I left the office of General Robert and rushed to the neurosurgery department at Coste Hospital."

Once again, Valérie found herself answering a call into an unknown situation. Her mind calculated the variables she would encounter from the information General Robert had given her. When she got to Coste Hospital, Valérie's first step was to find her faithful surgery room nurse.

"Mademoiselle Botto immediately assembled the material I needed," Valérie said. As she was making her preparations, she received a report that the weather had changed in the north, delaying her departure until the following day. The extra time was put to good use to make sure the mission would go as planned.

"Master Sergeant Bernard, a member of the airborne unit that would drop me at the designated DZ, personally had me try on my parachute."[5]

At 6 a.m. on the morning of July 23, Valérie reported to Tan Son Nhut for takeoff for Laos.[6]

"The weather was very cold and very poor," Valérie said of the flight conditions once it was underway. "We were forced to land in Vientiane, so we could embark onboard another aircraft as soon as the weather improved."[7]

At the airfield at Vientiane, the capital of the Kingdom of Laos, Valérie took stock of all the supplies that would be airdropped over the remote fort high in the Laotian mountains in the province of Xieng Khouang. While taking inventory of her supplies, she met again with Colonel Maurice Redon, who she had met previously at Tien Yen and whose new assignment had also brought him to Laos. Redon filled her in on the details regarding her patient.

"He explained that the patient was suffering from a severe pulmonary infection," she said. "His evacuation would require being carried for five days on a stretcher, and the patient could not withstand such fatigue."

Valérie thought to herself that it would have been perfect to use one of the Hillers to fly in and transport the afflicted soldier, except that the foul weather made it impossible. The outpost was extremely remote and far from any airfield, making a fixed-wing transport unfeasible as well.

"Air dropping a doctor was the only feasible solution," Valérie concluded.

The C-47 was loaded up with twenty containers; some held the medical supplies, and others held food, alcohol and other beverages, tobacco, and, probably just as important, the mail.

The outpost was at a place known as Muong Ngat and was as remote as any of the French fortifications were. The C-47 was ready to take off, and the pilot fully realized that the dense fog shrouding the ground below might well mean that airdrop that day might be aborted if the fort couldn't be accurately pinpointed. As for Valérie:

"My preparations were quickly made. I stuffed my red beret under my shirt and donned the regulation crash helmet. All I had left to do was to slip the parachute over my jacket."[8]

Valérie began studying the map detailing the flight plan for that day as soon as she settled aboard the aircraft.

"I pored over the map and studied the terrain surrounding the spot over which I was to jump. This wouldn't be the first time the Dakota would take off to resupply the Muong Ngat outpost and have to turn back. Will luck be with us this time?" Valérie wondered.

The view outside the windows of the aircraft revealed very little of the ground below. At times, the dense atmosphere cleared for brief seconds before completely obscuring the surface once again.

"The pilot signaled to me that he will gain some altitude and attempt to reach Muong Ngat by dead reckoning."

Again, Valérie fretted about whether they would have to turn back.

"Will he find a hole?" "Will the aircraft be able to break through?"

The C-47 also carried a powerful radio transmitter, and the radioman aboard monitored it closely, picking up the transmitter operating from Muong Ngat. The men at Muong Ngat were desperate not only for supplies but also for the doctor carried on board the airplane. For all involved, returning to Vientiane was not an option.

Even though the transport plane couldn't be seen from the ground, the distinctive sound of the C-47 Dakota's twin radial engines certainly could be heard. As the sound of the engines intensified, the radio operator at Muong Ngat relayed instructions to the pilot to maneuver closer to the outpost. As luck would have it, the clouds finally parted, and the outpost came into view.

"The outpost was in the middle of a basin surrounded by hostile looking peaks," Valérie observed. "The aircraft began to spiral downward."

It was only 1600 hours when the airdrop commenced. First to go were the twenty carefully packed containers. The pilot did his best to make his circles around the small fort as tight as possible so that the containers wouldn't be scattered far when they landed. When the last container was pushed out, it was Valérie's turn.

"I jumped and my descent was normal," she said. "I landed in the middle of the DZ (drop zone), a few meters away from a noncom, a blond-haired sergeant."

The young sergeant couldn't believe his eyes as Valérie unbuckled herself from the parachute harness. She was not who he expected the doctor to be.

"He stood there with his arms dangling," Valérie said of the dumbfounded soldier.

Suddenly an officer rode up to her on a slender horse.

"What are you waiting for?" the officer shouted at the soldier. "Help the doctor!"

"But, Lieutenant," the soldier answered. "I was expecting a guy!"[9]

Recovering his senses to some extent, the sergeant stepped forward to help gather up the now discarded parachute, as other men began to emerge from around the fort to retrieve the airdropped supplies.

The lieutenant introduced himself. His name was Faivre. He was well aware that time was critical in Valérie's mission.

"I was very anxious to see my patient," Valérie said. "So, the lieutenant loaned me his horse."

With a wave toward the general direction where the makeshift infirmary was, Valérie took off.

"It was my turn to trot. The journey allowed me a better look at the outpost."

As it turned out, the outpost itself was located on a small rise, but Valérie noted that the steepness of the surrounding peaks was impressive. Typical of how the war was now progressing, the complement of men at the outpost consisted of 15 Europeans and 140 Laotians. What was most interesting to Valérie was the way the fort was constructed.

"The walls, roofs, and gun emplacements were all made out of logs," she noted to herself. "Not the slightest bit of masonry. I was surprised by the skimpiness of the protection available to these men in the event of an attack!"

But Valérie had yet to learn of the fort's commander; his reputation struck fear in the Viet Minh, who were always a hidden but ever-present menace.

Once inside, Valérie could immediately sense the grave situation of the afflicted soldier.

"When I entered the outpost, I could read the anxiety in everyone's eyes," she said. "These men have feared for the past two days for the life of the sick man. Last year, two of their comrades died of acute pulmonary infections."

The soldier was Master Sergeant Marin. It was obvious from Marin's labored breathing that his lungs were filling with fluid. He was also burning up with fever. Bacteria were the likely cause of the infection, given the nature of working and living in a primitive environment that most Europeans were unaccustomed to. Valérie quickly confirmed that his condition was acute bronchial pneumonia.

"The antibiotics I immediately administered would eliminate the fever in a few days and free me from the role of being his nurse," Valérie remarked of her patient's hopeful prognosis.

Valérie had hoped that her visit to Muong Ngat would be brief, but an outbreak of brush typhus changed her plans.

"Two of the Europeans caught it," she said. "I needed to [obtain] chloromycetin. By radio, I requested some from the Laos Health Services Directorate. The radio was our only means of communication and we feverishly waited for the allotted airdrop time."[10]

The appointed time was announced, but once again weather became a major factor.

"As usual, the sky was overcast. But soon a cry rang out: 'The plane, the plane was coming!' Indeed it was circling up in the sky, almost invisible in the overcast, but we caught a glimpse of it."

The crew aboard the Dakota pushed out the container attached to a parachute, and soon the vital medicine was recovered. Valérie realized the danger of missions involving the highlands of Laos in zero visibility conditions.

"We were full of gratitude for the Dakota crew. Taking off from Vientiane with such weather was already unwise, but once over their target the aircraft should have wisely turned around."[11]

With treatment started, however, there was always a possibility for relapse. The two men would recover, but Valérie found herself needing to delay her departure back to Vientiane again. And with that delay, the legend of "the woman who came from the sky" began to take hold.

The people who inhabited the Laotian highlands surrounding Muong Ngat were the Meo, also referred to as *Montagnards* by the French, or "mountain people." The Meo were another of the many ethnic minorities of Indochina, culturally and physically distinct from mainstream Laotians.

Some of the Meo people had witnessed Valérie parachuting from the C-47 Dakota only a few days before, and others were simply told about "the woman who came from the sky," as Valérie became known. They also learned that she was a woman who could heal the sick, and soon Valérie was inundated by requests for aid.

"The news of my arrival had spread all around," she said. "The natives held the infirmary under siege, and the village chiefs urged me to come to their huts and visit the most severely stricken."

With limited supplies on hand, however, the demands of the indigenous population soon became an issue.

"My pharmacy was becoming rapidly depleted and I had to call out for a parachute resupply."

And material shortages were not Valérie's only concern.

"One morning, as I was pondering on a message to send out, a beautiful Meo girl came in. Her heavy rigid collars clanked on her bosom. With much grimacing and hand signals, she made me understand that she had a toothache. Pulling the tooth was necessary and I did it."

Following that one extraction case, more patients were to come.

"One the very next day, my patient brought in a good half-dozen women. All of them showed me teeth in awfully poor shape."[12]

The commander of the fortification was a captain named Revol, who also went by the name "Tigre." He was called "Tigre" for his ferocious reputation as a fighter who always kept the enemy at bay and trying to guess his next move. The captain knew that a female army surgeon would be an enticing target for the capture by the Viet Minh, so when it was time for Valérie to leave Muong Ngat, the only way to go was by the hazardous mountain trails that often cut through dense forests that lent themselves to becoming traps. The group's ultimate destination would be Xieng Khouang, where there was an airfield. But to get there, it was necessary for the group escorting Valérie to travel many miles by foot through the jungle for several days, where the travel would be bridged between armed fortifications and small villages friendly to the French.

Before the group could leave, however, Revol knew that they would have create a diversion.

"Captain Revol announced in a loud voice the news of my departure," Valérie recalled. "To fool the *Viet Minh*, who were on the lookout, a fake expedition was organized. As for myself, I would depart two days later."

Revol was correct in his suspicions that an ambush would occur. Not long after the diversionary party left the fort, they encountered an improvised explosive that went off. Fortunately, there were no casualties. The diversionary party would not be the only group leaving Muong Ngat. Revol himself left with a group on August 9 to perform an inspection of the other French forts in the region. Between the two separate groups, much of the threat from the Viet Minh would be relieved.

Valérie set out with her escort party on August 10.

"I said goodbye to Muong Ngat," she said. "[There were] twenty-four Laotian scouts with a cadre of three non-coms escorting me. We departed under torrential rain."

While the soldiers would be on foot, Revol provided Valérie with her own unique transport.

"The captain spoiled me," she said. "I was given a small horse that was as docile as it was intelligent. He was neither afraid of steep climbs or hair-raising descents along the trail. From time to time, I jumped off to help it."

Captain Revol had instructed his men to do everything in their power to see to the young doctor's safety.

"I had as a bodyguard a young Laotian, who never let me out of his sight," Valérie said. "Sometimes he was in front, sometimes abreast of me."

The soldier always kept an eye out for danger.

"Watch out, Captain," he would often cry out at a critical point along the steep trail. "The horse will fall down!"

The sure-footed creature was born in the highlands from generations of other ponies that were also born in the highlands and knew how to negotiate the rugged terrain as naturally as he moved through the air.

"My mount never failed," Valérie said. "When the slope was too steep, I got the feeling that he just squatted on its hindquarters and let himself slide down."[13]

The trek was not harassed by human foe as much as it was by the constant rain and an entirely different form of menace.

Leeches.

"The *Viet Minh* were less combative than the leeches," Valérie lamented. "Despite our clothes, they crawled onto our skin. We were forced to stop and pull them off. Theoretically, one should take the precaution of lighting up a cigarette and burning the infernal creatures to make them drop off by themselves. Although I was reminded of the infected wounds [caused by leeches] I had just treated on many of the Meo, I am forced to do like the others and pull off the nasty things. It was raining too much to think of lighting up, and the leeches would just launch another attack anyway."

The leeches were not just a menace to two-legged creatures.

"The ground just teemed with them; they were out in such profusion," she continued. "My horse became a prime target. Slippery and black, they clung to his chest, a few droplets of blood oozing out. I removed them as best as I could."

The Laotian soldiers, who were more accustomed to the leeches than the Europeans, also suffered.

"Although they took the precaution of coating their socks with soap, the Laotian scouts weren't spared any more than we were. Everyone had to stop at some point."[14]

As Valérie and her escorts progressed, the jungle grew even thicker with vegetation.

"To cross a particularly dense part of the jungle, the caravan slowed down," she noted. It was in this area that the first party that had set out from Muong Ngat, the diversionary one, had encountered the booby trap along the trail a few days earlier. The group went silent.

"At a sign from the master sergeant, I get off my horse. [I am told] that the *Viet Minh* prefer to shoot at mounted officers." Valérie's red beret made her an even more visual target.

The meandering trail was now so narrow that the group had to be in a single file to pass. The forest was vibrant with abundant animal life. Valérie and her group could hear the howling of monkeys, the constant banter and song between tropical birds, and the constant buzz of cicadas. But the soldiers had their ears tuned to other noises as well. They were ready to train their weapons in the direction of the sound of the slightest twig snapping.

And then it happened. Two shots rang out—both in quick succession, seemingly from nowhere. Then there was silence. Deathly silence. Even all the creatures of the forest had suddenly gone silent.

Were those going to be the only shots?

Would there be a firefight?

How many of the enemy were there, unseen, in the dense lushness of the forest?

The silence continued.

Fortunately, after what seemed an eternity, the master sergeant signaled the march to continue forward, confident that it was only a lone Viet Minh gunman who would have found himself quickly outnumbered if anything had escalated.

"Soon afterward, the master sergeant motioned me to get back on my horse," Valérie said. The lone gunmen had not entirely missed, however. "Laughing, one of the Laotian scouts shows his friends a bullet lodged in the wooden stock of his rifle. That young man had had a close call indeed. His good mood seemed how he greeted his good fortune."[15]

The group was not expected to reach the outpost at Pou-Soung that evening, so it became necessary to stay overnight at one of the villages they encountered along the trail.

"At nightfall, the village chief's hut welcomes us," Valérie said. "It was an opportunity to dry out our clothes. The roasted corn that the villagers gave us turned out to be excellent. The night was balmy and at dawn we resumed our journey."

Early the next morning, Valérie and her group reached the garrison at Pou-Soung. The French fortification there numbered some eighty men and was commanded by a Laotian chief warrant officer (CWO). The fort itself stood on a tall peak that dominated the valley below. The men at Pou Soung were already aware of the woman who was coming to visit them.

"Forewarned by 'jungle radio,' the CWO came to meet us," said Valérie. "He already knew who I was and under what circumstances I was para-dropped. The welcome I received was quite moving: at the outpost gate, the men presented arms."[16]

Valérie found that she wasn't the only woman present in the fort when she was invited to lunch there.

"At the table . . . [there was] the young wife of the CWO, who also lived within the post. She was shy and tried to retreat away from all the attention, but I insisted that she stayed. . . . [S]he agreed to have lunch with us."

The shy, young Meo woman responded in turn with her own kind gestures.

"As a souvenir, she offered me a silver Meo ring, a '*cour d'amour*'—a kind of small musical instrument—and an embroidered collar."

The gifts touched Valérie, who lamented the need to move on from Pou-Soung as quickly as possible.

"Alas! Three days march still awaited us, and we had to leave once again."

On August 12, the group reached the village of Muong Ngame, where the French maintained yet another outpost. At Muong Ngame, Valérie and her party were greeted by a group of village elders and others near its entrance.

"The most notable people of the village received [us] as a group along the path. They tied cotton bands around our wrists, for good fortune, which we would try to preserve as long as possible. And pretty girls offered me small bouquets of flowers," Valérie said, adding, "The sick needed to see me, also."[17]

As it turned out, there was quite a need for a doctor at Muong Ngame.

"Many of the sick were in several huts and I was so happy that I brought so much medicine with me. Quinine was all the more appreciated because it was so hard to come by." Quinine was commonly used to relieve symptoms of malaria, which was common this far into the brush.

"To entice me to give some quinine to them, some villagers brought me eggs and some chickens. My decision to hand out quinine only to the sick surprised them, I think."[18]

Back at the fort, Valérie met the commander, a French sergeant who was wearing a pair of dark glasses. There was a reason for that.

"I think I'm suffering from conjunctivitis," the sergeant told Valérie as he removed his glasses. "I've had it for more than a month."

Valérie immediately saw the inflammation in both of the soldier's eyes that must have been an utter plague to live with, even if it wasn't life threatening. The sergeant needed to go with Valérie and her escorts to Xieng Khouang to be flown to Saigon for further treatment at the eye care treatment center set up by the army there. There was nothing Valérie could do in the field for him.

But the sergeant was reluctant to leave his post and place his second in command in charge. Valérie stood her ground and told the sergeant point-blank that he risked going blind if his eyes were left untreated.

"I would win the argument with him, ultimately," Valérie later said. "The patient would leave with us the next day."[19]

But before the morning came, the people of Muong Ngame celebrated and made "the woman who came from the sky" their guest of honor. A major highlight of the celebration was the consumption of *bassi*.

Lots of *bassi*.

"This delicious beverage, composed mainly of rice alcohol, was placed in an enormous vat; each guest dips a long bamboo stem [into the vat] and sucks," Valérie said, describing the ritual. "The consideration a Laotian holds for his guest is directly proportional to the quantity of liquid the latter can absorb, as it was customary to drink to one's fill."

Even though Valérie conceded that the *bassi* was the best she had ever tasted, she also knew her limitations and did her best not to drink as much as her compatriots. But as the party wore on, the accolades for the now legendary doctor only grew.

"True to Laotian custom, my friends heaped upon me their wishes for prosperity, longevity, strength, and happiness. They bound my wrists in even more cotton ties which I was to keep on as long as possible."[20]

The next morning, the party set out once again, but Valérie had to say goodbye to one member before they left.

"I bid farewell to my nice little horse; he was too tired to continue," she said. The poor animal had marched on for miles and suffered greatly from the leeches, as they all had. Recuperation for the creature had become necessary. "The outpost lent me two other horses. Not without too much protest, the master sergeant I was bringing back with me was forced to become a horseman."[21]

Tha Thom was the next destination for the group. Before reaching Tha Thom, Valérie and her escort found it necessary to cross several riverbanks.

"Rivers in Laos are, in general, easy obstacles," she said, looking back on her experience. "Most of the time we ford them. The men had water up to their waist and I up to my knees. However, some of the streams are deeper."

The deeper areas in the river required creative thought before any attempt was made to cross them.

"[When the river was too deep] we then stopped and improvised a shuttle system," Valérie explained. "Pulling from the other bank and pushed into the water, our poor horses reluctantly waded in and swam as best as they could. Rafts, dug-out canoes, monkey bridges, all were put to use to cross these beautiful rivers."[22]

Continuing on the trail, the group encountered other travelers on the path as well.

"Along the way, our convoy grew by ten mules," Valérie said. "[They were] heavily laden and rather shy about when it came to going for a swim. Some of them were in pitiful shape."

Toward the end of the day, the group reached the village of Tha Thom, where Valérie once again encountered "Tigre."

"Captain Revol was awaiting us," she said. "Having left a day ahead of us, he had completed his regional inspection. A cheerful group of officers surrounded him. The chief of the elders put on a feast for us, and again, I was entitled to the little cotton good luck ties."

Tha Thom was somewhat different than the tiny villages Valérie and her group had passed through. As she described it, the village was almost like a "real little city" complete with streets, stone houses, a market, and even a bar.

"I was destined to further surprises when I was taken to my room," Valérie said. "It was spacious, clean, and had a bed with mosquito netting. I also appreciated the shower. Someone was kind enough to provide a pack of American cigarettes. But alas!, the Lucky Strikes were too mildewed and unfit to smoke."[23]

Tha Thom would prove to be an oasis for only a day, for it was necessary to continue the journey once again the next morning. The caravan had grown larger with the addition of more men and more mules carrying supplies. It would take two days to reach the final destination at Xieng Khouang. The trail was less rugged now, but there were still rivers to cross; the mules proved to be as difficult as before, only more so now because several had been added to the group.

And the leeches were still relentless.

As the August sun bore down, the heat and humidity from the tropical clime increased.

"The heat became oppressive," Valérie said. Along the way, children eager to earn a few centimes presented some relief. "Young children, as agile as monkeys, climbed to the top of coconut trees and dropped large green nuts. Milk from this fruit was the most refreshing drink we could find."[24]

The trail, however, also revealed one of the more impoverished villages that Valérie had yet encountered.

"We stopped for the night in a village of extreme poverty," she said. "Each hut sheltered a whole family, consisting of at least twenty people. At night, it's relatively quiet but there is an incessant nightlife, secret and lurking in every nook, that seems to haunt our modest refuge."

The threat of a surprise attack from the Viet Minh or their sympathizers was never far from anyone's thoughts.

The insect life also proved to be oppressive, especially for Valérie.

"[I was] prey to the attacks of tiny insects that devoured my face each time I lowered my cover. I lamented out loud the absence of my mosquito netting."

The next morning saw the beginning of the final leg of the journey. Xieng Khouang was now close at hand.

"Close to the city, a last river stood in our way," Valérie said. "No doubt eager to reach his stable, my horse spontaneously jumps in. Although I hold my legs at a right angle, this time I am thoroughly soaked. The two sergeants with me get a real laugh at my mishap."[25]

Xieng Khouang means "horizontal city" in the Lao language but is also of significant historical importance as the gateway to the "Plain of Jars"(Plaine de Jarres), the location of the ancient civilization that predated modern Laos. But the area around Xieng Khouang is characterized by grassy meadows and rolling hills.

"It was a rich and lively town, with a hospital," Valérie said of Xieng Khouang. "My first step was to go to the hospital, where I learned that a plane was to take me to Vientiane on the following day."

But Valérie was to also learn that poor weather conditions were settling back in. The shuttle from the Laotian capital had already turned back twice prior to her arrival there. And there was more rain in the forecast.

"As expected, the days went by and there was nothing in the skies except rain squalls. Rain, rain! And I quickly tired of walks between two downpours, or of poker or ping pong at the mess of the 7th Colonial Line

Battalion, whose officers were nonetheless charming companions. Unable to remain idle, I was anxious to get back to Saigon."[26]

The rain prevented regular service to Xieng Khouang for nearly a week. But shortly after daybreak on August 22, Valérie heard the drone of a transport plane's engine approaching the airfield.

"I jumped into a jeep and headed straight to the airport," she said elatedly. "[I knew] that there were several officers, like myself, who were waiting, and I feared that all of the available space would be at a premium."

The plane was a Noorduyn Norseman, a small Canadian-built bush plane that only had a capacity for ten passengers including the pilot. With packages and supplies bound for Vientiane, however, this particular Norseman had even less capacity.

The pilot was a young man named Lenthal who, by chance, knew Valérie from her frequent visits to Tan Son Nhut.

"I am taking seven people with me, no more," Lenthal told the gathering crowd. As several would-be passengers vied with the pilot for the limited spaces available, the petite doctor ambled her way into the empty copilot's seat in the cockpit.

In Indochina, there was often no such thing as "standard operating procedures," and sometimes that even applied to the departure of an aircraft in the more rural areas, as Valérie and her fellow passengers were to learn.

"It was a fairly easy task to get the onlookers to move aside and let us through, but a herd of water buffaloes turned out to be less docile," Valérie said. "The bovines, at times obstinate and dangerous, must be chased off with much stick wielding; the aircraft was heavy and the ground was soft. Lenthal had to taxi to the very end of the runway before he could take off."[27]

Lenthal was used to less than perfect conditions for takeoff. With adroit skill, he took the plane to the air with at least some meters left to spare on the runway.

"Soon, we were climbing to three thousand meters (app. 10,000 feet) before heading to Vientiane," Valérie said, clearly used to takeoffs like this one. "I grabbed the map and tried to get my bearings. Lenthal merely shrugged his shoulders."

The air was still thick with dense clouds when Lenthal cried out:

"It's all wrong," as he pointed to the map in Valérie's hands. "Somewhere around here there's a hump that's a least 3,300 meters (10,500 feet)!"

Lenthal's remark might have been a pilot's sense of gallows humor, but it went without saying that an unseen "hump" might not be exactly a desirable thing to encounter. The flight continued on, however.

"I was content with staring philosophically at the sea of clouds," Valérie said. "Everything was still socked in. I guess that the pilot felt, just as I did, that it was taking a long time. But suddenly there was a break in the clouds; Vientiane appeared to us."[28]

Vientiane was the capital of Laos and the home to the Laotian royal family. As it was in Vietnam, Laotian nationalists had attempted to make Laos an independent state in 1945 during the power vacuum following the occupation by Japan and before the return of the French to colonial rule. King Sisavang, however, remained loyal to the French, and the nationalist movement was at least temporarily forced to move into the shadows.

It was still early in the morning as the Noorduyn made its approach to the airfield.

"The charming capital of Laos, at the time an almost peaceful country, was asleep by the river," Valérie said. "I was already dreaming of the plane that would take me back to Saigon, mission accomplished."[29]

But the people of Laos were not ready to let "the woman who came from the sky" go just quite yet. When the plane landed, Valérie found someone to drive her to the military hospital in Vientiane, where she expected to stay for the evening.

"Just as I arrived at the hospital . . . I was informed that a cocktail party was to be given in my honor . . . at the royal palace," she said, astonished at the news. "In my honor, really? Nothing that I accomplished seemed to me to have merited the slightest honor. But in fact, a tale had begun to spread in Indochina where I already acquired a certain celebrity without having neither anticipated it nor wanting it."[30]

Indeed, the party in honor of Valérie André was to be hosted by no less a personage than King Sisavang's eldest son, Prince Savang.

"It was given at [the prince's] palace . . . where the Laotian aristocracy rubbed shoulders with French officers," Valérie said. But the honors hardly stopped at just a reception in her honor.

"During the party, the Prince presented me with a handsome medal, *The Million Elephants* and *White Parasol*." The honor was inaugurated by King Sisavang in 1927 to honor both military personnel and civilians in recognition of their exceptional service to the people of Laos.

Valérie found some playful irony in the title of her honor, however.

"When you thought about it, in spite of my long trek on both foot and horseback, I never encountered a single pachyderm!"[31]

But it was time for Valérie to leave Laos. The following morning, Valérie boarded a Dakota heading south to Saigon.

Upon her return to Coste Hospital, Valérie received orders to report to the office of General Robert. The general wasn't very pleased with Valérie's extended absence from Saigon.

"He greeted me coolly," Valérie said. The general questioned why the air drop into Muong Ngat had turned into such a long sojourn. "I just justified the facts, and obediently headed back to the hospital."[32]

Valérie wisely avoided emphasizing the honor she had received from the royal family for her service while she had been in Laos, as it probably would not have been prudent to test the pride of her commanding officer. Nonetheless, the tale of her selfless devotion to the healing of the sick and injured—both military personnel and the civilians of Laos—had spread, and it was evident that her acclaim was only growing.

A ceremony held in Saigon a few months later brought Valérie André the first of many accolades to come from her own peers in the French army. And it was none other than General Jean de Lattre de Tassigny who presented Captain Valérie André with her first formal military decorations, the medal for a military parachutist and the medal for combat field surgeon. The pride she felt from receiving these honors was evident in her words many years later.

"Among my photos, there is one that is the pride of my life. [In that photo] there is the commander-in-chief, de Lattre, in his formal uniform, slightly inclining his silhouette of imperious gentility towards me, speaking a few words of congratulations."[33] The photo's background also depicted three nurses standing in a row, receiving honors, as well as a squad of French Foreign Legionnaires presenting arms. It was an extraordinary image that foreshadowed even more extraordinary things to come.

The intersection of these two individuals, Valérie André and Jean de Lattre, had been many years in the making yet represented the pinnacle of the French expression of *esprit de corps*.

Valérie was representative of the younger and more modern generation of France, who had endured the fear and deprivation created from the German occupation of World War II, only to emerge as an individual who would devote her life not only to the betterment of France but also to the world. Jean de Lattre was of an older generation, who had also suffered the deprivation of war—in his case imprisonment by the German-backed Vichy government—who never gave up his idealism and devotion to his mother country and its causes. In that moment, regardless of the political turmoil in France over the course of the war in Indochina, the true course of the war was in the hands of the true believers.

There was no doubt that de Lattre had also gone through upheaval during the year 1951. His early successes on the battlefield against General Vo Nguyen Giap and the Viet Minh had come at a tremendous cost—the death of his only son. While it was true that there was nothing that gave de Lattre more pleasure than recognizing the outstanding achievements of the men and women who served under his command, such as Valérie, the somewhat somber and subdued continence of the commander in chief is also evident in the photograph taken that day.

Despite Valérie's depiction of the general as lordly and commanding—which he was—another battle loomed on the horizon for the general that would take on its own personal nature. And it would be a battle that Jean de Lattre would face to its bitter end.

As for Valérie, even though 1951 represented the culmination of her more than four years of experience in Indochina, it would prove to be the start of not only more extraordinary events in her life but also even more acclaim.

But as Valérie André would learn, acclaim could sometimes be a difficult thing to live up to or live with.

Chapter 22

A Test of Will

Alexis Santini knew that finding a replacement for Raymond Fumat wasn't going to be easy. After Fumat was sent back to France following his jeep accident, Santini was responsible for flying all helicopter missions. The need for the helicopter rescue service was increasing, and there was already talk of adding more helicopters to the two already in use. But who would pilot them?

Santini seriously considered placing Valérie André into a more regular role as a rescue pilot. He had tested Valérie's abilities by letting her fly supervised missions with him. But placing Valérie in a regular role as a rescue pilot wasn't solely Santini's decision. Although Valérie was the only other qualified helicopter pilot serving in Indochina, her service with ELA 52 posed a number of issues.

Valérie was under the command of CLAEO,[1] the quasi civilian/military administrative corps that included medical personnel. She was not part of the same command structure as Alexis Santini was in the air force. Her first priority was as a doctor, not a pilot, and her workload at Coste Hospital was already overwhelming. And she was also on standby with the ACP (*antenne chirurgicale parachutiste*) mobile medical unit. The different requirements of the two services often made coordination difficult—as Santini learned when General Robert offered Valérie medical missions in northern Vietnam and Laos during spring and summer 1951, and she was gone for weeks as a result.

There were also other issues that held Valérie back from full deployment as a rescue pilot. As a fully trained doctor and surgeon, she was considered a precious commodity at a time when doctors and surgeons of her caliber were in short supply. While her advanced medical training made her invaluable in saving severely wounded soldiers at remote outposts only reachable by helicopter, her potential loss or capture would severely impact the military's already overworked medical corps.

And, of course, there was another factor that had already been discussed among various circles. Valérie André was a woman, and in the prevailing thought of many at the time, a woman was just not supposed to take on such tasks as piloting helicopters and executing medical rescue missions.

But Alexis Santini dismissed this last rationale. With typical Corsican pragmatism, Santini concluded that Valérie's gender shouldn't preclude her service as a pilot. He had come to know Valérie well over the past several months, and he realized how tenacious the young woman was when she had set her mind on achieving a goal. And he also realized that the morale boost to the men in the field was beyond measure when a true angel of the air descended among them to perform miraculous rescues.

Valérie needed more training as a pilot before she could be released on solo rescue missions. Santini could confidently foresee that possibility. With Valérie away on assignments and not available to take Fumat's place, however, Santini found it necessary to shoulder the entire helicopter rescue program in Indochina by himself until another pilot could be added to the roster.

Santini's logbooks from 1951 read as a testament to his will and endurance in rescue operations. While Santini was not the only pilot engaged in aerial rescues during this period—fixed-winged aircraft were also used when the wounded could be brought to a landing strip—he was the only pilot capable of flying directly into remote outposts in dangerous combat zones to perform an evacuation.

The numbers from Santini's flight log tell part of the story. From March 24 to November 24, Santini flew seventy-one medical rescue missions in Vietnam—forty-seven in the south and twenty-four in the north. A total of sixty-eight men were saved with only four dying en route to hospitals.[2] The numbers in total for men rescued, hours of flight, and distances covered in only six months doubled the entire record for ELA 52 in all of 1950 when Santini was assisted by Sergeant Fumat.

In April 1951, Santini—along with the two Hillers and ELA 52's four airframe and power plant mechanics—was transferred to Gialam airfield near Hanoi in northern Vietnam in support of General de Lattre's continued offensive against the Viet Minh. For the next several months, Santini would be ELA 52's only helicopter pilot. The workload on one pilot was tremendous.

Several notable rescues performed by Santini occurred during this period with a Hiller helicopter, a very primitive machine lacking equipment and features that would make helicopters many times more effective in only a few short years to come. Time after time, Santini overcame these limitations and expertly performed with the Hiller like a virtuoso. A superlative test of Santini's piloting skills came on June 6, 1951, when he was ordered to evacuate four gravely wounded men near Ninh Binh.[3]

Ninh Binh was the area where the French had seen heavy fighting in recent months and was not far from Heron Rock where Bernard de Lattre was killed only weeks before. The Viet Minh were known to be all over the area in small cells, and the delicate helicopter—despite the prominent red crosses painted on its fuselage—was a prominent target. While it was optimal to fly rescue missions only in daylight, orders were issued to Santini late in the afternoon that day. The orders crackled over the radio at Santini's base of operations in My Co from a GATAC[4] air traffic controller in Hanoi.

"Toricelli, emergency evacuation required. Prepare to depart."

Toricelli was the radio call sign Santini used to communicate with air traffic control.

With only map coordinates furnished by the air controller to go by, Santini plotted his route from paper charts he kept neatly filed in a leather case for the entire area of operations. It was already late in the day. He could call off the mission for safety reasons, but the situation was urgent and men would die without his help. Not giving it a second thought, he climbed into the cockpit of the Hiller and started the engine, and the rotor blades began to turn. As Santini lifted off, daylight began to turn into dusk.

The Hiller was equipped with a pair of dual-beam spotlights at the bottom of its fuselage, and that was about all there was, besides the instruments, to assist the pilot in nighttime flying. The rural areas of Vietnam were in pitch black darkness at night. Even cook fires near where villagers lived were of no use for navigation purposes as they were often impossible to see from the air. In an era before night vision aids and global positioning satellites, a pilot like Santini could only rely on his instruments and dead-reckoning navigation skills to get to the wounded men.

Santini proceeded cautiously. Flying at night in the Hiller was incredibly dangerous. He had spent some time in the area of Ninh Binh and Phat Diem and knew some of the more prominent landmarks and navigational checkpoints. But his experience with flying the Hiller was only during daylight hours. At night, only a few landmarks were visible. Fortunately, it was a clear night, and the light of the moon helped illuminate the way to some extent. Inside the cockpit, the map light from the instrument panel provided a modest amount of illumination allowing Santini to recheck his charts; however, the margin for error was great as the helicopter clawed its way through the darkness.

GATAC had also radioed the platoon that the helicopter was on its way. They were told that they would have to light a fire to signal Santini where to land. They were also told to clear the area of debris as best as they could as the downwash from the helicopter's rotor blades could kick up dangerous projectiles.

A half hour into the flight, Santini caught sight of the fire. It was large enough that he knew it had been made from spare fuel from the platoon's jeep. Lighting a signal fire at night is always dangerous. There was always a chance that the Viet Minh would see it and stage an ambush on the position. But *mud soldiers* knew how to survive with little outside help.

Santini flipped the switch to the two spotlight beams on the bottom of the Hiller. He wanted to make sure that he could land safely enough without causing more casualties from an ill-prepared landing zone (LZ). Satisfied that the men had done their job Santini expertly landed the helicopter, and the men emerged forward from the safe distance they were keeping to meet him.

The Hiller's engine slowed to an idle allowing the rotor blades to slowly wind down their rotation. He was mindful of the battery failures that had happened before and kept the engine running. Santini didn't want a repeat experience so far from his base and in almost complete darkness.

The platoon's medic already administered triage to the wounded, and he established a priority for the two most severely wounded who would go first. It was times like this that Santini marveled at Valérie, who often boasted that with her petite frame an additional wounded man could make the journey back without being a burden to the Hiller's limited payload. But Santini was well aware of the weights involved and knew that bringing back only two of the wounded at a time would have to make do.

Santini wasted no time in preparing for liftoff once the two men were strapped to the helicopter's stretchers on the side. As soon as the rest of the platoon cleared away, Santini applied the collective control and throttle, and the Hiller was airborne once again. It had taken a half hour to reach the platoon's position, and it would take another half hour to return to base at My Co. The Hiller always felt different when it was fully loaded—the cyclic and collective controls were more sluggish, and the aircraft was less responsive. Yet Santini noted that northern Vietnam's comparatively cooler climate helped the helicopter achieve altitude with less difficulty.

When he returned to his makeshift base at My Co, Santini was met by a medical crew who transferred the wounded men to a waiting ambulance. Santini knew that there were still two men back with the platoon who would also require medical attention before the night was over. Once again he powered up and plunged his helicopter back into darkness, retracing his route to Ninh Binh. As an added precaution, Santini also switched off the aircraft's marker lights.

It probably won't make much difference, but it will give the Viets less of a target from the ground.

When he returned to the LZ once again, Santini wasted no time in evacuating the two remaining wounded soldiers.

The nighttime rescue Santini performed was not just remarkable for the lives saved. Flying the two rescue missions at night took a whole different dimension of piloting skills. Santini flew nearly the entire mission in darkness with few, if any, landmarks to guide him. This accomplishment left no doubt of his true skill as a pilot.

The rescue of downed fixed-wing aircraft pilots was also a regular occurrence for the crew of ELA 52. The precedent for retrieving pilots by helicopter had already been set by Sergeant Fumat when he maneuvered his helicopter over a marsh to rescue Lieutenant Jacquesson after he soft-landed his fighter plane in the Mekong following an engine malfunction. The loss of pilots from capture by the Viet Minh was a situation the French military wanted to avoid at all costs. The Viet Minh considered attacks from the air by means of bombing, machine-gun strafing, and napalm as among the most heinous acts of war committed by the French. As a result, pilots—even observation pilots—would be subject to some of the worst treatment meted out by the Viet Minh in prisoner of war camps.

On the morning of May 8, the two-man crew of a Morane-Saulnier Criquet scout plane took off from Gialam airfield. Their assignment was to provide aerial observations and positioning of ground-based artillery fire along the Black River. Scout planes were often used to more accurately direct bombardment from ground artillery through radio instruction as the plane-based crews could see the entire range of the battlefield from the air.

Twenty minutes into the flight the Criquet passed over a zone occupied by the Viet Minh near Cao Mai. Even though the aircraft was at an altitude of some 400 meters (1,300 feet), a lucky shot from the ground severed the fuel supply line, shutting the motor down almost immediately. With no other choice available, the pilot was forced to land on a strip of beach bordering the Black River.

It was a rough landing. The light aircraft struck the ground with tremendous force, rattling its two occupants violently inside the cabin. Not unconscious, but certainly dazed and injured, the two men managed to escape from the mangled fuselage. While the Criquet's crew managed to survive the crash, they knew they were in a bad situation, essentially stranded and far from any friendly aid. Making matters worse, the Viet Minh were not far away and no doubt saw the Criquet go down.

Fortunately for the Criquet's crew, their radio still functioned, and they were able to call in their position to GATAC in Hanoi. Word went out from GATAC not long after:

"Toricelli. Prepare for rescue of downed aircrew, one kilometer southwest of Cao Mai on Black River."

Santini quickly readied the single Hiller that was prepared for service. One of the two helicopters had been down for scheduled maintenance, and the available Hiller had just finished its overhaul and reassembly the night before. There had been no time for a shakedown test flight, so it would have to take place en route to the rescue.[5]

Because the Criquet's flight crew had radioed that they were forced down by Viet Minh artillery, two Grumman Hellcat fighter planes from the Corsica squadron were dispatched and immediately took to the air to locate the position of the two downed men. The task of spotting the two men was made easier when the Criquet's crew heard the drone of the approaching fighters and set the fuselage of their plane on fire with their remaining fuel to signal them. They knew that the fire and smoke would be a dead giveaway of their position, but they also knew that the two Hellcat fighter pilots would remain in the area and circle around until the rescue helicopter arrived.

The flight maintenance crew of ELA 52 had done their job well in reassembling the Hiller as Santini experienced no problems to Cao Mai. His radio was patched in with the Hellcats through GATAC, and he soon caught sight of the two planes circling the area of the burning wreckage. Despite the menace from the two fighter planes, the Viet Minh began advancing on the two downed pilots and from a distance started to open fire on them with a bazooka. Santini soon realized that a routine rescue had now turned into something incredibly hazardous.

The Hellcat pilots called in for reinforcements from their own squadron stationed at Gialam, and not long after the air was filled with even more fighter planes. The newcomers to the battle also had napalm canisters strapped to their bomb racks, and soon the whole area was engulfed in flame and even more machine-gun fire.

Amid this man-made hell, Santini seized his opportunity to go in and landed the helicopter close to the burning Criquet. At first, he didn't see the two wounded airmen because they had taken shelter from enemy fire by staying as close to the shore of the Black River as possible. The men found the remains of an abandoned sampan and kept themselves crouched as low to the ground to avoid detection. Santini managed to catch sight of them, however.

Santini realized that both men were injured far more seriously than he was initially led to believe. One of the men attempted to move away from the sampan but doubled over in pain almost immediately. Seeing no other alternative Santini jumped from the cockpit of the Hiller and raced to their position.

There was no time to lose as Santini reached down to help the man back to his feet. With the wounded man's arm slung over his shoulder, Santini partly carried the man back to the helicopter and pushed him into the cockpit. Bullets continued to whiz past him, but Santini ignored them. His mind was focused on getting back to the second man near the shore.

The second man had sustained more serious injuries than the first, and once again Santini found it necessary to virtually carry the wounded man back to his helicopter. It was almost a superhuman feat, but Santini found the strength to do it.

With their supply of napalm exhausted, the fighter planes concentrated their machine-gun fire in a succession of strafing runs that caused enough of a break from enemy gunfire that Santini was able to get the Hiller back up to speed and lift off from the area.

One Hellcat pilot, who had witnessed Santini's actions from above, marveled at how he had been able to successfully pull off the rescue at all. If Santini himself had thought that he had performed something extraordinary, there was no reflection of it in his official report. In his concise manner, Santini made the following entry in his flight log:

I have the honor to report the rescue was carried out on 8 May 1951 in the western sector of Viet Tri, one kilometer southwest of Cao Mai. Having taken off at 10 am from Bach Mai field, I arrived at 10:40 am at the crash. After spotting the crew of a Morane 500 on a beach on the edge of the Black River, I landed and took on board Captain Hector and Sergeant Bouneix. . . . I landed at Bach Mai at 11:35 am.[6]

The rescue may have gone unnoticed and just chalked up to another routine rescue that day; however, the men of the Corsica Squadron could not help themselves from recounting the story of Santini's courage under fire, both to themselves and to others. The fighter pilots could only admire a man who could almost magically land an aircraft in the middle of a pitched battle, unarmed, and manage to not only take off again safely but also save two men in the process. To them, it was a miracle.

It was the start of Santini's legend, even though the modest Corsican didn't consider his accomplishments to be greater than any other pilot. But if the modest Corsican would not promote his own exploits, then at least pilots who respected the bravery of a fellow pilot would.

Chapter 23

The Perils of Tenacity

Valérie André was at a crossroads in her military career, and she wasn't happy about it. She had successfully completed her mission in Laos and burnished her reputation among her peers. But the words that Dr. Carayon said to her in Cairo months before played over and over.

Will you be flying helicopters or performing surgery?

When that question was originally posed to her, Valérie said that she believed the two skills were compatible. Now she wasn't quite so sure.

"From August to November 1951, while the helicopter group lacked pilots, my flights were becoming scarce, decreasing my chance to become operational. I was angry, but once again I didn't rush into things."[1]

Valérie knew that ELA 52 was down to just one pilot, Alexis Santini, who had assumed responsibility for all helicopter rescues. She also knew that GATAC (Groupements aériens tactiques [Tactical Air Group]) was considering adding other pilots to meet the increasing workload and that she could very well be passed over as a replacement for Sergeant Fumat, even though she was the only other qualified helicopter pilot in Indochina at the time.

"The helicopter section needed pilots," she recalled. "Why not utilize me now that my helicopter training was already completed?"[2]

Her feelings were justified. General de Lattre had already put the French army on the offensive throughout 1951, and heavy casualties for both the French and Viet Minh were the result. Everyone believed that a new campaign along northern Vietnam's Black River region was in the offing, and there would be even more casualties. For wounded men located far beyond

189

passable roads or approachable river routes, the use of the helicopter was the difference between life and death.

Valérie brought up her irritation with Santini.

"There are two other pilots being considered," Santini flatly told Valérie.

Valérie repeated to Santini the question she already had in her mind.

"Why not use me? My training is complete."

"If you weren't a doctor, there would be no problem," Santini replied. "But I am forced to take Bartier."[3]

Twenty-nine-year-old Chief Warrant Officer Henri Bartier was born in Wambrechies near France's border with Belgium and had been flying aircraft since he was seventeen. Bartier enlisted in the French air force during World War II; he flew transport planes in and out of France's colonies in North Africa until the surrender in 1940 and was mustered out of the military the following year. As soon as France's air force was restored, however, Bartier resumed his service as well. He was among the first from France to arrive in Vietnam in late 1945. He initially flew aircraft that directed artillery fire but transitioned to flying medical Morane Criquets.

Most of Bartier's rescue missions were over northern Vietnam, and he soon gained a reputation for taking on especially dangerous missions. Despite the Criquet's medical insignias, Bartier often drew intense enemy fire. There was some who believed that the Viet Minh had attached a bounty on the young pilot, judging from the bullets that often riddled Bartier's Criquet following a mission. On one occasion, Bartier's aircraft, carrying a wounded soldier, was brought down by Viet Minh rifle fire that managed to damage its engine. He kept the aircraft aloft until he was able to set down on a rough road where he knew French troops were stationed nearby. Even though the plane wasn't able to take to the air again, the wounded man was transferred to a truck and brought to a medical way station. For Bartier's heroic actions he was promoted to the rank of chief sergeant.[4]

Bartier's missions took him to virtually every location in Indochina. He had an intimate knowledge of terrain and geography—especially northern Vietnam—far beyond that of most pilots. With more than five years of service with the French air force in Indochina, Bartier had flown nearly six hundred reconnaissance and medical rescue missions by 1951.[5] Yet his military career almost ended in 1949 when he came down with a severe case of yellow fever and was forced to return to France for several months of recuperation. But Bartier would return. He had met a young woman in Hanoi by the name of Marie Yvonne, who came from a Vietnamese/French family. He intended to marry her. If there was one thing that motivated Bartier above all else it was an inner drive, summed up by his own words:

"Indochina is a part of me."[6]

When Bartier returned to Indochina, his workload was unrelenting. As the war turned against the French in 1950, Bartier's efforts saved lives on Vietnam's northern frontier in places like Lang Son. There was no lack of recognition from his superiors. Not only was he recognized by inclusion in France's Legion of Honour but he was also awarded the French war cross, le Croix de guerre, along with multiple *palmes* between 1946 and 1954.[7]

When it became obvious that Alexis Santini needed a full-time pilot to replace Sergeant Fumat, GATAC put out a call for volunteers among its own ranks. It was no slight to Valérie that Henri Bartier, now promoted to the rank of chief warrant officer, was at the top of the list of new candidates.

There remained a problem, however.

Bartier would require training on the Hiller, with Helicop-Air in France and with Santini in Vietnam when he returned. It would be many weeks, if not months, before he would be considered fully operational. Bartier's absence opened up the opportunity that Valérie was seeking to prove her value in helicopter rescue.

In late November 1951, both Valérie André and Alexis Santini were ordered to a small airport near Bien Hoa, some forty kilometers north of Saigon. They were to be part of a relay team consisting of a medical rescue helicopter and primary medical emergency care. The idea was to immediately treat the wounded who would then be airlifted from the airport to Saigon by Morane Criquets, freeing up the helicopter so it could be used for continuous transport of the battlefield wounded.

"There were many casualties," Valérie recalled. "Santini was making runs between a spot in the Bien Hoa forest and the Laike airport. I climbed aboard [the Hiller] in the hope of making at least the return trip with Santini. . . . Tired after more than four hours of flight, Santini relinquished the controls to me. He appeared to not pay any attention to me, but I remained on my guard and strictly adhered to all instructions, not forgetting to ask Tan Son Nhut for permission to land."

The trip was uneventful, which was of course Valérie's complete intention.

"When we parted Santini didn't make the slightest comment regarding our little trip, and I took that as a good sign."[8]

The reserved Santini was not one to encourage anyone if he knew the inevitable outcome for success was a foregone conclusion, and Valérie knew that. He might not admit it to her, but Santini respected Valérie's growing skill as a pilot.

Three days after their return to Saigon, Valérie was free from her duties at Coste Hospital and used her downtime to visit Santini and the crew of ELA 52 at their base at Tan Son Nhut. She had hoped to be able to practice with one of the helicopters while she was there.

"As I neared the hangar, I could see that the mechanics were busy disassembling one of the Hillers."

At first, Valérie thought the helicopter was undergoing maintenance, but she soon learned otherwise.

"The thought that I wouldn't be flying that afternoon caused me some disappointment, but that quickly turned to real anguish. The aircraft—the only one available—was to be loaded the next day on board a Bristol and taken to Hanoi."[9]

The long-rumored military offensive along the Black River in northern Vietnam was launched, and the bulk of the battle was taking place near Hoa Binh not far from Hanoi. Hoa Binh ironically translates into "peace" in Vietnamese.

Valérie knew that her place should be with her comrades in the thick of the action.

"I had an idea at the back of my mind and I went to see General Robert."

Valérie hoped that the general would see the need to put her into service. With Bartier in the midst of helicopter flight training, Valérie knew that Santini would not be able to handle the duties of transporting the large number of wounded anticipated from battle solely by himself.

A meeting with General Robert was always fraught with some measure of uncertainty. While Valérie never doubted herself or her abilities, General Robert always saw it as his duty to determine what was best to serve the medical needs of France's military personnel in Indochina. In the general's eyes, Valérie André was first and foremost a doctor, and a neurosurgeon at that. In that capacity, she was an invaluable asset. But Robert realized that the helicopter section was courting disaster by relying on only one pilot.

General Robert was noncommittal at first, as he patiently listened to Valérie outline her request. As she spoke with the general, Valérie wondered if her qualifications and experience were enough to sway his decision.

"Would I obtain the permission I was seeking? Would he take into account the fact that I could replace Santini at the spur of a moment? Would he authorize me to load on board the Bristol with the medical team Saigon is sending to Tonkin?"[10]

Valérie was both surprised and relieved when the general finally said yes. She would also be required to fill in for any assistance needed by the medical team serving in the support of the mission. Valérie would accompany ELA 52 to northern Vietnam.

The Battle of Hoa Binh was the culmination of months of planning by General de Lattre to lure General Vo Nguyen Giap's Viet Minh army into a large, set piece confrontation. It was intended to deal a fatal blow to Giap and his insurgent force. As Valérie characterized it:

"It was General de Lattre's last wager. Eighty kilometers southwest from Hanoi, Hoa Binh was the center of the Muong population. The area was strategic for its roads, river transit, and communication lines."[11]

Valérie hastily made her preparation for her journey north.

"I forgot it could be cold in Tonkin and when we took off the next day I took only a few light-weight clothes. I was absolutely freezing when we got to Hanoi."

Valérie made herself familiar with Gialam air base in Hanoi almost as soon as she set foot on the tarmac.

"I made my way into the canteen of the 23rd Artillery Observation Air Group," she said. As a female officer and a pilot, Valérie was certainly a curiosity among the all-male flying fraternity. Nonetheless, a captain with the 23rd bought her a warm drink.

Meanwhile, the mechanic crew of ELA 52 had already offloaded the Hiller from the Bristol transport plane and rolled the fuselage into a corner of a hangar used by the Twenty-Third. There they began the work of putting the ship back together.

"Their task wasn't easy," Valérie said. "The mechanics didn't have their usual equipment available to them. The night barely sufficed for them to accomplish their feat."[12]

Time was not to be wasted. Santini ordered that the helicopter had to be ready for its next flight by dawn.

Initially, the battle at Hoa Binh did not produce as many casualties as were expected. The French planned to stage large maneuvers in the area to draw out General Giap's army. Control over Hoa Binh was seen as essential for both sides. With its network of road and river transport routes, ceding control of the area to the Viet Minh would allow them to continue to harass the capital in Hanoi.

French commanders were also counting on Giap's and Ho Chi Minh's fervor to end the war quickly with a massive force of both men and arms the Viet Minh had amassed since their alliance with the Communist Chinese. The French military was also stockpiling newer and more sophisticated weaponry thanks to the foreign aid coming directly from the United States. The French were confident that their supply and logistical superiority would deal a severe blow to the Viet Minh and the process for a truce between both sides could begin.

Giap, however, was not inclined to repeat the tactical mistakes he had made in past encounters with General de Lattre. He was fully aware that de Lattre would not hesitate to use the full might of the French air force against his troops. Viet Minh veterans who survived the battle at Vinh Yen still remembered the fiery terror that came from above when French planes dropped napalm for the first time.

Instead of a mass attack, Giap returned to his old tactic of assaulting the more isolated and vulnerable French outposts. That was precisely what occurred on December 9 when Giap ordered two regiments from the Viet Minh 312th Division and another regiment from the 308th to attack Tu Vu.

Tu Vu was located twenty kilometers upriver from Hoa Binh. The French outpost there itself was split into two camps separated by the Ngai Lai River that emptied itself into the Black River. The two sides of the camp were connected to each other by a rope bridge suspended over the Ngai Lai River, ostensibly to allow one side of the camp to evacuate to the other in case of an emergency.

The entire camp was also surrounded by ribbons of barbed wire while other parts of the approach to it were laced with landmines.

As part of the buildup in Hoa Binh, the outpost at Tu Vu had received some reinforcements. In addition to the more than two hundred Moroccan riflemen who defended the post, there was a tank platoon consisting of five Sherman tanks that had recently arrived as part of the military aid package sent from the United States. An artillery unit was installed on one side of the river to cover both sides.

Split in two by the river and with the slope of the hills to provide cover, the position was still incredibly vulnerable, however. The Viet Minh were able to use that to their advantage to avoid deadly contact from both artillery and tank guns. When the time came to strike, the Viet Minh used the cover of night to stage their attack. With more than two thousand men in all, they carefully set up a perimeter around one side of the outpost with mortars.

When everything was in position, the first volley in what was to become known as the "meat grinder" had begun.

Words pale in describing the carnage that was unleashed.

Mortar shells had rained down on the outpost for nearly an hour when hordes of Viet Minh infantrymen began screaming, "*Tiên-lên*," the Vietnamese word for "go forward."

And forward they went.

The Moroccans opened up with machine-gun fire on the first wave of the assault, and man after man was mowed down as each tried to climb over the barbed-wire barrier to reach the outpost. As Bernard Fall described the scene from *Street without Joy*:

[T]he enemy infantry threw itself across the barbed wire and the minefields without regards to losses. One "human-wave" attack after another was smashed by French defensive fires. . . . By 23:40, it was obvious that the southern strongpoint could no longer be held; the barbed wire entanglements, now covered with a carpet of enemy bodies, had become totally useless as a hindrance.[13]

Nothing could hold back the overwhelming human assault. One human life after another was destroyed as if its value had never even mattered, but the Viet Minh showed no sign of relenting. The tank crews continued to "fire into screaming human clusters,"[14] but soon they too were overwhelmed, and some of the surviving Viet Minh managed to jam hand grenades into the view slits cut into the armor. All five tank crews met violent deaths in what were now iron coffins.

The remaining survivors on the south had no choice but to evacuate to the north side of the encampment by way of the rickety rope bridge. But they soon found the north post to be equally untenable, as almost all their ammunition was exhausted.

The survivors on the French side saw an opportunity to escape to a sandbar island in the Black River, and they took it. They expected to be wiped out by the enemy, but the high cost of victory on the part of the Viet Minh saved the remaining French from oblivion as they chose not to pursue for the final kill. Perhaps, the Viet Minh commanders also felt that the demoralization from the battle would be enough when the survivors told of the fanatical charge.

For obvious reasons, the slaughter at Tu Vu was not widely reported. But to those who were taking part in maneuvers in and around Hoa Binh, both details and rumors quickly spread. Many couldn't believe the stories of human wave attacks. How could it be possible that men would die so willingly?

The question nagged at Alexis Santini. Four days later on December 13, Santini received orders to report to Rocher Notre-Dame to transport casualties. Rocher Notre-Dame was not far from Tu Vu. He asked Valérie to accompany him on the trip.

"Our helicopter was proceeding along normally. Some 800 feet below us, the Tonkinese landscape unfurled its carpet of rice field," Valérie later recalled. "Suddenly, Santini threw me a questioning look. I did the same. A fetid odor filled the aircraft."[15]

Valérie André and Alexis Santini were over the killing field at Tu Vu. And the corpses of the dead Viet Minh had gone uncollected by their comrades. The air was chokingly thick with the smell of decomposition.

"They said that there were eight hundred bodies caught on the barbed wire," Valérie said of the horrific scene.[16]

Tu Vu was only a preview of things to come.

Valérie and Santini continued on to Rocher Notre-Dame. On the ground they were met by Lieutenant Colonel Blankaert, who commanded a mobile group stationed in the area. There were six men to be evacuated back to Hoa Binh, so that meant successive trips for Santini and the Hiller. Valérie remained behind.

"Colonel Blankaert invited me to eat with him."

Lieutenant Colonel Henry Blankaert was among a new group of officers who had recently arrived in Indochina. Valérie discerned from his impeccably clean uniform shirt that he was a man who took pride in his military appearance, but his dedication was more than skin deep. Blankaert was an extremely competent commander and graduate of France's prestigious St. Cyr military academy. While Blankaert may have been new to Indochina, he was a battle-hardened veteran. During World War II, Blankaert escaped a German prisoner of war camp in Nuremberg and managed to get to Morocco where he joined de Gaulle's Free French Army. After being wounded in the battle for Corsica, he had joined General de Lattre's First Army in the second invasion of Europe, eventually earning five citations while commanding a battalion.

"Despite being newly arrived in Indochina, he appeared perfectly relaxed in the midst of the fray," Valérie noted, although she wasn't then fully aware of the colonel's background.

The brief respite for lunch did not last long.

"An alert interrupted our meal," Valérie said. "We immediately left our tent to see what was happening."

Perimeter lookouts had spotted a man in the distant no-man's-land approaching the camp in broad daylight. While it would have been highly unusual for the Viet Minh to move against a French outpost during the day, no one was about to take any chances in light of what had recently transpired.

Blankaert quickly grabbed a pair of binoculars and trained his eyes on the figure. It was one of the Moroccans who escaped slaughter at Tu Vu. As it turned out, he became separated from the rest of his company on the night of the attack and had been wandering several days in territory controlled by the Viet Minh.

"An order was given immediately to come to the rescue of the survivor," Valérie said. There was general amazement that the young Moroccan had survived at all.[17]

The Viet Minh were not finished with the French just yet. Changing their tactics to a less confrontational stance, they began to systematically attack communication lines, which were always precarious at best. Communications could be kept up through the steady traffic of Dinassaut attack boats that patrolled up and down the Black River, but they also became a target of Viet Minh mortar attacks that emanated from the thick brush growing along the riverbanks.

Battle flare-ups occurred everywhere, including the vicinity around Rocher Notre-Dame.

"There were many dead," Valérie said. When Santini returned for the final time to retrieve the last of the wounded and also Valérie, Colonel Blankaert had only one request.

"The colonel asked us to send out a priest," she said. "We couldn't find one in Hoa Binh."[18]

Nevertheless, the request was relayed forward, and Valérie noted that two days later a chaplain was parachuted into Rocher Notre-Dame.

As the war settled back into its pattern of sporadic hit-and-run tactics from the Viet Minh, an uneasy lull took place. Toward the end of December, Santini received orders to return to Gialam airfield in Hanoi. Valérie seized upon the chance to further hone her piloting skills. One of the things that Valérie discovered was that flying in the cooler northern climate of Hanoi allowed the Hiller to perform better than it did in the south.

"Practice flights were of much use to me," she said. "They allowed me to fly and familiarize myself with the Red River Delta. As seen from the air during this season, it differed greatly from the Mekong Delta. The air was relatively cool in Tonkin and we often flew under an overcast sky."[19]

With the Viet Minh showing no signs of relinquishing the fight, Valérie knew she could be ordered into service at any time. Each time she had the chance to practice with the Hiller, she also loaded sandbags into each of the sideboard litters to simulate casualties. Mastering control of the helicopter from the additional weight spread out from the aircraft's center of gravity presented a new series of challenges; however, Valérie knew it would be necessary to test her limits if she was to become a successful rescue pilot.

On December 23, the Viet Minh struck again at Ap Da Chong just north of Rocher Notre-Dame. Valérie was getting ready to take the Hiller up for another practice session when Santini rushed to the helicopter.

"Since you're already here, you might as well stay," he shouted at her over the din of the rotor blades. Valérie expected Santini to take the center seat control, but he surprised her when he allowed her to stay where she was.

"Head out for Ap Da Chong," he said to her as he unfolded a map in his lap. "I'm warning you, I am not going to say a thing." In his concise manner of speech, Santini meant this flight as Valérie's baptismal if she ever intended to fly solo missions. It would be upon her shoulders to either succeed or to fail with this mission. Santini would be on board as Valérie's monitor and would take control only if it was required. There would be no second chance.

Ap Da Chong was only the general direction for the flight heading. Their exact destination was a small dot on the map known as Xom Bu. Xom Bu was part of the line known as the "de Lattre line" in the Hoa Binh offensive and was regularly harassed by the Viet Minh. It wasn't the first time that Valérie had ventured into an active combat zone, but it was her first time while piloting the Hiller.

"The flight progressed normally and I approached a narrow LZ (landing zone) surrounded by stakes," she said. It was already late in the day, just past 1700 hours.

Xom Bu was held mostly by Foreign Legionnaires of the First BEP (Bataillon étranger de parachutistes, or "foreign parachutists battalion"). A German legionnaire lieutenant named Erhardt, who was acting as a medic for the battalion, stepped forward.

"We have sixteen casualties here," he reported. The large number of casualties meant that Santini was to assume control of the mission from here on.

"If everything goes right, we can probably evacuate four of the men this evening," Valérie said to Lieutenant Erhardt. She then told him that the two most severely wounded would go first. In order not to tax the Hiller's payload, Valérie would remain behind.

Valérie knew the dangers of night flying and hoped that Santini could make it back before the end of the day.

It was close to an hour later, with the last rays of sunlight gone that the familiar drone of the Hiller's engine and rotors signaled its approach. Valérie had not wasted time while Santini was away. With the help of Lieutenant Erhardt and some of his men, she had the stakes pulled out of the canvas holding back debris from being kicked up in the helicopter's rotor wash and enlarged the landing zone to a size more suitable for the aircraft to land on. With her direction, the men improvised the landing area.

"We only had a meager crescent of a moon shining dimly in the black of night," Valérie said. "When the helicopter came near it landed in the center of four empty shell casings into which straw had been lit; once again the soldiers had proved their ingenuity!"[20]

Santini probably appreciated the enlarged landing area but said nothing. It was dark now, which meant a flight back to Hoa Binh navigating only by instruments. To make matters worse, the Viet Minh were not far away, and the deadly accuracy of their mortar fire was a real concern.

"The helicopter took on a new load of wounded. That meant that twelve were still left," Valérie noted. As both Valérie and Santini tended to the two soldiers in the Hiller, Lieutenant Erhardt told them both that he had to leave and rejoin the First BEP that was moving on and couldn't stay with the wounded any longer.

"I informed Santini of my intention of spending the night at the outpost," she said. Santini knew that Valérie could not be dissuaded. With no choice but to approve her decision, Santini climbed back into the helicopter and lifted off into the darkness.

While Erhardt and the paratroopers had orders to be on the forward perimeter around Xom Bu, Valérie was not entirely abandoned with her wounded charges. The post was garrisoned with other Foreign Legionnaires manning artillery pieces who soon volunteered to help. Indeed, the Legionnaires were quite taken with the young doctor's courage in remaining with the wounded.

"The garrison adopted me as their *marraine*—their godmother," she said.

As Valérie became more accustomed to her surrounding, she took note of how the Legionnaires survived in a combat zone. Xom Bu was on the crest of a limestone bluff. Instead of constructing a concrete block fortification, as was the norm with many forward outposts, the soldiers used natural caves already bored into the hills.

"[There were] small connecting rooms equipped with camp beds and tables and chairs made out of bamboo logs. To ward off humidity, the soldiers had scattered wooden boards and straw matting on the ground."[21]

The first order of business for the night was to secure the wounded within the walls of the limestone caves. Makeshift hospital bunks were fashioned with used parachutes doubling as bedding to make the wounded more comfortable. While the remaining dozen men were not chosen to leave earlier, the medical condition of some of them was still very serious. One man was a captured Viet Minh officer.

"His wounds showed a penetration through the forehead that had exited through the temple which occurred at least ten days ago," Valérie observed. "The wound was beginning to look very nasty, but the man remained conscious and was very docile, though concerned. He followed our activity with worry and in perfect French kept asking me if he could be operated on."[22]

Valérie was later to learn the man was a political commissar, an officer within the Communist Viet Minh political structure responsible for ideology training among the ranks. French intelligence officers wanted to question the man, but his condition wouldn't allow it.

It was a long night for Valérie. Every sound was amplified. Sleep only came from sheer exhaustion. Everyone knew that the Viet Minh were there. Would another attack like the one at Tu Vu take place?

When morning finally came, Valérie looked to the skies for Santini.

"I searched the skies. An hour went by and then another. I kept on waiting as the morning wore on. At noon, I was worried and unable to understand what was going on, I sent a radio message."

With the help of the company's radio operator, Valérie wanted to know when to expect Santini and the helicopter.

"Request helicopter estimated landing time," she spoke into the transmitter.

"Helicopter grounded," came the reply.

"Request duration of grounding," Valérie called back.

"Grounding permanent," came the second reply.

There was no further word than that. Valérie had no idea if Santini had reached Hanoi or even Hoa Binh safely.

Was it possible that Santini was forced down or had even crashed en route? she thought to herself.

With no alternative on the horizon, Valérie had to assess her situation. With only an emergency first aid kit and a few nurse's tools, she was woefully ill prepared to treat her casualties with the supplies she had on hand. Quickly writing up a list of necessary items, Valérie got back with the company's radio operator to request an airdrop.

"It was now up to the radioman," Valérie said. "Fortunately, Hanoi quickly answered. They promised an airdrop for tomorrow if weather conditions were favorable."[23]

While attending to her patient, she was interrupted by the sound of two explosions. It turned out that one of the Vietnamese soldiers on the side of the French had set off two land mines.

"I rushed to the victim as his comrades were bringing him back," said Valérie. "He had carelessly wandered away from the barbed wire perimeter where he tripped the landmines. But to my amazement, he wasn't dead."

The land mines had caused considerable damage, however. The man's leg was broken, and he was riddled with shrapnel.

"His condition caused me great concern. I feared that some of the shrapnel fragments had pierced his abdomen." Valérie noted that requesting the airdrop of surgical tools and materials was probably a wise course of action since it seemed that it would be days before help would arrive to transport the wounded.

After another uneasy night, punctuated with occasional volleys of mortar shells lobbed in the direction of the limestone bluff by the Viet Minh, morning arrived once again.

It was the morning of Christmas Eve.

Traditions needed to be maintained and perhaps even more so on the battlefield, where home was so far away on a day that meant so much to so many.

"The Legionnaires strung their small trees with garlands, tinsel, and various decorations," Valérie observed. "Here and there they have put up candles."

Because of General de Lattre, who wanted his fighting men remembered for Christmas, there was an ample supply of food and beverage.

"Thanks to airdropped packages, bottles of champagne, cookies, and other treats were distributed soon before supper. An exceptional menu was planned."[24]

But the desolation and danger that the Legionnaires faced was not lost on Valérie.

"I admired the ingenuity of these able men, in the most tragic and precarious of situations, to celebrate Christmas with a child's happiness. I loved the generosity of heart and soul of these fighting men, who sacrificed their lives without limits. With them that evening, I drew additional reason for solidarity with the army. For me, it was the best of all worlds, the most straightforward and the most selfless."[25]

The ingenuity that Valérie referred to was how the Legionnaires took the time and care to construct makeshift furniture for her to treat her patients.

"In two hours, thanks to them, my operating room was readied," she said. "They had cleared a tent and made a table from bamboo. Above were lights. All was in readiness. All that remained was to wait for my instruments to be parachuted."

It was true. The medical supplies had not been airdropped yet. Valérie maintained a vigil over the more seriously wounded.

"Two lieutenants came up to me and invited me to share their meal," she said. "I thanked them and explained my work would keep me at my patients' bedside until late." With their own among the wounded, the two lieutenants pledged all the help they could.

It was after 10 p.m. when Valérie felt that she could leave the wounded for a few moments. One of the Legionnaires promised to remain on guard in the makeshift infirmary while Valérie stepped away and to notify her of any changes. Outside a thick fog started to envelop the hilltop. Valérie still fretted over whether her medical supplies would be delivered, but nothing could be done until the next morning. In another part of the encampment, she could hear the soldiers celebrating.

"The Legionnaires' song and laughter ring out in the still of the night," Valérie said. With the Legionnaires, Valérie felt safe, confident that the men had done everything within their power to keep the enemy at bay. "The *Viet Minh* could not be allowed to take advantage of the fog to stage an attack."

When Valérie entered the officers' quarters, four Legionnaire lieutenants stood at attention for the captain.

"I was touched by the welcome extended by my two lieutenants who were joined by two more, a paratrooper and a commando lieutenant. We sat down and dug into the meal that was far superior to the ordinary fare we were accustomed to."[26] Valérie had the feeling that it was an encouragement to the men for her to be there that provided some joy and comfort that otherwise would have been missed.[27]

When the clock struck 2400 hours, it was time to savor the most precious of French delicacies in their possession.

"Champagne flowed and it was excellent. Midnight! We raised our glasses. Outside there were sustained bursts of small arms fire. It was our Legionnaires who fire their weapons so as to 'mark the event.' This went on for some ten minutes. The enemy didn't return fire. They were aware of the routine."[28]

The "routine" may have been somewhat reminiscent of the Christmas armistice of World War I, where there was a brief cessation of hostilities on both sides of the trenches in observance of the holiday. But it was highly unlikely that the Viet Minh honored that history. Valérie later learned that, while Xom Bu was spared an attack by the *Viet Minh* on Christmas night, they did attempt an unsuccessful attack on the mobile group led by Lieutenant Colonel Blankaert at Rocher Notre-Dame.

Christmas morning found the hilltop at Xom Bu completely fogged in.

"The morning of the 25th was hardly suitable for an airdrop. The ceiling was low, and I was still worried and without news of Santini," said Valérie. Radio chatter was held to a minimum, as there was a distinct concern that the *Viet Minh* were intercepting communications.

It wasn't until the afternoon that signs became hopeful that the airdrop would happen.

"The weather cleared in the early afternoon and Hanoi advised us that a Dakota was getting ready for takeoff. All eyes turned to the sky."

With Hanoi less than an hour's flight away, it wasn't long before the C-47 reached Xom Bu.

"The aircraft finally appeared; it dove and flew right overhead and that was enough. Their drop was unbelievably accurate."

Among the packages dropped was of course the needed medical supplies, but a mail package was also sent to the soldiers at the outpost. One letter was of specific interest to Valérie.

"I finally found out what happened to Santini," she said.

As she read the letter, she found out that Santini's helicopter had developed mechanical problems on its last run back to Hanoi. It was at night so making any kind of emergency landing was a dangerous proposition. But at least the Hiller gave some warning before refusing to go on, so Santini was able to find a safe haven by landing at a French outpost at Trung La. Landing in total darkness without a lit landing zone laid out was almost an impossible task, but Santini somehow managed it. While the damage to the aircraft was not specified, it was evidently serious enough that the Hiller had to be transported overland back to Gialam, as were the two casualties.

Despite the hope that the Christmas airdrop brought to Xom Bu, rejoicing turned to consternation as Valérie scanned the contents of her medical supply kit. It was far from being as complete as she needed.

"The surgical catgut was left out."

Valérie searched all of the packages included in the airdrop, but the material to close up open wounds was nowhere to be found. Checking the inventory list, she found there was no mention of surgical thread.

"I was sure that the outpost's radio operator didn't omit anything," she said. "I would just have to be content with what was in the first aid kit that I brought with me when we landed at Xom Bu, plus the few tubes of suture thread that Lt. Erhardt left me. Even if I was stingy with what I had, I would only be able to perform three or four surgeries at best. I was relieved that we had been able to evacuate four of the most severe casualties by helicopter already."[29]

But the helicopter was no longer an option for the men who needed the most attention. Without stabilizing their condition on the spot, transporting them by jeep or truck could be a death sentence. Valérie André knew she had no choice but to prepare to operate within the confines of the primitive limestone caves of Xom Bu if there was to be a chance for their survival.

Valérie André and her family in Strasbourg, France, 1929. Valérie is standing to the side of her oldest sister, seated on the right. Valérie was one of nine children, with her youngest sibling born five years after this photo was taken. (Source: Valérie André)

Valérie André at Beynes glider port May 1945, while she was attending medical school at the University of Paris. Piloting a glider was a continuation of Valérie's fascination with flight dating back to her encounter with female aviator Maryse Hilsz when Valérie was only ten. (Source: Valérie André)

Valérie André from late 1947 at the time of her induction in the French Army Service de santé. Although Valérie was commissioned as a captain in the medical corps, her rank was not always seen as equal to her male counterparts in the French Army. (Source: Valérie André)

Alexis Santini and a Hiller 360 rescue helicopter at Tan Son Nhut airfield, Saigon, Vietnam, 1950. Santini was France's first military helicopter pilot. He would also go on to become the founder of France's first military helicopter flight training school in 1955. Alexis Santini and Valérie André would be married in 1963. (Source: Valérie André)

Alexis Santini (seated, center) and Raymond Fumat (standing behind Santini) along with Hiller UH-12A/360 in hangar at Tan Son Nhut, Saigon, Vietnam. Santini and Fumat were the first to establish a military helicopter service for France in Indochina. Fumat would later be sent back to France following an accident involving a jeep. (Source: Valérie André)

Valérie André undergoing training in a Hiller UH-12/360 at Helicop-Air's flight school at Cormeilles-en-Vexin, France. (Source: Valérie André)

Valérie André completing her final solo flight at Cormeilles-en-Vexin, August 11, 1950. (Source: Valérie André)

FÉDÉRATION AÉRONAUTIQUE INTERNATIONALE

FRANCE

Nous soussignés, pouvoir sportif reconnu par la F. A. I. pour la FRANCE certifions que

Mademoiselle ANDRÉ Valérie

né le 21 avril 1922

à Strasbourg (Bas-Rhin)

ayant rempli toutes les conditions imposées par la F. A. I. a été breveté :

PILOTE d'HÉLICOPTÈRE

L'AÉRO CLUB DE FRANCE

Le Président,

Date 1er septembre N° 33 1950

BREVET DE PILOTE D'HÉLICOPTÈRE

délivré par

L'AÉRO-CLUB DE FRANCE

6, Rue Galilée

PARIS

Photo du Titulaire

(Signature du Titulaire)

Valérie André's helicopter pilot's license, dated September 1, 1950. Valérie was the 33rd helicopter pilot licensed by the Aeroclub de France. (Source: Valérie André)

Valérie André and Hiller UH-12/360 following her first solo medical rescue mission to Bat Nao, Vietnam, on March 16, 1952, where she rescued two wounded French soldiers. Valérie's missions often placed her in dangerous combat zones and the Hiller provided little protection from enemy gunfire. (Source: Valérie André)

Valérie André receiving medals for her role as a military parachutist and combat field surgeon from General Jean de Lattre de Tassigny following her medical mission to Laos in the Summer of 1951. De Lattre was commander-in-chief of France's military force in Indochina. The death of his son, Bernard de Lattre, killed during combat near Phat Diem in May 1951, followed by de Lattre's own death in January 1952, dealt an emotional blow not only to Valérie André, but also to France's entire military mission in Indochina. (Source: Valérie André)

Valérie André not only served as a surgeon and medical rescue pilot in Indochina, but also as a field surgeon dropped by parachute into remote French outposts. When Valérie parachuted into Muong Ngat, Laos, on July 23, 1951, the native Meo people called her "the woman who came from the sky." (Source: Valérie André)

Valérie André en route to Bat Nao, March 16, 1952. The various rivers and other geographic features of Vietnam often served as landmarks to guide Valérie to remote outposts. (Source: Valérie André)

Alexis Santini, Valérie André, and Henri Bartier at Tan Son Nhut air base, Saigon, Vietnam, 1951. Bartier was brought in to replace pilot Raymond Fumat, who suffered a severe back injury in a jeep accident. (Source: Valérie André)

Alexis Santini, Valérie André, and Henri Bartier at Tan Son Nhut air base, Saigon, Vietnam, 1951. (Source: Valérie André)

Valérie André studying a map prior to a rescue mission, circa 1952. (Source: Valérie André)

Valérie André and the Hiller UH-12/360. Despite its occasionally temperamental mechanical nature, Valérie trusted the helicopter to get her through the toughest missions. (Source: Valérie André)

Valérie André in flight over northern Vietnam, 1952. (Source: Valérie André)

Valérie André helping to offload a wounded soldier at Lanessan Hospital, Hanoi, Vietnam, 1952. (Source: Valérie André)

Valérie André inspecting a bullet hole that tore through her helicopter on March 30, 1952, nearly hitting one of her two wounded passengers. (Source: Valérie André)

Henri Bartier rescuing a wounded soldier in northern Vietnam, undated photo. (Source: Robert Genay/Association Hélicoptères Air)

Wounded solider on a litter waiting to be transported, Xuan Mai, March 1953.
(Source: Robert Genay/Association Hélicoptères Air)

Valérie André and Hiller helicopter, Indochina, 1951. (Source: Marcel Poirée and ECPA Photo Cinema Video des Armees)

Valérie André and Hiller helicopter, Indochina, 1951. (Source: Marcel Poirée and ECPA Photo Cinema Video des Armees)

Valérie André and Hiller helicopter, Indochina, 1951. (Source: Marcel Poirée and ECPA Photo Cinema Video des Armees)

Valérie André preparing for inspection at Gialam air base, Hanoi, September 1952. When Alexis Santini left Valérie in charge of the helicopter section of ELA 53, she became the first female commander of an active aviation unit in the French military. (Source: Robert Genay/ Association Hélicoptères Air)

Valérie André and Hiller UH-12/360 over Gialam air base, Hanoi, October 1952.
(Source: Valérie André)

Loading wounded soldiers onto a Hiller H-23B rescue helicopter in a combat zone.
Danger from Viet Minh weapons fire was always present whenever the helicopter was
on the ground. (Source: Marcel Poirée and ECPA Photo Cinema Video des Armees)

Aftermath of a crash involving Valérie André at Gialam, in May 1952. The helicopter lost power during takeoff and crash landed only 30 feet off the ground. Valerie was unhurt, but checked herself into Lanessan Hospital suffering from both fatigue and amoebic dysentery. (Source: Robert Genay/Association Hélicoptères Air)

Helicopter pilots and mechanics of Escadrille de Liaisons Aériennes 53 (ELA 53), December 1952. Henri Bartier, Valérie André, *médecin général* Bergeret, and Alexis Santini are shown near the middle section of the helicopter. (Source: Michel Fleurence)

Hiller rescue helicopter loaded onto Bristol transport plane bound for Na San, Vietnam, November 1952. (Source: Robert Genay/Association Hélicoptères Air)

Georges Le Goff, Valérie André, René Fayolle, and Henri Bronner, at Na San land/air base in December 1952. Na San was a prelude to the battle at Dien Bien Phu a year later. (Source: Robert Genay/Association Hélicoptères Air)

Valérie André just before leaving Vietnam for the final time in March 1953. (Source: Robert Genay/Association Hélicoptères Air)

Henri Bartier's H-19 Sikorsky moments before it was destroyed by the Viet Minh during a rescue attempt at Dien Bien Phu on March 23, 1954. Bartier lost his leg in the attack and wounded soldier Alain Gambiez was killed in the subsequent fire. (Source: Michel Fleurence)

Henri Bartier receiving the Croix de Guerre with palm award from General Jean Dechaux, commander of GATAC Nord, Lanessan Hospital, April 1954. (Source: Michel Fleurence)

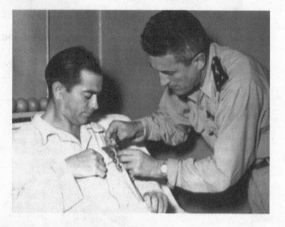

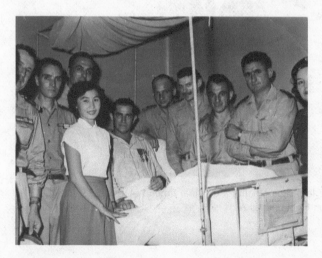

Henri Bartier next to his wife, twenty-five-year-old Marie Yvonne Bartier, at Lanessan Hospital, April 1954, Hanoi, following the presentation of Bartier's Legion of Honour and Croix de Guerre with palm award from General Dechaux, second from right. (Source: Michel Fleurence)

Valérie André receiving the Legion of Merit award from U.S. Secretary of the Air Force Harold E. Talbot, October 1953. Valérie's reputation as a rescue pilot in Indochina was well known all over the world by the time she returned to France in 1953. (Source: Michel Fleurence)

Valérie André and Alexis Santini with French Air Force General Martial Valin at a honors dinner at Hotel George V in Paris, 1954. (Source: Valérie André)

Valérie André returned to the battlefront in 1959 during the French war in Algeria. In Algeria Valérie flew the larger Sikorsky H-19 and H-34 helicopters into combat areas, transporting troops and supplies, and rescuing the wounded. She also served as chief medical officer at Reghaïa air base near Algiers. (Source: Valérie André)

Valérie André in command of a Sikorsky H-34, 1959. The war in Algeria has often been referred to as the first helicopter war because of the extensive use of helicopters for troop transport to battle zones. (Source: Valérie André)

Valérie André along with pilots and crew of her helicopter squadron in the Djebel mountain range of Algeria, 1959. In the background is a Sikorsky H-34, one of the most advanced helicopters used during the Algerian conflict. (Source: Valérie André)

Alexis Santini, prior to his retirement from the French Air Force in 1963. Valérie André often referred to Santini as the man who mattered most in her life. Valérie and Santini lived in Issy-les-Moulineaux until his death in 1997 at the age of 82. (Source: Valérie André)

Valérie André and Georges Agrissais's Sikorsky H-34 stranded at Sid bel Larbi, southern Algeria, January 23, 1960, after suffering an engine failure. (Source: Valérie André)

Valérie André receiving her promotion to general from French President George Pompidou on April 21, 1976. Valérie André was France's first female general and was instrumental in promoting equal rights in France's military during her career. (Source: Valérie André)

Valérie André and Alexis Santini celebrating Valérie's promotion on the evening of April 21, 1976. (Source: Valérie André)

Valérie André from 1976. Aviation remained a lifelong passion for Valérie. (Source: Valérie André)

President Francois Mitterand congratulating Valérie André after she was awarded the Grand Officer Legion of Honour on September 18, 1981. (Source: Valérie André)

General Valérie Edmée André.
(Source: Valérie André)

Valérie André in Paris,
May 2017. (Source:
Charles Morgan Evans)

Chapter 24

Operating in the Wilderness

Xom Bu, Vietnam, December 1951

The operating room the Legionnaires set up for Valérie André in their cave outpost was an improvised effort at best. With no hope of moving the patients to Hanoi any time soon, the shelter of the cave would have to suffice. The electrician who operated the camp's generator managed to gather every light fixture he had and had set them up in the area where Valérie was working, but the lighting inside was still poor.

"Primitive conditions always seemed to be the rule, never the exception," Valérie recalled.

Poor sanitation, nonexistent disinfection, and myriad sources of extraneous debris were just some of the issues Valérie had to deal with. Yet she knew that some of the casualties under her care would die without any sort of intervention. With the makeshift tables the Legionnaires fashioned out of scraps of bamboo, and the gasoline generator clattering away outside the cave to provide light, there was at least a facility she could put to use.

The Legionnaire medic, Lieutenant Erhardt, had returned to assist Valérie, who was preparing for her first procedure.

"To assist me, the one medic would not suffice."

Valérie put out a call for additional help from the other Legionnaires.

"I asked for two volunteers and several showed up."[1]

One of the Legionnaires' own, a warrant officer with a severe head wound, was carried by two men and placed on the table.

"I had to shave his skull. It was necessary for the procedure." Removing hair and debris was difficult, as a good part of the skin covering his skull was peeled away and torn from the wound he had received. Typical of the toughness of a Foreign Legionnaire, he was still conscious through it all.

"He smiled at me as he was given the local anesthetic," Valérie recalled.

The outward toughness of her patient, however, didn't necessarily apply to everyone in the operating room. As Valérie probed the open skull wound of the soldier, she noticed something wasn't quite right with one of her assistants.

"In the middle of the intervention, one of my helpers whispered something that I didn't understand. He rushed out of the room."

Valérie had seen this happen before.

"They may have been hardened from combat, but they weren't used to the atmosphere of the operating room."

One of the other soldiers donned surgical gloves and took his comrade's place.

"Cutting off and cleaning up the edges of the skin took only a few minutes," Valérie said. "Upon further scrutiny I could find no injury to the external bone structure."

While the procedure was relatively routine, the suture thread omitted from the airdrop of medical supplies immediately became a critical issue.

"I had to put a drain in place to relieve pressure," she said. "In view of the loss of skin tissue I had great difficulty in sewing up the edges of the wound."[2]

Valérie's next patient was the Viet Minh political officer with a severe gunshot wound to his head. Her enlisted medics placed him on the table, and Valérie worried that the man's condition had worsened. She could sense that the Legionnaires were not altogether happy with the idea of providing care to the enemy.

"He cast haggard looks at us. He knew he was in bad shape."

Applying anesthesia by hypodermic needle to the officer calmed him to some degree.

"He could sense that our ministrations were necessary, nevertheless he was understandably scared," she said of her patient. "He obeyed quietly but kept on asking if I will make him well."

Once he was sedated, Valérie began to cut away skin from both the entry and exit points through which the bullet had passed. Using a hypodermic needle, she squirted jets of antibiotic serum inside the wound both to cleanse and to flush out a mess of extraneous brain tissue and bone fragments.

Valérie lamented the lack of equipment and poor conditions.

"This type of emergency surgery work in the field is very difficult. I only had makeshift equipment. There was no possibility of aspiration or electro-coagulation and the center of infection was quite widespread."

Electro-coagulation devices provided a useful method of cauterizing tissue and staunching blood flow. The process promoted healing and allowed a surgeon to make more precise incisions. But the machines of that era were bulky and could not be airdropped into a combat zone. With no alternative, Valérie had to adapt to what was at hand.

"With streams of serum, I cleaned out the trajectory of the bullet as much as possible," she said. "I used a great deal of antibiotics, and once I dressed the skin and muscle wounds I closed off both orifices using standard procedures."[3]

The third man requiring surgery that day was the allied Vietnamese soldier who had accidentally tripped off a pair of landmines.

"He was much less receptive to local anesthetic," Valérie said of this particular patient. "But he was more reconciled [to anesthetic] soon enough when I showed him a large fragment, the size of a walnut, taken out from the back of his knee."

Valérie treated the man's wounds to the best of her ability, but she worried that he would need additional intervention.

"I kept an eye on the young Vietnamese who blew up on the mine. For him, I saved my small supply of catgut. It was impossible to know if a fragment had entered his abdomen or just remained stuck in the patient's side."[4]

With her supply of surgical thread nearly exhausted, Valérie limited surgery just to the three most seriously wounded. For the other men, she liberally administered antibiotics. Gangrene and tetanus were constant threats to full recovery.

December 26 and 27, 1951, were relatively quiet days for the Legionnaires in the area of Xom Bu. The Legionnaires had dropped into Xom Bu by parachute to secure the area, but the road leading out of there was still considered dangerous. A Viet Minh ambush was considered a high probability.

"The two lieutenants in charge of the platoon didn't know how long the hilltop would be cut off from the outside world and they organized things accordingly," Valérie said. The Legionnaires still required food and ammunition to be dropped by supply planes to continue the defense of their post.

Late in the afternoon of December 27, however, a patrol of Legionnaire paratroopers turned up with Lieutenant Erhardt. Valérie told the men that it was imperative to get the wounded to a hospital. Erhardt had patrolled the area and knew the dangers involved in evacuating.

"We discussed the chances of reaching the airfield at Ap Phu To by jeep so that the medical Morane could be used to evacuate the men to Hanoi," Valérie said.

Ap Phu To was not far from the hilltop at Xom Bu, but the Legionnaires' radio operator had not been successful in raising the French garrison manning the airfield.

Speculation and opinion for the evacuation of the wounded were hotly debated. Erhardt and his commandos had not encountered any of the enemy in their patrols but were still uneasy about the chances of slow-moving vehicles carrying casualties going unmolested.

"The discussion was lively," Valérie said. "But it was nevertheless evident . . . that an evacuation should be attempted."[5]

On December 28, Valérie readied her patients for transport.

"Again, I dressed all of the wounds and I examined the mine casualty with special care," she said. She still felt uncertain about the man's abdominal wound, and she hoped she was correct that it could wait for further treatment.

"I decided to leave with the wounded," she continued. "The convoy was to consist of an old Dodge ambulance, the only one in the region, and a truck. We displayed a white flag with a red cross to fully let the enemy know the nature of our transport."[6]

Just as uneasy as she felt about the condition of some of her patients, Valérie had real concerns about what would be encountered on the road to Ap Phu To.

"We arranged the litters in the truck and ambulance," Valérie said. Because space was limited in the two vehicles, the less severely wounded men would sit upright to make room for the wounded who required more care.

Once she was satisfied with the arrangements for her men, Valérie took her seat in the Dodge ambulance next to the driver.

"The signal for departure was given," she said. "The vehicles moved along slowly, as the road was not very good. Although driven by the hope of reaching Hanoi, I sensed the wounded were not very reassured."[7]

The small convoy started out with the Legionnaire commandos, but they had orders to remain at Xom Bu. After a few kilometers, Lieutenant Erhardt told Valérie that they could go no further. The medical convoy would be on its own without an armed escort.

An uneasy feeling permeated the air. The road was flat but felt seemingly endless, especially when an ambush could strike at any moment. All eyes and ears were tuned to any anomaly on the road ahead.

"The engine noise from the Dodge seemed deafening," Valérie said. "It disturbed the silence of the rice paddies. All were on alert."

As the two trucks rolled on, human figures that appeared to be crouched low to the ground—as if to train their fire on the oncoming convoy—came into view. The trucks slowed, but the figures remained still.

"They were dead bodies, abandoned several days ago already," Valérie said, unconvinced that danger was not present. "The *Viet Minh* never leave their own remain unburied. I concluded that the rebels had not yet returned to the scene of the fight. But they would be back."[8]

Fortunately, the dead were not an omen of worse things to come, but the road suddenly came up to a river crossing that stopped the two trucks from proceeding. There was a bridge, but it was under repair by a group of civilian Vietnamese workers supervised by a French lieutenant. The group had managed to travel four miles so far, but there were two miles to go before they would reach the airfield at Ap Phu To. Crossing the bridge at that moment didn't look very promising.

"In the condition the bridge was in, a jeep might have been able to make it through, but the ambulance was too heavy and the truck was completely out of the question," Valérie noted as she stepped out of the ambulance to speak with the lieutenant. She told the lieutenant that she was a doctor and was anxious to reach an airfield to transfer the wounded to Hanoi as soon as possible. As she spoke, she noticed the trucks on the other side of the river.

"I proposed a vehicle swap," Valérie said. "The officer was very understanding. He would lend me the vehicles that brought his workman out to the site and in exchange I handed over the truck and ambulance to him. I formally promised that I would return his property to him, and the deal was done."

The deal was not quite finished, however. What remained was the transfer of the wounded from the vehicles on one side of the bridge to the vehicles on the other side.

"Because the beams of the bridge were too shaky, the litter bearers labored on the steep slopes of the river bank and waded through the water. It took an hour to complete the transfer and then we were off again."[9]

With only a few miles to go and no known impediments to delay the journey again, everyone, including Valérie, began to breathe easier. But Valérie could see that the local inhabitants—many of whom were the ethnic minority known as Montagnards—were wary of any activity along the road.

"Scattered along the road, a few huts appeared. The noise of our engines sent their occupants into hiding. 'What was the purpose of this convoy?' they must have been asking themselves."

Many of the Montagnards were allied to the French, and that alliance often put them at deadly odds with the Viet Minh. Reprisals were commonplace.

Finally, the group reached their destination.

The entrance to the airfield at Ap Phu To was under guard, and Valérie immediately asked to speak with the radio operator stationed there. She was anxious to arrange evacuation by aircraft for her wounded men as soon as possible.

"Thanks to a field telephone, I was able to reach the zone commander," Valérie said.

But the zone commander—the one person who could authorize the dispatch of medical transport planes—replied back through the radiophone, "I'll be back in fifteen minutes."

Valérie found the zone commander's response unacceptable, especially after the long ordeal that she and her charges had already experienced.

"That wasn't exactly what I wanted and I told him as much," she said emphatically. "I insisted that he immediately authorize the evacuation of the thirteen casualties."[10]

"I will notify the commander of the liaison squadron," came back the terse reply.

Not long after that last transmission, Valérie saw a Morane plane on approach to the runway.

"I couldn't believe my eyes," she recalled incredulously. "No, it wasn't possible for Bach Mai airfield in Hanoi to have already responded. It wasn't a Morane ambulance plane."

Valérie was correct; it wasn't one of the Morane Criquets outfitted to carry the wounded, but it was transporting medical personnel.

"Out of the aircraft that just landed climbed Colonel Richet and Colonel Boron," Valérie said.

Colonel Pierre Richet's reputation was especially well known to Valérie. Dr. Richet had organized health services for the Free French during World War II and was highly decorated for his role during the liberation of France. After the war, Colonel Richet was instrumental in the organization of French medical services in Indochina and had a hand in the formation of the advanced surgical antenna units. General de Lattre personally requested Richet to return to Indochina to inspect medical services throughout the colony.

Richet and Boron were surprised to see Valérie.

"They thought I was still stuck in Xom Bu," she said. Boron, who was also a surgeon, asked Valérie if it was all right to examine the wounded men under her care.

"He was satisfied with their condition, but confided a concern to me," Valérie said. The concern centered on the Viet Minh political officer with the severe gunshot wound to the head who was still under her care.

"Shouldn't the *Viet* prisoner go back to Hanoi with guards?" Boron said to her.

The Viet Minh prisoner's condition had markedly improved, but Valérie maintained a vigil over the man for an altogether different reason.

"To tell the truth, I kept a close eye on him, not so much to impede his escape but to prevent our soldiers from doing him in," she confessed. "They kept throwing him dirty looks. To me a wounded man is sacred."

Valérie also added that she sensed little threat from her patient/prisoner.

"I have to admit that his antics were amusing," she observed. "As soon as he saw too many people around, he would hide behind me."[11]

, Boron deferred the Viet Minh officer to Valérie's care.

Later that same day, a welcome occurrence played out.

"Four young men in rags showed up," Valérie said. "They explained that their river convoy had come under bazooka attack from the enemy. They were the only survivors and miraculously unhurt."[12]

The battle between the French and Viet Minh had just started to flare up along the Black River itself. General Giap knew the river acted as a vital supply for the French's so-called de Lattre line of outposts and had directed the Viet Minh to attack shipping. French sailors navigated armed riverboats, known as Dinassauts, on Vietnam's waterways and rivers. *Dinassaut* was an acronym for Division navale assaut (Naval Assault Division).

Dinassaut patrols often took part in floating convoys escorting supply barges that brought food and ammunition to French fortifications in the area. As Valérie learned firsthand, the roads to remote outposts like Xom Bu and Rocher Notre-Dame were barely passable. Trucks traveling overland had to crawl along at slow speeds and negotiate poorly maintained bridges to move crucial supplies. The river was the more logical supply route for the French, and General Giap realized that as well. Giap and the Viet Minh began to shift their attack on French outposts to supply convoys on the Black River in late December 1951. As Bernard Fall described the conflict:

[T]he *Dinassauts* . . . render[ed] invaluable services to the hard-pressed defenders of the Hoa Binh pocket. Probably the bloodiest river battles since
the American Civil War were fought out between the French and *Viet Minh*
in the restricted confines of the Black River around Rocher Notre Dame . . .
ships [were] attacked by gunfire, mines, and even frogmen. . . . [The] small
self-contained "fleets" fighting on their own 250 miles inland on streams and
rivers for which there did not even exist naval charts and for which their craft
had never been designed.[13]

The four sailors Valérie encountered were survivors of one such assault.
Their convoy came under a "bazooka"[14] attack. After their boat began to
take on water and started to sink, they were forced to abandon the craft;
however, they managed to swim to shore and hide out along the shoreline,
evading capture. Eventually, they were able to reach one of the mobile
groups stationed at Rocher Notre-Dame and were transported to the airfield
at Ap Phu To.

The sailors bore no serious injuries but were nonetheless anxious to return
to Hanoi.

"For the past two days they have been waiting for a navy aircraft," Valérie
learned. "They asked if I could take them aboard the Morane ambulance
plane."

The Morane Criquet ambulance could only accommodate three individuals—the pilot, a passenger in the empty copilot's seat, and a man reclining
in a stretcher in a compartment aft of the cockpit—it was not possible for
Valérie to agree to their request when she had thirteen men who required
immediate evacuation.

"I'll tell the commander of the liaison squadron to send more planes," she
told the sailors. "It will be arranged."

Not long after this exchange, Valérie scanned the skies. To her relief, she
caught a glimpse of two small planes far out on the horizon. Two Morane
ambulance planes were now rapidly approaching the airfield.

"They landed in turn and one of them took on two casualties," Valérie
said. "One of the pilots, Captain de Grandpré, reassured the sailors that a
transport for them would be on the way."

De Grandpré was true to his word. As soon as he took off, another plane
dropped down on the runway.

"A navy anchor was clearly visible on the fuselage," Valérie said. "My
sailors were elated."[15]

Things progressed rapidly from this point on. Soon, three more Morane ambulance planes arrived. Along with the Dinassaut sailors, the most serious casualties had been evacuated to Hanoi.

"I learned from the pilot that two more aircraft were on their way. I was to take my place on the last one." In typical fashion for Valérie—who always believed her patient's care and comfort came first—she took her position in the stretcher compartment of the Morane Criquet, allowing the less seriously wounded soldier to occupy the copilot's seat in the cabin.

"The speed with which the evacuation took place was all to the credit of Captain Martin, who flew the aircraft in which I took off. Alas! A few months later Captain Martin would be killed during a night evacuation."[16]

Once in the air, the flight to Hanoi was accomplished in short order. It seemed as if no time had passed when the Morane plane with Valérie André touched down at Bach Mai airfield in the capital city. While that final airflight had been relatively smooth, the trip to the hospital was an altogether different experience.

"After we got off the planes at Bach Mai, we went by ambulance to the hospital," Valérie said. "The ambulance trip from the airport to the hospital was painful—the road was full of holes, the bumps jostled the wounded."

Along the way, Valérie thought to herself that there had to be a better way to transport casualties.

"Perhaps someday—when at last we have enough helicopters available— we will be able to transport the wounded directly from the theater of operations to the hospital courtyard."[17]

The thought was prescient. As the number of helicopters multiplied and improved in their capabilities, countless lives—both military and civilian— would be saved.

Valérie André would soon play her role in turning that idea into a reality.

Chapter 25

Ventilateur Calling

"King Jean" was dead.

General Jean de Lattre, whose only son gave his life in battle some seven months before, left Indochina for the final time in December 1951. He returned home to Paris, where he died on January 11, 1952. Only those closest to the general's innermost circle knew that he had advanced stage cancer. But the death of Bernard had also hung like a specter around de Lattre. A black armband over the left sleeve of his uniform served as a constant reminder of his loss. As he lay dying, General de Lattre's last words were:

"Where's Bernard?"[1]

The news of General de Lattre's death was met with shock in Indochina. The year 1951 was christened by many as the "Year of de Lattre." Under de Lattre, the French reversed the losses they had suffered in the previous year. But with de Lattre's passing, uncertainty about France's future in Vietnam was once again foremost on everyone's mind. Valérie André's thoughts were echoed by many.

"We felt like orphans, upset and distressed," Valérie reflected. "With de Lattre alive, we questioned little about the outcome of the war that still remained cruel and deadly. But with his passing, it was a time of doubt. The distress, the perplexity in the face of an unrelenting bloodbath, weighed on our daily struggle. It was like a bad premonition of what was to come."[2]

In the single year that de Lattre was in Vietnam, his impact was far-reaching. He had put the French army on an offensive footing—even though that entailed the controversial use of napalm and increased aerial bombardment. He had also started a program to include more Vietnamese to take up the fight against the Viet Minh. Even with his physical condition weakened by cancer, de Lattre went to the United States in fall 1951. During his visit to the United States, he successfully lobbied President Truman to send more military aid and equipment to the French in Indochina. Some felt that if de Lattre had continued in Indochina, there might have been a chance for France to negotiate an honorable withdrawal from Vietnam. But with de Lattre gone, there was a vacuum in French military leadership. The "orphans" left in the aftermath of de Lattre's passing would have to continue on.

Nha Ba Tha was one of the lonelier outposts in Vietnam that French troops endured. Although it was only a little more than an hour away from Hanoi by dirt road, it only merited a pinpoint on military maps of northern Vietnam. Nha Ba Tha was a remote village where another in a series of defensive French military outposts existed as part of the "de Lattre line."

If one were to look for Nha Ba Tha on a modern map, it would be as if it never existed. Yet in the early months of 1952, Valérie André found herself assigned to a military field hospital there. The assignment was temporary, as Valérie was now permanently assigned to ELA 52. Santini had lobbied on her behalf for formal attachment to the squadron, especially after her extended mission with the Foreign Legion at Xom Bu the previous month. She had proven herself to be an asset in Santini's estimation. Santini knew he wanted Valérie on the team he was assembling, as the medical role of the helicopter would be expanding very soon.

But Valérie wasn't altogether satisfied with her latest mission to Nha Ba Tha. She had hoped to be operational as a rescue helicopter pilot by now. But the mechanically unpredictable nature of the only two Hiller rescue helicopters serving Indochina had upset her plan. One of the Hillers was taken out of service, waiting for replacement parts to arrive at Gialam air base in Hanoi, where the helicopters were now based. Santini had left for Saigon to retrieve the only operating aircraft.

"I received orders to replace a colleague at the field hospital in Nha Ba Tha," Valérie said. The doctor stationed at the field hospital had been summoned to Hoa Binh to tend to an emergency there, although the campaign at Hoa Binh was winding down by February 1952.

The battle at Hoa Binh, initiated at the end of 1951, was Jean de Lattre's last gamble in Indochina; however, the battle did not yield an overwhelming victory. General Vo Nguyen Giap would not be baited into committing the bulk of his Viet Minh army against the better-equipped French army. Instead,

Giap fell back into the tried and true tactics of sporadic guerilla attacks with smaller forces on isolated French outposts, such as the massacre at Tu Vu that occurred in December. Once again, it was the Viet Minh tiger emerging from the dark jungle to claw at the back of the French elephant. As a result, by February 1952, General Raoul Salan, de Lattre's successor as commander of France's military force in Indochina, had ordered a substantial withdrawal from Hoa Binh.

Back at Nha Ba Tha, Valérie found herself in a mostly caretaker position at the field hospital. Fortunately, an airfield was located near the hospital so that casualties could be flown by plane to Hanoi.

"Rather than keep the wounded at the field hospital, I preferred to transfer the casualties by ambulance or airplane," said Valérie. "The surgical activity was very light, and I soon found myself idle. Air transport was only justified at night. From dusk to dawn, the road to Hanoi was dangerous."[3]

The assignment was brief, only ten days before her replacement arrived, and soon Valérie left for Hanoi. When she arrived at Gialam, Valérie's first stop was at ELA 52's temporary hangar to learn the latest news of her comrades.

"As always, I was warmly welcomed back to the base," Valérie said.

A number of changes had taken place while she was gone. Santini was still with the only operational helicopter in the south. Valérie learned that he would return north with the aircraft the following week. Additionally, most of the necessary parts to put the second Hiller back into service had arrived, with the rest expected to turn up shortly. The biggest news she learned, however, was that Chief Warrant Officer Henri Bartier was returning soon from France.

Although Bartier's record was undoubtedly above reproach, his return to Indochina sparked some degree of consternation in Valérie as to her own status. Valérie felt that her time as a solo pilot might not materialize with only one functioning helicopter at Gialam and Bartier now a part of the team.

"Will I ever really fly on my own?"[4]

While at Gialam, Valérie ran into a fixed-wing reconnaissance and medical rescue pilot named Francis Varcin. At thirty-nine years of age, Lieutenant Varcin had already spent nearly twenty years in the French air force, enlisting in 1932, with more than three years spent in Indochina. He was on his second tour of duty in the Far East.[5]

Varcin seemed anxious and wanted to speak out of earshot of any other officers there. It was as if a feeling of deep foreboding hung over him, and

Valérie sensed it immediately. He was reluctant to say too much while they were at the air base. Still, he wanted to meet with Valérie at Le Manoir, a small restaurant in Hanoi popular with French officers. Valérie agreed.

"One of the expectations of a doctor was to act as a confidant with soldiers and officers. Often, one confesses in all safety what cannot be said to those in command."

It also helped that Valérie was not only a doctor but also a woman. The compassion and understanding from that perspective were far different and, in many ways, more important than it would be from opening up to any male soldier.

As it turned out, Valérie's intuition proved to be correct. Varcin was troubled, but not in the conventional sense. While war fatigue was common among soldiers, Varcin, on the contrary, always passed on more straightforward assignments. In December, Varcin flew twenty-three reconnaissance missions over dangerous areas. If anything, the adrenalin from the danger was his constant motivation.

The conversation also touched on politics, especially the growing sentiment of the press and intellectuals in France that referred to the war in Indochina as *la guerre sale*, or "dirty war."

"France, for the most part, not only cared little for the fate of soldiers in Indochina but held this conflict to be despicable: 'the dirty war,'" Valérie opined.[6]

With Valérie, Varcin also spoke volumes about his wife and son who were back in France and how he desperately missed being with them. The long separation was especially hard on Varcin, as his infant son was born after his last leave to France, and he had not yet seen him.[7]

"We traded gossip of the happenings around Gialam airbase, but often the conversation returned to the subject of his wife, his family, and then his wife again," Valérie said, sensing the pain that Varcin felt and, perhaps, a premonition. "It was as if he were trying to give himself up to a pain, to exorcise a doubt. At that moment, I saw only a comrade . . . nostalgic of his family and who was speaking to a woman to indulge in confidences. It was as if to fight against a fatality that was becoming obsessive."[8]

Valérie was certain that Varcin was avoiding a deeply disturbing subject, thoughts that seemed to hang over him and were without resolution. After dinner that evening, Valérie and Lieutenant Varcin parted company. Varcin had an early morning reconnaissance mission that would take him over Viet Minh–controlled territory. But Valérie was left with a very uncertain feeling about the pilot.

The next day, Varcin arrived as usual at Gialam and met with an officer who was to accompany him on the reconnaissance mission as an observer. Varcin treated the mission as any of the many scores of reconnaissance missions he had flown in the unarmed Morane Criquet.

The high command had wanted an update on Viet Minh activity along Route Coloniale (RC) 6, the main road that ran between Hanoi and Hoa Binh to the west. Even though General Salan had withdrawn the majority of troops deployed in the November offensive, there was always the fear a push from Giap could once again place Hanoi in danger of being overrun.

The flight started routinely, mostly following RC 6 tightly and at low altitude. Suddenly machine-gun fire erupted from the ground and sprayed the air surrounding the Criquet. The Viet Minh had stepped up their firepower and were using machine guns supplied by the Soviet Union through China that had better range and accuracy. In an instant, bullets tore through the lightly skinned fuselage. Varcin's passenger emerged unscathed from the attack, and the shots had missed the vital functions of the aircraft.

But Varcin was hit.

At least one of the bullets that shot up through the plane's fuselage had managed to pierce the pilot seat and struck Varcin on the right side of his body. He was bleeding profusely. While Varcin maintained control of the Criquet, there was no way he would remain conscious long enough to return to Gialam in Hanoi; however, he knew there was a clearing with enough area to land his airplane near the French outpost at Xuan Pheo. With all of his reserve, Varcin guided the plane there and safely landed.

The observer leaped out and frantically called out to some soldiers who already knew that the plane was in distress. The observer had the door on the pilot's side of the aircraft already propped open, and with the help of the soldiers, he lifted Varcin from the plane. But it was already too late.

Lieutenant Francis Varcin was dead.[9]

The news of Varcin's death traveled quickly and in little time reached Gialam. Valérie was stunned when she learned what had happened.

"I couldn't bring myself to believe in this death and thought of our tete-a-tete from the past evening," Valérie said. "Was it a premonition of death that he dreaded last night and something that he couldn't tell me anything about?"[10]

Valérie's question would go unanswered. Lieutenant Varcin would be honored by his country and included in France's Legion of Honour. But the loss was just another reminder of how fleeting life had become in Indochina.

As for Valérie, she had begun to spend more time at Gialam. Gialam was twelve kilometers to the east of Hanoi and bordered the banks of the Red River. It was the second of two airfields used by the French near Hanoi, with a much smaller field at Bach Mai in the heart of Hanoi also active.

At the time, Valérie was temporarily living out of the Hotel Splendide in Hanoi. She would commute by jeep the twelve kilometers from the city's center near Hoan Kiem Lake to the air base. One morning, as Valérie prepared to go out to Gialam, she noticed a stray dog wandering near her hotel. In Vietnam, stray dogs are common to the point where they are often considered unwanted nuisances. It was a small, light brown dog living on the streets, probably since the day he was born. The likelihood was that the dog would wander the streets of Hanoi until he was hit by a car or truck.

Despite a hard life, the dog was not altogether skittish as most street dogs were in Hanoi. Presently, the dog singled out Valérie for attention and ventured up to her.

"*Another orphan*," Valérie thought to herself as the dog looked up at her with his pleading brown eyes. The dog seemed to understand her every word.

It was not her intention to adopt a stray, but the dog was not easily discouraged. The dog needed a home and had decided that he now belonged to Valérie. On impulse, Valérie decided to take the dog with her to Gialam. She noted that other air units had various animals as squadron mascots, and Valérie decided that ELA 52 would have one as well.

At Gialam, there was a steady influx of U.S. aircraft due to the increased military aid coming from the United States to Indochina. Because of this, the base was growing with more personnel from the increased activity with aircraft. With the completion of her assignment at Nha Ba Tha, Valérie was now spending nearly all of her time at the base.

When she arrived with her new charge, the flight crew immediately took to the little brown dog and agreed to adopt the mongrel as their squadron mascot. In a moment of inspiration, the little brown dog was named "Rotor," apropos for the mascot of a helicopter unit.[11]

In late January 1952, Alexis Santini returned to Gialam along with the Hiller. To save unnecessary hours on the mechanicals and airframe on the Hiller by flying from Saigon to Hanoi, the aircraft was partially disassembled and loaded onto a transport plane that arrived at Gialam. Santini and helicopter mechanic Adjutant Georges Le Goff supervised the Hiller's transport.

Valérie was still concerned that Bartier was to become operational as a solo rescue pilot before her. But as she learned more about the new addition to the team, even she had to concede that there was good reason for the young pilot to be activated for solo missions sooner.

"Bartier had accomplished real feats in terms of medical evacuation," Valérie admitted. "He had been flying a Morane all over Tonkin and knew the country thoroughly. It was only natural that he would have precedence over me and be released first."[12]

Despite Valérie's apprehension, ultimately it would be Alexis Santini who would have the final word. Although Bartier was an accomplished fixed-wing pilot, Santini recognized that Valérie had put in her time and was uncompromising as both a doctor and a pilot. Her time would come, but Bartier would indeed be "released" or activated first.

Henri Bartier had been in Indochina since 1945. Yet, in that period of time, the war had taken on something of a personal nature for him. It was not long before his assignment to ELA 52 that he had married a native of Hanoi, Marie Yvonne Chalumeau.[13] Marie Yvonne's family was well established in Hanoi; her grandfather was French and had traveled to Indochina in the nineteenth century where he married a Vietnamese woman and started a family, a rare occurrence in the era. French culture was predominant in the Chalumeau family; Marie Yvonne had received a French education in a French Catholic school. Through mutual acquaintances, Bartier met Marie Yvonne, and not long after they decided to marry.[14] The young couple was expecting their first child soon.

Bartier's first solo mission with the Hiller came on February 4. An outpost near Van Han was hit by intense Viet Minh mortar fire the night before. There were six wounded who required immediate evacuation. Van Han was slightly more than one hundred kilometers (sixty miles) north of Hanoi, so evacuating the men would require three round-trips. There would also be the threat of the mortar fire returning from the concealed Viet Minh once Bartier was on the ground retrieving the wounded. The mission was a test of endurance as the Hiller's overhead cyclic control stick would be incredibly fatiguing in the more than three-hour flight.[15]

Bartier would repeat the mission the next day, with six wounded evacuated from an outpost at Lang Tha Gia.[16]

With Bartier now activated, Valérie was hardly idle. On February 13, Santini scrambled to an emergency near Cam Giang—it was an attack on another small outpost. Fortunately, a mobile medical unit team was already in place at Cam Giang, where the wounded would be treated.

Santini knew that Valérie was champing at the bit to go on a mission.

"Santini took me along," said Valérie. "The helicopter was to be heavily loaded with jerry cans of gasoline."

They would drop the gasoline off at Cam Giang to have enough fuel to complete the mission. Santini had planned to evacuate the first two wounded from the outpost, and upon returning to the mobile hospital, he would hand off the helicopter to Valérie to complete the rest of the evacuation.

The Hiller proceeded on course and was hovering over the hospital at Cam Giang when suddenly the aircraft began to yaw violently to the right.

"We began losing altitude, and the helicopter began turning like a top. The gyrations began to pick up speed."

The situation was serious. Santini had lost control over the Hiller's tail rotor. The foot pedals that controlled the tail rotor were not responding, and the entire body of the helicopter was starting to swing uncontrollably on its axis. With the extra jerry cans of fuel aboard, the aircraft could become an explosive fireball if it struck the ground.

Santini had little time to react. The helicopter was plummeting. Loss of control over the tail rotor was one of the most critical malfunctions a helicopter pilot could encounter. Santini had practiced power-off landing many times in the event of an engine failure. As luck would have it, there was enough altitude left to perform the maneuver.

Shutting power off to the engine immediately slowed the twisting yaw, causing the helicopter to drop faster. But Santini anticipated that. With only a few meters left before impact, Santini pulled up on the collective stick, flaring the main rotor blades into a windmill slowing the helicopter's descent. It was a near textbook example of an autorotation landing.

"By what miracle Santini managed to land the aircraft, I will never know," Valérie marveled. "In fact, when we made contact with the ground, it was almost normal."[17]

Fortunately, neither Valérie nor Santini was injured, and even the Hiller emerged relatively unscathed. Upon inspection, Valérie and Santini saw that the cables running from the foot pedals to the tail rotor had bound up. When Santini manipulated the cables around their pulleys with some simple hand tools, he restored the tail rotor's function. But he deemed the Hiller's mechanical condition too dangerous to carry wounded until it could be inspected by Adjutant Le Goff back at Gialam. The casualty from Cam Giang would have to be evacuated by road to Hanoi. Santini and Valérie would carefully fly the Hiller back to Gialam.

While the helicopter would return to service in short order, Alexis Santini would not—at least not for the next ten days. Santini received orders to go to the port of Saigon to take delivery of four new Hiller H-23Bs that were recently delivered to replace the Hiller UH-12/360s that had been in operation since May 1950. Technology had progressed, and the four new helicopters promised vast improvement over the two older models that had their roots in civilian—not military—applications.

Valérie André wanted to replace Santini in the rotation during his absence and told him as much. But Santini denied the request.

"I want to let you go on your own, but I insist on clearing you myself," Santini told her emphatically. "I'll be back in ten days."[18]

Santini decided that Bartier would take over all rescue duties in his absence; however, Valérie took the opportunity to spend more time practicing with the one available helicopter. Nothing less than perfection would be expected on her part when she would finally be allowed to take on a solo mission. The recent incident involving the malfunctioning tail rotor taught her the value of being prepared for any emergency.

"Many times, starting from various altitudes, I practiced the maneuver of dropping the helicopter in a tight turn and landing on a precise spot."[19]

Even though Valérie had flown actual missions with Santini, she wanted to know how the helicopter would handle with just herself onboard.

"Sometimes I flew empty, and other times I had volunteers riding in the litter baskets. Also, because of the tropical heat, the aircraft was slightly overloaded to simulate the conditions encountered at most makeshift LZs, where take-offs were particularly tricky."

To be sure, flying in tropical Vietnam was far removed from the instruction Valérie received from Helicop-Air in more temperate France. With the marginally powered Hiller 360 struggling with its performance in Indochina's tropical climate, it was always a challenge to lift off with a full load.

"It was necessary to yank the helicopter off the ground, pick up airspeed close to the ground without leveling off, then pull back right away in order to jump any obstacles, like walls, hedges, trees, which were always where they shouldn't be."[20]

The practice that Valérie was putting herself through would prove to be incredibly valuable. As days wore on with Santini gone, Valérie noticed that Bartier was also under strain as the only operational pilot.

"Bartier, who was flying all missions, was beginning to show signs of fatigue," she observed. "I was, of course, happy with my little hops, but I was growing impatient."[21]

Valérie's impatience notwithstanding, the pace of the war in Indochina was about to change. With General Raoul Salan now firmly in charge of military operations, the French would go on the offensive once again.

In March 1952, the French high command prepared to launch Operation Mercure, a military offensive intended to neutralize General Giap's return to guerilla tactics that were grinding down French forces. Heavy casualties were expected on both sides. The success of Operation Mecure would heavily depend on the helicopter rescue unit.

Alexis Santini hurriedly readied the new Hiller H-23As for deployment but found both advantages and distinct disadvantages with the new aircraft. On the whole, he wasn't satisfied with the performance of the new machines. While Santini intended to ease the new aircraft into regular service gradually, he wanted to make sure the transition would be smooth. In the meantime, ELA 52 would soldier on with the two original Hiller 360s.

On March 15, Valérie arrived at Gialam, as now routine, to take one of the Hillers up for a practice run.

"I went up for my little ride as usual, and when I returned and landed in front of the hangar, Santini came up to me," Valérie recalled.

"Hello André," Santini said to her. "I see you've been working hard."

That much was true, and it showed. In the days that Santini had been away from Hanoi, Valérie devoted herself to perfecting complex maneuvers with the helicopter. But the question that remained in her mind was whether she would ever go solo. After all, Bartier had been certified as a solo pilot, even though his workload during Santini's absence should have justified the service of an additional qualified pilot.

"*He gave me no time to express my disappointment*," she thought to herself, anticipating more delays in her deployment. But Santini quickly cut to the chase.

"You'll fly the next mission," he told her, wasting no words.[22]

Valérie was beside herself with joy.

"I didn't dare leave the hangar. I felt if I should go away—even for a short time—Santini or Bartier would take my place in the event of an emergency."

On the following day, March 16, 1952, Valérie André's moment finally came. An alert came from Bat Nao to evacuate two seriously wounded Vietnamese soldiers allied to the French. Bat Nao is roughly seventy kilometers east of Hanoi and south of the coastal city Haiphong. The estimated time to reach Bat Nao was approximately an hour by air, which yielded very little preparation time before Valérie took off.

Santini and Bartier, along with the mechanics, fussed over the last-minute details with Valérie. Bartier, who had flown over virtually every part of Vietnam in his three tours of duty, described a distinctive cathedral as a landmark that dominated the village of Ke Sat. Ke Sat was a small town along the way to Bat Nao.

With intense Viet Minh guerilla activity in the area, GATAC—the military air traffic controllers—were to dispatch a pair of fighter planes to make a strafing run in the area surrounding the outpost, to be coordinated when Valérie was ready to land the helicopter. Strafing the area and dropping napalm, if necessary, would discourage the guerillas from firing on the helicopter.

Since there was no formalized uniform for the rescue helicopter service, Valérie André adopted a look that would become her personal trademark in Indochina: a floppy jungle hat, sunglasses, and a cream-colored flight suit.[23]

The Hiller had already been pushed out of the hangar and was on the tarmac. With almost everything ready, Valérie climbed into the cockpit of the Hiller and began the startup procedure. As the engine started and the rotors whirred to life, she had the map of her route spread out over the empty space of the seat next to her.

Valérie concentrated on the Hiller's instruments, carefully monitoring engine oil pressure, cylinder head temperature, and electrical and charging systems gauges. These were all essential as part of a preflight checklist before liftoff. Partway through this, a jeep drove up to the helicopter. An officer jumped out of the vehicle, crouching low. With one hand, he held on to his cap to keep it from blowing off in the downwash of the main rotor, and with the other hand, he clutched a sack.

"He waved at me and pointed to the sack," said Valérie. "I would be taking the garrison's payroll with me. The sum was significant."[24]

With the radio transmitter microphone in her hand, Valérie contacted tower control for clearance to take off.

"*Torricelli, Ventilateur* calling, over," she shouted into the microphone so she could be heard over the din of the engine and rotor blades. *Torricelli* was the radio call sign of GATAC-North operations. *Ventilateur*, which literally meant "electric fan," was the call-sign for the helicopter. "Requesting permission for lift off."[25]

The control tower confirmed her request and added that the two Bearcat fighter planes would rendezvous with her at Bat Nao.

The sky was dark gray and ominous. Although rain was not in the forecast, the ceiling altitude of the cloud coverage was low, meaning that Valérie would have to fly at a lower altitude closer to the road along the route. Low altitude made her vulnerable to enemy groundfire.

Setting the throttle to increase rotor RPMs and with an upward tug of the collective control, Valérie took off and pointed the aircraft east toward the coast. Santini, Bartier, the mechanics—and even Rotor—watched as the helicopter gained altitude, turned, and eventually disappeared from sight.

Almost an hour later, when Valérie was scheduled to meet up with her fighter escort over Bat Nao, the radio chatter from GATAC reported that the fighter pilots had not encountered the medical helicopter at the rendezvous point. They had scanned the area and found no trace of either the helicopter or its pilot.

Valérie André was presumed missing.

Chapter 26

Mademoiselle Ventilateur

En Route to Bat Nao, Vietnam, March 16, 1952

The Hiller was performing perfectly as it left Gialam. The southeast direction that Valérie André was taking toward Bat Nao would avoid flying over heavily populated Haiphong, northern Vietnam's large port city just east of Hanoi. Valérie had studied area maps for weeks in preparation for her first solo mission. Still, there was no substitute for the actual experience of flying over Vietnam's incredibly varied terrain.

The cloud coverage that day was extremely dense and low hanging. Rain was not in the forecast, which was fortunate since rain could come down in a virtual deluge in Vietnam and be extremely hazardous to fly in. But the low ceiling forced Valérie to keep the helicopter closer to the ground than she would have preferred. The delicate Hiller was quite vulnerable to ground fire. Even a lucky shot from a well-trained rifle could be fatal to both pilot and machine.

While she was well aware of these hazards, Valérie's full concentration was on spotting landmarks leading to Bat Nao.

"With the map spread out next to me . . . I was to head for the exact spot, and I was sure I would be successful. The southern portion of the Delta was still unknown to me, but on the map it appeared to present no problems. I had no room for any error."[1]

The route Valérie was following was well established for all military aircraft, which was important if an emergency should come up. By tracing

227

the route with key landmarks along the way, Morane scout planes could be dispatched to search the trail in case of a forced landing. The first major landmark, Ke Sat, was approaching.

"The cloud ceiling was not quite so low now. Bartier had gone to great lengths to describe the cathedral there, and I could see it. All was well, so far."[2]

Pressing on, Valérie followed the line of a rough road down below. It was the lifeline by land to the various forts and outposts that dotted the area.

"I flew from outpost to outpost," Valérie said. "The sky was becoming dense again, and I was flying only 200 (60 meters) feet off the ground. The hostile looking region was unknown to me and I was wary of dropping my altitude, yet I didn't want to fly upward toward the scud."[3]

Flying into the thick cloud coverage to avoid detection from the ground would be courting disaster. Valérie knew it would be too easy to become lost and disoriented without a visual grasp of her horizon. Despite the danger from ground fire, she realized there were no better alternatives.

"I was looking at my wristwatch at regular intervals," Valérie said, noting that she was already two minutes behind schedule. Nevertheless, Valérie was only ten minutes away from Bat Nao.

"Fight leader, *Ventilateur* calling. Do you receive? Copy?" Valérie shouted into her radio microphone. She repeated her call several times, but there was no response.

"Perhaps because of the bad weather, maybe the fighter planes have gone back to their base," Valérie speculated. The fighter planes would have been reassuring as an escort, but Valérie didn't dwell on their absence as Bat Nao was now up ahead.

"Down below, I could see my goal," Valérie said as she caught sight of the French outpost with relief.

The outpost had laid out a landing zone (LZ) with colored fabric panels firmly weighted to the ground by heavy whitewashed bricks arranged in a checkerboard pattern. A smoke marker showed the direction of the wind, and a tricolor fluttering on a mast close to the LZ helped confirm she was at the right spot.

"Docile, the helicopter descended toward the LZ. Slowly, I set the aircraft down. Once on the ground, I left the engine running, but I made sure that the collective stick was locked."[4]

Locking the collective control stick was a wise precaution, and one Valérie was repeatedly warned about. Without doing so, the vibrations of a still-running helicopter could cause the collective to creep, causing the aircraft to lift with no one aboard. One can easily imagine the disaster stemming from such an incident.

Once she was out of the helicopter, Valérie saw the men from the outpost approach, bearing two stretchers. The two wounded were Vietnamese soldiers allied to the French. As outpost soldiers came closer, it was apparent that, while they had expected the helicopter, they didn't expect the pilot.

A woman!

Valérie could easily read the astonishment in the men's eyes.

"Stupefaction was painted all over their faces," Valérie noted. She knew her whole appearance must have presented a bizarre sight. "What a get-up! My jungle hat, sunglasses, and flight suit—cream-colored once a week when it returns from the laundry—were all the targets of their stares. They finally dared to move up closer, even too close, I felt."[5]

The rotating main and tail rotor blades were a hazard to be near. Valérie ordered the men to exercise extreme caution around the helicopter.

"I removed the basket lids from the Hiller's side litters and signaled to the stretcher-bearers to duck their heads while approaching because of the rotor blades. The wounded were put in place each in turn, and I personally closed the covers. My watch confirmed that the operation took only five minutes. Perfect!"[6]

For Valérie, there was only one task left before returning to Hanoi.

"I produced the bag I was entrusted with, and everyone's face lit up. It was their pay. But what can they do with it in such a god-forsaken place? Nonetheless, it makes them happy."[7]

The men, however, signaled to her not to leave just yet.

"I am already back in the cockpit when the post commander—a large man with a beard—asks me if I can take a few letters. A bundle tied together with a coarse string containing at least ten pounds of mail was handed to me. Everyone was smiling."

"They drop mail to us every week," the commander told Valérie. "But it's been a month since we've been able to send anything out."

The mail was a two-way lifeline to the world. To receive letters from a loved one was important, but it was equally important for the men to know their loved ones also knew they were still alive and well.

Valérie was now ready to depart. She glanced at her two wounded passengers, and they appeared happy to be headed to the hospital.

"I waved at my spectators, who gave me a friendly salute, and I forgot everything that doesn't deal with the helicopter."

The helicopter now required all of Valérie's attention. Because the Hiller was loaded down with the two wounded men, its flight capabilities changed drastically. Valérie, however, had been practicing diligently.

"I 'milked' my RPMs to the maximum and pulled gently on the collective control while moving the cyclic stick forward. The aircraft lifted, gathering forward speed, and turned nicely at the edge of the trees before clearing them. The takeoff was successful. On to Hanoi!"[8]

Valérie reasoned that the two wounded Vietnamese were not too heavy, which helped considerably in getting aloft. Yet, there was another peril. Because the cloud coverage still loomed low, it was not possible to fly at a higher altitude. Also, Valérie's fighter escort was not present, so flying at low altitude out of Bat Nao still presented the Hiller as a tempting target from ground fire. The next few minutes were an excruciating test of nerves.

Valérie maintained her cool. It was pure *sang froid*. Each minute that passed without incident was a relief. The exhilaration of flying in this hazardous zone and skirting the danger that existed at every corner was incredible.

Presently, the bell tower of the cathedral at Ke Sat came into view. The relatively secure air route to Hanoi meant that the majority of the danger had passed.

When the hangars and runways of Gialam came into view, Valérie requested clearance from the control tower to land.

"I made a wide loop to execute a nice landing," Valérie said. "The full team was waiting for me in front of the hangar."[9]

It was with good reason that the entire crew of ELA 52 had maintained a vigil for Valérie's return. The two fighter pilots who were to rendezvous with Valérie at Bat Nao had reported no sign of the helicopter or its pilot.

"Santini was the only one who had faith in me; the others thought I was lost," Valérie said.

Santini filled Valérie in on how GATAC had declared her lost on the mission. Working backward in evaluating how well Valérie did on her first solo mission, Santini reckoned that the fighter pilots had mistaken another outpost for Bat Nao. Or they had arrived at Bat Nao earlier than Valérie's prearranged ETA.

"In any event, I told Santini—and not without a certain pride—that there's the proof. My casualties are here!"[10]

Valérie's first solo flight not only made an impression on Alexis Santini but also earned for Valérie respect and recognition from the French military's high command. Not long after, Valérie André received the Croix de guerre with one *palme* for her heroic action as a rescue pilot. The accompanying citation to her medal was composed by France's minister of defense, Georges Bidault, who wrote:

> During these operations she has constantly been the object of admiration from all for her courage, her calmness, her generosity, and her great modesty. She is a brilliant example of courage and feminine devotion, serving magnificently the French cause.[11]

The sense of modesty that Valérie assigned to her accomplishments allowed for some observance of her newfound fame.

"It was with still more astonishment—having not sought glory or honors—that my 'exploits' bring out the word 'legend' from journalists. The word 'legend' becomes attached to my name!"[12]

While Alexis Santini undoubtedly took some pride in his protégé's recognition, his main concern was that he was mostly satisfied with Valérie André's performance as a pilot; however, he was less satisfied with something even more pressing. The French air force had recently taken delivery of four new Hiller helicopters to relieve the wear on the two Hiller 360s and expand the service. The new aircraft were H-23As, a new designation now given to Hiller helicopters built to military specification.

A few significant revisions in the basic airframe yielded an easier flight experience with the new Hillers. The cyclic control was moved from overhead in the cockpit to a more conventional location on the floor. The relocated control alleviated the primary complaint of fatigue with the aircraft's flight control, which previously forced the pilot to uncomfortably hold their arm over their heads during a flight.

The new Hillers, however, were still powered by the same 178 horsepower Franklin engine. There was a more powerful, two-hundred-horsepower engine under development, but it had not yet been certified for installation in the new model. The same underpowered engine was now saddled with additional weight from improved but heavier radio equipment and a larger, more comprehensive instrument binnacle. Even the inclusion of khaki paint on the fuselage—compared to the bare aluminum skin of the first two 360 models—added a kilogram or so to the aircraft just from the weight of the paint alone.

As a result, the new ships' payload capacity suffered compared to the older 360 models, which were already marginal performers in Indochina's humid tropical climate. It was primarily for this reason that Alexis Santini was not altogether satisfied with the arrival of the new ships.

Two of the new aircraft were a gift from the people of Bordeaux, France, who had raised money for their purchase. The other two were purchased within the acquisition budget of the French air force. Santini wanted both Valérie and Henri Bartier to try out the new aircraft.

"Piloting these new Hiller H-23As was less tiring," Valérie quickly observed. "With the cyclic control now on the floor instead of overhead, we would no longer have to keep our arms raised hours on end."

The new helicopters' shortcomings were also readily apparent.

"From the very first flights, we noticed that even with a single casualty, the aircraft was overloaded. On these small helicopters, and particularly in tropical climates, weight is the enemy. But since these machines were given to us, we had to be content with them."[13]

Despite the mixed reaction to the new helicopters, there was other news Santini could now share with Valérie and Bartier. A dedicated hangar for the helicopters would soon be built at Gialam. The helicopter squadron would no longer have to share living quarters and maintenance space with the other fixed-wing units on the base.

Actual stick time on the Hiller H-23s was limited for the time being. Because of Santini's reservations about the new helicopters' weight-carrying ability, he was reluctant to deploy the new aircraft into service beyond practice flights.

"Santini was not very happy and not without justification," Valérie concurred, especially after taking the new Hiller up for her first test flight. For now, the two older 360s would continue to operate.[14]

On March 19, Valérie received orders to evacuate a wounded Vietnamese soldier from an outpost near Hung Yen. The outpost was located on the banks of the Red River some sixty kilometers south of Hanoi. Valérie had enough time to go over her maps.

"The outpost was actually at La Tieu, a dozen miles from Hung Yen," Valérie noted. "I studied the map of that region—yet unknown to me—until I knew it by heart. The loops in the river would constitute precious checkpoints."[15]

In an era long before satellite navigation, spotting unique geographic landmarks was indispensable. In the case of finding Hung Yen, one just had to look at the serpent-like route of the Red River with its prominent twists.

Flying southward along the road leading out of Hanoi to Hung Yen, Valérie and the Hiller operated with neither drama nor mishap. The weather was much better than it was on her previous mission so that Valérie could fly at a much higher altitude. Also, GATAC decided not to dispatch fighter planes for Valérie's protection that day, so maintaining altitude was crucial. Valérie was careful to observe how the Red River curved back and forth. She also took note of the various other French outposts along the river route for future reference. Valérie knew that familiarity with the outposts might well prove prescient.

"Upon reaching the fifth loop, which almost completely encircles something resembling an island, I prepared to make my turn," Valérie said. A small offshoot of the Red River split off from the main current and formed a circle around a parcel of land that extended for more than a kilometer. It was just another landmark noted on her map. "From that point I would be some six miles from Hung Yen."

Eventually, another landmark came into view.

"I saw the bamboo canal," Valérie observed. "I headed a little eastward until the helicopter intersected the road following the northern riverbank."[16]

La Tieu was just another dot on French maps of Vietnam in 1952 that no longer exists in today's world. This outpost was mainly composed of Vietnamese soldiers fighting against the Viet Minh—the results of the efforts spearheaded by the late General de Lattre to make the war more of a cause for the Vietnamese. Because the soldiers had not set out a smoke marker near the LZ, landing at the outpost proved to be a little more of a challenge for Valérie than it had been at Bat Nao.

"There was no smoke marker, but the flag told me the wind direction," Valérie observed as she scanned the site for the landing zone. Knowing from what direction the wind was coming was necessary to keep the broad sides of the helicopter from acting like a weather vane when landing.

As soon as she landed, Valérie and the helicopter were swarmed by men who rushed up to the LZ.

"I had to fend off the inquisitive. The Vietnamese always have a tendency to move in too close to the rotor."[17]

As was often the case when responding to an emergency far out in the field, the outpost's commander told Valérie that there were two casualties to bring back to Hanoi instead of one. With the initial payload problems of the newer Hillers not sorted out, it had been prudent on Santini's part to continue with the existing 360s. Maintaining weight balance with the helicopter was still an issue to deal with, however.

"Back at Gialam, I had loaded a jerry can of gasoline to serve as a counterweight, but it will have to be sacrificed. If a casualty weighs more than one hundred sixty pounds (72 kg), it was necessary to compensate this by placing a load in the other litter basket."

Because of the possibility of not restarting the helicopter so far out in the field, Valérie couldn't shut down the engine and pour the fuel into the Hiller's tank. Instead, she left the fuel with the post commander, who also handed her a bundle of outgoing mail.

With the wounded securely on board, Valérie was ready to take off. But she noticed that the excited Vietnamese soldiers—who had never before seen a helicopter let alone a woman pilot—were chattering one phrase over and over again.

"Quetak, quetak!"

The words were a mystery to Valérie, but she would soon discover what they meant.

"Later on I will learn that to all of them I am 'quetak'—the Ventilator Lady."[18]

Chapter 27

Allons-y

Gialam Air Base, Near Hanoi, Vietnam, March 1952

At Gialam air base, the Army Corps of Engineers broke ground on a new hangar for the helicopters. Valérie was especially keen to be a witness to its construction.

"Every day it became my custom to pay a visit to the future helicopter hangar," she said. "Sometimes I went with Santini and Bartier, and sometimes only with my dog, Rotor."[1]

There were significant changes in store for Valérie, as well as for Alexis Santini and Henri Bartier, with the transfer of the helicopters to Hanoi. The helicopter service was redesignated ELA 53 and served as a separate adjunct to the existing liaison squadron of fixed-winged Morane Criquets already at Gialam air base. ELA 52 would continue to provide rescue service in southern Vietnam.

Because of the unique operational characteristics of their aircraft, the helicopter crew of ELA 53 would have a certain degree of autonomy, which was the main reason for building a separate hangar. Sergeant Le Goff and his mechanics shared a maintenance hangar with a fighter squadron based at Gialam. But that was only a temporary situation until the completion of the new hangar.

Valérie was very impressed with the new helicopter facility.

"I kept an eye on the progress of the construction. The Corps of Engineers was spoiling us. The accommodations inside would be particularly refined."[2]

Meanwhile, Santini was preoccupied with the performance of the new Hiller H-23As that had recently arrived. Frustrated by the marginal

235

performance of the new aircraft, Santini wrote to the head of logistics for the French air force in the Far East concerning the shortcomings of the new aircraft.

"I respectfully draw your attention to the comparison sheet of these two types of helicopters and particularly to the usable weight for the wounded, in a tropical atmosphere, completely equipped and fully loaded, which is 500 kilos for the H23A's and 700 kilos for the older models (UH12/360)."[3]

The 200-kilogram (440-pound) payload deficit in the new Hillers meant that they were essentially useless in rescue work. Santini remembered how Valérie André had said that her light body weight was an advantage in flying the existing Hillers. With the new models, she would likely be the only pilot light enough to complete a mission with them successfully.

Ultimately a more practical solution needed to be found.

While Santini was still cautious in evaluating Valérie's performance, she had impressed him in carrying out her few solo missions so far. There was still a lot that Valérie had to learn, beginning with the fact that there was no predictability to any rescue mission—even if it took place in the same location.

On March 23, the outpost at Bat Nao reported two casualties for evacuation. Santini dispatched Valérie André since she had been there just the week before. Unlike the last time she ventured into the dangerous combat zone, GATAC made sure to provide her with fighter escort when she reached her destination.

At Bat Nao, the Bearcat pilots met up with Valérie and the Hiller. The standard procedure for a rescue helicopter flying into a dangerous area was to have the fighter planes strafe the area to keep any guerilla activity in the vicinity at bay. Often just the presence of the fighter planes flying low over the surrounding area was enough to keep the enemy away without a shot being necessary. Today was, fortunately, one of those days.

"I saw the two Bearcats a few minutes before I arrived at Bat Nao to start my descent," Valérie noted. As she approached the landing zone (LZ), she also noticed that something seemed out of place.

"The old LZ no longer existed. I noted with some reservations that the panels had been placed between the bamboo palisade and the blockhouse wall. The area seemed very small."[4]

Valérie was very tempted to use the LZ she had used the week before. It was only a hundred meters or so from the outpost and would have afforded a better area for landing and takeoff. Despite her reservations, she landed in the tight space near the outpost's main quarters. As soon as Valérie made contact with the ground, the bearded commander of the outpost rushed up to her, crouching low.

"I could tell that you wanted to land over there," he shouted at Valérie over the din of the helicopter, pointing to the old LZ. "We had to mine the old landing area. The *Viets* were sneaking into it and taking potshots at us."[5]

Fortunately, the loading of the two wounded soldiers took only a few minutes, and Valérie was able to lift off and return to Gialam without incident.

The next several days for Valérie were reasonably uneventful, with a brief lull in the action. Calls for emergency transport were light, so Santini and Bartier were able to take on missions. Valérie used her downtime to practice with the new Hiller H-23A, sharing her opinions about the limitations of the new aircraft with her colleagues.

Flying at night was rarely called upon, so when the day came to a close the crew could often be found spending their evenings in Hanoi's French Quarter.

"In the evening, we were bushed," Valérie later recalled. "Most of the time, all I wanted was to have dinner, alone or with Santini, at the Coq d'Or, which had become our unofficial headquarters."

Valérie encountered all types of people who came and went through Hanoi. Often when Valérie was by herself, she would be approached by young officers who were lonely and pining for home. Some were rather forward, but most just wanted to chat. One evening a young lieutenant, "N," stopped by her table at Coq d'Or. They had met in Saigon previously when Valérie was stationed there.[6]

"*He seemed frail,*" Valérie thought to herself, even though he was a combat soldier.[7] Valérie learned that the lieutenant was assigned to an outpost near Na San, some 250 kilometers east of Hanoi.

Once again, Valérie played the role of doctor and confidante to a soldier long from home. Her conversation with the lieutenant would inevitably lead to how he missed his family in France, especially his mother. Valérie couldn't help but think how the young lieutenant reminded her of the pilot, Francis Varcin. Although this lieutenant was not quite as morose about his future as Varcin was, he still seemed so young to her. Maybe this was because Valérie André had become something of a grizzled veteran after having been in Indochina for nearly five years. But in her eyes, he didn't seem well suited to the harsh conditions of Vietnam. She couldn't help but feel uneasy about his fate. And Na San—the area of the lieutenant's new assignment—would feature prominently in a future offensive against the Viet Minh.

But for now, the French military was focused on Operation Mercure, launched on March 27, 1952. It was General Raoul Salan's first major offensive against the Viet Minh since he assumed command of French armed forces in January. The maneuver intended to lure the Viet Minh general Vo Nguyen Giap into confronting a concentration of French force bolstered by the deployment of the military equipment provided by the United States. Salan was continuing the strategy of his predecessor, Jean de Lattre, to bring the enemy out into the open. But this course of action was almost becoming an obsession for French commanders. Giap was now less prone to take the bait. Only time would tell if Operation Mercure would break the cycle of stalemate between the French and Viet Minh.

Salan appointed General François de Linarès to head up a task force for operations around Thai Binh and Nam Dinh. With significant casualties expected, Linarès ordered a medical helicopter to be on standby near the battle zone at all times.

"To my great elation, I was the one assigned," said Valérie. The assignment spoke volumes about the confidence that her colleagues—especially Santini—had in her ability to carry out a field mission independently. She would not be going entirely alone, though. To keep the helicopter in working order, Master Sergeant André Tessier would also accompany Valérie. They would both stay in Nam Dinh until the completion of Operation Mercure.

Valérie had hardly arrived at the airfield at Nam Dinh when she received an order to proceed to an outpost at Lac Quan.

"I had just enough time to 'gas up,' which takes about ten minutes." It was already late in the afternoon. In moments, Valérie was airborne.

Late afternoons in Vietnam can bring on the worst in temperatures and humidity. These conditions were often amplified inside the fishbowl-like cockpit of the Hiller.

"Oil mixed in with the sweat and the dirt. The temperatures prevailing inside the helicopter cockpit are such that all we wear is our flight-suit."[8]

As Valérie came up to the outpost, the surrounding area was calm for the moment. There had been no need to send in fighter escort, and the LZ was laid out well enough for a reasonably straightforward landing. The stretcher-bearers brought out the wounded man.

"My patient was a very young Vietnamese, hardly bigger than I." Increasingly, more Vietnamese men were joining France's effort against the Viet Minh, and more were ending up wounded or killed as a result.

Valérie's return to Nam Dinh was routine. The field hospital was near the airfield. She flew low over it to signal the medics that she was carrying a casualty. Darkness was falling, and her timing was good that day. After the medics carried off her patient, the only task left was to secure the Hiller.

"Whenever possible, the helicopter must not sleep outside."

More so than fixed-winged aircraft, the helicopter was highly susceptible to damage that could affect its flight safety if left exposed to the elements. Sergeant Tessier was well aware that the Hiller was becoming a bit long in the tooth and was also determined to baby the helicopter in any way it took to prolong its service life. As luck would have it, the airfield bordered a cotton plantation, and its operators often used a small airplane for crop dusting weevils.

"The *cotonniers* have a small hangar for their airplane. It's temporarily empty and they loan it to me."

People in the surrounding area were undoubtedly awestruck by the young doctor piloting this strange flying machine, so much so that they presented every courtesy to her.

"The civilians of Nam Dinh extended me a welcome that I was not about to forget. One of them made available to me a room with a bath."[9] Valérie especially appreciated the latter luxury after spending a gruelingly hot day in the cockpit of the Hiller.

The next day Valérie André and Sergeant Tessier were up at dawn. They were ordered to bring the helicopter to Thai Binh, where General Linarès had established his field headquarters. Compared to Nam Dinh, the airfield at Thai Binh was considerably more active. Morane Criquet scout planes, Martin B-26 bombers, and Grumman Bearcat fighters came and went frequently. The Moranes were particularly busy with scouting missions. General Linarès had an intelligence report that the 316th and 320th divisions of the Viet Minh army had infiltrated the Delta areas around Nam Dinh and Thai Binh. But the problem was to find them in order to fight them. As Valérie André put it:

"The *Viet Minh* had infiltrated and spread throughout the countryside, fanned out like an oil stain."[10]

The Viet Minh had also perfected the use of camouflage as they dispersed. Mainly moving at night, they stayed within the deep underbrush of the jungle, often wearing the foliage of the forest plants to match the terrain exactly. Even the most experienced spotters would occasionally capture glimpses of some movement on one pass of the scout plane. By the second pass, however, the phantoms would completely melt into the brush once again.

"I just know the little bastards are somewhere around here," the scouts would often complain. "But go and find them in that mess."[11]

Not long after their touchdown at Thai Binh, an air force officer approached Valérie and Sergeant Tessier.

"Captain Fabères, a fighter pilot detached from air command . . . met Tessier and me and took us to an enormous camp. Judging from the number of officers and men moving among the many tents, *Mercure* must be an important operation, and its size surprised me."[12]

Despite the large-scale nature of the maneuvers, the first day at Thai Binh was relatively quiet.

"My first day called for no mission, and I was pleased. There were no casualties yet."

While the larger aircraft could be stored outside without a hangar on the makeshift airfield at Thai Binh, Valérie and Sergeant Tessier preferred to fly the Hiller back to Nam Dinh at the end of the day.

On the second day, Valérie and the sergeant repeated their ten-minute flight from the cotton field hangar to the base of operations, but the day passed uneventfully. On March 30, however, an attack close to Thai Binh shocked everyone back to the reality of war.

"I was assigned a new mission. The enemy was shoved back from the outskirts of town, and we had a few casualties. The coordinates I was given were near the seashore. I took off under a grey sky. Although I kept an eye on the ground, I navigated by compass heading."[13]

Martin B-26 bombers were sent in to repulse the attack. The Viet Minh feared little, but when the bombers dropped napalm, they fled from the rain of fire from the sky.

Valérie witnessed the aftermath of the carnage from a thousand feet above.

"Some six miles from Thai Binh, villages were still burning. The smoke was rising and blending with the rather low clouds. It was a moving spectacle; how could anyone ever be accustomed to the horrors of war? The sight of these large fires saddened and moved me. Nothing can erase the images of all the mutilated bodies."[14]

Valérie felt empathy for the enemy and the casualties they undoubtedly suffered, but she checked her thoughts. She reminded herself that both sides were capable of inflicting carnage upon each other. As a doctor, she was a witness to these horrors every day.

"I also couldn't help but think of the atrocities committed by the *Viet Minh*. My medical profession perhaps qualified me to be a judge of that. But what good is [it] to describe only abomination and cruelty?"[15]

Twenty minutes into her flight, Valérie was over rice plantations. According to the coordinates on her map, she was near her destination. But all she could see were rice paddies.

"Theoretically, I was to have fighter cover, or at least contact them if they were needed." For this mission, Valérie decided to go without them. But where was the outpost?

Valérie circled the area with the Hiller until some wisps of smoke caught her attention. She surmised that the men down below had not expected the arrival of the helicopter so soon. But the distinctive sound of the helicopter stirred the men into action, and two soldiers emerged from a bunkhouse. They hastily laid the fabric signal panels over the ground and weighed them down with heavy stone to designate the helicopter's landing area.

"I landed without bothering to check if the LZ was properly prepared. It was a good thing that I did, too, for I could hear detonations. Not far away, mortars were firing. Was it at us, or was it at the enemy? Impossible to know."[16]

The French Foreign Legion manned the outpost, and two of their own were wounded.

"They crawled out to the helicopter, dragging two stretchers. The first casualty had a massive leg wound, and the other one was hit in the abdomen."

Fortunately for the two Legionnaires, their wounds were relatively recent. Valérie checked the soldier with the abdominal injury and was reasonably certain he could be saved. But she could sense that the nearby battle was shifting rapidly.

"I was anxious to leave immediately. We were in a zone that provided no cover. Shots were coming from all directions, and I had no time to inquire about the situation."[17]

Valérie guessed that the Viet Minh were less than a kilometer to the northeast. She knew that the helicopter would be a target, even with prominent red crosses painted on the fuselage. Wasting no time, she brought her engine RPMs up and pulled upward on the collective to begin her ascent. A strong headwind was blowing directly at the front of the helicopter.

"We hardly reached three hundred feet when I heard a sharp crack. We had been hit!"

The Legionnaire with the leg wound was nearest to Valérie in the cockpit. She looked down at him, and she could read in his eyes that the stray bullet had been close. Just how close, Valérie didn't know. She got on the radio to request fighter escort. GATAC radioed back to her that the fighter planes were engaged on another mission in the sector and were not available.

Below were only rice paddies and no safe place to land. The helicopter would sink in the soft marsh.

"I just kept focused on the instrument panel."

So far, the helicopter continued to perform normally, and the gauges showed nothing unusual. But with two casualties aboard, Valérie decided not to take any chances. Getting on the radio again, she informed GATAC of her status and that she would land at Thai Binh, where there was also a field hospital.

As Valérie approached the last few kilometers before Thai Binh, two fighter planes appeared. They had heard Valérie's radio call and were able to break away to escort her into Thai Binh.

When Valérie finally landed, she first tended to the two wounded Legionnaires. As it turned out, the stray bullet pierced the litter occupied by the soldier with the leg wound and grazed him in the process. It was a close call. Sergeant Tessier checked out the helicopter and found that it had not suffered any further damage.

"You'll be able to continue," the mechanic reassured Valérie.[18]

Shortly after Tessier's inspection and approval that the Hiller was fit for duty, another call came in through the radio at Thai Binh. Two more wounded were reported in the area where Valérie had just rescued the two Legionnaires.

"This time the message informed me of the flow and ebb of the battle line. I was to return to the sector I had just left. If the panels for the landing zone were no longer in place, I was to pull back three kilometers further west to another LZ."

The orders caused Valérie some concern about how fluid the situation was becoming.

"*Were we now involved in a full-scale moving war? Was it tempting fate to bring the helicopter back to a place nearly fatal to it?*" she thought to herself.[19]

By now, it was late in the afternoon, and nightfall was approaching. Flying at night was always dangerous, but the two men had suffered abdominal wounds. Without intervention, their chances for survival were slim. The low cloud ceiling only compounded the danger.

"It was almost dark, and I knew that even with luck I would return only at night."

As Valérie journeyed back to the battlefield, the clouds seemed to get darker. As she approached the outpost where she had previously been, it appeared calm to her. Suspiciously calm.

"I spotted the flat area where I landed hardly more than an hour ago. Despite the engine noise from the helicopter, it seemed quiet."

As she maneuvered the Hiller closer to the ground, Valérie noted that there were no LZ panels laid out.

"Suddenly, the ground came alive. First came the mortar rounds, then, as the helicopter turned around, machine gun bursts. The *Viet Minh* must have captured the area."

It was one of the most dangerous situations Valérie had encountered to this point, but she remembered her instructions if she found the LZ no longer in place.

"I was rather happy to get away from there. *Let's head due west*," she thought to herself, remaining composed.[20]

A few kilometers due west, the situation brewing there was even more intense. The first sign of trouble was an entire village on fire. Next, Valérie caught sight of a Morane Criquet flying above her. She quickly realized that the Criquet was circling her next LZ, directing two Bearcat fighter planes where to train their machine guns and drop their napalm canisters.

"I radioed the Morane of my presence. He gave me the position of the LZ; when I saw it, I thought might as well try landing on a handkerchief!"

The landing zone was small because the whole outpost was under siege. As Valérie lowered the Hiller to around 50 meters (160 feet), she could see that only a narrow area existed between the barbed wire and the outpost. The panels barely covered an area of 3 square meters (10 square feet). Valérie knew to be cautious of how well the landing panels were laid out.

"The men were still not familiar with how the helicopter works. They thought that it functioned as easily as an elevator."[21]

In the heat of a fierce battle, however, Valérie saw no alternative.

"*Damn it*," she thought to herself. "*Let's go!*"[22]

The landing was almost a disaster. The Legionnaires used an old parachute to mark out the LZ, and it wasn't secure. As Valérie neared the ground, the rotor wash sucked up the thin nylon cloth into the rotor blades, where it instantly shredded. Valérie was immediately concerned that the fabric and debris kicked up from the ground had damaged the helicopter.

"*What a storm! . . . Should I kill the engine?*" she thought to herself, as she could still see bits of cloth caught up in the rotating mechanism. But she knew how stubborn the Hiller often was to restart. "Spending the night on the ground meant exposing the aircraft to *Viet Minh* fire."

Instead, Valérie locked down the Hiller's controls and leaped out of the cockpit. She saw some thirty men crouched behind a wall, with weapons drawn and ready, and she realized that the enemy must not be far away. Three young officers were standing nearby to her landing.

"Couldn't you have properly fastened your panels with rocks, not pebbles," Valérie shouted at them. The Legionnaires were tough and battle hardened, but Valérie let loose a stinging tirade—both in French and in German—to make sure her anger was clear to them.

Finally, regaining her composure, Valérie asked:

"Where are the casualties?"[23]

"On the other side of the levee," one of the officers replied. "But it's under fire."

From the violent sounds coming from across the divide, Valérie could guess that the fighting was fierce. But as she saw it, there was little choice but to plunge into the flames.

"We decided that only the helicopter was capable of jumping over the dangerous line of fire."[24]

But getting past the levee wasn't a clear shot. Valérie saw a row of trees lining an earthen berm built up along a channel of water flowing into a rice paddy. It was now late in the afternoon and getting dark quickly. Valérie wasn't taking any chances this time. She told the officers to get on the radio with the men on the other side to prepare the LZ.

"Tell them to light a fire and make sure the panels are weighted down properly this time," she told the radio operator.

The takeoff was easy, but getting over the tree line was intimidating.

"The trees appeared terribly high to me. With two wounded on board, such a feat would have been impossible. In one hop I was over the levee."

Crossing to the other side was only the beginning of the procedure. As Valérie came closer to the remainder of the outpost under siege, the barrage only grew in strength.

"The gunfire increased in intensity. Did the enemy anticipate my maneuver, or did they intercept the radio message? Considering the new equipment with *Viet Minh* battalions, the second hypothesis was plausible."[25]

When Valérie saw the signal fire, it directed her attention to the LZ the Legionnaires laid out.

"It was hardly an improvement, but at least the new LZ offered a wider opening."

The wind was not in Valérie's favor as she attempted to land. It was blowing fiercely. Because the layout of the LZ was not ideal, she wouldn't be able to take off with a more desirable headwind.

"Without hesitation and intending to take off any way into the opening, I landed downwind."

A major ran up to Valérie as she popped open the helicopter's door.

"We're surrounded! You've got to get them out of here quick."

Gunfire whistled all around as the Legionnaires brought out two of their most wounded. The big red crosses painted on the fuselage and side litter covers of the Hiller did nothing to interrupt the barrage. There were other casualties, but two of the Legionnaires were both shot in the stomach and their condition was critical.

Valérie sized up the two men and hoped her little helicopter could handle the load. They were both very large Bavarians. Their combined weight taxed the payload capacity of the Hiller, even with its lightweight pilot aboard.

"As I was about to take off, a thought made me hesitate. Perhaps I should only evacuate one casualty? But it was too late for me to return tonight, and the man I would have left behind would be lost."

Those thoughts flashed in Valérie's mind for only a brief moment. Inevitably she said to herself:

"*Allons-y!—Let's go!*"

Valérie applied the throttle, but the helicopter labored to climb a few inches, then fell back.

"I decided to take a chance on the second takeoff, and I cheated by over-revving the engine."

Over-revving the engine on the Hiller was not advisable, especially with an aircraft due for an overhaul soon. Too much power all at once could cause catastrophic damage. Valérie held on tight as the Hiller leaped in the air. The aircraft cleared the trees, but Valérie knew they weren't out of danger yet.

"Just as I feared, the instant it cleared the trees, a gust hit it in the rear."[26]

The wind was forcing the helicopter's tail to lift, making progress slow. The Hiller labored across a rice paddy, struggling to gain altitude. Valérie wanted to whip the helicopter around a half circle to get the nose to face the wind. The helicopter in forward flight against the wind was the most effective stance for the aircraft as far as performance is concerned. With the wind blowing at the rear of the tail rotor, the Hiller was significantly more difficult to control.

To compound the problem, the Hiller was losing power.

"From the sound of the engine, I knew the RPM was dropping. I have my eyes glued to the tach. We were crawling along the rice paddy. I had the throttle to the limit, and in spite of that, the Hiller couldn't cope."[27]

The aircraft was crawling above the swampy water. Valérie didn't dare let the helicopter drop its altitude.

"The Hiller was only inches from the water surface. Should it touch, it would get weighed down even more from the water and then settle into two feet of water covering the mud, and all would be lost!"[28]

The wind was still fighting the helicopter, but Valérie was as equally determined not to be defeated by the elements.

"I violently kicked the rudder pedals, and I finally managed to swing the aircraft into the wind. I struggled, clutching the controls, but not for long, fortunately!"

The engine started to respond, and the rotors began to pick up speed. Slowly, the helicopter began to climb. Valérie felt a rush of relief. She could now turn some of her attention to her two patients instead of only the helicopter.

"I glanced in turn at both my boys. The Legionnaire on the left seemed totally indifferent. The one on the right appeared worried to me. Despite the engine noise, he had heard me swearing and guessed I was in trouble. Fine! Sometimes a good swear word really helps."[29]

The Legionnaire might just as well have been worried about being a target of Viet Minh ground fire. Bullets were still whizzing past the helicopter during Valérie's struggle to regain control. Soon, however, the firestorm of battle decreased, and they were back on course heading to Thai Binh.

Valérie finally had time to radio Thai Binh that she was on approach.

"In the middle of a delicate maneuver—what with two sticks, the throttle, and the rudder pedals—a pilot is busy with both arms and legs. However, once I reached a safe altitude, I was headed for the hospital at Thai Binh and had the ambulance driver alerted on the airfield."

The touchdown was without any added drama. The two Legionnaires were transferred from the helicopter to the ambulance in short order. With the helicopter now powered down, Sergeant Tessier was crawling all over the Hiller for its post-flight inspection. He immediately spotted something wrong. One of the rotor blades showed two significant dents, no doubt caused by debris kicked up from the poorly prepared LZ on Valérie's first landing.

Tessier shook his head and asked Valérie if the helicopter exhibited anything unusual.

"Despite the damage, I didn't notice any abnormal vibrations during the flight," she told Tessier.

"I can't take responsibility for letting you fly again until this is checked out," he said to Valérie. Sergeant Tessier was a fully qualified airframe and powerplant mechanic but had worked around fixed-wing aircraft more than helicopters. He wasn't comfortable declaring the Hiller safe if there was any possibility of structural damage to the rotor blades.

"We'd better report the problem to Hanoi," he told Valérie.

Tessier was able to reach Master Sergeant Le Goff, the chief mechanic for ELA 53. Le Goff radioed back that he would be there in the morning to assess the situation.

"On March 23, a Hiller 23A landed at Nam Dinh," Valérie recalled.

It was Alexis Santini and Le Goff. Santini decided to come along after he heard how Valérie had placed herself in some incredibly hazardous situations. He was relieved she had emerged unhurt. He marveled not only at her skill but also her luck. With one concern out of the way, attention turned now to the damaged Hiller.

Le Goff performed a full field inspection of the aircraft. The damage was a lot less than was initially thought.

"Le Goff simply filled the blade dents with putty," Valérie said. "The aircraft would be grounded for only twenty-four hours, and the relief helicopter would remain on standby until that evening, then return to Gialam."[30]

In the evening, Valérie also returned to Hanoi for a few days of R&R. Santini would cover her missions while she was gone. But Valérie would soon find that Operation Mercure was only a warm-up for even more danger to come.

Chapter 28

On the Right Side of Luck

Thai Binh, Vietnam, Late March 1952

Operation Mercure was not the success the French had hoped it would be. Vo Nguyen Giap refused to let his army be baited into a large-scale battle that could settle the war once and for all. The French were becoming more deadly with weapons supplied by the United States, and Giap knew it. Viet Minh casualties were high, even with their reliance on guerilla tactics. Also, by 1952, thirty-five battalions consisting of 127,000 Vietnamese soldiers were allied to the French in Indochina. It was part of Jean de Lattre's legacy to make the fight against the Viet Minh a fight that the Vietnamese people would believe in. These troops were inexperienced and unproven, but they represented a genuine threat to Viet Minh supremacy in Vietnam.

It may have seemed as if the Viet Minh tiger was biding his time before striking with full force, but it was a waiting game with time running out for both sides.

This pattern of ongoing and deadly stalemate was becoming all too familiar to veterans of the war, such as Valérie André.

"Operation *Mercure* was drawing to a close. The *Viet Minh* seemed to have disappeared from the area swept by our troops. But instead, they were baiting themselves on the outposts that were isolated and relatively distant from Thai Binh."[1]

It was an effective strategy for the Viet Minh. Taking the war to the outposts inflicted damage to morale that proved to be more effective than

249

facing a massive French force in mass. Valérie found herself venturing many kilometers past the French base at Thai Binh to effect rescue missions. Outposts at Lai Quan, Chi Tien, and Tan Dau—more than forty kilometers (twenty-five miles) from Thai Binh by road—were out of reach by even the fastest French mobile groups. Yet these were the targets that took on the most harassment from the Viet Minh. A rescue helicopter could evacuate the most severely wounded in about an hour or so, but it was nearly impossible to dispatch a battalion over virtually nonexistent road surfaces to reinforce an outpost under siege in a short amount of time. Bomber squadrons could drop explosives or napalm to disperse the enemy; however, the Viet Minh would simply melt away into the thick forests or underbrush surrounding French outposts.

Dawn on the morning of April 1 was clear, as Sergeant Tessier readied the Hiller for another day of service. Every part of the helicopter required a visual inspection. Master mechanic Le Goff's repair to the damaged rotor blade from several days before was holding up well. All it took was some putty—similar to the filler used to repair a dent on a damaged car—to make the blade's leading edge as good as new. Tessier marveled at the simplicity of Le Goff's fix.

Valérie was also up early and joined Tessier in his inspection of the Hiller. As Valérie and Tessier walked around the aircraft, a radio message came in from GATAC. The garrison at Gia Thon[2] had been under fire for several hours, and two soldiers needed immediate evacuation. The helicopter had to leave as soon as possible.

Valérie immediately readied the Hiller for starting. As the helicopter began its rotor run-up, Tessier disconnected the auxiliary power generator assisting the battery in cranking the engine to life. Several minutes later, Valérie was airborne.

"On this clear morning, I felt like part of my aircraft. It flew without the slightest vibration. The coordinates of my destination were relayed to me, and the fighter planes were to catch up with me when I reached the site."[3]

Valérie's radio headset received an updated weather report. The skies were clear for the moment, but a weather front was rapidly moving in. Twenty-five minutes into the flight, Valérie arrived at what she thought was the right location.

"I was near a village and I could see the two fighter planes diving. I thought they were fighting, strafing the enemy. I was beginning to get used to seeing that. But I was wrong."[4]

The fighter plane pilots were informed that the landing zone (LZ) for the rescue helicopter had moved, but they were unable to reach Valérie by radio. Their diving maneuvers were an attempt to signal to her that the LZ was now in a different location.

"The fighters were diving over and over again to show me the way. By luck, I spotted the panels from afar, and I understood what they were up to."

The new landing zone was hastily prepared. Making matters worse, two trucks were also parked too close to the LZ.

"The prepared area was not very large but appeared doable. I made a fast approach, probably too fast. Antenna wires were strung in my path—I barely had time to 'pour on the coals' to jump over them and then drop down again."

Wires—whether for communications or electrical transmission—are always a deadly hazard to any aircraft. But for a helicopter landing in a restricted area, any rotating part caught up in a wire could whiplash the aircraft into an uncontrollable catastrophe for everyone in its path. Valérie was well aware of the disaster she narrowly avoided.

"It seemed to me that the people on the ground were not very sharp. Wouldn't it have been logical to clear the surrounding of the landing pad as much as possible?"[5]

Little time was wasted in loading the two wounded men into the litters on the side of the helicopter. The wounded men were Vietnamese but slightly larger than typical. Valérie calculated they would not pose too much of a weight issue for the helicopter. Still, a rolling takeoff on the Hiller's tricycle landing gear was desirable with a full load, and Valérie wasn't satisfied with the clearance area for her departure.

"I had the men move some of the trucks parked some ten meters (33 feet) in front of the aircraft," she said. When the trucks were moved, Valérie increased the rotor RPMs. Under full power, the helicopter rolled several meters before lifting off to return to the field hospital at Nam Dinh.

Rain began to fall, and Valérie had to keep the helicopter limited to low altitude. The rain steadily increased as she approached Nam Dinh. Making a soft landing, not far from the hospital, two medics with an ambulance took her two wounded soldiers away for treatment. As Valérie secured the helicopter, an air force captain rushed up to her.

"One of your escort fighters didn't make it back," the captain told her. "He got caught up in the storm and plowed into the ground."

"Probably his altimeter got stuck," he added.[6]

Valérie always felt the death of any fellow pilot as if a part of her also died. But it was war. There was never enough time to mourn the dead. Another rescue allowed another chance to save a life. Valérie felt that if she gave in to a feeling of helplessness, it would be a trap without escape.

Another radio message for a helicopter rescue came in that same day. An outpost on the Red River near Bich Ke had suffered multiple casualties. The dispatcher said that a French Dinassaut attack boat patrolling the river would evacuate the lesser wounded, but the two most severely wounded required the helicopter.

"I took off for Bich Ke. The landing site was on the bank of the river, and this time I can only compliment the ground crew for the way they have prepared the panels. A small Navy craft touches shore and takes on the light casualties. I took back with me to Nam Dinh a Frenchman and a Vietnamese more severely hit."[7]

Bich Ke proved to be the last rescue Valérie would perform for the next three days. A lull had set in again, and it was a welcome respite. Piloting the Hiller was an intense experience, and pilot fatigue was persistent. There was no such thing as an easy mission, only some missions that required somewhat less effort. Truly intense missions took every ounce of experience and resourcefulness that a pilot could muster. One such mission came on April 6, 1952.

The garrison at Luong Han near An Xa[8] was under attack. The force at Luong Han was all Vietnamese and had been under fire from the Viet Minh for several hours that day. The Viet Minh undoubtedly knew that the fort's defenders were Vietnamese, and in their eyes, they were traitors. The ferocity of the battle was even more intense than usual. The Viet Minh were intent on total annihilation.

Valérie and the Hiller were on standby at Thai Binh when the radio operator received the distress call from Luong Han. One man was shot both in the head and arm. According to the report, the man was already in a coma, and an emergency evacuation was needed at once. To help pinpoint the outpost, Valérie was told that a white cross was painted on the roof.[9]

Luong Han was only a half hour away from Thai Binh, but Valérie was bracing for a dangerous rescue mission. Ten minutes into the flight, two fighter planes eased up on both sides of the helicopter.

"We have orders to escort you," the lead fighter pilot told Valérie over her radio headset.[10]

Seeing the two fighter planes so early in the flight confirmed to Valérie that she was entering dangerous territory. As they approached the outpost, her feelings were confirmed. Chatter over the radio began to increase, with multiple voices overlapping each other, becoming unintelligible.

"As we flew for a minute or two toward the map coordinates, I could see a large black mushroom cloud; airplanes were whirling," she said, describing the melee. Valérie knew that the black smoke meant that napalm had been dropped.

"There were quite a few of us in the sky. I had never seen so many over one target. And all of us were talking over the radio at once."[11]

The scene was chaotic. The outpost was isolated from a regular supply line, so resupplying the garrison required an airdrop. While a firefight was going on, a C-47 Dakota supply plane was circling the outpost, looking for an opportunity to drop provisions by parachute to the men who were under siege. In turn, two fighter planes were escorting the supply plane to protect it from enemy ground fire. Above the Dakota and its escorts was a Morane Criquet, whose onboard observer attempted to coordinate the entire battle scene from his aerial vantage point via radio instruction.

As Valérie came closer to the outpost, she was surprised by the abrupt maneuvers performed by the pilots in the Bearcats escorting her.

"My fighters passed by so close they almost touched me—too close, judging from the prop-wash shaking the helicopter. I disapproved of these useless aerobatics."[12]

The Dakota dropped its supplies. When the parachutes deployed above the crates, the big plane lumbered away from the area.

"Its work was done, and the Dakota seemed to be departing. But my mission had yet to begin. I tried to inform my fighters that I was going to land, but I couldn't get my message across. There were aircraft everywhere. I had to look out in every direction."

Getting a radio message from the helicopter to the fighter pilots was difficult. The handheld radio microphone was attached to the center instrument pedestal. Valérie would have had to take one of her hands away from the cyclic or collective controls. In a situation where it was crucial to maintain absolute control of the helicopter, using the microphone was nearly impossible.

The fighter pilots were still coming dangerously close to the Hiller as Valérie maneuvered over the fort.

"Why did they insist on still buzzing me?" she asked herself. She knew that the fighter pilot's job was to fire their machine guns in the direction of the Viet Minh to discourage any firing upon the helicopter as it landed. But their close-quarter activity was not the usual procedure.

"They dropped down on me, cutting me off. I could no longer grab my mic, as I needed to keep my hands on the controls. All the shouts over my headset were meaningless, so I ripped it off, thus achieving relative silence. I then plunged into the fray."[13]

The outpost was small with a wall surrounding it, but she could clearly see the white cross on the roof; however, Valérie quickly surmised that the space within the walls was too small for a helicopter to land. She saw no other choice but to land outside the fort, exposing herself and the helicopter to enemy fire.

"I flew around the outpost at a low altitude and noticed that the men were crouched along its walls and the low hanging roof of the building. What were they waiting for? Shouldn't they at least fetch the containers that were dropped?"

As Valérie assessed the situation, it dawned on her that the Viet Minh were so close that the soldiers dared not venture far from the relative safety of the outpost.

"There must be some *Viet Minh* sharpshooters around, who zero-in on the defenders each time they leave their shelter."

Just as Valérie was bringing the helicopter in for a landing, a burst of machine-gun fire crackled in the air around her. With the Viet Minh, there was no such thing as a warning shot. Valérie knew she was now a target.

"Less than fifty meters from the fort, I noticed the only spot where I could land. There was a casualty to pick up, and I came to get him. I had to go in."

A second volley of bullets rang out, followed by a third as Valérie approached her landing zone.

"I figured out approximately where the fire was coming from. When I finally plopped the aircraft down on the ground, I got the feeling that I would be better protected there than in the air."

As Valérie locked down the controls of the Hiller and then opened the door, she immediately knew that something was amiss. She motioned to the soldiers with her hand to bring the wounded man to the helicopter, but they wouldn't budge from the fort.

"I kept insisting, and I called out to them. It was as if they were paralyzed with fear. I had an urge to swear at them, but the racket from a weapon spewing fire on my right cut me off."

The Viet Minh repositioned. Even though they were many meters apart from Valérie's location, they intensified their fire on the helicopter.

"I had a feeling that this time the helicopter was irretrievably done for. It had to be punctured like a sieve."

Fortunately, the enemy fire was not as severe as Valérie first imagined. But there was little doubt that the longer she stayed, the machine-gun fire would find its mark.

Finally, from the fort, one of the men frantically gestured back at Valérie.

"He signaled to me to take off again, and I immediately ducked back down. There seemed no other alternative for me, and I took off without the wounded."

The takeoff was equally hazardous as the Viet Minh had shifted their fire to intercept the helicopter. The fighter planes were still buzzing the area, and their presence was the only thing saving Valérie from being obliterated on the ground. The Vietnamese garrison was also firing back in the direction of the enemy as Valérie took to the air.

"Caught between two fires, I weaved the Hiller back and forth in the hopes of throwing off enemy fire. My aircraft fluttered like a butterfly."

Valérie was lucky, and she knew it.

"Quickly, I put my headset back on."

With the crescendo of battle rapidly subsiding, she could hear the normal radio transmissions once again.

"The fighter pilots told me that I had orders to return to Thai Binh and await instructions there. I feared this sounded more like a lecture that was coming."[14]

It turned out that her feeling was correct. General Jean Gilles, who was assisting General Linarès in paratrooper deployment during Operation Mercure, was waiting for Valérie when she arrived. Gilles had followed the aborted rescue at Luong Han over the radio and was not pleased. He immediately informed Valérie that she had needlessly endangered herself in the mission.

"The observer in the *Criquet* tried to radio you to reroute your course," Gilles told her. "The fighter pilots tried to reach you, too. The *Viets* were all over that fort."

Valérie immediately realized her mistake.

"*No person is as deaf as the one who has removed her headset,*" she thought to herself.

It turned out that fighter planes had resorted to buzzing as close to the helicopter as they dared in an attempt to warn her off from landing.

"You were lucky, Captain," Gilles continued with his dressing-down. "One of the fighter pilots told his leader that if you don't want her to land, just fire a burst at her!"

Valérie accepted the criticism as constructive.

"I am sorry that I didn't hear the pilots' comments. In the future I will never again remove my headset; the lesson was a good one."[15]

Despite Valérie's unsuccessful rescue attempt at Luong Han, the men there were not forgotten. According to Valérie, the wounded man was rescued on the following day by Alexis Santini, while Valérie was on another mission. Santini's task was made somewhat easier when six fighter planes were sent in to strafe the area surrounding the outpost with machine-gun fire. On the day after that, a relief battalion marched to Luong Han to shore up the defense of the beleaguered Vietnamese garrison.[16]

Operation Mercure drew to a close not long after. Valérie André and Sergeant Tessier returned with the Hiller to Gialam in Hanoi. The tempo of the war, however, was still unrelenting.

"Both the helicopter and I settled back into a daily routine which lacked in neither interest nor diversity. We were in the dry season, and the war was getting twice as active along the Delta."

Not all of Valérie's missions involved the living. On April 9, another Vietnamese garrison in Hoa Mac was attacked on the previous night. Their leader, a lieutenant, was killed while on patrol. Ordinarily, the helicopter was only used to expedite the severely wounded to a hospital, but an exception was made in this case. French high command knew that it was necessary to maintain the morale of the Vietnamese troops that they were nurturing to take a more active role in the war. The men at Hoa Mac were devastated by the loss of their commander. They had requested that his remains were to be treated with the highest possible honor.

"My feelings were quite different from those that usually prevail as I fly to some outpost requiring a medical evacuation," Valérie noted. "The small Vietnamese outpost had lost its lieutenant—the officer had stepped on a mine. As I flew over the outpost, I could see that the men have provided an honor guard around their chief in the courtyard. They had cut some branches and woven wreaths."[17]

The men were solemn as Valérie completed her landing maneuver. Not for a moment did they break from the gravity of the farewell ceremony for their fallen comrade. Their display of reverence was not lost on Valérie.

"The body was placed in one of the baskets, and the wreaths were arranged in the other. In a last goodbye of the officer to his men, I took the helicopter on a wide circle upon its departure."

Each man remained at attention until the helicopter faded into the distance. Afterward, for the men left behind, it was a return to the art of survival.[18]

Back at Gialam, life also went on. The plan to expand the helicopter service was taking shape. The new storage/maintenance hangar and crew quarters for the helicopter squadron was nearing completion. There was also word of new and larger British-built Westland helicopters arriving soon to join ELA 53. In southern Vietnam, the helicopter service was also expanding. Henri Bartier was busy flying missions from the new heliport recently opened at Tan Son Nhut. The heliport was named in honor of Bernard de Lattre, the son of General de Lattre, killed in battle nearly a year before.

Bartier's workload was just as intense as Valérie André's. From March to the first week of April 1952, Bartier performed thirteen rescue missions, bringing back fifteen wounded to Saigon. Unfortunately, three of Bartier's wounded came in dead on arrival at Tan Son Nhut.[19]

Back at Gialam, Valérie André found the milder April weather in northern Vietnam a pleasant relief.

"In Indochina the weather can rapidly turn foul. At least in April we were yet far away from summer thunderstorms."[20]

Valérie would learn firsthand not to take the weather for granted in Vietnam in the course of one mission. On April 12, Valérie was ordered to proceed to Vu Tien, where a detachment of Moroccans carrying out a reconnaissance mission was ambushed.

Vu Tien was close to one hundred kilometers (sixty miles) from Gialam. Valérie estimated that the round-trip would take roughly ninety minutes. The weather started in her favor as she reached the somewhat isolated area with no problem. Upon landing, Valérie learned that the Moroccans had suffered severe casualties in their firefight with the Viet Minh. A lieutenant acting as medic told her that there were already several dead, and the wounded man was in desperate condition.

"He might not make it," the lieutenant said to Valérie. "But let's give him a chance anyway."[21]

Valérie was especially taken with the lieutenant's choice of words: *Let's give him a chance.*

"*That sentence summarized our vocation well,*" she later thought to herself. "The helicopter was a *chance* for these threatened soldiers. Yes, to give a *chance* to this one as with all the others."[22]

With the wounded Moroccan strapped securely into the litter, Valérie took off in the direction of Hanoi, using the Red River as her guide.

A weather front was moving quickly into the area, and the skies grew darker. Valérie had to decrease the altitude of the Hiller, bringing it closer to the river. Soon the wind was increasing, and it wasn't long after that sand from the banks of the Red River swept in swirls around the low-flying aircraft.

"The sand was whirling, literally choking. The helicopter danced, yawed, and pitched itself upward, caught up in the turbulence. It was a real tornado sweeping the area."[23]

The winds were wildly unpredictable. The helicopter was becoming increasingly difficult to keep airborne.

"I struggled with the controls, but the Hiller was sucked in and turned upwards and downwards, climbing and descending."

Valérie knew her situation was once again dire. Luck would play a role as much as skill to get back to home base safely.

Having flown the route from Nam Dinh and Thai Binh—which were both near Tu Vien—many times already, Valérie knew she was only ten minutes away from Gialam. But the storm was also increasing in intensity.

"The aircraft was flying backward in the wind, rather than forward."

Valérie needed to reach down deep in the bag of pilot's tricks to try to save herself and her patient.

"I gave it *all it's got* for power, full cyclic stick forward, and waited. Still shaking and tossed around, the Hiller, nevertheless, gained some ground."

At least the helicopter was now making forward progress. In what seemed to be an interminable several minutes, Valérie was finally over Gialam air base.

The tower control at Gialam was monitoring her flight as she came into view, and Valérie could hear their instructions over her headset.

"Warning, helicopter, you've got a forty-knot wind, warning, helicopter. Acknowledge!"

Valérie couldn't reply.

"I had too much need for both my hands to keep the aircraft flying."

As she approached ELA 53's hangar, the wind may have subsided for just a moment.

"I was able to execute a sweeping turn, worthy of a bomber, which at least brought me into the wind. Held in check, the aircraft descended obediently."[24]

The entire crew came out of the hangar to welcome Valérie back. More than one of the crew commented on her skill in getting back to Gialam. Others were in wonder as to the incredible luck that must have been on Valérie's side.

Even Valérie reflected on the role chance played in a pilot's success:

"It was without a doubt that luck often accompanied me, like a faithful friend. In a mission, luck is what comes from elsewhere. It was the indispensable supplement. There was no way to count on it or to hope that it will lessen pilot error. No, luck is something else; a mysterious presence that one must know how to capture and never refuse."[25]

Avoiding pilot error was an ever-present thought in every aviator's mind. It was not long after that Valérie André was to see the aftermath of just such an incident involving other aircraft.

On April 14, an urgent call came into Gialam for a helicopter rescue on the open sea. The French aircraft carrier *Arromanches* was stationed off the coast of northern Vietnam in the Gulf of Tonkin and had suffered a disaster. A Hellcat pilot misjudged his approach to the carrier and crash-landed on deck, mowing down everything in his path. Five men were killed instantly, and three others were severely injured. Fortunately, fast action from the accident crew kept an inferno from erupting aboard the ship. But it was a major catastrophe, nonetheless.

"I was to fly out toward Haiphong and from there to the airbase at Cat Ba where a naval officer was to brief me," Valérie said. The *Arromanches* was somewhere off the coast but now limping back to port while her crew assessed the damage."

The officer told Valérie that at least two casualties required immediate transport to a military hospital from the ship. Her mission was to land onboard the *Arromanches* and assist with their evacuation.

"I was told that the two sailors were rather corpulent. I immediately gauged the gas in my tanks so as to keep only the strict minimum."

Extra fuel added weight to the helicopter. With a pair of stout casualties, it was necessary to be precise and take only what was required to complete the mission.

"A quick check of my aircraft revealed that the brakes were working poorly. If the aircraft carrier was rolling and pitching, the helicopter with its tricycle landing gear would meander all over the flight deck."

The Hiller was notorious for having underperforming brakes on its wheels. The aircraft's designers presumed other measures would be taken to secure the helicopter on the ground. Valérie would not take any chances. She asked the officer to radio ahead for the *Arromanches* crew to be ready to tie down the helicopter as soon as she landed. She also said to tell the men to be especially careful around the Hiller's main and tail rotors. The Hiller would be the first helicopter to land on the *Arromanches*, and Valérie was determined not to be the cause of any other accidents.

"What is the exact position of the *Arromanches*?" Valérie asked the naval officer. She realized that a ship underway on the open sea—even a large ship like the *Arromanches*—might be tough to spot, especially in the dense mist that often shrouded the Vietnamese coast.

"There is no haze," the officer replied. He then provided what seemed to Valérie to be somewhat vague coordinates of the ship's last known position, adding, "from a thousand feet above you'll see the *Arromanches*."

The officer's instructions didn't completely reassure Valérie, but she realized that time was of the essence.

"Without adding any fuel, I fired up my meager 178 horses that would have to fly the two casualties back to the hospital." And with that, Valérie lifted off.

Flying over the ocean is an incredibly daunting task for any helicopter pilot. Everything associated with an aircraft needs to perform flawlessly. There was nothing to be saved if a forced landing was required. At least within Halong Bay, there are more than sixteen hundred islands—both large and small—that could be used as landmarks. But over the open ocean itself, there was nothing but water.

"High up above the surface of the ocean, I saw nothing. Heading out for the assumed position of the ship, I progressed over a calm sea, crisscrossed by sampans and pretty junks under sail. As I feared, haze blanks out the horizon. But trusting my watch and my compass, I go on."

"It felt like a long time," she added.

Presently, Valérie spotted something different on the ocean up ahead. As she flew closer, the mass came into focus. It was indeed the *Arromanches*, along with a destroyer acting as its escort.

"The *Arromanches* was heading my way. I couldn't help but feel that luck was with me," she thought to herself joyously.

It was the first time that Valérie saw an actual aircraft carrier, and its size astonished her.

"The naval officer back at Cat Ba mentioned the word 'island,' and my ignorance had shocked him. But the superstructure and the bridge do form something shaped like an island."[26]

Valérie was instructed to maneuver the helicopter behind the ship when she was ready to land. The carrier seemed to glide over the water. Valérie could see from the fluttering windsocks and flags that her landing would be without any unnecessary drama. As the entire length of the flight deck came into view, Valérie could see evidence of the carnage. The badly damaged Grumman Bearcats were piled in a heap at the front end of the ship. It was quickly apparent to Valérie that casualties could have been much worse.

Turning her attention away from the wreckage, Valérie picked out markings in the shape of a *T* on the deck of the *Arromanches*. This was the LZ for the Hiller. The landing signal officer stood in front of Valérie and the helicopter as it came in contact with the deck. As soon as it touched down, several sailors rushed out to secure the helicopter.

As had become standard operating procedure, Valérie kept the Hiller's engine running. She thought about refueling the Hiller but was still concerned that the helicopter would balk at a restart, even on an aircraft carrier.

"In a pinch—although this is not permitted—I could shut the engine down and take on some gas. But the *Arromanches* only had available 100 octane gasoline, whereas the Hiller used 80 octane. My current fuel supply appeared sufficient to me, so I busied myself tending to the wounded."[27]

Gauging the somber mood of the men of the *Arromanches*, Valérie could tell they were still in deep shock over the accident.

"As I climbed out of the aircraft, I could see the deep sadness that was written all over every face," she observed. "I avoided asking any questions regarding the accident."[28]

Two officers approached Valérie. One was the commander of the *Arromanches*, Captain Emile Granger-Veyron. Valérie was quickly brought up to speed as to the medical condition of the injured men.

"There are three men who need to be brought back to shore," Captain Granger-Veyron told her. "We had to amputate a leg on one man. He lost a lot of blood, and they are still trying to stabilize him. We think he'll be able to go on the next flight, but the ship's surgeon hasn't cleared him for evacuation yet. You may have to spend the night here when you come back."

The first two casualties were brought out on litters with small floats attached to them that were designed for ship-to-ship transfer, not to aircraft.

"The floating litters were so bulky I had trouble closing the baskets," said Valérie. Additionally, one of the injured men was indeed large. "One of my passengers, a large bearded man, weighed at least a hundred kilos (220 lbs)."[29]

Once the men were secured to the litter baskets, Valérie wasted no time getting the Hiller ready for takeoff.

"On my signal, the landing signal officer ordered the chocks pulled out, and I took off into the wind. The aircraft climbed slowly."

With the additional weight on board, the Hiller labored somewhat as it flew away. At least there wasn't the usual urgency to make a quick getaway. As Valérie pointed out:

"Forget the altitude—there was no fear of the *Viet Minh* for now."[30]

The coast of Vietnam was still far off into the distance, and the sea seemed to stretch on forever. Valérie was very mindful of the helicopter's fuel supply; both time and gasoline were precious commodities.

"This trip seemed horribly long to me. For want of a clock on the instrument panel, I wore a watch around my neck. Minutes went by, and the wind must have picked up."

Cat Ba was farther than the fuel onboard the helicopter would allow Valérie to travel, but she knew there was a supply base at Doson where she could pick up extra gasoline.

"*Ventilateur* calling Doson, request landing for fuel resupply," Valérie called out over the radio.

When Valérie landed, two mechanics rushed out to meet her, carrying jerry cans of gasoline.

"I handed them the funnel and a chamois," Valérie said. The chamois served as a filter that strained the fuel as it entered the Hiller's tank to prevent contaminates from fouling the engine's carburetor.

"The sailors seemed happy to be back on firm ground. The large bearded man was smiling."[31]

From Do Son, Cat Ba was only a few minutes away by air, but Valérie felt more confident with more fuel onboard. Once she arrived at Cat Ba, medics quickly unloaded the two sailors, and the Hiller was again topped off with more fuel. Daylight, however, was beginning to fade.

"I had to hurry as dusk was approaching," Valérie said. "The skipper of the *Arromanches* had specifically asked me to come back, even if I had to spend the night on board."[32]

Valérie was sure that if she had to spend the night aboard the aircraft carrier that the Hiller would be well taken care of in the company of the fighter planes stored below the flight deck.

Finding the *Arromanches* on the open sea proved to be easier on the second attempt. After repeating the previous landing procedure, Valérie brought the helicopter to rest. The men darted out from their shelters to secure the aircraft to the deck once again.

As Valérie emerged from the cockpit, an officer ran up to her, ducking down low to stay clear of the rotor blades.

"The ship's doctor gave the okay to move the patient," he shouted to her over the din of the still operating helicopter.

Again, no time was wasted. The injured man was brought to the flight deck and quickly strapped into the helicopter. With no time to say a formal farewell to the *Arromanches* and its crew, Valérie gave the signal to release the Hiller and for them to stand clear. No sooner was she airborne than she took note of the darkness.

"On my way back, night falls suddenly around me. I turned on my running lights and lit up my instrument panel."

Fortunately, Valérie saw lights coming from the coast and zeroed in on their location. It wasn't long that she reached Cat Ba with her patient.

"We reached the airfield without incident."

After a long day of work, both Valérie and the Hiller retired for the evening—the Hiller on the airfield tarmac and Valérie André in the officers' quarters at Cat Ba.[33]

The crew of the *Arromanches* did not forget the rescue. A few days later, the aircraft carrier's captain sent a cable to Valérie conveying his thanks for her effort:

Aircraft Carrier *Arromanches*
17 April, 1952

Mademoiselle Andre,

I wish to express my deep gratitude for your invaluable assistance in transporting our wounded from the *Arromanches*, thus avoiding a long and painful journey for them by ship.

Also, you are the first woman to have landed on the *Arromanches*, which you did with ease. I would like to express my congratulations."

Captain Emile Granger-Veyron[34]

It was no small feat that Valérie André was now officially recognized for her efforts in the air, on land, and at sea.

Chapter 29

No Place for the Dying

Northern Vietnam, Summer 1952

Changes were coming to Vietnam in summer 1952. Most ominously, the Communist Chinese were increasing their support of the Viet Minh. The volume of weapons pouring into Vietnam from China was substantial—some 40,000 rifles, 450 mortars, 120 recoilless guns, 50 antiaircraft guns, and 35 field guns during the year 1952 alone.[1] These numbers paled compared to the volume of weapons and equipment coming from the United States to aid the French in Indochina. Yet, the net effect of improving the Viet Minh army would have dire consequences in campaigns to come.

Valérie André saw these changes and how they affected the French on the battlefield. One of the most immediate signs of change was the expansion of the medical rescue helicopter service. The service had proven itself to be an overwhelming success. Santini's time was now in great demand creating a second helicopter squadron.

But if there was one overall feeling that was beginning to take its toll with the personnel, and even the equipment of ELA 53, it was fatigue. The pace of performing rescues was unrelenting. Valérie's flight log during spring and summer 1952 spoke volumes: in March, eleven rescues; in April, nineteen rescues; and in May, twenty-one rescues. When the monsoon season reduced the war to a relative lull during June and July, Valérie still managed to pull off medical evacuations for fourteen wounded soldiers. Some of the missions included making multiple roundtrips in the course of a single day.[2]

"I felt the fatigue. With the prevailing heat in Tonkin, flying a helicopter every day became more painful. The lower part of the cockpit door forms an integral part with the basket cover, and when there are casualties on board, the pilot had to close up the cabin."[3]

There were times when the Hiller's cockpit's interior temperature easily exceeded 40 degrees Celsius (100 degrees Fahrenheit).

It was not only the physical exhaustion starting to impact Valérie. Being a daily witness to the war's indiscriminate destruction of life had its effect, too. As a doctor, Valérie placed a high value on her skill to save lives, and the helicopter was a tool that often made that possible. But all too often, there were limitations as to what the doctor and the machine could do.

"An evacuation was requested by the outpost at Gian Khau. The Phu Ly region is very beautiful, with impressive chalk hills dominating the road leading to Ninh Binh. But each gorge there appeared to hide frightening mysteries. The *Viet Minh* were masters of those ravines, and it was better not to risk entering."[4]

Valérie had strict orders to land in Phu Ly before proceeding onto Gian Khau. She was to wait for fighter escort to arrive and stay with her the rest of the way. But while she and the helicopter were on the ground at Phu Ly, the Hiller became a source of endless fascination for the local populace.

"The helicopter had hardly landed that it attracted the curiosity of the Annamese (Vietnamese). A crowd of them invaded the airfield," Valérie said. "I was forced to get angry. They marveled at the sight of the *ventila-teur*, and they felt a violent urge to touch with their own hands this bizarre object. They were especially drawn to the tail rotor. 'Are the blades strong?' they would ask. They absolutely wanted to see for themselves."[5]

The situation grew so intense that soldiers at the airfield had to step in with their weapons drawn to disperse the swarm. Fortunately, the crowd complied, and there was no further incident.

The sky grew dark as another weather front began to move in. Valérie wanted to get on with her mission but had no choice but to wait for the fighter planes to arrive.

Presently, the drone of two radial engines grew louder as two Bearcat fighter planes approached. Flying low and at high speed, the two fighter pilots flew over Valérie and the Hiller. They split off and made a wide 180-degree turn, this time heading back a little slower on their second pass. It was a signal for Valérie to take off immediately and follow.

Gian Khau was only thirty kilometers (twenty-two miles) from Phu Ly. Valérie knew she could arrive at the outpost in less than thirty minutes. The two Bearcat pilots wasted no time getting to Gian Khau before Valérie. They strafed the area surrounding the outpost with machine-gun fire to drive away the Viet Minh before Valérie and the helicopter arrived. She knew that the pilots would do whatever was necessary to keep her, the Hiller, and the wounded soldier she was to transport safe from enemy fire.

There was very little Valérie knew of the wounded man at Gian Khau. GATAC usually didn't specify the status of a wounded man over open radio channels over concern that the enemy could be monitoring transmissions.

As she flew on, the first drops of rain splattered the Plexiglas canopy of her aircraft. Santini had recently put Valérie and Bartier through extensive instrument flight rules (IFR) training.[6] Pilot disorientation was a common cause of accidents. Valérie piloted the Hiller with a greater degree of safety by relying on her aircraft's instruments for navigation at night or in inclement weather. Over the radio, Valérie could hear the chatter from the Bearcat pilots as they flew low over the area, dispersing any remnants of enemy presence. She was still a few minutes out from Gian Khau.

"Watch out, *Ventilateur*," one of the pilots warned through Valérie's radio headset. "You're going to hit a squall."

Valérie acknowledged and thanked the pilot, but she already knew that she was flying into a storm. With a glance at her altimeter and compass, she reported her position and ETA back to the pilots. A moment later, the rain came down in a torrent, thoroughly drenching the helicopter. Visibility through the canopy was down to zero. Valérie kept her eyes on the artificial horizon on the instrument panel to maintain her flight attitude. There were no landmarks visible from the ground, and the compass kept her on course. A blanket of gray enveloped the helicopter.

The rain continued for several minutes; but typical of the weather in Vietnam, the deluge suddenly stopped, and the sky began to clear. Valérie could see the dirt road that led up to the outpost, and she soon caught sight of the fighter planes making their low passes over the surrounding area. As she drew nearer to the landing zone (LZ), Valérie noticed that something wasn't right.

"As soon as I landed, I noticed the disorder prevailing at the outpost."

Three men from the blockhouse in the center of the compound ran up to the helicopter, as Valérie opened the door to her cockpit.

"It's our sergeant," one of the men told her. "He's dying."

The soldiers motioned to Valérie to follow them back to the blockhouse. As she peered inside, she saw the gravely wounded soldier lying prostrate on a stretcher. The unit medic had done his best to stabilize the sergeant's injuries, but Valérie could see that his wounds were extensive.

"One glance was enough. I won't bring him back alive."

The wounds were as severe as they could be and yet spare a man from immediate death. The young sergeant had caught the full force of a fragmentation grenade. Shrapnel riddled his abdomen, and his left wrist was bandaged back together and only held in one piece by gauze and his own sinew. He had lost a lot of blood and labored strenuously as he breathed.

Valérie injected a shot of Sedol into the man's arm, and the pain deadener seemed to have some effect. His eyes relaxed a little, but Valérie knew his time was running out.

"He barely had a breath left in him. But must I try everything?"

The soldiers brought the young man to the helicopter with an abundance of care. They placed him in the left side litter, just below Valérie's position in the cockpit. A quick getaway was necessary as the Viet Minh were returning to reclaim their position, and fire from several hundred meters away began to erupt once again.

Nam Dinh was only forty-one kilometers (twenty-five miles) to the northeast, and Valérie opened the Hiller's throttle wide open with the hope of getting the sergeant to the field hospital there. She knew the route to Nam Dinh by heart.

"Not for an instant did I lose sight of the face of this tall and handsome boy, gradually slipping into agony," Valérie said.

"Water, water," the young man silently said to Valérie through the Plexiglas cover of the side litter. She could read the words on his lips. With his stomach wound, Valérie knew giving the young soldier water was out of the question even if they were on the ground.

"How far the hospital seemed to be."

As the flight went on, the soldier's condition only worsened. The Sedol was starting to lose its effect, and pain wracked the young man's body. In a feverish, manic impulse to seek relief from the pain, the young soldier clawed away at his bandages with his still usable right hand, exposing the raw stomach wound. He even managed to tear away the bandages and splint that held his mangled left wrist together.

Valérie André could only watch as her patient suffered, helpless to relieve his misery.

"I began to lose all hope of arriving in time at the hospital. Little by little, the signs of his agony became more evident. Awful spasmodic tremors shook his body. Undoubtedly, he was suffering an internal hemorrhage."

Finally, Valérie could see the field hospital at Nam Dinh. She wasted no time setting the helicopter down and was out of the cockpit even before the medics arrived.

"Perhaps this man was still alive?" Valérie hoped against all logic. But as she opened the cover, she saw what she knew was inevitable.

"All I brought back was a dead body."

Valérie later characterized that flight as "one of the most painful memories of my flying days."[7]

The attempted rescue of the sergeant would not be Valérie André's last painful memory. In another rescue mission around the same time, Valérie would feel not only some of the same pain but also a more personal connection.

On July 29, Valérie received instructions to evacuate a wounded officer at Thai Luong. When she got there, Valérie wasn't at all satisfied with the landing zone.

"I had been there before," she said. "To my great surprise, the landing platform was located on a former dike that had been widened and was now surrounded by an earthen wall. A little further away stood a new blockhouse. It really seemed like all the many memos concerning the preparations of LZ's, which Air Support sent out to units in the field, were never read!"

Faced with a choice to either use the area set aside for the helicopter's landing or abort the mission, Valérie elected to carefully squeeze the Hiller into the tight space. There was barely any room to spare.

"I landed close to the blockhouse in a rather foul mood. When I climbed out of the aircraft I noticed that my fears were justified—the tail rotor was less than a meter (three feet) from the little wall. How could I ever pull the aircraft out of such a trap?"[8]

As Valérie was planning a takeoff in her mind, an officer ran up to the helicopter. Before he could say anything, Valérie told him in no uncertain terms that the inadequately prepared LZ was a hazard to her.

"I explained to him the reason for my ire—did he think the helicopter is nothing but an elevator?! I directed him to issue instructions to all the post commanders under him."

But the officer was oblivious to Valérie's concerns.

"Oh, I know, I know," he said to Valérie. "In France, I have already seen helicopters in action . . ."

Valérie tuned out the oblivious officer when the casualty was brought to the helicopter. She gasped as she recognized the face of Lieutenant "N," the young man who had just recently stopped by her table at the Coq d'Or in Hanoi.

The young man had suffered a severe abdominal wound.

"When I saw the lieutenant on the stretcher, my heart cringed. He was the young man I had met several times before. When he was healthy, he already seemed delicate. I wondered how he would find the strength to survive."[9]

Valérie's anger over the LZ evaporated as she plotted a safe liftoff.

"The take-off turned out all right. The helicopter rose between the walls, then skimmed the blockhouse. I flew back to Nam Dinh."

Just as with the sergeant, Valérie could not help but feel the ebbing of another life. This time, however, Valérie's patient arrived alive. But his condition remained grave.

"On the following days—each time I could—I would pay a visit to the young lieutenant. He seemed to be holding on."[10]

Each day in Indochina grew increasingly hazardous from the war. The psychological pressure of witnessing wartime atrocities eroded personal resolve. Even the aftermath of a horrific event could have lasting consequences. One such event occurred at Cape St. Jacques during summer 1952.

Cape St. Jacques was the gateway to Saigon. It was on the coast of southern Vietnam off the banks of the Saigon River and well known for its vast expanses of idyllic, black sandy beaches and palm trees. The French maintained a convalescent resort and recreation area for soldiers who were wounded or on leave. Sometimes soldiers were accompanied by their families, who often traveled long distances to visit them.

On July 20, an elite squad of a Viet Minh terrorist unit wearing stolen French Expeditionary Corps uniforms infiltrated the compound at Cape St. Jacques. The Viet Minh had been carrying out terrorist attacks, particularly in the south, that should have put the French more on guard for just this possibility.

The squad stormed a dining hall where a group of French officers, along with their wives and children, were settling down to dinner. The Viet Minh attacked without mercy. Beginning with a salvo of grenades lobbed into the dining hall, the terrorists followed up with a fusillade of machine-gun fire. The ensuing chaos was almost indescribable in its savagery. Eight officers, six children, two women, and four Vietnamese servers were killed. A small boy managed to survive by hiding behind a chair, going unnoticed during the brutal attack.

By coincidence—and only a few days after the massacre—Valérie André had to return to Saigon for a few days. At Gialam, Valérie was assigned a seat on a Dakota bound for Saigon that also included General Raoul Salan and his staff. After settling into her seat, the passenger next to Valérie told her that the plane would make an unscheduled stop at Cape St. Jacques.

"The officers accompanying General Salan were making mysterious comments, but I avoided questioning them. What happened at the Cape?"

News of the incident had not been made public yet. Valérie was to learn of the tragedy firsthand.

"When we landed on the peninsula, I was to find out."[11]

Valérie had seen many horrible things in Indochina since she first arrived in 1947, but the scene of the massacre took the horror of war to a different level. General Salan insisted on seeing every detail involved with the attack.

"I shall never forget our visit to the villa used as a mess hall by the convalescents and their families. The dining hall and the kitchen were in shambles. Blood was spattered on the walls; the tile floors were covered with food, broken glasses, and dishes, and the broken furniture attested to the violence of the drama."[12]

The French military and *agents de Sûreté* were still investigating the crime, but it was not hard for Valérie to have a sense of how the moment of the attack transpired.

"The panic felt by our poor compatriots, attacked and massacred in the middle of their meal, was easy to imagine. We went to the hospital to visit the survivors. Terror was still there in the eyes of the men, as well as those of the women and children."[13]

Another poignant memory came when the group left the hospital. General Salan had not only come to meet the survivors but also to pay tribute to the dead.

"Finally, we stopped and paid our respects to the coffins lined up in the hospital courtyard," Valérie said. She also noticed the smaller coffins. "I thought of the children who were massacred."

Valérie could see that Salan was very affected by the carnage. He wanted answers, but answers were not forthcoming. Before his arrival, Salan had ordered that all local Vietnamese village chiefs and officials be present also. Valérie listened in as Salan attempted to get to the bottom of what had happened.

"Can you give us information on those responsible for this massacre?" Valérie heard the general tell an interpreter.

The various elders understood the general's question, but there was only silence.

"The village chiefs just stared at each other. No one seemed to know anything."[14]

With nothing to be gained from staying longer, General Salan and the rest of the party returned to the airfield for the short trip to Tan Son Nhut.

Valérie André didn't remain in Saigon for long.

"As soon as I returned to Tonkin, I resumed my duties and my work."

Not long after Valérie was back in the north, however, she had yet another sad encounter.

"Because Santini was back for a few days, I spent some quieter days out at Gialam. At the end of lunch the two of us were having at the airport, an Air France pilot came up to our table. He told us that one of his passengers would like to talk to me. She had just arrived from Paris and was waiting for me on the terrace, in front of the dining room."

The woman was the mother of Lieutenant "N." The young soldier had been transferred from the field hospital at Nam Dinh to Lanessan in Hanoi, where he had bravely clung to life. The military sent word to the young man's mother in France, who boarded the first available flight to Vietnam to see her son. En route to Vietnam, the woman learned of the story of how her son was spirited away from the battlefield by a courageous angel. It was so fantastic. But when the Air France pilot heard the woman's story from one of his attendants, he knew that the angel she spoke of could only be Valérie André.

But the flight from France to Vietnam took several days, so she couldn't have known what Valérie already knew.

"The young officer died two days before at Lanessan Hospital. This woman, who came all the way from France, didn't know it yet."

Valérie could not tell the woman what had happened in any less painful manner.

"I was sure she could read the truth from the expression on my face. I signaled to Santini, who rushed over. It took both of us to tell this mother the truth she already guessed."[15]

There was a limit to everyone's endurance and health in Indochina, and Valérie proved to be no exception. Even with the most cautious hygiene precautions, it was only a matter of time before one would eventually succumb to one or more maladies. As a physician, Valérie could self-diagnose, and she realized that she wasn't well.

"In the days that followed, the rhythm of the evacuations picked up. No sooner had the helicopters returned to the field, they were off again. The routine demanded the full use of our faculties. The war in the Delta seemed to me to have no beginning, no end. Our missions took us to the four points of the compass rose and for the first time . . . I felt really tired."[16]

There was a breaking point for Valérie, and it came one morning on the tarmac at Gialam. As she prepared for a mission that was to take her to Dong Ly, she waited for clearance from the control tower while a C-47 transport was landing nearby. When the plane landed and was taxiing to its terminal, Valérie was given clearance to begin her flight.

"As I laid the map down next to me—I knew the route by heart—I took off."

But almost immediately, Valérie could feel there was something wrong with the Hiller.

"Thirty feet off the ground, there was a sudden drop in RPM, causing the aircraft to flutter. I tried to level it. The nose dropped, the helicopter fell and crashed smack in the middle of the parking apron."[17]

The Hiller came down hard, and it pancaked into a crumpled heap. Valérie had the breath knocked out of her, but the Hiller's structure held together. The basic lap seatbelt did its job, preventing her from sustaining serious injury. She looked up and could see a man in the control tower, waving his arms. Men were running toward her and the helicopter from all directions.

A captain with one of the aerial artillery observations groups based at Gialam was the first to get to the crash. But Valérie had already extricated herself from the wreck.

"Do you need help, Captain?" he asked.

"No, I don't need a thing," Valérie replied. "I don't even have a scratch."

But as she turned around to survey the damage to the Hiller, her heart sunk. The engine had likely experienced a problem with its fuel supply, causing the RPM to drop while the helicopter was still in ground-effect mode. The damage might have been less severe if the aircraft was at a higher altitude when the engine became balky. Valérie could have performed a much softer, power off / autorotation landing.

"Its tail was bent in two like an inverted 'V.' Its landing gear was crushed. My helicopter looked in such sad shape that I had to walk away."[18]

It was almost as if Valérie felt the pain of her aircraft more than any pain that she may have suffered in the accident.

"I would have liked for them to remove the poor aircraft as soon as possible, but the investigating team is never in a hurry. They would photograph it from every angle."[19]

As Valérie turned to walk back to the hangar, she caught sight of Alexis Santini and mechanic Georges Le Goff standing transfixed.

"I could also see Santini and Le Goff, motionless at the hangar entrance—they appeared petrified," Valérie recalled. "They would confess to me later that they recovered the use of their legs only after they saw me emerge from the cockpit."[20]

But just as her helicopter had suffered, Valérie knew she wasn't well either.

"That same day, I suddenly decided to check myself in the hospital," Valérie said. "The laboratory confirmed a case of amoebic dysentery that I suspected for a long time. I might as well undergo a proper treatment; the sooner I could get rid of these parasites, the sooner I would be able to resume my flights."[21]

Chapter 30

Taking Command

Hanoi, July 1952

Lanessan Military Hospital was one of the most prominent buildings on rue Concession in Hanoi. Overlooking the banks of the Red River, it was part of the French army headquarters in the old Citadel part of the city. Lanessan was built in the 1890s and was originally designed to accommodate four hundred patients. Now, after six years of war, the hospital was filled beyond its original capacity, often accommodating more than fifteen hundred patients.

As fate would have it, Valrie André found herself to be among the infirmed at Lanessan.

"The stay at the hospital broke the rhythms of my daily life. Barely one hundred meters from the room I occupy, Santini and Bartier landed several times a day. They never failed to pay me a visit."[1]

Valérie was dejected, and her proximity to the helicopter landing pad only served to heighten that feeling. The hospital had recently installed a helipad to spare transporting the wounded through the streets of Hanoi by ambulance after they arrived at either the airstrip at Bach Mai or Gialam air base. The constant landings and takeoffs near her room only increased her desire to return to active duty.

Valérie still suffered from a severe case of amoebic dysentery that could prove fatal if not completely treated. A standard treatment at the time was intravenous injections of emetine, a drug derived from the ipecac root. A side effect of emetine was severe nausea. Until a patient was declared free of the microscopic parasites, a hospital stay was mandatory.

As a doctor, Valérie found it challenging to be a patient. But as a pilot who personally rescued several of the men who were still patients at Lanessan, Valérie found she had many admirers.

"Often . . , I would hear a knock on the door and see some of the wounded men I had evacuated who came to visit me."[2]

In time, Valérie's condition improved to the point where she was released from the hospital. But she would not be cleared for flight status for another two weeks.

"I waited, trying to kill time and soothe my impatience. Life in Hanoi was austere compared to the hectic and carefree city of Saigon. But I like the Petit Lac [Hoan Kiem] and its pagoda, and the Grand Lake [Ho Tay], the rue Paul Bert [Trang Tien street], and venture into the fascinating and mysterious streets of the capital of Tonkin. My dog *Rotor*, impressive by his size, served as my bodyguard."[3]

The Vietnamese capital may not have been the vibrant place it once was, but it afforded enough diversion for Valérie to get through the final days of her recovery. On June 17, she reported for her last checkup with the flight surgeon, Major Cantoni, who certified her fit for duty once again. Valérie's return to active service proved to be good timing. When she arrived at Gialam, Valérie learned that Alexis Santini had received new orders.

"Santini was urgently recalled to Saigon. He told me that I was to be in charge of the helicopter section."[4]

Placing Valérie André in charge of the helicopter operations of ELA 53 was significant. It symbolized the trust Santini had in her ability to command and manage the squadron. But it also marked the first time a woman would be in charge of an aviation unit within the French military. It was also a time of pride for the rotorcraft section of ELA 53, as the new facilities for the helicopters and their maintenance were now complete at Gialam.

"What a pleasure to have a perfectly landscaped hangar, the most beautiful one on the base. The Corps of Engineers had done well," Valérie noted with great satisfaction. She had personally chosen the plants and flowers from Hanoi's many flower markets to decorate the new headquarters' exterior and interior.

"I remained with Bartier, Le Goff, and the other mechanics. Harmony prevailed within our little group, and the change of hangar further enhanced our spirits."[5]

Command did not exempt Valérie from service. On the following afternoon, Valérie André found herself back in the thick of the action. Orders came through for her to leave for Nam Dinh. She was to transport a non-commissioned officer to replace the commander of an outpost who had become seriously ill. The weather was atrociously hot and humid.

"I took my place at the controls. The heat is unbearable under the Plexiglas. What I would give to leave the doors back at the hangar."

She immediately dismissed the notion of flying with an open cockpit.

"Were we to fly without covers over the litters, the casualties would feel too insecure. Even when a mission theoretically involves only one passenger, we can't take the chance of removing one of these doors. The helicopter could receive another assignment en route."[6]

The flight from Gialam to Nam Dinh posed no challenge as Valérie had flown the route so many times by now that she knew every kilometer of it. When she reached the airfield at Nam Dinh, it wasn't long before the soldier she was to transport to Hill 71 marched up to the helicopter. He was outfitted for combat, with grenades hanging from his belt and a submachine gun slung over his shoulder.

"I don't want any weapons on board," Valérie flatly told the soldier.[7] "If I were to take you out equipped as you are I would have to cover the red crosses on the basket covers. My mission is, and must remain, strictly a medical one."[8]

At first, the soldier didn't comprehend Valérie's order. He had not expected a female officer who was also a helicopter pilot. Without his weapons, he felt naked and said as much to Valérie. But Valérie remained firm, and ultimately the soldier complied.

"Very well," he replied somewhat reluctantly as he peeled off his weapons and ammunition to leave with an ordinance officer in Nam Dinh.

Hill 71 was only a fifteen-minute flight from Nam Dinh, but it was impossible to land at the outpost itself. It was situated at the top of a mountain peak with no place for the helicopter to land.

"According to the information received in Nam Dinh, I would only be able to land at a road crossing."

As they approached the landing area, Valérie could make out the topography surrounding Hill 71. She made a wide circle with the Hiller as they came nearer. The road at the base of the hill was easy enough to find with a rice paddy that ran along one side of it. There were also pockets of thick brush uncomfortably close to the road. Valérie examined the area for human activity. An ambush was always a possibility.

"The road was deserted, but the peasant farmers continued their work in the rice paddies," Valérie observed. "When a battle starts, they vanished. When things quieted down, they were back."[9]

The circling helicopter had signaled to the men defending the elevated outpost to move down to the road. But just as the helicopter landed, shots rang out. The soldier Valérie was transporting from Nam Dinh leaped out of the Hiller's cockpit, swearing about the machine gun he'd left behind.

"Although the men from the fort shouldered their weapons, the alert was only short-lived," Valérie said. "I was only half worried. The *nhaques* had not fled their rice paddies, and that was generally a good sign."[10]

With combat averted for the time being, a sense of calm prevailed. The men of Hill 71, along with their commander, approached the landing site.

"Their commander was thin and visibly exhausted. He had doubtlessly spent several months on this hilltop. I could only imagine those anxious nights. From dusk to the following dawn, the commander of an isolated outpost most often could only rely upon himself."[11]

The young man had requested his own evacuation the day before but now had second thoughts about leaving his hill.

"But I am in perfect health," he protested to Valérie. "This defies understanding."[12]

Valérie would have none of it. She recognized battle fatigue, and the young noncom exhibited all of the classic symptoms of having spent too much time in the field.

"Your replacement is here. I'm taking you with me," Valérie said to the soldier. "Like it or not, you'll return to Nam Dinh."[13]

Almost as soon as the young soldier climbed into the cockpit, fire erupted again from the brush. The men who remained behind, along with their new commander, scrambled back up the hill to the relative protection of their fortified perch.

The following day witnessed a flurry of activity inside and outside the helicopter hangar at Gialam. General Chassin, commander of the French air force in Indochina, was scheduled to inspect the new facility.

"The helicopter hangar was humming with cheer, in spite of the prevailing heat. All of us were eager for the Air Force Commanding General to be satisfied with his inspection."

Valérie took pride in the crew's work. The Hillers, including the new H-23A models, were precisely lined up on the tarmac. The hangar was also ready for the new and much larger Westland S51 helicopters that were to enter into medical rescue service soon. The Westlands were something of an emergency acquisition, as the newer Hillers were still plagued with payload issues. Alexis Santini was overseeing the delivery of the new helicopters at Tan Son Nhut air base in Saigon where they would undergo trials. Also, there would be new pilots joining both ELA 52 in the south and ELA 53 in the north to fly the new Westlands.

"The hangar, the offices, the rooms, everything was ship-shape," Valérie noted. "I have never seen men doing such a neat clean-up job—everyone pitched in."[14]

All was in readiness, and General Chassin was expected to arrive at any minute. But Valérie would not be there for the inspection.

"Alas! I would not be present for the general's arrival in the hangar I was so proud of. A few minutes before the appointed hour, I was sent out on a mission."[15]

Valérie was wary of her assignment almost from the start.

"*The region stretching from Gian Khau to Ninh Binh was controlled by Viets*," she thought to herself, contemplating the dangers she may encounter. In an area where the Viet Minh were known to be operating, it was normal procedure for GATAC to send in fighter planes to accompany the helicopter. For this mission, however, Valérie would not have the advantage of their cover.

"The fighters were quite busy elsewhere and I was not to be provided with an escort. Theoretically, the mission was to be an uneventful one."[16]

Valérie's mission would be far from uneventful. Not very long into her flight, she began to feel acutely ill.

"Suddenly I felt dizzy," she said. "The emetine was playing tricks on me. My last injection was barely two weeks ago, but the drug was not fully eliminated. The dizziness persisted."

Valérie began to sense that she could lose control of the helicopter as the disorientation refused to subside. Flying over territory that was thick with a Viet Minh presence also meant that landing was not an option.

"Although my urge to land was great, I knew I had to hold on."

Valérie was seriously concerned. Even maintaining consciousness now posed a serious challenge.

"I bit my lips until they bled. Fortunately, the remedy was effective."

Gian Khau was only moments away, and Valérie was relieved when she finally caught sight of the fort there.

"I kept flying despite my grogginess. Without paying too much attention to the smallness of the LZ, I landed inside the outpost."[17]

One of the soldiers ran out from the outpost to meet her. Ordinarily, Valérie would be focused on getting details about the patient she was to transport, but she quickly spied a bottle of beer in the young soldier's hand. Greeting pilots with beer upon landing was a French custom, and on this occasion, it was an especially welcome one.

"How could he have possibly known to what extent his foresight was welcome? I literally yanked the bottle out of his hand. It was just what I needed. I was dying of thirst and the beer revived me."[18]

With much of her equilibrium restored, Valérie supervised the loading of her casualty into one of the Hiller's litters. The man's wounds were not serious enough to warrant an evacuation back to Hanoi, so Valérie's destination was the field hospital at Nam Dinh.

Once in Nam Dinh, the helicopter was met on the airfield by an ambulance crew, who took the wounded soldier with them, leaving Valérie with an opportunity to refuel the Hiller before returning to Gialam. As she waited for fuel, she received a message from the air controller at GATAC that heavy rain was quickly moving into the region and to hurry back to Gialam. Valérie revved the helicopter into action and headed north. The flight time between Nam Dinh and Hanoi was only forty-five minutes, but Valérie knew that she wouldn't be able to outrun the storm.

"I barely covered half the distance . . . when a squall of unbelievable violence engulfed the helicopter. At times, the rain stopped, lightning flashed, and then new gusts hit the aircraft."

Small aircraft take tremendous punishment in bad weather. It almost always takes exceptional piloting skill to come out unscathed. Light helicopters are even more highly susceptible to wind buffeting. Valérie commanded every ounce of her reserve to steady the machine as the wind increased its ferocity.

"I was no longer moving forward; I was moving backward. I tried without success to go around the storm."

There was a way out of the tempest, however. Valérie realized that she could reach a small airfield at Hung Yen.

As it turned out, Valérie was not the only pilot experiencing problems. She saw a medical Morane transport plane also parked on the airfield with its engine cowling removed. After she landed, she walked over to the plane's pilot, Captain de Grandpré. De Grandpré told Valérie that he was transporting a seriously wounded paratrooper back to Hanoi when he encountered mechanical problems. Now in the middle of bad weather, de Grandpré and his patient were stuck on the ground as they waited for a mechanic to arrive from Gialam. Valérie and de Grandpré discussed their next move.

"In view of the weather condition, help would likely be delayed. We agreed that as soon as the weather cleared, I would take off with the casualty."[19]

It took nearly an hour before the high winds began to settle down. When Valérie felt the time was right, she lifted off with the Hiller. She headed back to Hanoi with her wounded passenger, flying directly to the helipad at the hospital.

"The sky was still grey, but I got back to Lanessan. When it was all added up, I saved the paratrooper several hours' travel."[20]

Back at Gialam, Valérie found that command had numerous downsides.

"Santini's absence stretched out longer than was expected. The thousand and one details of running the helicopter section tied up a lot of my time."[21]

Administrative work seemed to be a never-ending chore. Parts requisitions for the maintenance and operation of the helicopters was an ongoing headache, especially with the supply chain for many vital components reaching out over thousands of miles away in either the United States, France, or Great Britain. Personnel issues were also a significant concern. One of the mechanics came down with a case of dysentery and required hospitalization. The additional workload transferred to the remaining mechanics often meant longer hours and occasional delays in getting an aircraft ready for a rescue mission. Valérie was determined to keep the helicopters available at all times and rarely left the hangars at Gialam during this period.

"The few friends I had in Hanoi complained of never seeing me."[22]

Meanwhile, the war continued to take its toll on the French at an even more relentless pace. While a brief respite occurred in early July—a lull that Valérie André described as a period of "easy missions"—as the month progressed, so did the war's intensity. On July 7, Valérie was alerted that two officers were wounded in the region of Mao Khe, northeast of Hanoi. The Hiller was rolled out of the hangar immediately. The support crew could have a helicopter prepped for takeoff in ten minutes or less.

Instead of an outpost, the helicopter rescue was requested for a mobile group on reconnaissance on a road near Mao Khe. The French army mobile groups often suffered the most casualties as their patrols usually operated far away from the relative shelter of a reinforced and mine-protected outpost.

Lieutenant Colonel Henry Blanckaert commanded Groupe Mobile 7. Blanckaert was a graduate of St. Cyr and a World War II combat veteran decorated numerous times for bravery in action.

Blanckaert had a wife and five children back in Rabat, Morocco, and could have opted for less hazardous duty. But instead, he chose to command a mobile assault and reconnaissance unit. During his first months in Indochina, Blanckaert took part in the battle of Hoa Binh and was instrumental in holding points at Rocher Notre-Dame and Tu Vu. Throughout the spring and summer, Blanckaert and Groupe Mobile 7 saw hard fighting in the areas between Hanoi and Haiphong.

But Blanckaert's luck came to an end on July 7 during a reconnaissance mission when the unit ran into a minefield planted in the road. Blanckaert and another officer were seriously injured with shrapnel wounds. Of the two men, Blanckaert was more severely wounded and lost a considerable amount of blood as his unit waited for the helicopter to arrive. Since the mobile group had no fixed position, Valérie was contacted by GATAC over the radio, informing her of the unit's exact location on the main road.

"The aircraft skimmed some of the chalky hilltops and entered the valleys with rugged surfaces. Mao Khe appeared, and soon I spotted the white panels."[23]

From the air, Valérie could see that the mobile group consisted of several jeeps and light armored assault vehicles. The vehicles formed a tight circle around the wounded in an area already laid out as a landing zone (LZ) for the helicopter. The arrangement resembled a makeshift fort. Valérie took some relief in the preparations the men had made in case the Viet Minh were in the area.

"The presence on the ground of the mobile group spared me the need for fighter plane cover. But the markings on the edge of the road traveled by the trucks and jeeps for the LZ was only some three to four meters (10 to 12 feet) square."[24]

The landing zone was too tight for the Hiller. Valérie made several circles above the unit with the helicopter, gesturing with her arms to the men below to move the vehicles further apart so she could land.

Once on the ground, Valérie learned that the situation had changed. Colonel Blanckaert had suffered a severe vascular wound—likely a femoral artery—and was losing too much blood to be stabilized at the LZ. It was decided minutes before Valérie landed to drive the colonel and the other injured officer by jeep up the road to a field hospital where Blanckaert could undergo a blood transfusion.

"I went to the wounded man's bedside. He was perfectly lucid, but too weak to be transported in my opinion."

Valérie quickly assessed Blanckaert's condition. His handsome facial features were ghostly pale from the blood loss. The injuries below his waist were considerable, the result of shrapnel from a mine penetrating deeply into the colonel's vital organs.

"Take me with you, Doctor," Blanckaert weakly said to Valérie, looking directly into her eyes. "I prefer to leave with you. I don't want to remain here."[25]

Valérie told the colonel that she couldn't move him yet. His blood pressure was dangerously low, and the transfusion process could not be rushed.

"As gently as possible I told him that he must first complete the blood transfusion . . . in order to get his blood pressure back up. My colleagues and I all agreed, and decided we must delay the time of departure as long as possible. The helicopter would take off a half-hour before nightfall."[26]

While her orders were to return the casualties to Hanoi, a strong front of thunderstorms was moving in quickly, and GATAC sent new orders to avoid the area. There was no doubt that Colonel Blanckaert needed medical attention as soon as possible, and Valérie struck upon an alternative plan.

"A few days earlier I had conducted a series of reconnaissance flights and found a landing point in Haiphong."

Haiphong was the third-largest city in Vietnam and had a fully equipped hospital.

"Although that LZ was not yet officially sanctioned, I knew where to land. Lt. Colonel Blanckaert would not have to endure the fatigue of a long ambulance ride."[27]

Valérie radioed ahead to the medical personnel in Haiphong to be ready to meet her with an ambulance at her coordinates.

"The sun was setting low on the horizon, and the helicopter was ready. Stretcher-bearers very gently brought Lt. Colonel Blanckaert. I settled him into the left litter basket. He was tall, so in order to compensate for his weight, I placed some of his personal effects in the right basket."[28]

Nightfall was quickly approaching, but Haiphong was less than an hour by air from Mao Khe.

"The Hiller took off without any problems and flew over a few chalky hilltops that were already turning grey as we headed for the Haiphong road."

Before long, Valérie could see a concentration of city lights as Haiphong came into view. She recognized the landmarks leading to the landing zone she had sought out a few days before, but the medical team added an extra step in guiding her to the landing area by igniting a marker signal. As she trained her vision to the smoke rising from the ground, Valérie could see that a large group from the hospital was waiting.

"The hospital surgeon was there, as he insisted on meeting in person the severe casualty."[29]

Valérie marveled at the colonel's composure.

"This was not his first wound, and he remained stoically calm."[30]

With Lieutenant Colonel Blanckaert in the hands of the medical center in Haiphong, Valérie needed to leave quickly. It was now evening and necessary to reach the French air base on Cat Ba Island to find a safe haven for her and the Hiller. When she arrived at Cat Ba, Valérie was notified over the radio that Blanckaert was still undergoing surgery, although the massive internal hemorrhaging had been stopped. Ultimately, Blanckaert would not count in Valérie's successes.

"Eighteen days later, when we thought he was out of danger, this glorious soldier would die of uremia [blood poisoning]," Valérie said. "Those who knew him will never forget him."[31]

Chapter 31

Breakdown

En Route to Tuyen Quan, July 8, 1952

There were times—even when flying over the most dangerous areas of Vietnam—that Valérie André felt the sheer exhilaration and joy of being a pilot. She often reflected that she had realized her dream of hurtling through space with the help of her plastic bubbled aircraft.

"In the midst of this daily slaughter, there were also . . . some privileged moments of contentment. The mission would be over, and the happiness of a return flight—without a wounded patient—was a relaxation, a new freedom, an escape. It was like suddenly returning to my childhood dream."[1]

After a successful mission to the outpost near Tuyen Quan, Valérie was lulled into a sense of calm. Tuyen Quan was south and to the west of Hanoi, not far from the Red River. The rescue of a Vietnamese soldier who stepped on a mine was performed almost flawlessly with no significant problems encountered. The weather was ideal, and even the landing zone was laid out correctly for once.

"I heartily congratulated the sergeant, a young Vietnamese, for his preparation of the landing pad."[2]

The enlisted man was severely wounded and had lost a lot of blood. The Hiller was running low on fuel, and it would be necessary to fly to the airfield at Nam Dinh, only a few minutes away by air.

"I . . . dropped him off at the Nam Dinh airfield adjacent to the hospital."

Valérie felt that the young soldier would be better off if he received immediate care at the field hospital in Nam Dinh, instead of enduring the long flight back to Hanoi.

Without a wounded man to take back to Hanoi, Valérie settled into what she believed would be a less stressful flight.

"The return flight without a load . . . had a lot to offer. I could relax and was happy to be flying."[3]

A few minutes into the return flight, however, Valérie's hopes for a serene journey were suddenly dashed.

"All at once, a sharp crack interrupted my train of thought. I turned around and noticed nothing abnormal."

Any unusual noise coming from the usual cacophony of sounds made by the Hiller was always a cause for concern. Valérie kept a sharp eye on the helicopter's instrument panel.

"I heard a growling noise over the regular purring of the engine, and in a few seconds the oil temperature rose from 90° to 110° (C)."

The sudden rise in temperature was an immediate sign that something was wrong with the Hiller.

"The needle kept climbing, and I detected a burning smell. Without hesitation, I cut power and put the Hiller in autorotation."

Cutting power to the helicopter at four hundred meters (thirteen hundred feet) altitude allowed the rotor to turn freely, like a windmill. The aircraft descended slowly and controllably to the ground. Fortunately for Valérie, she had been following the main road from Nam Dinh to Phu Ly, so there was at least a decent surface for a landing. But rice paddies flanked each side of the road.

"I had but one thing in mind: reach the road which I could see . . . between the flooded rice paddies. Should the aircraft get mired in the mud, it would be irretrievably lost."[4]

It was sometimes difficult to maneuver a helicopter and precisely land where one wanted in autorotation. There was no possibility of a second chance in case of error; however, Valérie was able to land the Hiller so that it perfectly lined up on the road. But now Valérie was stranded.

"Although the road between Nam Dinh and Phu Ly was fairly frequently traveled by daylight . . . by night the *Viet Minh* were in control of it. With the benefit of darkness, they would swarm onto the Hiller."

With the aircraft on the ground and at a dead stop, Valérie emerged from the cockpit. Her first task was to find a stone to chock the tires and keep the Hiller from rolling on the uneven ground as the helicopter had a very weak parking brake on its landing gear. As she looked up into the engine cradle, Valérie noticed wisps of smoke.

"With my finger, I attempted to spin the cooling fan. As I expected, the fan freewheels. In a way, I am reassured, and I return to studying the road."[5]

The road and the rice fields were deserted; not a single being was in the area. This made Valérie feel uneasy. The rice field almost always had workers tending to them, and it was often a bad sign when they weren't there.

"As far as the eye could see, it was empty. . . . The helicopter made a forced landing halfway between two main villages. Should the *Viet Minh* turn up, my fate would hardly be more enviable than that of the Hiller. The red crosses on the aircraft wouldn't protect one of us any more than the other. The rebels sometimes spared the men, never the women, and there was no point in dwelling upon the reasons for this."[6]

The silence only amplified the sense of danger. Valérie's thoughts momentarily turned to a dark contemplation.

"It had been often said that pilots in Indochina carried with them a *mercy pill* or vial. For my part, I have never seen a single one of either. Tales are so easily started."[7]

Valérie gathered her maps from the cockpit. She was sure there was a French outpost not far from her position. But Valérie wasn't about to leave the helicopter unguarded, even if that meant placing her own life in danger. Using the radio to notify GATAC also wasn't an option. If the Viet Minh were to intercept a radio transmission signaling a downed aircraft, they would move immediately on Valérie and the helicopter.

As Valérie began to spread the map out, the silence was broken by a truck coming up the road. She had hoped it was a French military vehicle, but it wasn't. It turned out instead to be a bus loaded with Chinese civilians. The vehicle was so overloaded that some of the passengers and their parcels were forced to find space up on the roof. With the Hiller blocking part of the road, Valérie positioned herself in front of the aircraft with her arms outstretched to force the driver to stop.

Undoubtedly, the Chinese bus driver was puzzled to encounter a petite French woman dressed in a light-colored jumpsuit, sunglasses, and floppy safari hat posed next to an incredibly bizarre-looking machine on a road traveled mainly by military personnel and the local population. To the driver, she looked as if she had come from another planet. Nevertheless, he stopped the bus.

"The Chinese driver climbed down from the bus and waited as I scribbled a few words on a scrap of paper, and with a sign of his head, he acknowledged my instructions. I wanted him to carry the instructions to the nearest outpost."[8]

Consulting her charts, Valérie knew that the outpost at Binh Luc was not far.

"I wanted him to deliver the message on foot to the outpost. I didn't want him to climb back behind the wheel of the bus."

Valérie was still acutely aware of her predicament and didn't want to chance that the man would ignore her instructions. The driver, however, was not willing to comply. As Valérie maintained her insistence that the driver deliver her message, the passengers on the bus were agog at the curious scene. Even Valérie could not help but notice that she was the center of their full attention.

"I didn't really know what I looked like with my jungle hat askew, my sunglasses, and my flight suit stained with oil, and the helicopter there to impress these intrepid travelers. They remained quiet, cooking in the sun, either on top or below the bus roof, while their driver walked away philosophically."[9]

Valérie speculated that she may have seemed more menacing to them than she believed, which was probably why the bus driver finally bowed to her order.

"Perhaps they feared that I was armed, or perhaps they feared that the *Viet Minh*, attracted by the bait, might descend upon the Hiller, and by the same token, ill-treat them."[10]

Fifteen more minutes went by when Valérie noticed a man running in her direction.

"He was a sergeant, out of breath, who ran over from the neighboring outpost. With his binoculars, he saw me land. His lieutenant sent him to my rescue."[11]

The sergeant was Vietnamese. Valérie was relieved that she was indeed not far from help. Feeling confident enough to write a note instructing the outpost to contact GATAC by radio about her situation, she sent the sergeant back to his outpost with the message. The outpost would send more soldiers to her position soon.

Valérie thought about how her message would be received back at the helicopter hangar.

"This wouldn't be the first time Le Goff would have to make a repair out in the field," she thought to herself.

Another fifteen minutes went by. But then a squad of men appeared trotting down the road. The same Vietnamese sergeant called out to his men to fan out on the road along the rice paddies to form a line of defense. Valérie was satisfied that the Hiller was now protected. The bus driver had returned by this time, and Valérie signaled to the men to allow the bus and its passengers to move on.

"Captain, he arriving," the Vietnamese soldier told Valérie in his rough French. "Us wait and guard you."

A jeep moving at full speed, kicking up a cloud of dust, was soon spotted coming from the direction of Binh Luc. A French captain and his lieutenant made a dramatic stop behind the broken helicopter.

"We saw you drop with our binoculars," the captain excitedly said to Valérie. "We even noticed some smoke."

The captain went on to explain that his unit was engaged in an operation with the Viet Minh ten kilometers away when they saw Valérie's helicopter experiencing trouble. They broke off from combat and rushed as soon as they could to the site of the landing.

"We thought you had been shot at," the lieutenant added. "And that you had crashed into a rice paddy."[12]

The two officers were concerned about Valérie's safety and insisted that she accompany them back to their compound at Binh Luc. Valérie was reluctant to leave the helicopter, even under armed guard. But she was eventually convinced. After the Hiller was moved to the side of the road to allow traffic to pass in both directions, and making sure that a sufficient number of men would watch over her machine, Valérie climbed into the jeep with the two men.

Despite the precautions, Valérie continued to worry over the helicopter. At the outpost, Valérie sent her own message to GATAC over the radio, describing the problem with the Hiller that caused the forced landing. She also described her observations concerning the aircraft's cooling fan, hoping that Le Goff would bring the necessary parts to restore the Hiller to flight readiness.

"It already seemed like a long time had passed. I figured it would take at least two hours for Le Goff to fly from Hanoi to Phu Ly in a Morane, and then to catch up to us by road. I was anxious to know that my aircraft was safe."[13]

At Binh Luc, Valérie was offered lunch with the men.

"Worry spoiled my appetite," she said. "In spite of that, the luncheon offered by the two officers was good. But the beer was warm and didn't quench our thirst. I finally requested that we go back down to the helicopter."

More time went by. Knowing that the unit had engaged the Viet Minh only ten kilometers away weighed heavily on Valérie's thoughts. Every moment that passed was both a relief and also a sense of dread until the next moment. Every sound was amplified; every vehicle that came in the direction from Phu Ly was scrutinized for hopeful signs. The wait was an eternity.

Finally, after more than two hours, a jeep was spotted speeding toward the site of the downed helicopter. Valérie could make out the face of the mechanic, Georges Le Goff, in the passenger seat. It wasn't long before the jeep pulled up to her.

"When he caught sight of me, he shook his head. His face was a riot. He appeared to be both flabbergasted and satisfied."

"Captain," Le Goff said to Valérie. "You're living on borrowed time!"[14]

Valérie watched as Le Goff diagnosed the broken helicopter. He also spun the engine's cooling fan and concluded what Valérie already suspected—the drive gearbox that connected the engine to the cooling fan had disintegrated inside. Any attempt to restart the helicopter without a replacement gearbox would cause the same overheating problem.

"There's no way to make repairs before nightfall," Le Goff said to Valérie. "We'll have to push the aircraft all the way to Phu Ly."

Phu Ly was more than ten kilometers away and in an area where an intense engagement with the Viet Minh had just occurred.

"We all looked at each other. Towing the helicopter almost ten kilometers would be a Homeric task. Also, the *Viet Minh* were likely on alert for several hours by now and ready to attack. In any event, they weren't far away."[15]

The Hiller was on tricycle landing gear, but the wheels were relatively small in diameter compared to the tires and wheels of a jeep. The landing gear wasn't meant for travel over rough, unpaved roads for long distance. As a result, progress would be agonizingly slow.

With an arrangement of ropes and straps, Le Goff supervised and improvised hitching the Hiller to the back of a jeep tow vehicle. A sense of some relief was felt when a contingent of Legionnaires pulled up in an armored car. The Legionnaires told Valérie that they would take the forward point, and the squad of Vietnamese from Binh Luc would make up the rear guard.

After Le Goff was satisfied with the Hiller's tow straps, he signaled that it was okay to pull forward. The convoy moved at a "walking man's pace."[16]

Le Goff remained behind the helicopter, steadying the tail skid on the stinger-like tailboom with his outstretched hands. The Hiller would have otherwise wandered on the rough road surface without Le Goff's steadying it. The French officers wanted Valérie to ride with them, but she chose to walk alongside Le Goff.

The long walk was hard on both of them.

"The sun was bearing down on us," said Valérie. "We were sweating, and we had nothing to drink."[17]

Moving at not much more than a snail's pace, the party managed to put some distance between the landing site and the ultimate goal of reaching Phu Ly. The rice paddies gave way to heavier vegetation with banana groves interspersed.

It was a perfect place for an ambush.

"I noticed the Legionnaires increasing their vigilance," Valérie said.

"This is a lousy spot!" one of the soldiers whispered to Valérie.

Shots rang out, and everyone's blood froze.

"It was only the Legionnaires firing off a warning salvo," said Valérie.

But she knew that her group was not the only one present. Valérie could make out human figures dressed in black dropping to crouch in the dark recesses of the jungle.

"I couldn't make out their weapons—perhaps they had some, or perhaps not. In any event, the sight of the armored car forced them to keep quiet."[18]

Or at least that's what Valérie hoped.

Time and distance pressed on, but the heat was no less oppressive. Even Valérie, exhausted and with her flight suit soaked in sweat, had to finally accept the offer to ride in the tow jeep with the officers. Le Goff continued to trudge behind the helicopter. At least the number of thatch-roofed huts and increased signs of life meant that they were beginning to approach the outskirts of Phu Ly.

Unfortunately, the helicopter proved to be an unwanted attraction. As the group made its way to the center of Phu Ly, more and more people, especially children, gathered to see the strange machine slowly making its way through their village. It was not the first time that Valérie had encountered this phenomenon.

"Every half-naked urchin in Phu Ly was there to watch us go by. Minute by minute, the crowd swelled, and now the adults were taking an interest in us."

This attention brought on another worry.

"How many in the crowd were *Viet Minh*?"

The crowd that had at first maintained a distance now clamored around the Hiller. Though thoroughly worn out, Le Goff tried to keep his pace while steadying the machine as it moved down the street. Le Goff struggled to fend them off as they tried to put their hands on the helicopter. Valérie feared for the safety of both Le Goff and the Hiller. It was a situation that threatened to get out of control quickly.

Finally, the Legionnaires, who were still maintaining the path at the front of the group, made their way back to the helicopter. They raised their guns as if they meant they were ready to fire. The message was received, and the crowd began to disperse. Fortunately, no shots were fired, and the mob retreated to the sides of the road to watch at a more respectful distance.

The Legionnaires knew of a barn in Phu Ly that would be suitable to stow the helicopter overnight. The helicopter was unhitched from the jeep, and some enlisted men helped Le Goff push the Hiller to its resting place. Guards would be with the machine at all times. Valérie noticed how thoroughly rung out the mechanic was.

"He sat down, mopped his brow, and smiled up at me," she said. "We were both finally entitled to a little rest."[19]

It was now twilight, and the sun was dropping into the horizon. It had been another day that Valérie cheated fate. The Viet Minh had more than a foothold in the area, and the threat of a firefight and capture was a distinct possibility.

The Legionnaires arranged for a hut with a cot for Valérie for the night. But the heat and humidity were as oppressive at night as during the day.

"The night was sweltering. Unable to sleep, I tossed and turned on the cot. The wide-open door and window did not let in the slightest breath of air. I couldn't recall such heat, and I was forced to keep the mosquito netting on."[20]

Valérie found that the men opted to sleep outdoors, so she moved her cot out of the hut. Valérie wondered how the climate in the usually more temperate Tonkin region could be hotter than in Cochinchine to the south. Other thoughts flooded her mind. She worried that she wouldn't be able to fly the Hiller out of Phu Ly. It was a restless night with little sleep for her. When morning came, Valérie was still awake.

"I thought I would be the first one to visit the helicopter, but Le Goff had beaten me to it. He was casting a reproachful look at the inside of the fan gearbox."

"It's completely shot, Captain," he said turning to Valérie, showing her the parts he held in his hands.

"I need not be told. I could see the roller bearings were either twisted or melted."

The small gearbox was a part very specific to Hiller helicopters.

From Valérie's description of the Hiller's problem relayed to Hanoi while she was still stranded at Binh Luc, Le Goff anticipated that the breakdown centered around the gearbox. From his toolbox, he pulled out a replacement part and proudly showed it to Valérie. But his pride turned to bemusement when he removed an inspection plug on the unit.

"My message had put him on the right track," Valérie noted. "But one can't think of everything. Le Goff forgot to bring the special oil."[21]

The omission meant another delay in getting the Hiller back in the air; however, with a radio message to GATAC in Hanoi, a bottle of the correct gear oil was soon on its way to Phu Ly via supply plane. Two hours later, the "precious liquid" arrived.[22]

For Le Goff, the rest of the procedure was fairly straightforward. After filling the new part to the proper level with oil, Le Goff fitted the new gearbox in place of the old using simple hand tools. Le Goff stowed his tool kit in the Hiller when his work was complete and took a seat next to Valérie.

"Around noon, all was in readiness," Valérie noted triumphantly. "The engine was running smoothly. After thanking our hosts and all who helped us, we took off, flew in a small circle so we could say goodbye to our friends, and headed off for Gialam."[23]

Chapter 32

Recognition

Hanoi, July 14, 1952

A muted excitement surrounded the atmosphere on the tree-lined rue Borgnis Desbordes in Hanoi. It was *La Fête Nationale*, more commonly known outside of France as Bastille Day. Although the day's significance extended beyond the military, the French armed forces used the occasion to honor its troops, both at home and abroad.

The various representatives of France's overseas expeditionary force were readying themselves for a display. Valérie André, Alexis Santini, and Henri Bartier were also there. Each of them was receiving decorations and awards for their service in Indochina. Valérie received the third "palm" to her Croix de guerre, or "war cross." The French air force usually awarded a palm— i.e., additional merit—to the Croix de guerre for every twenty-five combat missions performed. By July 1952, Valérie André had flown more than fifty combat missions.[1]

The streets around Hanoi's Hoan Kiem Lake were clogged with military personnel and vehicles getting into formation. The military provided its own security force, but *agents de Sûreté* were also circulating in the crowd, wary of a possible Viet Minh terrorist attack.

For the most part, the Vietnamese population of Hanoi shunned the military display. There were Vietnamese in attendance who served in the military and also in local government affairs aligned to the French and their still omnipresent colonial rule. But over the last seven years, the native Vietnamese population of Hanoi was exhausted from the war. Instead of turning out to the parade route and risking suspicion as Viet Minh collaborators, most chose to tend to their own affairs on a day that meant more to a foreign power occupying their country than it did to them.

For the pilots of ELA 53, however, the day meant recognition of their service. In only a short period of time, the helicopter rescue service brought hope and salvation to a war that often seemed futile and hopeless. The French air force gambled when it purchased the two Hillers, but the hard work of the pilots and crew had paid off. The program was a success and would only improve as time moved on.

Along with the military honors presented on July 14, Valérie's work as a rescue pilot earned her an additional distinction.

"When my *Croix de Guerre* received a third palm, it prompted my inclusion in the Legion of Honour."[2]

The Legion of Honour was one of France's most prestigious institutions, established during the age of Napoleon for the recognition of deeds of merit by both civilians and the military. Valérie was inducted at the first rung as *chevalier*, or "knight."[3] Valérie André admired the Free French Army that liberated France during World War II, whom she characterized as "modern-day knights." Now she would formally take her place among them.

Alexis Santini was also admitted to the Legion of Honour. As for Henri Bartier, he had not only achieved the rank of *chevalier* in the Legion of Honour but also, by this date, had performed more than five hundred combat zone missions in a Morane and nearly a hundred in a Hiller. The number of palms that he had been awarded since his arrival in Indochina in 1946 was nothing short of incredible.[4]

"After the ceremony, we asked Bartier, 'how many [palms] does that make?'" Valerie asked.

"Nine, ten, eleven . . . !" Bartier answered nonchalantly, pretending to count them all off one at a time.

Valérie believed that Bartier had achieved his thirteenth palm to date.[5]

The day's ceremonies also cited Valérie's "contributions to the maintenance of troop morale."[6] The wording of the citation may have sounded underwhelming, but the sentiment had much greater significance. Where it once seemed as if hope didn't exist for the "mud soldiers," Valérie André brought compassion, and, maybe most important, a female presence to the front.

Valérie was also honored by a letter she received from the commander of the French air force, General Lionel-Max Chassin:

Mademoiselle,

I personally consider your activity in Indochina as symbolic for two reasons. Firstly, because it reflects our country's human and civilizing mission in the Far East; secondly, because it shows how essential it is for theaters of operation to have women capable of quiet courage and modesty committed to the highest professional virtues.[7]

In the context of the era, Valérie's citation from Chassin represented a breakthrough. She regarded the letter as something more than just a personal acknowledgment of her efforts.

"It was a salute to the role of women in the war."[8]

When Valérie arrived in Saigon five years earlier, the attitude toward a female officer was often prejudicial and dismissive. There were still many obstacles to overcome, but Valérie's tenacity and dedication carved out significant inroads. And as Valérie André made immeasurable strides for herself, she also made it possible for other women to follow her.

With well-deserved acknowledgment from the military, however, there came another aspect of recognition—attention from the press.

The French military desperately needed positive press exposure to justify France's presence in Indochina and attract recruits to its overseas mission. To that end, the exploits of Captain Valérie Edmée André served to capture the imagination of a war-weary public and inspire a new generation of women. Valérie found herself to be a reluctant subject of interest.

"Although I was not really disposed to expose my life to the press. I agreed to receive journalists to better talk about 'us' and 'our' common fight."[9]

Claude Guigues, a war correspondent for the weekly *Samedi soir*, was one of the writers Valérie encountered. Guigues spent some time out in the field, talking with men at remote outposts who depended on helicopter rescues to keep their fallen comrades alive.

"We were expecting a man," a soldier told Guigues about his first encounter with a rescue helicopter. "Now we don't wait for a man anymore. Everyone knows Captain André in Tonkin."[10]

The newspaper *Caravelle* featured photos of Valérie in a story on the contributions of women to the war in Indochina. An excerpt read, "in Indochina, where the climate slowly wears the most resistant, women have not hesitated . . . to serve the wounded with their courage and compassion."

"On page one of *Caravelle*, I appeared in flight gear with my brush hat standing in front of the helicopter," Valérie remarked of her newfound fame, adding that the "journalist gave a good overview of the work of the helicopter section."[11]

The spotlight was not at all Valérie's choice. One journalist noted she was reluctant to talk about herself or her exploits for his article:

Answering questions in this noisy airport bar obviously annoys her. While smoking and drinking her coffee with hot milk—it's raining, and it was cold—she is curled up in her field-jacket that she put on her shoulders. With each sentence she adds:

"I think I've said enough."[12]

Valérie believed that the focus should be on all military personnel engaged in Indochina, not on herself.

"The people in Paris will never know enough of the sacrifice of the soldiers in Indochina." [13]

Valérie André's story was newsworthy beyond France and its colonies. Blake Clark wrote a feature article about Valérie for the French publication *France Illustration*, later condensed for the American monthly *Reader's Digest*. Typical of American magazines of the time, the piece was titled "The Adventures of Mademoiselle Helicopter."[14] Clark, who was a "roving editor" for *Reader's Digest*, interviewed Valérie about her work and spoke with some of the men Valérie rescued from the battlefield:

Sgt. Joseph Lerouge told me while he was still in the hospital how Mlle. André had rescued him. He was in a column which was ambushed. A bullet lodged in his leg and shrapnel plowed into his back. He was nearly dead when he reached the landing strip where Mlle. André met him.

"Having her pick me up in that faraway place was like having your mother suddenly show up in the jungle," he said. "When she patted my cheek it felt wonderful. And getting to the hospital was as smooth as flying on a cloud."[15]

A combat photographer shared his perspective about Valérie:

"Before she came, a soldier hit in the belly wanted to shoot himself rather than suffer the inevitable gangrene. Now, when a fellow's hit, he thinks: "The little doc with the wings is on the way."[16]

The American publication *Collier's* also ran an article about Valérie titled "Pretty Doctor in a Copter," by Peter Kalischer. The opening paragraph read:

"Captain Valérie André [is] the most remarkable woman in anyone's army since Joan of Arc (a whopping claim the captain will writhe at)."[17]

While the point may have been broad, the author was able to find a definite admiration of Valérie's talents among the men who served with her, such as mechanic Georges Le Goff:

> How do we feel toward her? You mean how do we feel about a woman pilot in war? Some of us have worked so long with her it's routine. She's a captain, but well—not a captain, you understand. We address her as *mon capitaine*, but we refer to her among ourselves as *Mademoiselle*. The sex business, honestly, no one thinks about it. On the base, she wears coveralls and a slouch hat, she flies her missions like the men, she gives orders, and we take them.
>
> But every so often it hits you. For example, when we hear her voice on the radio calling for fighter support. She's trying to land at a besieged outpost to pick up wounded, and the *Viets* are shooting at her helicopter. Then it comes over you: *mon dieu*, it's a woman doing this.[18]

When Kalischer interviewed Valérie he found her to be "devout, dedicated, and shy, but with a will of iron." When he asked Valérie why she volunteered for service in Indochina and why "this kind of job was not usually considered women's work," she told him:

"I am a doctor. And this is where my job took me."[19]

Kalischer wrote extensively about Valérie's numerous missions as both a helicopter pilot and, before that, as a doctor who also parachuted into remote areas. The article especially took note of Valérie's skill as a pilot, honing in on her narrow escapes on some missions.

"She is a crack pilot. She has twice brought back her craft with five bullet holes in it and once, flying dangerously low, landed without mishap with a dead stick—the trickiest maneuver in the book."[20]

But the writer also had the audacity to broach the subject of Valérie's personal life.

"She leads a life of unromantic rectitude that it started rumors of a previously unhappy love affair. To the question of whether she contemplated marriage, she replied blandly, 'I am unmarriageable (*sic*). My husband and I could never be together. My work would not give us the time.'"[21]

Another anecdote related by Kalischer told of how Valérie was stopped by French military police while on her way by jeep to Gialam.

"She received a delinquency report from an MP for driving in Hanoi without proper papers," wrote Kalischer. "The report found its way to

Lt. Col. Paul Davy, the base commander, to note what action he would take. Davy airily wrote, 'To be shot at dawn' in the margin and sent it back to the MPs."[22]

Besides print media, Valérie André was also the subject of a short film made by a French military camera unit intended to prop up morale among the troops serving in Indochina.

"A mission brought me to Xuan Mai, where a passenger turned up by the name of Jean Leriche," Valérie later recalled. "The young man had received authorization to film some footage."[23]

Leriche was a camera operator for SCA (Service cinématographique des armées). SCA produced a series of informational films covering the armed forces serving overseas. For the far east theater of operations, the series was called *Regards sur l'Indochine* (Indochina at a glance; ca. 1952). There was, of course, a propaganda element to the films; however, SCA filmmakers also made an effort to document life in Indochina.

Leriche captured footage of Valérie during a typical rescue mission in an installment titled "Medicine Capitaine Valérie André." The mission, however, was simulated, as it would have been difficult and dangerous to film Valérie under actual conditions. But the events were true to what she ordinarily encountered.

The film opens with a brief shot of Valérie André at *La Fête Nationale* commemoration in Hanoi, receiving her second and third palm to her Croix de guerre. The next sequence jumps to a scene of Valérie and the Hiller on the tarmac at Gialam. Valérie consults with one of the mechanics as the helicopter goes through its rotor run-up.

The narrator introduces Valérie as doctor/captain, surgeon, helicopter pilot, and parachutist before explaining her mission as a medical rescue pilot. Soon the film audience is alongside Valérie on a rescue mission. She flies toward Hoa Binh over rice paddies and the Red River to retrieve a wounded soldier. Sheets of white cloth are carefully laid out and weighted down with stones to designate a safe landing zone (LZ). As Valérie touches down, the next scene cuts to two Bearcat fighters flying low over the LZ while firing their machine guns to ward off any guerilla activity.

With the area secure, Valérie emerges from the helicopter's cockpit as its rotors turn at idle speed. A quick cut shows five soldiers approaching the aircraft. Two of the men are bearing another man on a stretcher. Throughout the scene, machine-gun sound effects are added to the film's soundtrack, but in real life, Valérie would often be close to enemy fire.

Next, Valérie tends to the wounded man before he's loaded onto one of the litters on the side of the Hiller. With a quick cut to a shot of Viet Minh sharpshooters aiming at the helicopter, Valérie is soon back in the air with her patient, heading back to Hanoi. After landing, Valérie lands at Lanessan Hospital, and attendants carry the patient away. Valérie André completes yet another mission. She casually lights up a cigarette as the film fades to an end.[24]

The film was widely distributed to military installations in Indochina and only enhanced the legend surrounding Valérie; however, there was an unfortunate coda marking the production of the film.

"A few weeks later, I would regretfully learn that my nice movie-photographer was captured in the Moc Chau district while accompanying a patrol," Valérie said.

Jean Leriche would remain a prisoner of the Viet Minh until April 1954.[25]

Chapter 33

Pyrrhic Victory

The summer monsoon season in northern Vietnam played havoc with rescue operations. Valérie André had gone more than a week without a mission because of the heavy rains that grounded the helicopters. Fortunately, the poor weather also inhibited the French and Viet Minh from fighting, so casualties were relatively light. Alexis Santini, who had recently returned from the south, took on the few rescue missions that came up. But early on the morning of September 9, Valérie received orders to fly to Nam Dinh and then on to an outpost at Do My.

When Valérie reached Nam Dinh, she topped off the Hiller's fuel tank before heading off on the next leg of her mission. A noncom told her that heavy flooding washed out roads to Do My and that the Viet Minh were in control of the only route accessible by motor vehicle. For the moment, the weather was fair if somewhat windy, and rain was not in the forecast. But the soldier told Valérie to expect heavy fighting in the area.

It took Valérie only a half hour to reach Do My. As she approached the flat, muddy plain surrounding the outpost, she saw that it was under siege. Fighter planes were already making their strafing runs to both sides of the blockhouse to force Viet Minh guerillas away from the landing zone (LZ). On the other side were the rice paddies and shallow water ponds. As she hovered the helicopter closer to the LZ, she could see extensive flooding around the outpost.

"I spotted the landing area immediately. It consisted of a few square meters of muddy soil, sprinkled here and there with a few clumps of grass."[1]

It was another seemingly impossible landing site. The downwash from the Hiller's rotors wrinkled the thin layer of water coating the mushy clay surface. Valérie decided that she would tentatively touch down and see if the helicopter was contacting anything solid before putting its full weight down.

"With my hand on the collective and the throttle, I steadied the aircraft, ready to yank it back up if it got bogged down."

It was a careful balancing act, but by and by, Valérie felt that the helicopter's footing began to firm up.

"The equilibrium appeared set; the Hiller no longer budged. I lifted off my seat, and suddenly the aircraft began pitching downward."

Valérie's heart dropped almost as much as the Hiller sank. With the helicopter's engine still running and its rotor operating at idle speed, the situation could turn fatal at any moment.

"One leap into the liquid mud allowed me to examine the damage. Its nose wheel and front landing lights had vanished into the mud."[2]

The helicopter was up to its belly pan in porous earth. At least Valérie took some solace that the rear two landing wheels seemed to be holding up their share of the helicopter's weight above ground. If the tail rotor became bogged down in the mud, the aircraft would be irretrievably lost. Yet Valérie wondered if it would be possible to extricate the helicopter from the bog, especially once the wounded men were on board.

"*Will I be able to take off under load?*" she fretfully thought to herself.[3]

The post commander, also immersed in mud, waded over to Valérie from the blockhouse.

"We've been under attack up until the fighter planes arrived," the commander told her. "It wasn't possible to prepare a place for your helicopter to land. We would have laid out some bricks and wooden boards, but the *Viets* fired at everyone leaving the perimeter."

The excuses were moot while the helicopter remained stuck, and Valérie was angry.

"I had water up to my knees and couldn't help myself from chewing out the commander."[4]

Fortunately for Valérie, there was only one wounded man, meaning the takeoff load would be lighter. But she knew the helicopter would struggle to pull itself free from the mud. As a group of men brought the wounded soldier on a stretcher to load in the Hiller's litter, Valérie told the post commander to have his men help free her aircraft.

"Solely preoccupied with wrenching the aircraft off the ground, I asked the men to dig out my wheels. They did this with sticks, rifle butts, anything. The men scooped out the mud with their bare hands."[5]

The fighter planes were gone, and the enemy was once again approaching the outpost.

"Rifle shots rang out; the *Viet Minh* started firing again. I had to hurry and press everyone on. I jumped into the cockpit. While the soldiers backed away, I applied power. The rotor downwash sucked the water. The helicopter rose obediently and pivoted over a handful of soldiers."

Valérie later learned her cursing the men as they dug out her helicopter had some repercussions when an inspector followed up with the men about the evacuation of their comrade.

"Oh yeah! *It* [the helicopter] came . . . with a woman on board," one of the men told the officer. "But, boy, what a foul temper she had!"[6]

After returning to Hanoi and dropping off her patient on the helipad at Lanessan, Valérie returned to Gialam. Santini was among the first to inspect the pitiful sight of Valérie and her mud-caked helicopter. As the mechanics began cleaning the mud from the Hiller before rolling it back into the hangar, Valérie could tell Santini was visibly displeased.

"André," he said to her. "You should have put off the evacuation until later."

"Yes," Valérie replied after explaining the situation she encountered. "But wouldn't you have taken the same risk?"[7]

As Santini assessed the negligible damage to the Hiller, he tried to picture in his mind how Valérie once again escaped from catastrophe. He took out a cigarette. After lighting it and taking one long drag, he blew out the match, snapped it into an inverted V, and held it up to Valérie's eyes. It was a wordless reminder of the morning a few months before when Valérie's helicopter had lost power on the tarmac at Gialam and crashed to the ground, causing the tailboom to crumple in the shape of an upside-down letter V.

"Not prone to long speeches, Santini just winked at me," Valérie later recalled. "We understood each other."

Valérie knew that Santini, or even Henri Bartier, would have assumed the same risk under similar circumstances. The wounded man would not have survived any delay in transport. But Santini's message was clear.

"In advising caution, Santini was only doing what he had to do."[8]

Santini was to leave for Saigon a few days later. ELA 52 in the south was preparing to become operational with fresh pilots who trained in Great

Britain to fly the new Westland WS-51 helicopters. The WS-51s were built in the United Kingdom under license from the American firm Sikorsky. The new and much larger aircraft were soon to be introduced in the north to supplement the work of the smaller and overworked Hillers. During Santini's absence, Valérie André was in command of ELA 53's helicopter section.[9]

The arrival of the new helicopters was well timed. While hostilities were in a lull thanks to the monsoon season, another kind of storm gathered. So far, 1952 had proved to be a stagnant year in the war, with neither the French nor the Viet Minh gaining the upper hand. But that was soon to change. On October 14, the 308th, 312th, and 316th divisions of the Viet Minh army attacked French outposts near Nghia Lo and Son La, two hundred kilometers west of Hanoi, where the French army was at its weakest.

At first, it appeared that the Viet Minh were advancing rapidly, much as they had at Dong Khe, Lang Son, and Cao Bang near the Chinese border in late 1950. On October 16, a regiment from the Viet Minh 312th surrounded a French garrison at Tu Le a few kilometers southeast of Nghia Lo. The outpost was reinforced by the Sixth Colonial Parachute Battalion (6e Bataillon colonial de commandos [6e BCCP]) under the command of Major Marcel Bigeard. Bigeard was a towering and somewhat controversial leader in the French military whose personal motto was, "If it is possible, it will be done. And if it is impossible, it will still be done." But the situation at Tu Le taxed even Bigeard's resources. By some estimates, the French were outnumbered ten to one. Soon the garrison and paratroopers at Tu Le were in a fallback retreat where even the wounded were left behind. The casualties on the French side were staggering. But the survivors, including Bigeard, managed to lure the pursuing Viet Minh to more heavily armed fortifications along the Black River at Son La and Na San, where more than fifteen thousand French soldiers were waiting. The end result was a bloody firefight that lasted for several days. General Giap, who was expecting weak resistance from the French, intensified his attack by throwing three divisions into the battle. The French were well equipped, however, with the recent arrival of five 105 mm howitzer batteries. The pushback from the French was more than Giap expected.

As Valérie André observed the unfolding events:

"General Salan organized his response about the airbase at Na San, which allowed regular resupply of the combat units by airlift. This allowed for reinforcements of men and supplies to be sent to positions at Lai Chau and Sam Neua, as well. The purpose of the strategy was to attract the enemy on a true battleground where they would be restricted in their ability to maneuver."[10]

The French turned the tables on Giap. Taking advantage of fair weather conditions, Salan ordered an around-the-clock presence of Bearcat fighters and B-26 bombers to strafe and bomb the Viet Minh by day and to drop flares at night to keep the battlefield lit for deadly French artillery strikes.

Back at Gialam, the daily routine for ELA 53 accelerated during Operation Lorraine. Santini rejoined ELA 52, and there were also other new arrivals. The new Westland-Sikorsky WS-51s finally made their way to the north, along with several new pilots. Valérie André and Henri Bartier weren't checked out to fly the new helicopters, but they both were intensely interested in the new machines.

"Are these big 'bumble-bees' going to swipe all our missions?" Bartier said to Valérie, marveling at their size and overall look.[11]

Indeed, the larger Westlands appeared to be superior machines in comparison to the Hiller. They were more powerful, with a greater payload capacity, capable of carrying four wounded—two inside the cabin and two on Stokes litters mounted on each side of the fuselage.

The WS-51 design, however, was far more complex than the Hiller. The French acquired their nine WS-51s from Westland Helicopters in Great Britain. Westland built the WS-51 under license after Sikorsky started to phase the S-51 out of production for the much improved S-55. The *W* in the designation WS-51 denoted the Westland version. The British version of the WS-51 also differed significantly from its U.S.-built counterpart and, as a result, suffered from quality control and reliability issues. As Valérie André noted:

"During November, the S-51s would break down one after another, and in between two evacuations, the Hillers had to come to their rescue."[12]

One notable Westland breakdown occurred on November 13 at Moc Chau. One of the new pilots assigned to ELA 53, Sergeant André Voirin, was ordered to transport medicine and medical supplies to Na San. Chief Warrant Officer Pierre Pellegrin accompanied him. Pellegrin had not yet flown a mission in the Tonkin region and was supposed to be familiarizing himself with the mountainous terrain in the area of Na San.

After completing their supply mission to Na San, Voirin and Pellegrin moved on to Moc Chau, where they were to evacuate two injured Moroccan soldiers. After securing the two wounded men to the interior of the aircraft, Voirin took the Westland up to an altitude of four thousand feet. Suddenly, a loud noise rang out from the S-51's rotor head assembly, just to the rear of Voirin and Pellegrin. In an instant, the entire helicopter began vibrating violently, making even the instruments impossible to read. Voirin had no choice but to cut power to the engine and place the helicopter into an autorotation.

In most emergencies with a helicopter, a power-off autorotation usually results in a controlled crash landing; however, Voirin was not aware that one of the three main rotors had become detached from the rotor hub. With only two of the three rotor blades windmilling against the force of air pressure, the aircraft's descent was much more rapid than it should have been. Fortunately for the crew and the wounded, Voirin was able to flare the two remaining rotor blades before the aircraft touched down, cushioning the rough contact with the ground to some degree. But the hard impact from the landing sent a massive shock to everyone onboard.

Voirin and Pellegrin were both considerably shaken by the landing. With the fuel system shut down, the danger from fire was minimal. Voirin and Pellegrin knew that they had landed in Viet Minh territory. It wouldn't be long before the downed helicopter would be discovered. A cursory inspection of the aircraft indicated that it was severely damaged. Both pilot and copilot realized that they were fortunate to walk away from the wreck. The two wounded Moroccans became a priority and required attention at once. After being unstrapped from the litters, the two wounded men were capable of walking with some assistance. Voirin decided to leave the crash site and move on in the direction of Ban Hoa, where there was a small outpost.

"We walked for four hours in the brush before we were recovered by a company of the 1st RTM (*Regiment Tireurs Moroccain*—Moroccan Artillery Regiment)," Voirin later wrote in his report.[13]

The next day a team of inspectors and mechanics returned to the crash site. The helicopter was declared a total loss, but the inspectors wanted to know what caused the aircraft to lose control. Close examination of the rotor hub indicated that a faulty main control damper yoke was at fault. In their official report, the air force inspectors wanted to know if other Westland S-51s suffered similar malfunctions and if operations in the tropical climates were a contributing factor. Before leaving the crash site, the stricken WS-51 was stripped of its radio equipment and some salvageable parts and then destroyed so that it would be of no use to the Viet Minh.[14]

In a footnote to the incident involving the WS-51, Valérie André noted that the two wounded Moroccans "vehemently refused to set foot inside another helicopter that seemed so dangerous to them."[15] Presumably, the two men were eventually evacuated by truck over the crude road that wound through Ban Hoa back to Hanoi.

Sergeant Vorin's WS-51 was not the only Westland-built Sikorsky to suffer mechanical difficulties in the field. On November 29, another WS-51 experienced mechanical problems at Phu Ly. Valérie André was assigned to complete the remainder of its mission in a Hiller.

"I was ordered to take off for Yen Phuc. Seven wounded Legionnaires required evacuation. One of the 'bumblebees' was experiencing problems. My passenger was to be Sergeant Gerbollet, the mechanic assigned to perform the repairs. I was to drop him off at Phu Ly. Together we get airborne, and a half-hour later I left him next to the Sikorsky [Westland] and continued on to Yen Phuc."

The Legionnaires proved to be more adept at setting out helicopter landing zones, and Valérie found the LZ acceptable. But she could sense an uneasiness among them when she landed.

"I sensed their impatience as soon as I landed." The Legionnaires expected the larger helicopter to take at least four of the seven wounded. Evacuation with the smaller Hiller meant more trips, and they said as much to Valérie. Valérie could give no assurance whether the "*bumble-bee*" would be back in service anytime soon.

"The first two casualties were already there, on stretchers. Their weight didn't concern me. In every direction the area is clear, and I took off for Nam Dinh without any problem."

When Valérie reached the mobile hospital at Nam Dinh with her first two wounded, she received orders to return to Yen Phuc for another round of evacuations.

"*Ventilateur*, this is *Toricelli*—continue your shuttles. The Sikorsky [Westland] is not available."

The news of continued problems with the supposedly more sophisticated and capable S-51 struck Valérie as amusing.

"In five hours fifteen minutes, this good old Hiller transported the seven casualties to the hospital and then returned to Gialam."

When Valérie touched down at Gialam, Sergeant Le Goff ran up to meet her.

"I see that you scored nicely against the Westland-Sikorskys today," he said to Valérie as he rolled the Hiller back inside its hangar. His tone reflected his admiration for the underdog aircraft.

But it wasn't really a competition between the Hiller and the Westland, and Valérie realized that. The Westland-Sikorskys were supposed to fill a need, and they were not living up to their promise.

"The Hillers frequently had to come to their rescue," Valérie recollected. "If our personal pride found satisfaction in this, Bartier and I nonetheless deplored the capricious behavior of the newcomers. Had their performance not been so deficient, medical evacuations could have been organized on a much larger scale."[16]

Despite their criticism of the larger helicopters, both Valérie and Bartier looked forward to the day they would take control of the Westlands. In the meantime, they would carry on with the Hillers, although they were not immune to mechanical problems. Being the first and oldest of the operational rescue helicopters, the Hillers had accumulated a considerable amount of flight time.

"Our Hillers are really exhausted," Santini said to Valérie while discussing upcoming flight duties with her. "They are not far from reaching six hundred flight hours."[17]

While Valérie was aware that the aircraft were due for major overhaul, the news was not particularly assuring. Major overhaul of the Hiller's airframe and power systems meant that they needed to be shipped back to a factory-authorized repair station. Hiller lacked such a facility in Southeast Asia at the time. That meant the aircraft would likely have to be sent back to Helicop-Air in France to carry out the necessary repairs. Valérie was not concerned about making the transition to becoming a Westland pilot. But the larger helicopter's troublesome nature placed the entire helicopter rescue program in jeopardy.

Meanwhile, mechanical issues were not the only maladies plaguing ELA 53. The pilots and support crew also suffered from a host of medical ailments. To treat some of the more minor problems, Valérie André opened a first aid station at the hangar "to treat cuts, bruises, and hangovers."[18]

Many times the illnesses exceeded what first aid could cover. During the height of Operation Lorraine in the Na San campaign, Henri Bartier was suddenly bedridden and was out of commission for several days.

"His illness could not have come at a worse time," Valérie remarked. "Santini was in Saigon, and the WS-51 pilots were not checked out to fly the Hiller. Only one Sikorsky [Westland] was on flight status."[19]

But even Valérie André was not entirely well.

"I forced myself to get a certain number of hours' sleep so as to be in good shape at dawn should a mission call for an immediate departure. But bacillary dysentery was sapping my strength, forcing me to visit [flight surgeon Cantoni] at Gialam. I was thinking of interrupting my flying for a few days.

The medical captain expressed the same opinion and gave me the medication I asked him for."[20]

Military operations continued at Na San throughout November and well into December. Even with the problems cropping up with the helicopter and personnel, the need for rescue services was acute. Orders were issued to send helicopters to remain on standby at Na San in the event of more casualties. Despite early prognostications of Operation Lorraine's success, General Giap continued assaults on the more vulnerable outposts close to Na San.

"During the latter part of December, the positions at Moc Chau and Yen Chau fell despite bitter resistance," Valérie said. "It was now impossible to refuel at the airstrips in between, and the range of the Hiller didn't allow an un-refueled flight. The sole operational Westland would be the only helicopter able to fly between Na San and Hanoi."

Again, there was a problem. In the aftermath of Sergeant Voirin's accident, the squadron mechanics were increasingly reluctant to certify the Westland as airworthy. Even the sole operational Westland exhibited an unusual driveline vibration that required further diagnosis, and it was advised not to fly the aircraft more than necessary. As a result, a decision was made to load one of the Hillers into a Bristol transport plane and bring it to Na San, thus bypassing the problem with fuel range.

But there was another problem. Santini was still involved with ELA 52 operations in Saigon, and Bartier—the only other pilot rated to fly a Hiller—was out of commission. The responsibility fell upon Valérie to take on the task of moving the wounded from outlying outposts to Na San.

"We were ordered to depart within three hours," Valérie said. "Four mechanics—including Sgt. Le Goff and Corporal Robert Genay—were to reassemble the helicopter in Na San with minimum delay. The prospect of the journey filled us all with enthusiasm."[21]

With the disassembled Hiller on board, the Bristol transport made quick work of getting to Na San. Flying into the Thai region of Vietnam afforded a spectacular view of mountains and valleys carpeted with lush, green vegetation. But danger always lurked in the deceptively beautiful landscape.

"I thought of the Dakotas and other transports that have crashed or were shot down by the enemy," Valérie reflected. "Despite these losses, the airlift kept operating night and day."[22]

As the fortified encampment of Na San came into view, Valérie and her companions could see how well armed it was. The hilltop locations, where some of Giap's battalions had attempted to assault the French position, could be easily detected by the burned and defaced vegetation caused by napalm and heavy artillery barrages. When Valérie could finally see the breadth of the battle camp, it was a sight that completely amazed her.

"Artillery batteries were scattered all around the brown soil. Like chopped-off tree trunks, the barrels of the artillery guns were aimed at the sky and shined in the sunlight. Over on one side, a small artillery unit was firing, spewing out small whitish puffs."[23]

Valérie expected to see tents, but there were none to be seen. With the aid of the Corps of Engineers, the French had managed to put most of their operations at Na San underground. When the Bristol finally landed, Valérie began to learn some of the secrets that Na San was hiding as she and the mechanics waited for the unloading of the Hiller.

"I had time to spot ten, twenty shelter access doors. It was an invisible city buried at the bottom of the valley."[24]

It turned out there was an intricate series of corridors that connected offices and large rooms filled with the latest equipment in warfare. Kitchens, storage rooms, and ammunition depots were all interconnected. Fiber matting covered the earthen walls to prevent dampness. Gasoline-powered electric generators hummed away at various sections that powered the vast array of yellow-tinted floodlights. There was even a fully stocked hospital capable of treating all but the most seriously wounded. White sheets covered the walls and ceilings of the operating room.

The entire complex at Na San was under the command of General Jean Gilles. Gilles was a graduate of St. Cyr and a veteran of World War II. He was a battle-hardened paratrooper and received a field promotion to general only the week before.

Valérie met briefly with the general before finding her way to her quarters.

Back up on top, Le Goff and the other mechanics finally unloaded the Hiller and immediately got to work on its reassembly. Anticipating nearly everything he needed for the job, Le Goff erected a portable overhead chain hoist to help in the reinstallation of the long rotor blades. Every component that came off the aircraft so it would fit inside the Bristol now had to go back on.

"My four characters have located a quiet corner and, bare-chested, they pull, hoist, assemble, screw, tighten nuts."

Valérie watched their progress until she suddenly heard Le Goff exclaim:
"Merde!"

It turned out that one of the tires on the helicopter's tricycle landing gear was flat. It was neither repairable nor replaceable with the spare parts they had brought with them.

The problem was not insurmountable. The operations officer at the base put out a radio message to Hanoi to bring a spare tire in on one of the transport planes that landed on the airstrip every fifteen minutes during daylight.

With work completed for the day, Valérie André, Le Goff, and the other mechanics made their way to the underground bunker's mess hall for dinner. During dinner, Valérie learned that a paratrooper battalion dropped over Chine Dong had suffered casualties.

"I went to bed early, but I thought about all of the broken arms and legs of those who fell smack into the forest. I'd have to go and retrieve them as soon as possible."[25]

By the following day, the Hiller—complete with a new landing gear tire and wheel—was once again whole. Le Goff and his mechanics stood nearby as Valérie took a short shakedown run around the airfield to see if the aircraft was ready for its first mission.

"All four remained by the runway watching me as I test flew the machine. The flight was entirely satisfactory, and without cutting power to the engine, I radioed Central Operations:

"The helicopter is ready!"

The message that crackled in reply over Valérie's headset instructed her to take off for Co Noi, an outpost near a small village in the Tonkin Delta. It was a mountainous country, and Valérie worried about the capabilities of the freshly assembled helicopter's performance.

"Wouldn't it have been better to conduct a few practice flights? Be that as it may, alone on board, I notice the Hiller flies well, and I headed east."[26]

Co Noi was a fairly well-entrenched camp but considered vulnerable. Paratroopers were sent in to keep the camp from falling to the Viet Minh. Nearby outposts at Moc Chua and Yen Chua had already fallen recently. As Valérie approached the LZ, a C-47 Dakota circled the area, dropping supplies by parachute to the troops on the ground. As Valérie got closer, she could see the men had laid out panels for her landing zone.

"The Dakota's drop zone was some fifty meters from the panels intended for my use. Very kindly, the pilot acceded to my request and interrupted his work until the Hiller had landed."

When Valérie landed, the two wounded men were waiting along with the battalion doctor. The condition of one of the men was grave.

"The lieutenant was in deep traumatic shock as a result of a massive shoulder fracture. The internal hemorrhage was certainly important."

"I did all that I could do for him," the battalion doctor told Valérie. She looked over the second man, a sergeant. He was less severely wounded, despite an open fracture of his thigh and a chest wound.

Valérie was concerned that the lieutenant might not survive the journey back to the base hospital at Na San. The second man was not as seriously wounded. Still, he was considerably larger than the lieutenant, and Valérie was concerned that the weight differential would hinder the helicopter's responsiveness. Deciding to make a return trip for the sergeant, Valérie instructed the doctor and his men to secure only the lieutenant to one of the Hiller's litters. Seconds later—after making sure he was indeed secure—Valérie was underway, allowing the still circling Dakota to resume the remainder of its supply drop.

While en route to Na San, Valérie read out the lieutenant's condition to Na San's Central Operations officers.

"I gave out all the required information so that, upon my arrival on the field, not a second would be wasted. The lieutenant needed immediate trauma emergency treatment."

The message was received and relayed to the medical center in Na San's bunker. As soon as Valérie touched down on the tarmac, the base doctor and his medics immediately pulled the young lieutenant underground.

"Hibernation!" was the operative word that got Valérie's attention when it came to treating the lieutenant's trauma. It was a relatively new and radical treatment, and Valérie was surprised that the field hospital could implement the procedure. As she later explained the treatment involving "hibernation":

"It was a method that consisted of disconnecting the neuro-vegetative system, as applied by Medicin Colonel Chippeaux. It had already saved several lives."[27]

With the lieutenant now in the care of Na San's medical team, Valérie lifted the Hiller back into the air. She headed back to Co Noi to retrieve the sergeant. Soon Valérie and the helicopter were over the hilltops leading to the outpost. As she pressed on, Valérie was careful to establish landmarks along the way and took note of the narrow, twisting ribbon of road that led back to the outpost.

Curiously, as she approached the outpost, Valérie noted how the topography surrounding the bunkhouse and tower had changed in only an hour.

The paratroopers were stripping vegetation and leveling the ground with shovels to prepare a landing strip for Morane Criquets.

"The helicopter could only be used for medical evacuations. Several other liaisons needed to be established between Na San and then set up at Co Noi, which involved three or four battalions."

The battalion doctor met Valérie with the wounded sergeant after she landed.

"The sergeant was rather heavy. My machine labored when I wanted to pick it off the ground and gain altitude. A difference of fifty or sixty pounds was noticeable."

It was late in the day, and dusk was rapidly approaching. Valérie was relieved when she caught sight of the runway at Na San. With efficiency, the medical team again met Valérie on the tarmac. With little time wasted, the sergeant, just as the lieutenant, was swallowed up by the underground complex.

With the day coming to a close, Valérie turned her concern to her helicopter.

"Once the sergeant was in the hands of the medics, I tended to the Hiller. The terrible dust and humidity of the night air would be fatal to it. In a few days it would have a shelter available to itself."

Le Goff had the foresight to bring tarps and canvas from old tents to create some temporary protection. The evening passed uneventfully, although artillery cannons boomed throughout the night.

At dawn, Valérie and her team met again near the helicopter. A tanker truck slowly rolled up and down the red clay airfield, spraying a mist of water to check some of the ever-present dust. Under Le Goff's supervision, the men performed a thorough check of the Hiller before allowing Valérie to leave for her next mission.

It was to be a very long day.

The first mission was not too difficult. A Vietnamese private, not too seriously injured, was flown from Co Noi back to Na San.

"I had only returned to Na San, killed the engine, and drunk the traditional bottle of beer brought to me by Le Goff when Operations dispatched me to Co Noi again."[28]

The Viet Minh in the area had taken up sniper activity while Valérie was gone. The next casualty was a young French soldier with a bullet wound to his stomach. Again, back to Na San, where Valérie hoped that it would be her last mission for the day.

But it wasn't to be. Late in the afternoon, Co Noi sent out a message requesting a third evacuation. Darkness was rapidly approaching, and it would be a race against time to complete the mission before nightfall.

By now, Valérie believed the helicopter "knew the way" to Co Noi just as well as she did. As she descended between the hills, she learned that there were two casualties to evacuate. One of the casualties was a journalist by the name of Jacques de Pottier. He had a bullet embedded in his thigh. The second casualty, a private, was not severely wounded. Valérie reasoned that he could have waited for a return flight, but the sun was already setting.

It was not a good situation.

Valérie knew that the higher altitude combined with the heated air would create very little lift for the Hiller's two rotor blades. Gaining altitude with the weight of the two men aboard would be difficult. But she went ahead with the decision to evacuate both at the same time.

It was fortunate that the soldiers had constructed their runway for fixed-winged aircraft. Valérie would need its full two-hundred-meter length to get the Hiller airborne.

"The Hiller skimmed the grass and picked up speed but was only willing to climb after a run of some fifty meters. During these few seconds of almost horizontal flight, I detected a certain anxiety on the faces of the onlookers. It was useless to ask the Hiller to climb even more—the air in the region provided very little lift. Skimming the tops of the trees, the aircraft dragged along every curve of the path I followed. I feared crashing in the middle of the forest. A first strange shudder, then a second, shook the cockpit. If Santini could see me, would he break more matches in two?"

Valérie held her breath, twisting the throttle fully open and working both the collective and cyclic control. The Hiller achieved its miracle. It cleared the top of the forest.

With night enveloping the world in darkness once again, Valérie touched down at Na San. Her thoughts, again, were with her trusted mechanical companion.

"The poor thing was tired. Its daily work had been carried out under particularly difficult conditions. It would soon be entitled to a major overhaul."

The Hiller made it back to Na San despite suffering some damage that occurred during its rough takeoff. Le Goff discovered the damage and radioed Gialam to send additional spare parts to Na San in the morning.

When the next morning dawned, it was December 31, the final day of 1952. As the sunrise took its full effect, the morning run of Dakotas began to arrive from Hanoi. Onboard one of the aircraft were the parts needed to make the battered helicopter whole once more. Once again, Valérie André's mechanized partner was ready for a new day.

"Doubtless refreshed and eager to go after a night's rest, the Hiller was quickly repaired and readied. I was about to test it with one or two laps around the field when 'Operations' notified me that a sergeant was seriously wounded. . . . On the way out, I tested my old companion. It seemed to respond normally—jumping around, climbing, ascending."[29]

This mission was not far from Na San, and Valérie could quickly cover ground arriving at the LZ in little more than five minutes.

"I landed in the middle of a group of paratroopers. The sergeant they handed over to me had multiple wounds. Carried to the field hospital in slightly more than fifteen minutes, he was immediately given emergency care and operated upon. The speed of the intervention would ultimately save him."[30]

While the war recognized neither holiday nor commemoration, the remainder of December 31 was relatively peaceful for Valérie André.

"Hey! This is New Year's Eve!" Le Goff exclaimed to Valérie.

And so it was. And as evening came about, Valérie felt that it was possible to finally relax, knowing that there would be no missions to fly during the night. And as the minutes ticked away toward midnight, the men at Na San also felt that they could finally relax.

"Without the feverish activity prevailing throughout the camp, I would have thought about celebrating the passing of the old year. A gala dinner awaited us. At the mess hall entrance, General Gilles stopped to congratulate a soldier who appeared outrageously young to me. His face was that of an adolescent."

The young soldier was tougher than Valérie first surmised. He had led a squad that successfully engaged the Viet Minh and had brought back three prisoners.

"They also brought back two rifles and an automatic," an officer said to Valérie.

Upon closer examination, Valérie could see how the young man was changed by his experience in Indochina.

"I could detect a certain male stoutness. His face was hard. What a tough learning ground this war in Indochina was. What a tough ambiance was that of a fortress buried in the jungle which celebrated New Year be fending off enemy attacks."[31]

The Dakotas had supplied Na San well for the holiday evening. The meal was excellent and in the best French tradition, and champagne flowed. While the festive mood would last until midnight and beyond, Valérie decided to retire early to her quarters near the base hospital.

"I needed my sleep, and the first day of the year may have some early morning missions. In the gallery occupied by the field hospital, there was silence. One could sometimes hear the nurses moving back and forth between beds. Tomorrow, some of the men would be evacuated by Dakota, but others will also take their place."[32]

The first day of 1953 opened to a crystal clear sky in the morning. The relative peace from the end of the previous day did not carry over, however.

"Co Noi advised that there were ten casualties to evacuate. Neither war nor nature had changed in one night!"[33]

Depending on the weight of the casualties, evacuation by helicopter would have required five round-trips or more. Fortunately for Valérie, the airstrip at Co Noi had been completed. It was now able to accept a Morane Criquet medical plane. Chief Warrant Officer Papon would assist Valérie with the evacuations that day.

The situation at Co Noi had gone from bad to worse over the last forty-eight hours. A few days before, Valérie flew the same route over the twisting dirt road that led to the LZ at Co Noi without any need for an escort. Today there would be two Bearcat fighter planes to meet her there when she was ready to land. But en route to Co Noi, Valérie was on her own.

"Nine to ten kilometers from Co Noi, a shot rang out. Was this an isolated shooter? I had neither the time to ask the question nor for the reply. Automatic weapons opened up. Mortar shots joined the action. To start its descent, the Hiller had just lost some altitude. How could I have guessed the *Viet Minh* were present in the clump of trees over which I was flying? Who could help me out?"[34]

There was no choice for Valérie but to "pour on the coals" and hope she could fly over the dangerous part of the forest before one of the bullets or shells would find its target.

Mercifully, the danger subsided, and up ahead, Valérie could see the two Bearcats, as their pilots were already engaged in strafing runs beyond the perimeter of the camp at Co Noi. Presently, Valérie could also see that Papon's Morane had already landed. Still somewhat shaken up by her close call, Valérie brought the Hiller in for a landing not far from the Criquet.

Some of the men on the ground had seen Valérie come over the heavily wooded area they knew was heavily held by the Viet Minh. They were amazed that she had survived the equivalent of an aerial minefield.

"Papon and a few officers surrounded me. The pilot wanted to know why I had followed a route that was now off-limits. Like the other spectators, the Chief Warrant Officer expected to see the helicopter fall out of the sky in flames."[35]

Unbeknownst to Valérie, Papon had received new routing instructions from Na San's operations to avoid the route over the dirt road leading to Co Noi and to go farther north over some of the higher mountain peaks. Valérie, however, had not received the new instructions.

"Before taking off with two casualties on board, I wanted to glance at the map. Papon pointed out the new routing that Na San forgot to point out to me."[36]

Despite the barrage of bullets that Valérie experienced, both she and the helicopter came away virtually unscathed. But the return to Na San would also present a new set of challenges.

"From the very beginning, the return trip got off on the wrong foot. With two casualties aboard, the Hiller protested. Twice—and those circles seemed to take on an awfully long time—I was forced to fly around one of the peaks until the helicopter was willing to climb to a decent altitude. A tree-covered range stood in my way. I thought I could go over it. The aircraft skimmed the treetops while air currents slammed it downward. While keeping an eye open for small clearings where the Hiller could land if necessary, I juggled and cheated and prayed to the updrafts and downdrafts."[37]

The danger was real. High altitude and the thin tropical air, combined with a marginal payload, had always been the Hiller's Achilles' heel. Now those deficiencies were throwing every bedevilment they possessed at once at Valérie André as she fought to keep the helicopter in the air.

"The helicopter was every moment on the brink of catastrophe, *in extremis*. I wrestled it two or three times without even believing that the stick motion I applied could restore its speed or to force it over a tree."

The unwieldy helicopter had the flight characteristics of both a straw in the wind and a lead ball combined. But finally, Valérie was able to maintain her mastery of the controls.

"The last knolls were not as bad as I feared, and I finally reached Na San."

Papon had a much easier time negotiating the mountainous peaks back to Na San. He had already offloaded his casualties and was on his way back to

Co Noi when Valérie landed. Valérie, too, was to return to Co Noi to retrieve two more casualties. Valérie began to feel a severe fatigue setting in, but she was determined to complete her mission; however, she wondered what the two wounded men at Co Noi would think if they only knew the difficulties with her previous trip.

"If they could have suspected my troubles, they might have preferred to wait for another Morane shuttle. But it was getting late."[38]

It only took less than five minutes to strap the last two casualties into their litters. Valérie didn't refuel the Hiller at Na San, and she hoped this would be an advantage as she took for the northern mountaintops once again.

"How many times would I have to turn around the peak to gain altitude again? I wanted to gain thirty more feet. With less gasoline on board, such a goal might be possible. The Hiller didn't play games, and once it reached a proper altitude, it agreed to head straight for the stable. We landed at Na San at dusk."[39]

That was the cap to a harrowing day. When she was met by Le Goff on the tarmac, even Valérie wondered how she had managed to emerge victorious over fate again.

The next day when Valérie awoke and reported to the airfield, she was met with a surprise when one of the early morning transports brought in an unexpected but familiar face.

"Bonjour, mon capitaine. I have been assigned to replace you."

Henri Bartier had fully recovered from his illness and was ready to take over where Valérie left off.

There was relief on Valérie's part that Bartier had arrived. The previous day had proved to her that she wasn't indestructible. There were limits to what the human body could endure despite the mind and the will remaining indomitable. And Valérie André understood this.

"I had to admit the long months of daily missions had gotten the better of my endurance. The fatigue I suddenly felt prompted me to climb on board the first Dakota headed for Hanoi."

At Gialam, Valérie saw the flight surgeon, Major Cantoni.

"Operational fatigue and iron-deficiency anemia," the major bluntly told her. Cantoni ordered Valérie to take a prolonged rest at the beach resort at Nha Trang.

"And to think that in the old days, such a diagnosis appeared to me as vague and lacking in precision. It now represented something real."[40]

*   *   *

Operation Lorraine came to an end by January 1953.

Superior weaponry and air power by the French proved to outmatch General Giap. When Giap finally withdrew, Viet Minh wounded and dead numbered more than three thousand.

The final number of roughly one thousand dead and wounded was considered a soft enough blow for the French to declare themselves the victors in the campaign. Moreover, General Salan and his generals were convinced that the strategy of grouping smaller fortified artillery units around a fully functioning resupply air base to draw out Giap's army could be used in a future campaign. In that sense, Na San would become the blueprint for something much larger.

It was no small quirk of fate that there was a signpost at Na San that pointed toward a small Vietnamese province known as Dien Bien Phu, some 170 kilometers to the west. It would be there that something much larger would soon happen.

Chapter 34

To Breathe Again

Nha Trang, January 1953

The idyllic beaches of Nha Trang stretched on as far as the eye could see. Soft sand countered gentle waves. The central Vietnam coastal resort city was the perfect place for Valérie's extended rest and recreation. The weeks spent in rescue operations at Na San capped an arduous year for the young doctor and pilot. The balmy ocean climate was soothing to a soul wracked by hardship and travail.

"The red corpuscles did not resist thirty months of active life in Indochina," Valérie said in her inimitable manner. "However, the calm region on Nha Trang seemed to be kind to them. And I even managed to put on some weight."[1]

The extended leave allowed Valérie to think of not only her present but also her future. Her thirty months with the helicopter rescue service had been both the most rewarding and grueling times of her life. And the helicopters were never very far from Valérie's mind.

"One morning, as I was lazing on the beach, a familiar noise drew me away from my reading. What was a Sikorsky doing in Nha Trang?" Valérie asked herself. "Are battles that we have not heard about taking place in the area?"[2]

Actually, the Sikorsky was coming in from the sea. As the helicopter came into view, Valérie could see an anchor painted on the helicopter's long fuselage. Curious about its mission, Valérie took off in the direction of the airfield.

"The pilot, a comrade I met while I was on the *Arromanches*, explained to me that the fighter planes from the aircraft carrier were operating nearby in Qui Nhon."[3]

The pilot was on standby as support for the fighters.

Valérie was to learn that the aircraft carrier would no longer need the services of the Hillers or Sikorskys from ELA 53. The French navy recognized the value of aircraft capable of vertical takeoff and landings and recently acquired new machines.

While the tranquil shores of Nha Trang were a curative retreat for Valérie, she relentlessly yearned to rejoin ELA 53 at Gialam. The intertwining of flight and rescue heightened her desire to return to action; however, Dr. Cantoni, Valérie's flight surgeon, refused to shorten the length of her convalescence. Valérie chafed—each day was a month in her mind.

Valérie's appointment for reexamination came on January 28, 1953, in Hanoi.

"Once again, I confronted Dr. Cantoni. This time I know my blood count is good. The doctor can no longer deny me the right to fly."

But contrary to her wishes, Cantoni would not certify Valérie to resume rescue flights. Valérie refused to believe it, but the flight surgeon's verdict would send her back to France.

Cantoni's decision was a crushing blow. Ever since Valérie's arrival in Vietnam in 1947, she had persevered against incredible odds and endured virtually every obstacle thrown in her path. Confronting death and human destruction had taken their toll, but Valérie's dedication to healing always brought her through to the next mission. The adrenaline rush from beating the odds and surviving another day kept her going. But now, she faced the end of five turbulent years.

With heavy sadness, Valérie ventured out to Gialam the following day. The hangars at Gialam had been her true home ever since her assignment to Hanoi. She knew every square centimeter of the buildings. The sights and sounds of the airfield were often a source of joy and delight for her when the darkness of war clouded everything else. But now, Valérie's trip to the hangars at Gialam brought her sorrow, as she knew this visit would be among her last.

When Valérie arrived at the hangar, she learned she wasn't the only departing member of ELA 53.

"Abandoned in the back of the hangar, my two dear Hillers await the time of their overhaul, that is to say, their dismantling and departure back to France."

She further lamented, "They no longer have the right to fly and, unfortunately, neither do I."[4]

The older Hillers were making way for the larger Westland-Sikorsky S-51s, which already took up most of the hangar space; however, the hangar would also be home to newer-model Hillers and improved versions of the Sikorsky.

Valérie was somewhat dismissive of the British-built machines as their service reliability had proven to be "capricious" at best. Valérie wanted to be certified to fly the larger and more powerful helicopters. Still, the diminutive and somewhat primitive Hillers would always hold a special place in her heart.

"Three Hiller type H-23Bs have been sent to us from the United States. Pilots will now be able to take off without worrying about the weight of the two injured people installed in the baskets. With two hundred horsepower instead of 178, the power difference is small, but in reality, this additional power greatly improved flight conditions. The higher horsepower engines would spare many difficulties to those who were to pilot them."

But Valérie kept coming back to the question that nagged her the most.

"Will I be one of those pilots?"[5]

It was a question that had no answer. At least not for now.

Valérie learned from Sergeant Le Goff that the two oldest Hillers would be flown to Cat Ba Island and loaded on a transport ship bound for Marseilles. It would be their last flight in Vietnam, and, it would turn out, Valérie's final flight as well.

Alexis Santini was still on assignment in Saigon, but Henri Bartier remained in Hanoi. Both Valérie and Bartier would take the Hillers on their final flights to Cat Ba.

"It was not without some emotion that we met near the parking apron of the hangar," Valérie recalled. "The mechanics were attending to the fueling and the engine run-up of the helicopters that were about to take their last flight. I took off, and Bartier followed me. Alone in our cockpits, we headed out for Cat Ba. There, the two crates that brought the H-23Bs from France were waiting. The two Hillers were to be dismantled and loaded up without any delay."

The prospect of saying goodbye to her mechanical companion saddened Valérie profoundly.

"There was a last photograph, a last look, and we abandoned them. A Siebel brought us back to Gialam."[6]

On March 25, 1952, Valérie André ventured out to Gialam for one last time. With her Hillers gone and her flight status in limbo, there was very little reason for her to remain in Hanoi. She had already met the officer who was replacing her, and their meeting had been rather abrupt.

"He was full of vim and impatience. I felt that my presence was no longer indispensable."[7]

While ELA 53's new commanding officer had no history with Valérie, it was not the same for the rest of the crew. Each of them had assembled to be reviewed by their former commander one final time. Even the little brown dog, Rotor, that Valérie had rescued off the streets of Hanoi was there. Rotor was now in the care of Le Goff, who made him squadron mascot.

Alexis Santini, her mentor and commander, was the only person who wasn't there. Santini was still in Saigon performing rescue missions with ELA 52. It pained her to miss one of the most significant people to have ever entered her life. She truly hoped she would see Santini again.

"I bid farewell to the pilots, the mechanics, and all my companions on good days and bad. They were as moved as I was, but each one tried as much as possible not to show anything.

"I took one last look at the office I loved so much, the hangar and the helicopters. Suddenly images flowed into me that tightened my heart—Rocher Notre-Dame and the retreat of Hoa Binh. The daily trips across the Delta under a grey and rainy sky in February and March, light in the Spring, and the color of lead in August. My long flights out of the Thai country, and of course, my mission to Na San.

"So many faces too—soldiers, women, children, caught in the flood of this inextricable war."[8]

The memories of her experiences in Indochina were overwhelming, but Valérie, like her comrades, faced them bravely.

A flight on an Air France Constellation bound for Paris was reserved for Valérie André on April 5.

Valérie wrote to her family that she was returning. The flight was long, and sleep came swiftly despite the constant droning of the Constellation's four radial engines.

"Please fasten your seatbelts; we will be arriving at Orly in twenty minutes," came the announcement over the aircraft's intercom. The flight attendant also relayed the current temperature on the ground from the pilot. It was 8 degrees Celsius (46 degrees Fahrenheit) in Paris, relatively temperate for the time of year but downright cold for anyone emerging from the tropical climate of Indochina. She raised the collar of her coat in anticipation of the change.

When the landing was complete, Valérie gathered up her belongings and made her way to the mobile stairs leading off the plane. As with all trips from Asia to France, the flight time and layovers for fuel and maintenance were long. After such a long period of inactivity, Valérie had to regain the use of her legs, and moving seemed to require some considerable effort.

As Valérie and her fellow passengers approached the concourse, dissonant cries erupted from the crowd of friends and family gathered to meet the new arrivals. Valérie heard her name called out through the commotion and craned her neck to catch sight of her sisters and brothers and their respective husbands, wives, and children, who had all turned out to meet her. She also saw her mother, and most surprising to Valérie, her father was there.

Philibert André had opposed Valérie leaving Strasbourg to pursue her education in medicine during the German occupation. He had also disapproved of her joining the French army in Indochina. Still, Philibert André was there, proudly clutching a scrapbook of articles he had collected detailing Valérie's exploits over the past several years.

Feelings of joy, relief, and pride resounded in the voices that overlapped one another in the reunion with her family. While not the end of Valérie André's story by any means, her story, at least for now, had come full circle.

Chapter 35

Dénouement Dien Bien Phu

Dien Bien Phu, Vietnam, March 23, 1954

Dr. Grauwin was waiting for word on whether the helicopter would arrive soon. A patient needed evacuation to Hanoi. He knew that several more would need to be airlifted out of the base by tomorrow. Worried, he lit a cigarette and inhaled deeply.

"Will the airstrip even be operational by tomorrow?" Grauwin thought to himself.

Grauwin had good reason to worry. A month earlier, he had been there when Viet Minh artillerymen trained their opening shots in battle at one of the base's two airfields. The explosions of 105 mm shells came during dinner time. Grauwin and the other men ran from the mess hall toward the first detonations. It turned out that a disabled C-119 Packett transport plane awaiting spare parts from Hanoi was now in flames as fuel from its tanks burned out of control. Grauwin later wrote:

"They hit the Packett. For a first attempt, it was truly masterful. One shell to the right, another to the left, and then bang on the target."[1]

From then on, the shelling never seemed to let up.

Thirty-nine-year-old Paul Grauwin was the commander of the mobile surgical unit attached to the French army base at Dien Bien Phu. Born in Belgium, Grauwin was a compact man distinguished by his round, wire-rimmed spectacles and shaved head that gave him the appearance of a studious eagle. He had served as a surgeon with the Free French Army during

World War II. He had been in Vietnam since 1947, with his latest assignment at the military hospital on Cat Ba Island.

Grauwin should have been on his way back to France by this time. His tour of duty in Indochina was over. But the lead surgeon at Dien Bien Phu had become seriously ill, and a replacement was needed only for a few weeks. Grauwin was given the assignment. Two weeks had soon stretched to more than a month, however, and Grauwin found himself stuck at the base, as the wounded and the dead piled up all around him.

The base at Dien Bien Phu was the French military's latest attempt to regain its dominance in Vietnam. Dien Bien Phu was a sparsely populated Vietnamese province only ten kilometers from the Laotian border and more than three hundred kilometers from Hanoi. The idea for the massive military base came in the aftermath of the French victory at Na San a year earlier. At Na San, Viet Minh general Vo Nguyen Giap threw three divisions of his army up against a force of fifteen thousand French defenders and suffered more than seven thousand dead and wounded as a result. In terms of sheer numbers, it was a victory for the French, with little more than three hundred killed and another six hundred wounded. To the French, Na San proved that a heavily manned land base supplied by aircraft around the clock could be a successful strategy against the Viet Minh.

With that in mind, the French high command approved a plan to build a larger version of the Na San land/air base at Dien Bien Phu.

It was an ambitious plan. The French high command under General Henri Navarre rationalized that by placing the base at Dien Bien Phu, the Viet Minh's access to neighboring Laos would be cut off, along with their supply line from China. Choking off the source of munitions and support was seen as crucial in crippling the Viet Minh. An even more ambitious objective, however, was to draw General Vo Nguyen Giap and the Viet Minh into a direct battle with the heavily armed French position, just as they had at Na San. With heavy artillery pieces brought into place at the camp, the French felt confident that they would be more than a match for the Viet Minh.

Or would they?

The French didn't conceive of the possibility that the Viet Minh would bring their own heavy artillery pieces to the densely forested hills surrounding the valley at Dien Bien Phu through sheer strength of will to even their chances in battle. Underestimating the will of the Viet Minh would be a fatal miscalculation by the French.

The massive military buildup in the area began in November 1953, focusing on a small valley of roughly 6 kilometers (3.5 miles) by 20 kilometers (12.5 miles). The base was surrounded by rolling and densely forested hills on all sides. On November 20, the French airdropped the first of more than nine thousand men and four thousand tons of supplies into Dien Bien Phu. The massive airdrop even included a bulldozer to level the area and construct subterranean earthen shelters. The bulldozer was also used to extend one airfield built by the Japanese during World War II and create a second landing zone (LZ) for rescue helicopters.

By March 1954, the base at Dien Bien Phu had grown to ten thousand combat soldiers and more than eighteen hundred support personnel. The Viet Minh were estimated to have had more than fifty thousand combat troops at Dien Bien Phu and an additional fifteen thousand civilian men and women in roles of support and resupply. Much of the supply work was done either on foot or by bicycle, physically carrying everything from food to artillery shells into the hills. Large artillery guns mounted on wheeled caissons were laboriously dragged uphill. It was a feat unparalleled in modern warfare.

On March 13, the Viet Minh fired their first volleys at the French. It marked the beginning of fifty-seven days of hell.

By March 23, the situation at the base was dire. As casualties mounted, Grauwin grimly noted:

"I counted up to a hundred and fifty wounded. Seventy of them were superficially or not too seriously wounded and could be sent back to their battalion infirmary. Eighty would have to be examined more closely, and I believed that fifty of them would require an operation."[2]

What was even more appalling was the camp's morgue. The number of those killed in battle was reaching staggering proportions:

"The morgue . . . was full up. Outside between the hole [dug into the side of a trench] and the barbed wire, there were a hundred bodies, dropped there in confusion, either on stretchers or on the ground, fixed in grotesque or tragic attitudes. Some were sheeted in canvas, and others were wearing their combat uniforms, motionless in the position in which death had caught them."[3]

The Viet Minh had inflicted so many fatalities that the camp's commander—General Christian de Castries—ordered that the dead be buried on the spot where they were killed.

Normal surgical practices were often abandoned due to the overwhelming number of cases. Grauwin and his colleagues often operated bare-chested as the supply of surgical gowns was exhausted early on. Most of the time, surgical gowns proved to be impractical anyway, as the heat and humidity in the poorly ventilated bunker hospital made for an incredibly stifling environment.

Initially, the French believed the base was undefeatable. Colonel Charles Piroth, the base's artillery chief, confidently declared before shooting began that "I've got more guns than I need" to defeat the Viet Minh. Three days after the heavy bombardment commenced, it became apparent that the enemy's guns outmatched French artillery. Piroth committed suicide in his quarters. He felt that he had dishonored his command.

The perimeter around the land/air base at Dien Bien Phu that had once seemed impenetrable was now like a noose tightening around the French. The Viet Minh steadily choked off the area despite suffering massive casualties on their own side. Keeping the two airfields open was essential to transporting the most seriously wounded out of the camp and allowing vital supplies in. Without this lifeline to Hanoi, there would be no hope for the French.

March 23 saw no let up from the Viet Minh. The French military complex at Dien Bien Phu was divided into eight defensive hillocks, all with female names supposedly named after past mistresses of Colonel de Castries. The farthest-reaching position from the center of camp that the French held was a hillock known as Isabelle. On that morning, the Third Foreign Infantry Regiment of the French Foreign Legion withstood a severe shelling from the Viet Minh. Grauwin received word to expect casualties.

As it turned out, the regiment repelled the Viet Minh with a superior offensive, beating their attackers back into the surrounding brush. As a result, casualties on the French side were much lighter than expected. The most severely wounded that morning was twenty-three-year-old Lieutenant Alain Gambiez, who took a bullet to his knee cap during the siege and was in severe agony.

Gambiez was the son of General Fernand Gambiez, who was General Navarre's chief of staff. Lieutenant Gambiez was among the first who arrived at Dien Bien Phu in November when the buildup in the area began. As with many of his comrades, Lieutenant Gambiez realized the deadly hazards of the valley early on. In a letter to his wife, Gambiez wrote: "For my part, I have been afraid, but I thank the Lord for it. We can understand the fear others have more easily afterward. We manage to think about death, but, despite this, we still have tremendous confidence."[4]

As a general's son, Alain Gambiez could have opted for a safer post in Hanoi or anywhere else. But Alain Gambiez did not seek or want special treatment. Even Dr. Grauwin was puzzled why Gambiez would not accept an easier posting:

"Why did [the sons of generals] refuse a quiet post when they had more than done their duty as section leaders or company commanders? Was it the fear that people would say, 'Oh, he's a general's son.' No. It was simply love for the profession of arms, in which they were no different than their comrades whose names were less known."[5]

When Gambiez arrived at the camp hospital, Grauwin examined the young soldier and briefly considered amputation. By now, Grauwin was used to performing amputations many times over. Upon further examination, Grauwin thought it was possible to save Gambiez's leg. To do so, he would need to be airlifted by helicopter as soon as possible to Hanoi.

The helicopter rescue pilots had their work cut out for them since the French moved into the area. ELA 53 still bore the brunt of the medical evacuations by helicopter, although now they were operating out of the airport at Muong Sai, Laos, forty-five kilometers to the east of Dien Bien Phu. There the pilots kept their aircraft on continuous standby to facilitate rapid evacuation.

Once the wounded arrived at Muong Sai, they would be loaded onto transport planes for evacuation to Hanoi. One new element for ELA 53 was the introduction of U.S.-built Sikorsky H-19s that entered into service in October. The new helicopters were a vast improvement, superior in terms of performance and reliability to the Westland WS-51s that the French were still using but starting to phase out. The smaller Hillers were entirely unsuited to the demanding tasks required at Dien Bien Phu.

The extreme danger of flying in and out of Dien Bien Phu—surrounded on all sides by enemy fire—presented an ever-increasing gamble to pilots. The large, lumbering Sikorskys were highly vulnerable when they slowly hovered into landing position at the base's LZ. But their workload was enormous. Since November 1953, there had been well over six hundred medical evacuations by helicopter from Dien Bien Phu.[6] Adjutant Henri Bartier was responsible for sixty-one of those evacuations to date.[7] And this flight would mark his 1,092nd mission as a rescue pilot in Indochina.[8]

Dr. Grauwin was well acquainted with Bartier's work.

"I had known Bartier long ago when he was piloting a Morane for the medical service. He was a sergeant then, and he had evacuated hundreds. He knew all the landing areas in Indochina."[9]

Lieutenant Gambiez was now well sedated, and his wounded knee was dressed and stabilized. The camp medics waited with Gambiez for the helicopter to arrive. The French artillery was holding the Viet Minh at bay, and the area around the LZ seemed secure.

Sergeant Henri Bernard accompanied Bartier as copilot for this mission. The H-19 was a more complex helicopter to fly than the Hiller and required more monitoring of its vital systems. A copilot was considered necessary for the safe operation of the aircraft.

Approaching the camp at Dien Bien Phu at high altitude from the southwest, Bartier and Bernard braced for entry into the danger zone. The Sikorsky H-19 had a higher cruising ceiling compared to both the WS-51 and Hiller H-23. Bartier made sure to take advantage of staying out of range of enemy fire before making his descent into camp.

Bartier effortlessly made the transition from flying Hillers to the much more complex Sikorsky helicopter and had grown accustomed to flying them into dangerous areas. The French base at Dien Bien Phu had proven to be the most challenging landing area yet, and there had already been several close calls for other pilots. Onboard the helicopter were also boxes of medical supplies for the camp hospital. As there was only one casualty to pick up, Bartier hoped the medics would quickly get the wounded man aboard his aircraft.

Bartier landed close to Isabelle to facilitate the transfer of the wounded. He was aware of the danger. The Viet Minh were becoming more deadly accurate with their shells. Even the airfield in the middle of the camp was now a frequent target.

Bartier backed off on power with the LZ in sight and began his descent. As always, his landing was precise. Once on the ground, a group of soldiers ran up to open the helicopter's side door to retrieve the supplies inside. At the same time, two medics carrying Gambiez on a stretcher worked quickly to get him inside the cabin and strapped to the floor of the helicopter. Up in the cockpit, Bartier and Bernard were separated from the cabin and were only able to watch with the hatch door propped open to make sure the men had closed the access to the fuselage and were clear of the rotor blades when they finished. Each second that went by was interminable. Bartier knew that Viet Minh in the surrounding hills had eyes trained on the helicopter. The prominent red crosses painted on both sides of the aircraft meant nothing to the Viet Minh. As soon as the men were clear, Bartier twisted the throttle and pulled up on the collective for a quick upward thrust.

The helicopter managed to gain only a few meters of altitude when a sharp, metallic sound pierced the cockpit. Bartier felt a searing pain in his left leg and knew he was hit. A split second later, another artillery shell pierced one of the Sikorsky's fuel tanks. There was an explosion, and then fire erupted all around the helicopter. The fuel tanks were located under the cabin floor where Lieutenant Gambiez was strapped in.[10]

There was no control. Bartier and Bernard were helpless as the helicopter plummeted violently back to earth. The force of the crash was such that Bartier forcefully struck his head on a bulkhead in the cockpit, which knocked out one of his front teeth and caused a concussion. Sergeant Bernard was thrown through the windshield. He suffered several broken ribs but was relatively unhurt. A Legionnaire saw the crash and was the first to reach the burning helicopter.

Sergeant Bernard and the soldier pulled at the door to the cockpit and managed to pry it open. The cockpit was on fire, and Bartier was still strapped in. The smoke was dense and toxic.[11]

Bartier could feel hands on his body, undoing his flight harness and pulling at him. Part of his flight suit was burning. The noise was like an immense roar, and the pain from his lower leg was excruciating. Smoke and fire were everywhere. Sounds and sights blended together in a blur. But then the din became fainter and fainter, and even the pain began to subside as Bartier lost consciousness. The nightmare ended as everything started to fade out.

* * *

The sight of the helicopter crashing in flames set off alarms all over the camp. At first, it seemed the men inside the burning wreckage couldn't be saved. The highly flammable magnesium that made up the Sikorsky's fuselage only added to the intensity of the fire. The rescuers used only dry chemical extinguishers and buckets of dirt and sand to fight the flames. Any water making contact with magnesium would only worsen the fire.

Fortunately, the helicopter had partially rolled over on its side when it impacted the ground. Bernard and the Legionnaire were able to pull Bartier to safety, but Gambiez was not as fortunate. The flames quickly overtook and consumed the interior of the Sikorsky. The rescuers could hear Gambiez cry out for help, but it was no use. The intense fire fueled by the helicopter's outer metal skin made it impossible to extract Gambiez in time. Sous

Lieutenant Alain Gambiez, the son of General Fernand Gambiez, joined the list of men allied to the French who would give their lives at Dien Bien Phu.

Sergeant Bernard and Henri Bartier were more fortunate. The men rushed the seriously injured and unconscious Bartier to the base hospital. It was not possible to save Bartier's mangled leg, and there was no choice except to amputate below his left knee; however, the remainder of Bartier's injuries were survivable. Bartier suffered a concussion from the impact that also knocked out his front tooth. There were also multiple burns on his body from the fire, especially on his right leg. But it appeared that he would survive.

Henri Bernard was less seriously injured. The pain in his chest was considerable, but he tolerated it. Bartier was the priority patient.

As Bartier regained consciousness, he became aware of his new situation. There was a reverence for the pilot who laid his life on the line so many times for others. Although living quarters were scarce in the beleaguered camp, Bartier was quartered in one of the shelters near the base's command center until he could be evacuated to Hanoi.[12]

Medical evacuations out of Dien Bien Phu were now seriously in question. It was not only an issue for Bartier and Bernard but also for others. The destruction of Bartier's Sikorsky by Viet Minh artillery demonstrated the vulnerability of both the airfield and the LZ on the south end of the base near the stronghold at Isabelle. The airstrip near the camp's center was still considered to be well protected, and transport planes were able to fly in and out. But it was becoming a question of how long this would be possible.

Three days after the attack on his helicopter, Bartier was placed on a C-47 and flown directly to Gialam in Hanoi. Sergeant Bernard was left behind to make room on the plane for the more seriously wounded.

As for Bartier, he was taken to Lanessan Hospital when he arrived in Hanoi. There he was reunited with the central person in his life, Marie Yvonne Bartier.

Marie Yvonne was relieved to learn that her husband would recover, although the loss of his leg meant that his days of flying into combat zones were over. Marie knew that the transition would be difficult for her husband.

"As soon as there were wounded to bring back, he was always 'Bartier the volunteer,'" Marie would say in an interview many years later. "He had the impression that he was protected by the red crosses on his helicopter."[13]

It would be a difficult road to recovery for Henri Bartier. Bartier suffered from depression from not being able to save Gambiez and losing his leg in the incident.

"This time they had me," Bartier said to his wife in private. "I'll never be like I was before."

"You're still here, and that's all that matters," Marie answered back. "Why would you say that?"

Henri raised the blanket covering the lower part of his body. Marie only reassured him.

"So, you have half a leg? We'll get you a pair of crutches. You're a winner. You will fly again."[14]

Marie would be proven right. And from that day on, Marie Yvonne Bartier never left her husband's side until he was ready to fly again.

As for the French defenders at Dien Bien Phu, the battle raged on. The Viet Minh were relentless in their assault on the base. On the same day as Henri Bartier was airlifted to Hanoi—March 28, 1954—another C-47 medical transport plane landed at Dien Bien Phu late in the day. Twenty-five casualties were brought aboard, including Sergeant Henri Bernard.

The plane taxied on the base's airstrip preparing for takeoff when its starboard engine sprung an oil leak. The pilot shut the aircraft down and ordered the wounded and the medical staff to disembark. Twenty-nine-year-old flight nurse Genevieve de Galard-Tarraubes was among the medical crew onboard.

Repairs wouldn't be carried out until morning for fear that work lights would give the Viet Minh a beacon to target their artillery on the aircraft, but the precautions made no difference. Mortar shells rained down on the airfield beginning that evening, cutting the stricken plane into ribbons and irreparably damaging the runway. The now destroyed C-47 was the last plane to use the airfield during the siege. The air and medical crew—including de Galard-Tarraubes—along with Henri Bernard and the twenty-four other wounded were stranded at the base. Genevieve de Galard-Tarraubes was the only female French military nurse to serve at Dien Bien Phu for the remainder of the siege.

For the next thirty-nine days, the situation at the base became an unrelenting nightmare. The Viet Minh pounded the French position mercilessly as the camp's perimeter shrank day by day. With the airfield gone, it was no longer possible to resupply the base by landing transport planes. Supplies dropped by parachutes often went wide of their targets and fell into the hands of the Viet Minh. All the while, monsoon rains poured from the sky.

There were attempts at sending in reinforcements. Marcel Bigeard led a battalion of parachutists airdropped into the camp. But they were not enough to fend off the ever-increasing bombardments.

Meanwhile, French diplomats held frantic meetings with their counter-parts from the United States. Desperate appeals were made for the U.S. Air Force to bomb the hills surrounding the camp at Dien Bien Phu to stop the Viet Minh onslaught. It was even suggested that the atomic bomb should be used to destroy supply lines from China. Ultimately, President Eisenhower declined to intervene.

The end finally came on May 7, 1954. General de Castries surrendered to the Viet Minh. It was the final blow to the French cause in Vietnam. The remaining French combatants and support personnel at Dien Bien Phu—including flight nurse Genevieve de Gallard-Tarraubes, Dr. Paul Grauwin, Sergeant Henri Bernard, Lieutenant Colonel Marcel Bigeard, and General Christian de Castries—were taken prisoner. The final numbers for losses by the French at Dien Bien Phu were devastating: 2,293 killed, 5,195 wounded, and 10,998 captured.[15]

The Viet Minh also suffered great losses at Dien Bien Phu. It is estimated that as many as 8,000 Viet Minh were killed, and an additional 15,000 were left wounded. General Vo Nguyen Giap didn't believe the French were finished in Vietnam in the immediate aftermath of the Viet Minh's victory. The French still maintained a considerable military force in Vietnam—some 470,000 troops versus approximately 300,000 Viet Minh. Half of this force aligned to the French cause were Vietnamese, a legacy of General Jean de Lattre's attempt to make the war a Vietnamese cause against communism. And the French were still in control of Vietnam's major cities.

But the defeat at Dien Bien Phu ended the French will to continue the fight. France entered a period of mourning for the losses at Dien Bien Phu.[16] Opposition to the war in France was intense, with less than 10 percent of the population supporting the war in public opinion polls. When the Radical Party's Pierre Mendès-France became France's president in 1954, the end to the war had finally come. With massive support from the National Assembly to withdraw from Vietnam, Mendès-France agreed to an international peace conference to be held in Geneva, Switzerland.

Similar to the hopes held for the ill-fated Fontainebleau Conference of 1946, Ho Chi Minh and his followers believed they held the upper hand in Geneva. The Viet Minh People's Army of Vietnam had just handed a major defeat to a formidable colonial power, and Ho Chi Minh had great support among the people of Vietnam.

But Vietnam would once again become a pawn to greater powers. This time the Soviet Union, China, and the United States would be the deciders of Vietnam's fate. The United States, in particular, dreaded the specter of communism gaining more of a foothold in Asia. As a result, Vietnam was divided into two regions, north and south—split at the 17th parallel line on the map. Ho Chi Minh's Democratic Republic of Vietnam would control the northern part. The south's government would be appointed by Vietnam's on-again, off-again emperor, Bao Dai. A national referendum would take place in July 1955 to determine who would lead a unified nation. Unfortunately, when the national referendum was held, Bao Dai's choice for prime minister, Ngo Dinh Diem, rigged the election in the south to reject unification with the Communist north.

The decisions made at the Geneva Conference dealt a blow to Ho Chi Minh's ambition of a united and independent Vietnam. The repercussions from Geneva would carry through to another war with another country.

This time it would be with the United States.

CASUALTIES OF THE FRENCH INDOCHINA WAR, 1945–1954

French armed forces: 75,581 dead (20,524 French nationals, 55,057 from French colonies and the French Foreign Legion), 64,427 wounded, 40,000 captured[17]

Viet Minh People's Army of Vietnam: 191,605 dead or missing,[18] 300,000 wounded[19]

Civilian casualties in Vietnam: 175,000 (estimated)[20]

Chapter 36

Challenges and Disillusion

Valérie André followed the events that unfolded in Vietnam during spring 1954 with both alarm and resignation. She had returned to France a little more than a year before but desperately wished to reconnect with her comrades still engaged in the struggle.

Months before the climactic battle at Dien Bien Phu, Valérie tried to return to service in Vietnam and wrote to General Fernand Gambiez about rejoining ELA 53.

"I received a reply. [Gambiez] expected my return to the Far East. He wanted to entrust me with medical evacuation by helicopter."[1]

With support from General Gambiez, Valérie hoped that her life in the military in Indochina would be different this time. She wanted to be fully integrated as an officer within the regular French army, not just the Service de santé. Her service record in Indochina was ample evidence that justified her inclusion as an officer in the regular army. But resistance to her request was immediate.

"[My integration] raised a multitude of objections, everything from the state of my health to the absence of possible assignments. In short, there were many bad pretexts, all of which were based on antifeminism. The military, at that time, was delighted to have women under their orders as nurses or secretaries. But they would not consider making them one of their own."[2]

Valérie did not back down from this rejection. Her next appeal was to France's minister of defense, René Pleven.

"[Pleven] was concerned with the promotion of women in all fields. . . . One of his daughters had not been able to enter the Polytechnique—a school closed to women. He considered the discrimination that affected me to be completely unfair and outdated."[3]

Pleven possessed a degree of influence to upend some of the status quo of France's military regarding promoting equality among its ranks. Keeping in line with attitudes that existed in 1950s France, the defense minister's changes to the military's structure were more incremental than monumental in scope.

"[Pleven] decided to create a women's military medical corps, where doctors and pharmacists would have the same rights and prerogatives as male personnel. . . . With the rank of captain, my integration into the corps was published in the Official Journal of the French Republic."[4]

The Women's Military Medical Corps was a small step in the right direction, and Valérie was fully aware.

"The Army didn't hide its reluctance to admit women as full officers. It was not until the 1970s that sexual discrimination between medical officers in health services was eliminated by creating a single corps."[5]

When the Women's Military Medical Corps became official on September 5, 1953, Valérie André was among its first inductees. René Pleven acknowledged Valérie's new status at a ceremony in Paris.

"Captain, you have chosen to make the military your career," the defense minister told her. "I congratulate you, and I am happy about it. But do not forget, in the army you will meet the best and the worst."[6]

After spending nearly six years in Indochina, Valérie André was already well aware of how true that was.

As Valérie waited for new assignments, she passed her time in Paris. As a result of her fame in Indochina, widely reported by the French press, Valérie found herself invited to various social engagements. At a cocktail party, however, there was an instance that reminded Valérie of the jealousies and prejudice that persisted even among civilians.

"I caught two women in their forties, one explaining to the other with an informed air, 'But you know, it was not *her* who was actually flying the helicopter!' Why is it hard for women to believe in the accomplishments of one of their own?"[7]

Time after time, Valérie André encountered people who didn't believe it was possible that she had flown solo rescue missions in a helicopter in combat areas. But her record in Indochina spoke for itself:

Valérie André flew 129 combat flight missions and rescued 168 wounded.[8]

It was frustrating for Valérie to hear disparaging accounts that cast doubts on her record. Nothing was handed over easily or was a "given" in her career. Valérie's aversion to self-promotion and publicity often allowed dismissive attitudes to prevail. But Valérie knew that the only way to overcome prejudice was to continue demonstrating her capabilities and to fight for her rights.

In July 1953, Valérie André took to the air again at the Paris Air Show, the first time the international event was held at Le Bourget Airport. Valérie put a military-spec Hiller H-23B through its paces before a packed crowd.

"I performed a flight demonstration of the aircraft's capabilities. It was a dazzling display, very much appreciated by the public, judging by the ovation that greeted my landing. I was asked to land at the foot of the presidential rostrum, where President Vincent Auriol congratulated me and introduced me to the crowd."[9]

President Auriol's daughter-in-law, Jacqueline Auriol, was also at the air show. Jacqueline was an avid aviation enthusiast, even in the aftermath of a crash involving a SCAN 30 amphibian where she almost lost her life. Jacqueline overcame several years of reconstructive surgery following the accident, but she continued in aviation. Jacqueline Auriol qualified as France's first female military test pilot in 1950. She would become one of the first women to break the sound barrier in August 1953.

Valérie André found a kindred spirit in Jacqueline Auriol, and the pair established the beginning of a lifelong friendship. Jacqueline discussed her work as a test pilot at the aviation test center in Brétigny-sur-Orge. Jacqueline was testing prototypes of the new Dassault Mystère II, France's first jet fighter—the plane that she would use to break the sound barrier. She encouraged Valérie to look into the possibility of joining the team at the test center.

But Valérie still held out hope of returning to Indochina. She believed that the rigid policies toward women in the military had eased, especially now that she was fully commissioned as an officer in the army. Valérie still wanted to rejoin her old unit, ELA 53; however, her request was now somewhat more problematic because she was part of the regular army. The air force would have to approve her reinstatement. In September 1953, Valérie received word from General Jean Dechaux, commander of GATAC North in Vietnam.

"The general informed me that I couldn't be assured of a proper place in the helicopter unit in Tonkin. Bitter disappointment? Why not admit it? The motives for the refusal remained vague and ambiguous, but I didn't dwell on the reasons. The only thing that mattered was to let the adventure continue—even if my present life was made up of jerky, fragmented experiences that were less rich and coherent than they were in Indochina."[10]

Valérie missed the sense of purpose she had found in the Far East and would have to find fulfillment somewhere else. Through Jacqueline Auriol, Valérie contacted Dr. Louis Bonte, the general director of the flight test center at Brétigny-sur-Orge.

"Dr. Bonte offered me an assignment as a doctor and pilot."[11]

It was the perfect situation for Valérie, combining her medical and aviation passions in a technological field that was expanding on an almost daily basis. French aviation corporations were investing heavily in new aircraft designs for military and civilian applications. Valérie would soon expand her experience from piloting Hiller helicopters into different aircraft. Even in this new environment, however, Valérie faced some of the same issues at the test center as she did in the army.

"Denis Prost, a future world record holder, introduced me to the Bell 47D, a helicopter which differed little from the Hiller. Because he was probably afraid I might steal his image of being the most experienced helicopter pilot at the test center, he couldn't avoid a certain aloofness towards me."[12]

Valérie shrugged off Prost's attitude as she was able to find camaraderie with other pilots and personnel.

"Test pilots form a kind of *caste*, an aristocracy if you will, driven by a constant pioneering spirit, concerned with modernism and perfection. They were dedicated to their profession with a magnificent passion."

Valérie proudly added, "I was quickly admitted among them. And thanks to Dr. Bonte, I kept my flying privileges."[13]

Valérie expanded her piloting skills with the variety of aircraft available at Brétigny-sur-Orge. In addition to piloting the Bell 47, Valérie graduated on to fixed-wing aircraft, including the Morane 733 and Nord 1101. The test center also gave Valérie a chance to test other types of helicopters, such as the diminutive Sud-Ouest Djinn, France's first production helicopter.

More important, Valérie also found professional fulfillment in her work. She was tasked with establishing the first medical heliports for hospitals in France at Melun and Clamart.[14]

Valérie would later say that the test center was her "Eden." Yet the war in Indochina remained at the forefront of her thoughts. She had heard of plans to build the large air/ground base in northwestern Vietnam, and she knew it would be a significant challenge for the military—much like Na San had been in 1952. But as reports of the ensuing debacle at Dien Bien Phu began to filter back to France, it was apparent that Vo Nguyen Giap had learned from the mistakes he made at Na San.

"I persisted in believing that my presence in Indochina would be desired—I had heard that there were not enough helicopter pilots there. I wrote to Saigon and offered to take responsibility for light helicopters and the organization of air medical aid. The not very encouraging replies I received were reasons to understand that my return was not desired by everyone."[15]

The news out of Vietnam went from bad to worse during spring 1954.

"At Dien Bien Phu, the expeditionary force resisted heroically but was doomed," Valérie observed. "I was upset and hurt like everyone else in France."

Valérie felt the toll from the war on a more personal level than it was felt by many others in France. Her involvement as a doctor in Indochina meant that she suffered every casualty and death as if it had happened to a close personal relative. She was especially shocked when she received word of Henri Bartier's crash after his helicopter was struck by Viet Minh mortar shells.

"I learned that Bartier's H-19 was shot down while he was trying to get the injured out of this hell. He was seriously wounded and had to have his leg amputated without being able to rescue the son of General Gambiez."[16]

After more than seven years of the conflict in Indochina, French attitudes toward the war ranged from *la guerre sale* (dirty war) to *la guerre oubliée* (forgotten war); however, when the defeat at Dien Bien Phu was announced on May 8, France went into a period of mourning. Many theaters and restaurants were closed for two days throughout the country. Radio stations canceled entertainment programming and played somber classical music. Church bells pealed in respect for those who died and for those who survived.[17] It was a time of introspection for many.

The Indochina war was over. It was the end of an era and marked the end of France's colonial ambitions. France's other colonies would also see independence as their end goal post-Indochina. The next trouble spot for France to deal with was Algeria in North Africa.

Meanwhile, it was homecoming in France for the veterans of Indochina. Henri Bartier was among the first to be sent back to France. His recovery was progressing well with his new prosthetic leg. Marie Yvonne's strength and support had made a lot of his rehabilitation possible.

In France, Bartier sought out Henri Boris at Helicop-Air, the Hiller helicopter agent in France now based in Issy-les-Moulineaux near Paris. Boris was expanding his business and had already hired Bartier's predecessor in helicopter rescue, Raymond Fumat.

Boris needed qualified flight instructors/demonstrators, and Fumat had fit into his program perfectly; however, Fumat only lasted a short time with Helicop-Air and found employment at France's Sud Aviation. He was "chief pilot" and a demonstrator for the Djinn and Alouette II helicopter programs. Because of Fumat's brief time serving in helicopter rescue, he is sometimes called *le pilote oublié*, the "forgotten pilot."[18] He would be remembered as one of the early pioneers of helicopter rescue, however. Raymond Fumat died in Courbevoie, France, on June 27, 2001, at the age of eighty-one.

Unlike Fumat, Henri Bartier opted not to enter private sector aviation. He refused discharge from the air force based on his disability. Because of his war record, he was allowed to remain in active service. In 1955, he was recalled to active duty—despite a 95 percent disability rating due to his injuries. He was promoted to the rank of lieutenant with the distinction of "helicopter flight officer."[19]

He was initially assigned to French air force base 721 near Rochefort, France. But in January 1955, his unit was transferred to the newly commissioned air force helicopter training center in Chambery. His commander was Alexis Santini.

From 1955 to 1963, Bartier served as a light helicopter instructor, head of the flight training division, test instructor, and pilot leader. Michel Fleurence, a pilot trainee at Chambery in 1955, had fond memories of Bartier at dress parades, who proudly wore "his Croix de Guerre comprising about fifteen palms and his many other decorations that jangled [as he walked]."[20]

Bartier's continued service in the air force was often accompanied by a recurrence of injuries he suffered at Dien Bien Phu. He required hospitalization multiple times over the remainder of his life. Bartier, however, managed to accrue an additional 1,979 hours as a helicopter flight instructor at Chambery.

When Bartier retired in 1966, he had been promoted to the rank of commander. He was also awarded the rank of commander in France's Legion of Honour. Of his war experience, he was always immensely proud that he earned a reputation as a rescue pilot. He was said to have remarked to a friend:

"In all my military career, I only shot my rifle once. . . . I killed a duck because I was hungry."[21]

Henri Bartier died in Aix-en-Provence, France, on May 18, 1994. He was seventy-four. He was survived by his wife, Marie Yvonne Bartier.

Henri Bartier performed 1,092 combat flight missions in Indochina, including 262 rescues.[22] He earned the Croix de guerre with fifteen palms.[23]

As for Alexis Santini, he returned to France in 1955. Santini had overseen a rapid expansion in the use of medical rescue helicopters over the past five years. By the time Santini left Indochina on July 14, 1955, France's rescue helicopter fleet grew from the original two Hiller UH-12/360s to forty-four aircraft, including more advanced Hiller models, Westland-Sikorsky WS-51s, and Sikorsky H-19As.[24] The helicopter service's personnel also grew. A total of forty-four pilots and forty-eight mechanics served in Indochina between 1950 and 1955.[25]

Upon his return to France, Santini was promoted to the rank of major. He found that he was very much in demand for his expertise and organizational skill in military helicopter medical rescue services. The Hiller Aircraft Company invited Santini to come to Palo Alto, California, where he shared his opinion of their helicopter and its operational use in Vietnam. After he visited California, Santini traveled to the East Coast to see the Sikorsky factory in Connecticut and the Piasecki helicopter factory near Philadelphia. He evaluated the latest aircraft from both companies in order to make a recommendation to the French air force for future purchases.

"I stayed a month to make my choice," Santini said in an interview years later. "I realized that the Sikorsky H-34 seemed to be more suitable than the Piasecki H-21. I submitted my report at the end of August and recommended the purchase of the H-34 for the Air Force."[26]

When Santini returned to France, he was given another assignment. This time he would go to Algeria to assess the state of military helicopter operations there.

"There was a lot of equipment breakage happening, and I was asked to think about training pilots," Santini said. "[While I was in Algeria], I trained pilots to fly by day and by night.

"When I returned to France, I was called on by the Air Ministry to create a helicopter training division."[27]

France's first military helicopter training school was established at Base aérienne 725 in Bourget du Lac-Chambery. Major Alexis Santini was its first commander. Located in the French Alps region, Base aérienne 725 was recognition of the expanded role that helicopters now played in the French military. Initially, the school made do with the Hillers, Westland Sikorskys, and American Sikorskys brought back from Indochina. But new aircraft, based on Santini's recommendations, would soon be arriving. While helicopters in

Indochina were used strictly for support and medical rescue missions, the air force saw the potential of an expanded role for rotorcraft.

Algeria was now the principal reason for the French military's need for more pilots and more helicopters. After the capitulation in Indochina, Algerian nationalists saw their opportunity to break away after 124 years of French rule. On November 1, 1954, the war began when the National Liberation Front (FLN) declared Algerian independence. There were more than one million French and European settlers in Algeria in 1954, who vehemently opposed self-rule by more than eight million Algerians. The French government was initially determined to keep Algeria as part of France and committed the full force of the French military, including conscripts, to the conflict. Unlike Indochina, drafted soldiers from France could not elect exclusion from overseas service. More than four hundred thousand troops from France were sent to quell the uprising; however, the war soon turned into another quagmire, with heavy casualties mounting on all sides.

Valérie André was at a crossroads in her career. She was well aware that the medical situation in Algeria was as dire as it had been in Indochina. While she found her work at the aviation test center rewarding and the variety of new and experimental aircraft endlessly fascinating, Valérie felt compelled to do more. In July 1956, Valérie received authorization to report to Base aérienne 725. She was reunited with Alexis Santini for the first time since they were in Vietnam. Valérie was impressed with the facility that Santini had put together in only a year.

"The fleet amounted to fifty aircraft that performed laps and exercises in the mountains. [The school] supplied the manpower of two helicopter squadrons in Algeria. About twenty pilots were declared fit for departure at each promotion, with about eighty hours of flight time to their credit."[28]

Compared to the twenty hours of flight time required to obtain a helicopter pilot's license on a Hiller at Helicop-Air only six years earlier, the additional hours reflected the complexity of the new Sikorsky aircraft at Chambery. Valérie finally had the opportunity to earn her certification on the larger H-19 helicopter.

"My instructor was Chief Warrant Officer Wachter, an excellent teacher. The notes I got at the end of the course made me feel good: 'Particularly gifted pilot . . . a safe, flexible, precise and regular pilot.'"[29]

While Valérie was stationed at Chambery, an incident occurred at nearby Mont Blanc. Jean Vincendon and François Henry, two amateur mountaineers, were lost on the mountain as they attempted to scale the 4,810-meter (15,780-foot) peak in late December 1956. A separate pair of mountaineers had encountered Vincendon and Henry the day before, and it was believed they were stranded on an icy precipice overlooking a void at the 4,000-meter level. Extreme weather conditions on the mountain made a land-based rescue attempt difficult, if not impossible. The *gendarmerie* at Chamonix contacted Base aérienne 725 and the French army's École de haut montagne (EHM—High Mountain School) to assist in the search. Commander Yves Le Gall from EHM headed up the overall rescue, while Alexis Santini was in charge of helicopter operations. Valérie André accompanied Santini to Chamonix as part of the medical support team.

On December 27, the first helicopter search of the mountain found no sign of Vincendon and Henry. But the crew of a helicopter flight conducted the following day finally spotted the two men. The helicopter crew examined the surrounding area and concluded that the two exhausted and frozen men would have to hike two hundred meters from their position to a relatively flat plateau where a helicopter could land. Later that day, the helicopter returned to drop a supply package and instructions to move to the landing zone.

This was the first time a mountain helicopter rescue had ever been attempted in France; however, the plan to rescue the two men ran into problems almost immediately. Despite heading up EHM, Commander Le Gall had no experience in mountaineering or mountain rescues and rejected advice from experienced civilian mountain climbers from the area. Some local mountaineers suggested that a helicopter could take them partway up Mont Blanc to reach the stranded men. Le Gall made it clear that only the military would carry out the rescue.

Unfortunately, Le Gall also had the authority to overrule Santini's choice of helicopters to perform the rescue mission. Le Gall wanted to send two of his cadets from EHM to facilitate the rescue. The Sikorsky H-34 was the only helicopter capable of carrying the two rescuers, a pilot and copilot, and Vincendon and Henry.

Santini believed the smaller Alouette II was better suited for the high-altitude rescue, despite only accommodating a pilot and three passengers. The Alouette was the world's first turbine-powered production helicopter manufactured in France by Sud-Est Aviation. The Alouette's turbine engine was not affected by high altitude, and the aircraft's service ceiling was much higher than the H-34. Santini had concerns about the Sikorsky's performance at four thousand meters; however, the Alouette II had only been in production since April 1956 and was still undergoing high-altitude testing. Despite Santini's reservations, Le Gall ordered him to use the Sikorsky.[30]

The weather on Mont Blanc continued to be atrocious, delaying the rescue until December 31. The conditions still weren't optimal to launch an airborne rescue, but the operation went ahead anyway. Warrant Officer André Blanc piloted the H-34 while Santini chose to go as copilot. They were accompanied by Honoré Bonnet and Charles Germain from EHM. As the helicopter approached the landing zone, Blanc and Santini could make out that Vincendon and Henry were still alive. As they hovered close to the fine, powdery surface of the plateau, the downwash from the Sikorsky's rotor blades created a blizzard blinding both Blanc and Santini in the cockpit. The phenomenon also caused a snowload to accumulate on the rotor blades simultaneously. Blanc lost control of the helicopter, and it rolled over on its side not far from the stranded mountaineers.

Back in Chamonix, Valérie André was distraught when she heard that Santini's helicopter had gone down. At first, there was no word if anyone had survived. A flood of emotions ran through her. Santini was the man who approved of her, mentored her, and entrusted the command of ELA 53 to her in Vietnam. She was where she was in her career because of Santini. At that moment, Valérie realized that Alexis Santini was the most important man in her life. She felt helpless that she wasn't able to do anything.

Santini and Blanc, along with Bonnet and Germain, were shaken up but mostly uninjured from the crash. The helicopter was destroyed, but at least its fuselage would serve as a shelter. Bonnet and Germain were able to reach Vincendon and Henry and pulled them to the downed aircraft. Their arms and legs were extensively frostbitten—almost like "blocks of wood"—but the men were still lucid and able to communicate. But now, six men needed rescuing from Mont Blanc.

A second helicopter spotted the wreckage of the first and was able to send word that the downed crew was still alive. A plan was devised to drop two more cadets from EHM by helicopter to reach the stranded men. They would then help them get to the Vallot observatory station in the mountain, where they could be airlifted back to Chamonix. Santini and Blanc were ambulatory, as were Bonnet and Germain. But Vincendon and Henry were now unable to move at all. The best that could be done was to pull them into the wrecked helicopter and hope for the best.

Once the party reached Vallot, Alouette helicopters ferried the survivors back to Chamonix. A helicopter was also sent over the wreckage of the

Sikorsky. When no signs of life were found, the rescue of Vincendon and Henry was called off. Their bodies were not recovered until spring.

As for Alexis Santini, Valérie André was standing ready when his rescue helicopter landed in Chamonix. He had suffered extreme exposure from the elements and required hospitalization. Valérie stayed with him until his recovery was complete.

The failed rescue at Mont Blanc gave Valérie much to consider. She was relieved that Santini would recover, but the experience reminded her of her time in Indochina when she made a difference as a rescue pilot. She knew she had more to contribute than just a passive role at the aviation test center. Her recent certification on the H-19 gave Valérie the confidence to launch an audacious plan to bypass the military command structure to join a helicopter medical rescue team in Algeria.

"I was thirsty for a new adventure, similar to the one I experienced in Indochina. The four years that had passed since my return had been, for the most part, an expectation that was often disappointing. I took the initiative to write to Colonel Felix Brunet, commander of the helicopter squadron in Oran-La Senia."[31]

Brunet was a former fighter pilot who converted over to helicopters at Bourget du Lac-Chambery in 1956. He commanded Escadron hélicoptère 2, Helicopter Squadron 2 (EH 2). Valérie requested to participate in operations with EH 2 while on summer leave from the test center. She was elated when she received a positive reply from Brunet on June 24, 1957.

"I apologize for being so late in responding to your letter," Brunet wrote to Valérie. "You did not have to make such a request. With great pride, EH 2 and I will welcome you when you arrive and for as long as you please. Your time at EH 2 will be extremely useful to all, and I thank you sincerely for thinking of my unit."[32]

Valérie's maneuver was a backdoor approach to reenter regular military service. She knew that if she applied through formal channels her request would be denied.

"The annual closing of the test center in July prompted me to request a 'leave' in Oran. Officially, the regulations didn't authorize a soldier to carry out operational missions during a leave."[33]

Writing directly to Brunet was Valérie's workaround to rejoin a combat zone squadron. While her role with Brunet's unit was supposed to be limited to an "observer" capacity, Valérie hoped for more out of it.

When Valérie landed at the French air base in Oran, she learned that there were already 270 helicopters in use in all of Algeria, primarily Sikorsky H-19 medium and Sikorsky H-34 heavy helicopters. She had never seen so many helicopters in one place. There were similarities between the French missions in Indochina and Algeria. Brunet's squadron was responsible for a 340,000-square-kilometer (211,000-mile) territory of forests, deserts, and mountains. They were engaged with an adversary that employed similar guerilla warfare tactics to the Viet Minh. The Algerian rebels were known by the French as *fellaghas*, an Arab word for "bandit."

The *fellaghas* possessed much more lethal and accurate weapons than the Viet Minh. The helicopters were frequent targets, with the traditional tricolor rondel providing a perfect bull's-eye. French mechanics took to painting small stars and crescents over the bullet holes they found in the fuselages of the Sikorskys.

Valérie immediately had an affinity for the imposing, often bellicose Felix Brunet.

"Colonel Brunet's welcome could not have been friendlier. A stern, imperious, and frank face with an epic appearance. . . . He was an exceptional fighter pilot, an incomparable trainer of men, and a man of unfailing courage."[34]

Brunet was open to Valérie's idea to pursue more than an observer's role with his squadron. She had already earned her certification on the medium H-19 and Bell 47, so she was not a novice. Valérie had gone through preliminary approval with influential officers in the past, only to be disappointed with denial of her operational status by others in the command chain. Felix Brunet, however, had tremendous influence in Algeria and a degree of autonomy within his unit.

"After discussing with authorities representing the 5th air region, Brunet announced that I had been given the green light for operational missions. I was certain that he had taken it upon himself to allow me to fly as a pilot."[35]

Passing her check flights in a Bell 47 and Sikorsky H-19, Valérie moved up to the largest helicopter in the French armed forces at that time.

"I learned to fly the H-34. This 'heavy' aircraft seemed extraordinarily easy to fly. Equipped with a miraculous servo-control system, I had the impression that I could control it with my fingertips."

Valérie's days were full at Oran. She flew both practice and operational missions with several of Brunet's most trusted pilots. In many ways, it was almost like a return to Indochina—complete with the danger, adrenaline, and the accomplishment that came from rescue. But it was also much different from Valérie's days of flying delicate Hillers in the extreme environments of Vietnam. Lessons were learned in Indochina, and considerably more attention was paid to pilot safety in Algeria.

"There was no question of escaping from wearing a bulletproof vest, however heavy and uncomfortable it may have been. Or dispensing with the armored 'bucket' of protection attached to the seat we sat on. Each aircraft was closely monitored during a mission, whether it was a Bell, where the pilot sits alone, or a Sikorsky with a crew of two pilots and a mechanic."[36]

But the helicopter's role was changing in warfare, and Valérie would be a witness to why the war in Algeria would become known as the "first helicopter war."

"On the evening of July 23, I received word to go to the Sebka firing range on the following day at the controls of a Bell 47. I was told no more. But I knew that a flight test of the armed helicopter, 'Mammoth,' was being prepared. There I saw the first demonstrations of firing from a helicopter. The helicopter was overloaded with various weapons—12.7 mm machine guns, rockets, and 20 mm canons. Targets in the shapes of cones were scattered on the ground. The 'Mammoth' proceeded with its tests, putting out a terrible noise."

After witnessing the demonstration of the massive gunship, Valérie concluded:

"The time of the *ventilateur*, used only for medical evacuations, was over."[37]

Chapter 37

To Fight and to Save

Some called France's intervention in Algeria a "police action." Still, there were all too many similarities to the recently concluded war in Vietnam. Algerian independence was at the root of the conflict. French generals abhorred a repeat of the debacle in Vietnam. They campaigned for a heavy political and militarized hand to clamp down on the independence movement. But the home population in France was resistant to more bloodshed for another futile cause. Even Valérie André expressed her reservations.

"Will the Indochina drama be repeated [in Algeria]? Would French troops have to face again an adversary whose first asset is their knowledge and mastery of the terrain?"[1]

The Algerian situation, combined with the unforgotten defeat at Dien Bien Phu, prompted a crisis in confidence for the French government. Even though the military tried to discourage negative press coverage of the Algerian war, there were reports of roundups of Algerian civilians into massive relocation camps and widespread torture of individuals suspected to be aligned to the Front de libération nationale (FLN; National Liberation Front) and other independence groups.

Protests and demonstrations for and against France's policies in Algeria were taking their toll on the country. Terrorist bombings of civilian targets in Algiers and Paris by pro-Algerian independence groups spread fear. There was a massive outcry for a return to firmer and more stable rule. With the future of France hanging in the balance, the National Assembly appointed the only man who seemed to be able to unite the French people once again.

Charles de Gaulle.

Many believed that the staunch anticommunist, pro-colonial wartime general would find a way to repair the latest crack in France's colonial foundation. The only question was what would be de Gaulle's solution?

Valérie returned to Brétigny-sur-Orge later that summer with a new awareness and sense of how serious the situation was in North Africa. The other test pilots were impressed with Valérie's opportunity to fly advanced rotorcraft in a hazardous combat zone.

"I enthusiastically recounted my life in operations, and I noticed that some of [the pilots] were a little envious and a lot sympathetic. Everything operational was always of interest to the test pilots. It seemed that my flight requests were now honored more easily."[2]

Valérie was able to earn her certification on the Alouette II helicopter shortly thereafter. But Algeria continued to weigh heavily on Valérie's mind.

"How could I envision living longer in the comfort of the test center when many of my comrades were going to the 'slaughterhouse' in Algeria every day?" she asked herself.

Valérie's devotion to duty and to "fight and save" for others outweighed her temptation to remain in the comparably safe confines of the aviation test center in Brétigny. She requested a transfer back to Chambery to complete her certification on the Sikorsky H-34.

"I was won over by the H-34, a powerful aircraft whose fine and flexible handling is surprising in relation to its weight and volume. I still appreciate its flying qualities in operations and in load and altitude. I was very confident."[3]

With confidence came a new driving ambition for Valérie. No longer did she feel compelled to accept rejection from a faceless review panel within the military hierarchy's command structure. With the help of Dr. Bonte at the Brétigny test center, Valérie was able to obtain an introduction to air force general Edmond Jouhaud, commander of the Fifth Air Region in Algeria. Jouhaud was also a *pied-noir*, the son of French parents born in Algeria. The *pied-noir* in Algeria were the most vociferous opponents of Algerian nationalists. They were determined to keep the country under French control at any cost.

Valérie was also single-minded in her ambitions but in a different way.

"After my training on the H-34, my determination was stronger than ever. I wanted to serve as a doctor and a pilot at the same time. Jouhaud knew that I had seen the usefulness of helicopters in Algeria and that my competence in this field was no longer in doubt."[4]

Jouhaud approved Valérie's request. She arrived in Algeria in January 1959 and was assigned to Escadron hélicoptère 3 at Boufarik air base. She was EH 3's assistant medical officer at the base infirmary.

Alexis Santini was also bound for Algeria. He had felt some responsibility and regret over the failed rescue mission of Vincendon and Henry at Mont Blanc[5] and wanted to serve his country in time of war once again. He was appointed the head of helicopter operational standards in the Fifth Air Region, which included Boufarik air base. Along with Santini's new assignment came a promotion to lieutenant colonel. One of the biggest challenges Santini faced was homologating the inventory of helicopter squadrons. The variety of aircraft used—Sud Alouettes, Bell 47s, Sikorsky H-19s and H-34s, and Piasecki H-19s—made parts and maintenance issues difficult. Also, some of the aircraft were proving not to be well suited for use in North Africa. While Santini was an admirer of the Alouette II, he often found it lacking in durability compared to other aircraft, noting that the leading edge of the rotor blades "crumbled in the rain," and a short circuit in its wiring system "could ignite the whole helicopter in ten seconds."[6]

Operational use of helicopters, as well as the pilots, was also among Santini's concerns. Officers often ordered young pilots to "take off, day or night, sometimes in hazardous weather conditions." Santini criticized officers who had too much of a tendency "to take [helicopters] as taxis" whenever they wanted.[7] Even Valérie André observed this callous practice:

> The life of light helicopter pilots in operations meant that they were constantly available and on the move. Called in at any time, often just as they began their meal, they were always subordinate. . . . A non-commissioned officer *Alouette* pilot, who had been fasting since the day before and whose state of fatigue was unmistakable, confided his complaints to me when his passenger, a senior Army officer, came and said:
> "Where's my driver? I need him immediately."[8]

Santini was well aware that the abuse of pilot resources and pilot fatigue were recipes for disaster and did his best to curb such excesses.

As for Valérie, she quickly became accustomed to her new life at Boufarik. Twelve years earlier, she arrived in Saigon as a young army doctor from France, with little knowledge of what her life in the military would entail. Now, as an officer with full standing, Valérie André approached her new role at Boufarik with a confidence far removed from that past moment in time, fraught with uncertainty and spurious resentment from her male peers. Yet there was a peculiar attitude toward Valérie that still prevailed.

"My arrival did not provoke an explosion of joy. It wasn't hostility, but at least a certain apprehension. What reputation did I have? Would I be difficult to deal with? Fortunately, this unfortunate impression soon dissipated."[9]

At least she wasn't treated as an afterthought when it came to her quarters.

"My installation in the building reserved for officers was easy. I got along very well with the chief medical officer, Dr. Pierre Batard."[10]

The pilots and mechanics eventually warmed to Valérie. She came to refer to them as her "merry men." They took rescue and transport missions seriously, however, and suffered many casualties during their time in North Africa. Mechanics were also often placed in danger, as the Sikorskys required an onboard technician if a problem occurred in flight.

Within a few weeks of her arrival, Valérie was approved to fly medical evacuation missions. In addition to the bulletproof vest she wore on missions with Felix Brunet's squadron, the situation confronting helicopter personnel in Algeria required her to go one step further.

"It was deemed essential that all pilots and mechanics be armed during missions."[11]

Initially, Valérie found a certain reluctance from the air base's armament officer to provide her with a weapon. But a directive was issued that read, "Captain André is to be issued a PM MAT 49 each time a mission justifies the use of this weapon." A MAT 49 was a French-made submachine gun capable of firing six hundred rounds a minute.

Also, she was no longer limited to flying only one type of aircraft. The primitive Hiller she had trusted as her mechanical flying companion in Vietnam was no longer viable in this new era of warfare. She was allowed to fly the three aircraft types in EH 3's inventory, the Sud Alouette II, the Sikorsky H-19, and the Sikorsky H-34.

"It was a privilege to fly all three types of helicopters, as this was reserved only for wing command officers. Every day I told myself to take full advantage of the opportunities I had been given and live intensely in the present moment."[12]

Another career breakthrough for Valérie came when her mission in Algeria was expanded. Algeria was vastly different than Indochina in troop transport. Instead of the mass airdrop of paratroopers, as in Indochina, helicopters brought commandos directly to the front line. Instead of fixed-wing fighter pilots strafing the battlefield before landing, the French had a new weapon in their arsenal known as the "Pirate." It was the operational successor to Felix Brunet's "Mammoth" that Valérie saw in action a year earlier.

"The Sikorsky H-34 quickly became the most suitable means of transporting fighters to places that were difficult to access," Valérie explained. "The fire support aircraft was named 'Pirate.' It was armed with a 20 mm cannon and two 12.7 mm machine guns. Its mission was to protect heli-lift operations by orbiting in a small circle during the duration of the landing mission. The gunners were selected from among the best shooters of the air commandos. . . . Their efficiency was formidable."[13]

Valérie was involved in many types of transports and more during her tour of duty in North Africa—flying generals to and from meetings, performing aerial reconnaissance, and transporting civilians. But the most dangerous missions involved bringing commandos into areas where they would engage *fellaghas.*

On July 6, 1959, Valérie was briefed on a mission that would involve several helicopters, including the "Pirate," moving French soldiers into position in the Hodna Mountains. It was part of an overall strategy put together by air force general Maurice Challe and often referred to as the "Challe Plan." The Challe Plan entailed using elite troops who were dropped at known FLN strongholds by helicopters. Their objective was to destroy the FLN's military wing.

The July 6 mission involving Valérie was a massive operation that included fifteen rotations at three different drop zones. The French army was also participating in this operation with their own helicopters,[14] the American-made and aptly named Piasecki H-21 "Flying Banana."

The "Pirate" led the formation of helicopters. For the first drop, the gunners on board the lead ship were prepared to fire on anything that moved when they were in range of the drop zone. They were battle hardened and inured to the consequences of taking their enemy's life. But the gunners were exposed, too. The large side door of the Sikorsky was open for one gunner, and a small window was cut out for the second. There was little to no protection from the aircraft's metal fuselage.

"Onboard each aircraft we took 8 or 9 armed commandos. . . . Our infantrymen were by the door of the cargo hold and would jump out even before the helicopter had touched the ground."[15]

After a grueling first day, there was no letup on the next. Valérie and her copilot, Sergeant Le Chenadec, were at the embarkation point at Aïn Arnat near Setif. The outside temperatures were unrelenting, more than 40 degrees (104 degrees Fahrenheit).

"We could see from afar the groups of infantrymen ready to board. For the first time, we received orders to refuel without turning off the aircraft's engine, an order that seemed absurd because of the risk of fire."[16]

The commander in charge of loading the commandos onto the helicopters wanted to rapidly dispatch the men to the field with the least amount of downtime. But as Valérie feared, a fire broke out near one of the helicopters when fuel accidentally ignited.

"A corner of the wheat field [adjacent to the airport] caught fire. The flight of the helicopters to escape the flames was spectacular."[17]

The operation was not without further incident. Switching roles from transport helicopter to *évasan*, Valérie and Le Chenadec also rescued two combatants wounded during the assault on the Hodna Mountains.

"We managed to escape from automatic weapons fire. The *fellaghas* generally let the helicopter load the wounded and start its takeoff before firing."[18]

Valérie never revealed how many stars and crescents were painted on her aircraft's fuselage after a mission.

The Sikorskys were also not immune to mechanical maladies. Valérie and her copilot, Sergeant Georges Agrissais,[19] were assigned to deliver animal feed to *meharistes*. The *meharistes* were the Algerian camel cavalry unit allied to the French army that patrolled the Sahara region in the south. A mechanic and an Algerian infantryman were also on board the Sikorsky H-34.

The mission got off to a bad start when the cavalry unit captain complained to Valérie that they had delivered the wrong kind of food for his camels.

"He had a habit of checking the food before the helicopter left and was very upset," Valérie said. "It was not the first time this had happened. He insisted that we take the 800 kilos of grain back with us."[20]

On the way back to the supply depot, the H-34 began experiencing a problem.

"I was at the controls, and it seemed that the throttle was a bit soft. My eyes were riveted on the tachometer. Something abnormal was happening, and Agrissais felt it, too."

Agrissais was a helicopter mechanic who transitioned to pilot. He opened the side window of the cockpit and saw thick, black smoke pouring from the exhaust pipe. He knew immediately that the Sikorsky's engine was shot.

"We've had a breakdown," he shouted at Valérie.

They were kilometers away from their base, and the helicopter's altitude was not optimal for a power-off autorotation landing.

"I opened my window, strapped myself in tighter, [and shouted back at Agrissais], 'Everything will be fine. We have a hole in front of us.'"[21]

The "hole" was a valley ahead of them that dipped downward just enough to perform the delicate maneuver. Agrissais, who had more hours in the H-34 than Valérie, took control. The landing area was strewn with massive boulders, making it even harder to find a safe place for the large aircraft to land.

"The landing area was narrow, and the speed [of our descent] seemed huge," Valérie noted.[22]

Agrissais proved to be a skillful pilot, avoiding the larger obstacles in his path. When the helicopter came to a rest, the cargo door below the cockpit was thrown open. The mechanic and infantryman were the first on the ground, both with their weapons drawn. Once Agrissais and Valérie climbed down from the cockpit, Agrissais opened the clamshell doors of the Sikorsky's engine compartment for a quick assessment of the aircraft's powerplant. As expected, the engine was damaged, and there was no way to repair it in the field.

Although the helicopter was stranded in an inhospitable area, at least its radio still functioned. In the barren area bordering the Sahara, the crew was reasonably confident that they weren't in imminent danger from *fellaghas*. Still, without assistance, that situation could easily change. Agrissais got in contact with the nearest base.

"After a few minutes, a T6 fighter plane flew over us at very low altitude, waving its wings to reassure us. A little later, a Sikorsky H-34 landed beside us, followed by a second."[23]

Not only were the helicopters swift to arrive, but shortly thereafter the *mehariste* cavalry was also on the scene, led by the captain who objected to the feed brought for his camels.

After a thorough inspection of the inoperable Sikorsky, it was decided that a new engine would be brought to it and swapped out. The operation would likely take two days. The cavalry captain offered his hospitality to Valérie and Sergeant Agrissais, as they awaited transport back to base.

"The captain offered us tea in a tent, drawn up in haste. [Afterwards] he granted me the privilege of a brief ride on one of his animals, which caused great hilarity among my companions."[24]

Valérie's flight logs revealed the unrelenting workload under which she worked. In an eight-day period in September 1959, she flew sixteen missions in eighteen hours and fifty-five minutes, transporting 240 people, including 100 commandos and several tons of cargo.[25] All of this was combined with Valérie's work as a doctor at the infirmary at Boufarik, which required her to spend her nights on medical watch.

The Challe Plan was only one of many attempts by the French to gain control in Algeria. The cost in human lives was also high. More than seven thousand French soldiers and more than twenty thousand FLN insurgents were killed. But the offensive did succeed in driving FLN leadership across borders to Tunisia and Morocco.

As military action increased against the FLN, however, retaliatory acts by FLN supporters and operatives also increased. In the capital of Algiers, intense fighting and terrorists bombings took a massive toll. Clandestine elements within the French army sought vengeance and employed torture to ferret out the perpetrators. Executions were rampant.

Algeria weighed heavily on all of France, and no less so than on its president, Charles de Gaulle. De Gaulle was proving not to be the staunch pro-colonialist ally that the *pied-noirs* in Algeria had hoped.

De Gaulle came to Algeria in September 1959. He had concerns over how the military was exerting increasing political influence in the affairs of North Africa. A significant part of the military's leadership was deeply aligned with the transplanted Europeans and their struggle to maintain their dominance in Algeria. De Gaulle recognized this as a threat to French democracy and was determined to derail this growing problem before it eroded his presidency.

Valérie André was among those gathered in the Soummam valley near Algiers when de Gaulle reviewed the troops.

"We know today that it was here General de Gaulle revealed his point of view: the end of colonial Algeria, the need for Algerians to choose their own destiny, and a call for discipline within the Army," Valérie wrote, years after the occasion.[26]

De Gaulle arrived at this position pragmatically. Despite the success of the Challe Plan, he knew his armed forces would ultimately be in a losing position, much as it was in Indochina. But it was also necessary for de Gaulle to maintain military pressure on the FLN in order to save face by negotiating an honorable withdrawal. France needed to retain its economic interests in the region, including access to the rich oil fields at Hassi Messaoud. It was a fine line to walk. De Gaulle was often accused of ambiguity in his choice of words, which only made the separation of Algeria from France more difficult.

On September 16, 1959, De Gaulle made a televised address where the subject of Algerian "self-determination" was put before the French people.

"The fate of the Algerians belongs to the Algerians through universal suffrage," de Gaulle declared.[27]

De Gaulle's stance triggered a reaction from elements within the French military that vehemently opposed any concession to the Algerian nationalist movement. The Organisation de l'armée secrète, or OAS, was an ultra-right-wing and clandestine unit of officers that plotted revenge against Charles de Gaulle, who they regarded as a traitor. Many members of the OAS were veterans of Indochina, and they resented the defeatist governments that throttled the military from attaining victory. They initially worked behind the scenes to help bring de Gaulle to power in 1958 but soured on the former general by 1961. The OAS had aligned themselves with the interests of the European *pied-noir* minority in Algeria, even if that meant the overthrow of the government in France.

Valérie André was determined to remain apolitical in a volatile environment.

"Loyalty to orders remained my personal philosophy. The ambiguity that surrounds General de Gaulle's policy in challenging circumstances cannot justify in my eyes that one refrains from the duty of obedience and silence in the ranks."[28]

But disobedience of de Gaulle's orders and vocal opposition to his government was at the core of the OAS. The activities of the OAS increased after a referendum vote put to the people of France and Algeria in January 1961 overwhelmingly supported Algerian "self-determination." Despite the clear message that the vote signified, the OAS set out to ignore the wishes of the majority of French and Algerian voters and plotted the overthrow of the French government.

The situation came to a climax on April 21, 1961, when generals Raoul Salan, Maurice Challe, Edmond Jouhaud, and André Zeller—who had all been relieved of command duties by de Gaulle—seized control of Algiers, with the help of both military and civilian operatives allied to the OAS. The insurrection also spread to Paris, where OAS supporters attempted to foment a coup.

The timing of these events coincided with a new assignment for Valérie André. A few days before, she received orders to replace Dr. Batard as chief medical officer at Reghaïa air base. For Valérie, it was affirmation that her

skills and efforts were now fully recognized. She was also elated because
she would be allowed to continue flying. But her satisfaction from the promotion was decidedly muted by the news reports that streamed in on her
transistor radio early on the morning of April 22.

"I realized very quickly that something abnormal was happening. General
Challe was broadcasting a message."[29]

Challe's prepared statement quickly got to the point:

I am in Algiers with Generals Zeller and Jouhaud and in communication with
General Salan to uphold our oath, the oath of the Army, to keep Algeria so
that our dead will not have died for nothing. A Government of abandonment
. . . is today on the verge of definitively delivering Algeria to the external organization of the rebellion. . . . Would you want Mers El-Kébir and Algiers to
be Soviet bases tomorrow? . . . The Army will not fail in its mission, and the
orders that I would give you will never have any other goal."[30]

Challe's radio message went on to say that the insurrection had also
spread to Paris. The rebel general's message was an appeal to the army to
overthrow de Gaulle. Everyone in Algeria immediately felt the depth of the
conspiracy.

"During the night of the 21st and 22nd, [several paratrooper and commando regiments] seized the key sectors of Algiers, arresting many representatives of the civilian government and military. Who was in on it at Reghaïa?
I didn't know at the time. In any case, the secret was perfectly kept."[31]

Valérie remained glued to the radio as long as she could before racing off
to the morning flag ceremony for the base. Reghaïa was only thirty kilometers from Algiers, and it was certain that many on the air base were in league
with the rebel generals.

"I scrutinized the faces, which seemed to me to be very serious. Everyone
knew. Usually, we chatted and talked happily before separating to join our
respective units. But this morning, the dispersal of the troops was instant—
each of us wrapped up in our thoughts."[32]

The atmosphere on the base was one of uncertainty. Many who worked in
the base hospital were *pied-noirs* with family living in Algiers. Throughout
the day, assistant doctors expressed their anxiety to Valérie, who did her best
to maintain calm and order. But it wasn't easy. Valérie was upset to her core.

"These events hit me like a dagger. It was a brutal challenge to everything
I had built around me as an ideal."[33]

General Edmond Jouhaud's inclusion in the junta of insurgent generals was especially jarring. Jouhaud had approved of Valérie's first official assignment in Algeria at Boufarik. Valérie's advancement in her career owed much to Jouhaud. Now he was part of a plot to not only seize control in Algeria but also to overthrow France's elected government.

"Jouhaud could not accept the abandonment of his homeland and rebelled against power," Valérie said. "He was *pied-noir* to his soul."[34]

Valérie could understand Jouhaud's reasons for his participation in the insurrection, but they were not her own. A few months before, Valérie took a week's leave in Paris, where she met with General André Martin. Martin was the chairman of the joint chiefs of staff under de Gaulle and had served as air commander in Algeria. The national referendum on Algeria's self-determination caused confusion in the military. While it was evident that de Gaulle "wanted to get rid of the Algerian burden," casualties on both sides were still mounting.

"I expressed to General Martin my concern about the government's intentions, which had changed in relation to previous declarations and promises. Men continued to fight, and men continued to die."

Valérie was seeking clarification of France's mission in Algeria.

"We must follow General de Gaulle," was General Martin's succinct answer to her.[35]

Valérie was mindful of Martin's words when she received a letter from General Pierre Bigot, the new commander of the Fifth Air Region appointed by the junta.

"I read it and verified its origin. I locked it up in a filing cabinet and decided not to let anyone around me know its contents."

It was a proclamation of "legitimacy" for the Salan, Challe, Zeller, and Jouhaud regime. Valérie considered it an illegal order; however, later that same day, an OAS operative, Lieutenant Colonel Maurice Emery, began asserting his newfound authority.

"[Emery was] dry, tall, authoritarian, pushing everyone around him. He was an animated propagandist of the putsch—scolding some, chastising others, acting as if he had already taken over power at Reghaïa. He announced his position without ambiguity, telling us to be at his disposal to receive orders later."[36]

The situation was tense and threatened to spiral out of control, but an eerie calm prevailed in the early stage of the revolt. Salan chose not to arm civilian *pied-noir* partisans, which probably limited bloodshed in the streets of Algiers. But the OAS junta needed to quickly consolidate power—especially over the mostly conscripted military force in Algeria—if they were to achieve a complete takeover. The plotters, however, overlooked one detail in their plan that proved to be their undoing: the transistor radio.

On the evening of April 24, President de Gaulle, dressed in his general's uniform, took to the airwaves. Most of the enlisted men and officers, including Valérie André, had inexpensive Japanese portable radios and immediately tuned in de Gaulle's address. The president denounced the generals as "partisan, ambitious, and fanatical" and were "distorted by their delirium" in their understanding of France and the world. He told the nation that the generals had no authority and ended his appeal with, "Frenchwomen! Frenchmen! Help me!"[37]

"De Gaulle's . . . speech greatly affected me," Valérie said. "I left my office and went to the officer's mess. Everyone had heard the speech, . . . and they were absorbed in a silence that spoke volumes of their unease. The atmosphere was gloomy."[38]

Reghaïa air base shared barracks with paratrooper/commando units, and there were many OAS loyalists embedded in their ranks. Colonel Emery commanded an elite squad of commando/paratroopers on the base, trained to be ruthless in the face of any enemy. There was a real fear that the situation would devolve into civil war. Valérie found herself in a position of keeping order among her staff at the base infirmary.

"[The staff] was upset by General de Gaulle's appeal and wanted to know my position, my opinion of what to do. I began by calming them down, telling them clashes would likely break out, and there was no point in making them worse."[39]

As Valérie was speaking, a commotion broke out from the barracks occupied by the commandos. Now that de Gaulle had declared their insurrection illegal, many of the commandos believed they would soon be hunted down as traitors. Some of the men were demanding to take action. Sporadic scuffles broke out that night and into the next day between men loyal to de Gaulle and men aligned with the OAS.

On Monday, April 24, the crisis reached its pinnacle.

"Incidents occurred during the ceremony of the colors. The men broke ranks to demonstrate their opposition to the insurrectionists."[40]

But the coup was starting to lose its momentum. Without support from the conscript army, the OAS had no hope for success.

"General de Gaulle's appeal had deprived the coup plotters of a large part of their manpower," Valérie concluded.

Only twenty-five thousand enlisted men out of four hundred thousand stationed in Algeria supported the revolt. More important, only six hundred officers out of thirty thousand were involved with the insurgent generals and OAS.[41] Without broader support, the generals' coup attempt—or "putsch," as it became known—ultimately failed. De Gaulle began withdrawing French troops from Algeria later in 1961, ending France's dominance in the country. On July 5, 1962, Algerian independence was declared.

As for the *pied-noirs*, more than 1.4 million left Algeria over the next two years. Most returned to Europe. Many harbored bitterness and anger over being forced to leave Algeria. But the toll of the war in Algeria was also staggering. By France's own estimate, more than 350,000 were killed during the war, with more than 250,000 Algerians dead.

Valérie André was left with a bad taste in the aftermath of the generals' putsch.

"I came out of this tragedy very bruised," she said. "Officers of great value, judging their honor lost, threw themselves into an impossible adventure . . . and by doing so went to their doom. As for me, while I understood their reasons, I did not accept their actions."[42]

Many military participants in the OAS plot were arrested. Of the four generals who instigated the coup, Zeller and Challe were sentenced to fifteen years in prison, while Salan and Jouhaud fled and evaded arrest. OAS terrorist activities continued after the revolt. A nearly successful assassination attempt on the life of President de Gaulle and his wife was carried out by OAS operatives in August 1962, as they were being driven in their Citroën DS to Orly Airport. Despite a hail of bullets that struck the car, no one inside was injured, and the plot was thwarted by de Gaulle's chauffeur, who managed to escape the attack by skillfully driving on four blown-out tires.

Violence increased in Algeria, with the FLN seeing the war's end coming and the French army demoralized. Valérie remained at Reghaïa another year, but it was with difficulty.

"I lost all enthusiasm and had to force myself to maintain a good mood," Valérie said. "In April [1962], unable to stand it any longer, tired of so many horrors, I asked for a ten-day leave in Paris. Algeria already belonged to the past. . . . I asked for an assignment to the Villacoublay Air Base as chief medical officer. I received a positive answer and was told that the position would be available during the summer of 1962."[43]

When Valérie left Algeria for the last time in August 1962, she witnessed the misery of the *pied-noir* exodus from the airport in Algiers. Even though Europeans dominated the native Algerians for more than one hundred years, the North African country had still been their home.

"The hall was drowning under the uninterrupted flow of terrorized and haggard men, women, and children, who would sometimes have to wait several days before being able to take a plane. Many, who thought their turn had come, were turned away and had to wait again. In their eyes there was a flash of anger, that was then veiled by a dull resignation.

"It was how we felt, as well."[44]

Epilogue

Triumph of an Indomitable Spirit

Valérie André's return to France in August 1962 marked another new chapter in her life. The Algerian war would be her last foray into a combat zone. Still, Valérie would continue to find new challenges in her career as the world evolved around her.

Villacoublay air base, some thirteen kilometers (eight miles) from Paris, had played an important role in French aviation development dating back to the early days of ballooning and airplanes. Valérie's assignment as chief medical officer at Villacoublay was a significant appointment, but the job also posed massive challenges right from the start.

"My first contact at Villacoublay was far from warm," Valérie recalled. "The base infirmary was not very attractive; scaly, moldy exterior walls, dilapidated and poorly maintained interior facilities. And very quickly, I realized that my presence disturbs some people. . . . I was going to upset the established rules and the way of life on this very quiet airbase."[1]

Contrary to logic, Valérie found that being a veteran of the Algerian and Indochina wars was not advantageous. Villacoublay was home to France's Military Air Transport wing. Many of the base's personnel had not served in active combat areas in France's overseas wars; however, this would change as more veterans returned from Algeria. But initially, Valérie "was not well accepted . . . by the sedentary people" already established in their positions.[2] But as was typical of Valérie's character, she persevered.

"With passing months, I managed to transform the infirmary, renew the paint and appearance, change the furniture, and modernize the technical equipment. Even the staff was visibly invigorated."[3]

One other notable arrival at Villacoublay in fall 1962 was Alexis Santini. After serving four years in Algeria as head of the Fifth Air Region's helicopter operations, he had just been promoted to the rank of colonel in September. He was now assigned to Villacoublay as inspector of helicopters.[4] Valérie was overjoyed at the prospect of reuniting with the man who mattered most in her life.

"We were comrades in arms," Valérie said. "We had many common tastes. This explains everything."[5]

Santini revealed to Valérie that he planned to retire from the air force on his forty-eighth birthday, October 31, 1962. From the moment they met in Henri Boris's Paris office many years before, Valérie and Santini found an attraction to each other, along with a common sharing of hopes and ideals. While they both still served in the military, their respective dedication to duty and professionalism prevented them from maintaining anything more than a platonic relationship. But Santini realized that Valérie was the woman who mattered most in his life as well.

On the day of his retirement, Alexis Santini proposed to Valérie André. They were married on December 12, 1963.

Valérie and Santini's nomadic military life had also prevented them from laying down roots anywhere for very long, but Valérie's work continued at Villacoublay. To be in close proximity to the air base, Valérie and Santini found a fifth-story apartment on a hill overlooking the Paris suburb of Issy-les-Moulineaux. It was an appropriate choice for them. Issy-les-Moulineaux was also home to France's first civilian heliport, established by Henri Boris of Helicop-Air and others in 1949.[6]

Valérie was very pragmatic about her new living quarters, as she told an interviewer:

"You know, before being 'stable,' I only knew suitcases, hotel rooms, military tents, rented places. Nothing of my own, and that nothing suited me perfectly. Here, I liked the clear windows of this pigeon house, the space, and the air. I wanted a lot of sky."[7]

Indeed, there were many times, especially in her later years, when Valérie would spend her time gazing contentedly from her perch over the modern city that Issy-les-Moulineaux built itself into over the course of several decades.

Valérie's career continued to flourish in the 1960s. Her tenacity and professionalism had worn down her most vociferous critics. Without a doubt, prejudices still remained in the French military, but Valérie made considerable strides. In late 1964, Valérie's name was entered into the promotions list for the upcoming year.

"I was very proud, not only for myself but for all women," Valérie later said. "Until then, female soldiers had never been promoted beyond the rank of commander. On September 29, 1965, I was promoted to the rank of doctor lieutenant-colonel."[8]

Valérie's new rank was a first in the French army, but it would not be Valérie's last promotion. Five years later, on January 1, 1970, Valérie André was promoted to full colonel.

The intervening years brought their shares of challenges and adventure. Besides her duties at Villacoublay, Valérie often had assignments that took her around the world. As a passenger on a shakedown test flight of President de Gaulle's Caravelle jetliner to North Africa, or as part of a team investigating the fatal crash of a military DC-6 on the island of Réunion in the Indian Ocean, Valérie's life was full and varied. But as she grew more secure in her position as an esteemed veteran of the French army, she exercised increasing influence in bringing the issue of equal rights for women in the military to the forefront. The political and social foment of the late 1960s opened up a new awareness of women's rights in society. Valérie did not identify herself entirely with the women's liberation movement of that era. Yet, her sense of fairness and equality prompted her to take a stand when the French National Assembly attempted to reform the health services of France's armed forces. Instead of furthering the ideal of equality, as René Pleven tried with the establishment of the Women's Military Medical Corps in 1953, the new legislation proposed by the National Assembly was a step backward.

While the Women's Military Medical Corps was essentially a "separate, but equal" organization within the French military, it did establish that women of the same or superior rank to their male counterparts were no longer subordinate because of their gender. There were, however, concerted efforts to block women from entering into the Women's Military Medical Corps altogether. Most notably, women were banned from admittance into the Health Service School in Lyon and the Naval School of Health Services in Bordeaux. Valérie characterized the ban on women at these institutions as "arbitrary and deliberately misogynistic."[9]

The Military Reform Act of 1968 threatened to eliminate the Women's Military Medical Corps, without substituting a measure to ensure equal rights for women serving in the French military. Valérie André was personally outraged with the proposed changes and took on the challenge of righting the inequity.

Valérie attended a meeting in Paris on June 7, 1968, to debate the wording of the proposed legislation. The meeting was chaired by the spokesman for the Center for Information and Research of Aeronautical Medicine.[10] At the conclusion of the presentation, Valérie had questions that demanded answers.

"What happens to female physicians and pharmacists who are not mentioned in Bill No. 601?" Valérie asked.

"Indeed, you are right to ask the question, and the problem has been raised. But the Women's Military Medical Corps is doomed to extinction because of the cessation of recruitment at the basic level."[11]

The statement stunned Valérie. She had been instrumental in establishing the Women's Military Medical Corps. The incremental gain for women's equality among the ranks was now about to vanish.

"I was shocked, but I immediately made a decision," Valérie said. "I reported the proceedings to the commander of Villacoublay Air Base and announced my intention to combat this injustice about to be committed. I took care to specify that I would not act as Chief Medical Officer of Villacoublay, but in my capacity as a female medical officer of the highest rank."[12]

Valérie lobbied her senator from Upper Marne, Dr. Raymond Boin.

"Dr. Boin had a great understanding and a beautiful spirit of equity," Valérie said. Boin proved to be a staunch ally and carried considerable influence because of his seat on the Defense and Armed Forces committee. Boin saw to it that wording was included in the Military Reform Act that would clarify the role of women in France's military. At the convening of the National Assembly on July 16, 1968, Boin read into the record:

"Let us add that all provisions that concern the doctors and chemists of the armed forces also applies to the female personnel of these corps, who have been known—especially in Indochina and Algeria—to have fulfilled their duty heroically. Our commission owes them a deserved tribute."[13]

It was a victory for women's rights in the military.

"The cause was won," Valérie said after the amended bill was adopted. "Female medical officers were now integrated into the new single corps without distinction of gender. Women could now finally benefit from a career path identical to their male comrades. At least in theory."[14]

There were still hurdles to overcome. When the military health science schools in Lyon and Bordeaux readmitted women, the number of positions open to women was limited to a quota system that persisted for many years.

"There were restrictions, regardless of the grades obtained by women," Valérie noted. "When I was later in charge of presiding over the 1979 competition, I was able to raise the number of places allotted to young women to 25, although 140 places were allotted for young men. But it was clear that the test results for the 25th woman were better than that of the 140th man."[15]

Becoming a champion of women's rights was not a mantle that Valérie sought. Still, her innate sense of justice and fair play and the prominent role she held in the French army during this tumultuous time destined her to become an outspoken advocate.

"I was happy to effectively defend the cause of women, as I have always done without prejudice or bias, and with a constant concern for equity. To be exemplary in their eyes? Yes, I have always wanted to be. It was an honor to be a model of a woman who lived a life outside of traditional constraints and conventions, without complacency towards oneself."[16]

Complacency was a trait that Valérie abhorred. Adventure constantly stirred in her spirit. In 1974, Valérie was given the opportunity to visit mainland China with a civilian and military delegation from France, including Bernadette Chirac, the wife of France's prime minister and future president, Jacques Chirac. For Valérie, it was a glimpse into a hidden world, one that had greatly influenced her life while she served in Vietnam. Valérie was fascinated by her journey and its revelations.

But an even greater revelation awaited Valérie upon her return to France. Rumors began to circulate that she was being considered for promotion to general.

"This would be a spectacular promotion and one that would not go without embarrassing the conformists! I would become the first woman general."[17]

On November 7, 1975, Valérie received an invitation to Matignon, Prime Minister Chirac's residence in Paris, along with fifteen other male officers. Chirac subjected each of the invitees to a round of questions.

"It was obvious he knew perfectly well the course of our respective careers. The precision of his questions attested to his interest in the armed forces and state of the military. He asked me at length about my work as a doctor and pilot. In a few minutes alone, he asked me if I would like to be a general. I was convinced that I was in the presence of a strong ally."[18]

Chirac and the council of ministers made their decision official not long after. On her fifty-fourth birthday, April 21, 1976, Valérie André became France's first female general.

"It was one of the most beautiful days of my life," Valérie said of that day.

Valérie's formal rank was *médecin général* (doctor general), which was the equivalent of a brigadier general. The promotion elevated her to a select group of women from other nations who attained similar rank. By Valérie's estimate, there were four female generals plus one admiral in the United States, one in England, and perhaps one in Bulgaria in 1976.[19]

In France, however, Valérie's promotion created a media frenzy.

"A large number of journalists and cameramen crowded the gates of Villacoublay. The crowd mobbed me as the star of the day. The three television channels and all of the radio stations were present."

Valérie was astounded by the response. The line of questions asked by the various reporters present set the tone for numerous interviews that were to follow:

"What shall we call you?" was a question asked of her multiple times.

"*Madame le général* or doctor general," Valérie would repeatedly answer. "'*Madame la generale*' is reserved for the wives of generals. Better to say '*Madame le général.*'"

"How is your promotion welcomed in the traditionally anti-feminist army?"

"There is no more anti-feminism in the army than elsewhere, maybe less. I know that my promotion is well received."

"Do soldiers who approach you show some hesitation?"

"More and more rarely. It has happened that people who meet me for the first time don't really know what to call me. But they get the hang of it very quickly."

"What about civilians? What do they do?"

"They can do whatever they want."

"Don't you think that the promotion of a woman would be more convincing if it were a woman who was chief of staff for the army? You are a general, certainly, but you are also a doctor. Isn't this appointment simply putting a uniform on roles traditionally attributed to women to feed, educate, or provide care?"

"I don't think so, and, in any case, we will one day see a woman as chief of staff. Since we choose the best people to reach the highest positions, there is no reason why it shouldn't be a woman. She will not be appointed because she is a woman, but because she is the best."[20]

Another question Valérie fielded hit close to home.

"Isn't it a problem in your relationship with your husband that you're a general while he is only a colonel?"

Valérie shot back at the reporter.

"This is proof that people still have incredible prejudices. My husband is very proud of me for becoming a general, and it's never been a question for him to think that he's 'only a colonel.' He's almost prouder of it than I am!"[21]

And it was true. When Valérie concluded her long day at Villacoublay, she went home to Issy-les-Moulineaux. Valérie found Alexis Santini answering a steady stream of phone calls that had poured in throughout the day. When he saw Valérie, he left the phone off the hook. There would be no more calls that evening. Santini had brought home a perfect bottle of champagne and poured a glass for Valérie and himself.

Without a doubt, Alexis Santini was secure with who he was and with his own accomplishments. After his air force retirement, Santini entered the real estate profession and found success in Issy-les-Moulineaux, which grew by leaps and bounds starting in the 1970s. But Santini's military record was never in doubt.

As the founder of France's military helicopter rescue corps, Alexis Santini performed a total of 246 missions in Indochina, rescuing 430 wounded.[22] Of his total of sixty-two hundred flight hours, he spent more than fourteen hundred hours in combat zones. Santini also received numerous awards and citations and was a commander in France's Legion of Honour. And in recognition for his work in establishing France's first military helicopter flight training program in 1955, he was given the honor of having France's present-day helicopter flight training base in Vaucluse named after him:

Helicopter Crew Training Center 341, Colonel Alexis Santini.[23]

As for Valérie André, her new position also meant new responsibilities. After a ceremony where she was formally installed as *médecin général* by French president Valéry Giscard d'Estaing, Valérie was made director of health services for France's Fourth Air Region—a post never held by a woman prior. A perk with her new job meant that she was allowed to pilot a military helicopter to visit the various air bases in her region.

"The territory of the Fourth Air Region covers the southeast quarter of France and Corsica. There were about twenty airbases with very diverse missions. I went to each of them on board my favorite aircraft, the *Alouette*."[24]

It was a joyous time in Valérie's life as she immersed herself in all aspects of aviation. It was the dream of a little girl fulfilled. Her mind went back to her youth in Strasbourg after encountering Maryse Hilsz for the first time and deciding from that moment on to become a pilot.

"I will be a pilot. Soon," Valérie said to her parents. "And a doctor."

Her parents smiled.

"Pilot, doctor, all that?"

"Why not?" Valérie replied.[25]

Aviation, however, was not all that mattered to Valérie. She felt that there were still issues resulting from the Military Reform Act of 1968 that needed resolution. The quota on female enrollment at the health service schools in Lyon and Bordeaux was especially troubling. Valérie presided over the competitive examination jury for entrance at these schools in 1977 and 1978. The scores of the finalists revealed the true extent of discrimination that women experienced in advancing their careers in the military.

"I noted that the last boy admitted obtained an average of 12.525 on his exams, and the last girl, 13.850. This meant that if the bar were the same for boys and girls, 58 female candidates would have been admitted instead of 25."[26]

Valérie took her findings to the director of health services, who listened to her report but passed off her concerns in a vague reference to "problems with personnel management."[27] To her surprise, the conversation turned to the prospect of another promotion for Valérie.

"After the usual praise and a reminder of the achievements in my military life, he said that I would be promoted to the rank and privileges of a three-star general. But, . . ."

The director had an ulterior motive.

". . . he proposed to shorten my career somewhat!"[28]

It was a blatant attempt to remove Valérie as a squeaky wheel in France's military command structure.

"The suggestion fell on me like a cold shower. The timing seemed wrong. I remained stoic and didn't let my disbelief show."

Valérie had expected to remain in service for another three years. She felt she still had contributions to make. But the promotion upended these plans. Yet, *médecin général inspecteur* (doctor inspector general) was the highest rank attainable for a member of the medical corps, male or female, in the French army.

"The promotion was announced by the Council of Ministers and published in the Official Journal on April 9, 1981. It was still a great first, and I had reached the top of the hierarchy accessible to a military physician. But this euphoria was also tinged with a little melancholy."[29]

President François Mitterrand presided over Valérie's last promotion on September 17, 1981. The ceremony also included her elevation to grand officer in the Legion of Honour. It was a bittersweet day for her. It marked the end of a career without precedent in French history.

Valérie's retirement did not mean that she had abandoned her battle to improve the working conditions of females in the military. In spring 1982, Valérie joined the Commission for the Prospective Study of Military Women.

"The name of the commission was rather barbaric," Valérie said. "Charles Hernu, the minister of defense, asked me to chair it. We were to examine the conditions for better integrating women into the armed forces."[30]

Valérie presented stark figures to show that France had a long way to catch up with other countries in incorporating more females in the ranks.

"I had no difficulty demonstrating how far France was behind in this area. In the United States, women made up 8.9 percent of the army, 7 percent of the navy, and 11 percent of the air force. In France, it was 1.1 percent in the army, 0.57 percent in the air force, and 2 percent in the navy."[31]

The commission seriously examined the problem. On May 9, 1985, the Ministry of Defense instituted a number of measures to ensure women were better integrated within the military community. While underrepresentation of females in France's military persists even into the present day, women made up 15 percent of total service personnel in 2022;[32] however, as a testament to the efforts made by Valérie André as a trailblazer in the Health Service Corps, 58 percent of the corps' personnel is composed of women today.

Throughout her post-military life, Valérie never slowed down. In 1983, she became a founding member of the French National Air and Space Academy. In 1988, she published a memoir, *Madame le général*, her follow-up to *Ici, Ventilateur* that she wrote in 1954 on her life in Indochina. She continued to receive numerous awards and accolades and became an inspiration to anyone who came to know her and her story.

Valérie and Santini lived contentedly in their rooftop apartment on a hill overlooking Issy-les-Moulineaux. They led a full life. They would attend the many reunions of veterans who took part in the wars of Indochina and Algeria. Valérie was always philosophical about her participation in France's overseas conflicts.

"Lost wars, dead wars. . . . From Indochina to Algeria, we suffered terrible, unjust, but never mediocre ordeals. This journey through fire has been a school of life, where we learned to go as far as we were able and reach beyond that point to surpass ourselves. The purpose of military life was also an exaltation of the noblest values; the honor of serving, the sense of duty, the gift of self, and the will to be. I don't know of anything more beautiful.

"A soldier, like a doctor, never ceases to experience humility; no victory is ever final, no diagnosis irreversible.

"Various obstacles have stood in my way because of the 'female fact,' but I believe that far from discouraging me, these obstacles served to galvanize me."[33]

Valérie never forgot those who helped her along the way. No one in that category surpassed the help and support from Alexis Santini. He would always be the "man who mattered most" in Valérie's life.

In 1996, Santini's health began to fail. To make his last days more comfortable, especially during the torrid summer months, Valérie had air conditioning installed in their apartment in Issy. Valérie nursed Santini and took care of him to the best of her ability, and she stayed with him until the end.

Colonel Alexis Santini died on January 31, 1997. He was eighty-three. When once asked if he ever regretted giving up piloting a plane for a helicopter, Santini answered without hesitation:

"Not at all. I was very happy to take part in this adventure. If I had to do it again, I would do it again!"[34]

Valérie's life continued. She was never alone in her later years. She remained in her Issy apartment, where she received friends and visitors from around the world. But she was never sedentary, another trait she loathed. She owned a BMW 3 series compact that she expertly piloted through the streets of Issy-les-Moulineaux and Paris. It may not have been an Alouette, but she enjoyed the lively performance of the little car. Even while driving, she was always impeccable when it came to attention to detail, right down to the leather gloves she invariably wore.

She also frequented cafés and restaurants in and around Paris, where she was known and welcomed by all. A fond memory for me came on my first encounter with General André when I was invited to dinner at Les Closeries des Lilas in the Montparnasse district of Paris. General André confided that it was a place where celebrities and politicians could be found, not realizing that she was the most special person there that evening.

Valérie also enjoyed air travel whenever possible. Another fond memory for Valérie comes from when she had turned ninety, and she was about to travel to Washington, DC. She excitedly spoke of how she was going on a "girls' weekend" and that she would be in the company of the world champion aerobatic pilot and director of France's Air and Space Museum, Catherine Maunoury, and Patricia Haffner, the pilot of the Air France Boeing 747 taking them to the United States. The highlight of her trip was a visit to the National Air and Space Museum.

As she approached her centenary in 2022, Valérie André's friends and admirers gathered with her in Issy-les-Moulineaux on March 8 to bestow yet another honor. The historic heliport in Issy—the first private heliport in all of France—was renamed "Héliport Paris—Issy-les-Moulineaux Valérie André." It was hardly a coincidence that this occasion coincided with International Women's Day.

The wars that Valérie André took part in have faded in the collective memory of France and the world, but they should never be forgotten. The sacrifices, the sadness, and the horror of what humanity is capable of forever etches itself in our history. But the individuals who reached beyond convention—especially those who tried to make the world better, when things were at their worst, and went beyond themselves—gave humanity hope.

"In my own way, I have always been a rebel," Valérie André once said. "I rebelled against outdated injustices or outdated traditions. But I was always a rebel who liked order . . . and risks."[35]

Notes

CHAPTER 1

1. Valérie Edmée André, *Ici, Ventilateur!* (Paris: Calmann-Lévy, 1954), 119–20. Unless otherwise indicated, translations throughout this book are mine.

CHAPTER 2

1. Valérie Edmée André, *Madame le général* (Paris: Académique Perrin, 1988), 9.
2. André, *Madame le général*, 9.
3. André, *Madame le général*, 10.
4. Universal male suffrage in France was established in 1914. The vote was extended to French women on April 29, 1944, by the French Provisional Government while still in exile in Great Britain.
5. André, *Madame le général*, 11.
6. André, *Madame le général*, 11.
7. André, *Madame le général*, 11.
8. André, *Madame le général*, 14.
9. André, *Madame le général*, 21.
10. André, *Madame le général*, 21.
11. Three thousand French francs was the equivalent of approximately US$90 in 1939, or roughly US$1,800 in 2021.
12. André, *Madame le général*, 14.
13. André, *Madame le général*, 15.
14. André, *Madame le général*, 16–17.
15. Pinot would later become an instructor for Charles de Gaulle's Free French air force that relocated to England during World War II. See Vital Ferry, *Croix de Lorraine et Croix du sud, 1940–1942* (Paris: Éditions du Gerfaut, 2005), 45.
16. André, *Madame le général*, 16.

CHAPTER 3

1. Valérie Edmée André, *Madame le général* (Paris: Académique Perrin, 1988), 16.
2. André, *Madame le général*, 17.
3. André, *Madame le général*, 17.
4. André, *Madame le général*, 17.
5. André, *Madame le général*, 17.
6. André, *Madame le général*, 18.
7. André, *Madame le général*, 18.
8. André, *Madame le général*, 19.
9. André, *Madame le général*, 19.

CHAPTER 4

1. Valérie Edmée André, *Madame le général* (Paris: Académique Perrin, 1988), 19.
2. André, *Madame le général*, 19.
3. André, *Madame le général*, 20.
4. André, *Madame le général*, 20.
5. André, *Madame le général*, 21.
6. André, *Madame le général*, 21.
7. André, *Madame le général*, 22.
8. André, *Madame le général*, 22.
9. André, *Madame le général*, 22.
10. André, *Madame le général*, 23.
11. André, *Madame le général*, 23.
12. André, *Madame le général*, 23.
13. André, *Madame le général*, 23–24.
14. André, *Madame le général*, 24.

CHAPTER 5

1. Valérie Edmée André, *Madame le général* (Paris: Académique Perrin, 1988), 40.
2. André, *Madame le général*, 40.
3. André, *Madame le général*, 40.
4. André, *Madame le général*, 40.
5. Jacqueline Bromberger et al., "October 1941—Resistance Starts in Clermont-Ferrand," in *The Strasbourg French University Is Transferred to Clermont-Ferrand* (Paris: Délégation à la mémoire et à l'information historique du

Ministère des anciens combattants et victimes de guerre, 1993), http://mapage.noos
.fr/jibro/resistance-universitaire/en/Chapitre_Premier_partie2.html.

6. A. J. Liebler, comp., *After the Drama of Clermont*, in *L'Université libre*, January 15, 1944, reproduced in *The Republic of Silence* (New York: Harcourt Brace, 1947), 305.

7. André, *Madame le général*, 25.

8. Georges Livet and Francis Rapp, eds., *Histoire de Strasbourg des origines à nos jours* (Strasbourg, France: Éditions des dernières nouvelles de Strasbourg, 1992), 4:487.

9. Gaélle Talbot, "Commemoration de la rafle de l'Université de Strasbourg repliée à Clermont-Ferrand (1943) 70e anniversaire, 1943–2013," 2013.

10. André, *Madame le général*, 25.

11. Eric Panthou, "PRAT Henri, Albert, Eugène [pseudonyme dans la résistance: Sinfer 571]," Maitron, last updated February 20, 2022, https://maitron.fr/spip .php?article221611.

CHAPTER 6

1. Valérie Edmée André, *Madame le général* (Paris: Académique Perrin, 1988), 26.

2. André, *Madame le général*, 26.

3. Charles Whiting, *The Home Front: Germany* (New York: Time-Life, 1982), 142.

4. André, *Madame le général*, 27.

5. André, *Madame le général*, 27.

6. André, *Madame le général*, 44.

7. André, *Madame le général*, 44.

8. André, *Madame le général*, 44.

9. André, *Madame le général*, 28.

10. André, *Madame le général*, 28.

11. André, *Madame le général*, 28.

12. André, *Madame le général*, 28.

13. André, *Madame le général*, 29.

14. André, *Madame le général*, 29.

CHAPTER 7

1. Valérie Edmée André, *Madame le général* (Paris: Académique Perrin, 1988), 29.

2. Larry Collins and Dominique Lapierre, *Is Paris Burning?* (New York: Simon & Schuster, 1965; reprint, New York: Grand Central, 1991), 210. Page references are to the 1991 edition.

3. André, *Madame le général*, 29.

4. André, *Madame le général*, 29–30.

5. André, *Madame le général*, 30.

6. André, *Madame le général*, 30.

7. André, *Madame le général*, 30.

CHAPTER 8

1. Valérie Edmée André, *Madame le général* (Paris: Académique Perrin, 1988), 30.

2. Bertram M. Gordon, *Historical Dictionary of World War II France: The Occupation, Vichy, and the Resistance, 1938–1946* (Westport, CT: Greenwood, 1998), 216, 280.

3. Anthony Beevor, *D-Day, the Battle for Normandy* (New York: Viking, 2009), 451, 448.

4. Gordon, *Historical Dictionary of World War II France*, 243–44.

5. Gordon, *Historical Dictionary of World War II France*, 365.

6. Rod Kedward, *France and the French: A Modern History* (New York: Overlook, 2005), 311.

7. Jean Lacouture, *De Gaulle, the Rebel 1890–1944* (New York: Norton, 1990), 569.

8. André, *Madame le général*, 30.

9. André, *Madame le général*, 30.

10. Gordon, *Historical Dictionary of World War II France*, 213.

11. André, *Madame le général*, 30.

12. André, *Madame le général*, 30.

13. Jean Lartéguy, *Le guerre nue* (Paris: Stock, 1976).

14. André, *Madame le général*, 37.

15. André, *Madame le général*, 37.

16. André, *Madame le général*, 37.

17. André, *Madame le général*, 37.

18. Valérie Edmée André, *La patholgie du parachutisme* (Paris: R. Foulon, 1948).

19. André, *Madame le général*, 38.

20. André, *Madame le général*, 38.

CHAPTER 9

1. Thomas Landenburg, "The French in Indochina," Digital History, 2007, 3, http://www.digitalhistory.uh.edu/teachers/lesson_plans/pdfs/unit12_1.pdf.

2. Elliott Roosevelt, *As He Saw It* (New York: Duell, Sloan and Pearce, 1946), quoted in "Roosevelt and Churchill on Colonial Questions, August 10, 1941," Mount Holyoke College, n.d., accessed June 6, 2022, https://www.mtholyoke.edu/acad/intrel/fdrwc.htm.

3. Fredrik Logevall, *Embers of War* (New York: Random House, 2012), 104.

4. CLAEO, or Corps de liaison administrative pour l'Extrême-Orient (Administrative Liaison Corps for the Far East).

5. Valérie Edmée André, *Madame le général* (Paris: Académique Perrin, 1988), 37.

6. Maurice Vaisse, *L'Armée française dans la guerre d'Indochine (1946–1954)* (Château de Vincennes, France: Editions complexe, 2000), 124.

7. André, *Madame le général*, 37.

8. André, *Madame le général*, 37.

CHAPTER 10

1. Valérie Edmée André, *Madame le général* (Paris: Académique Perrin, 1988), 41.

2. Valérie Edmée André, *La pathologie du parachutisme* (Paris: R. Foulon, 1948).

3. André, *Madame le général*, 39.

4. André, *Madame le général*, 39.

5. André, *Madame le général*, 39.

6. André, *Madame le général*, 40.

7. André, *Madame le général*, 40.

8. Christopher Goscha, "Colonial Hanoi and Saigon at War: Social Dynamics of the Viet Minh's Underground City, 1945–1954," *War in History*, April 2013, 226.

9. Goscha, "Colonial Hanoi and Saigon at War," 227.

10. André, *Madame le général*, 40.

11. André, *Madame le général*, 40.

12. André, *Madame le général*, 40.

CHAPTER 11

1. Valérie Edmée André, *Madame le général* (Paris: Académique Perrin, 1988), 35.

2. André, *Madame le général*, 35.

3. André, *Madame le général*, 42.

4. André, *Madame le général*, 16.

5. Valérie Edmée André, *Ici, Ventilateur!* (Paris: Calmann-Lévy, 1954), 16.

6. Peter Wallace and Arnold M. Meirowsky, "Repair of Dural Defect by Graft: An Analysis of 540 Penetrating Wounds Incurred in the Korean War," *Annals of Surgery*, February 1960, 175–76.

7. Seckin Aydin, Baris Kucukyuruk, Bashar Abuzayed, Sabri Aydin, and Galip Zinhi Sanus, "Cranioplasty: Review of Materials and Techniques," *Journal of Neuroscience in Rural Practice* 2 (July–December 2011): 162–67.

8. André, *Madame le général*, 41.

9. André, *Madame le général*, 41.

10. William McFall Waddell II, "In the Year of the Tiger: The War for Cochinchina, 1945–1951" (diss., Ohio State University, 2014), 202.

11. André, *Madame le général*, 41.

12. André, *Madame le général*, 41–42.

13. André, *Madame le général*, 42.

14. André, *Madame le général*, 43.

CHAPTER 12

1. Alan Bristow (with Patrick Malone), *Alan Bristow: Helicopter Pioneer* (Barnsley, UK: Pen & Sword, 2010), 113.

2. Bristow, *Alan Bristow,* 112.

3. Bristow, *Alan Bristow,* 113.

4. Bristow, *Alan Bristow*, 113.

5. Bristow, *Alan Bristow*, 113.

6. Bristow, *Alan Bristow*, 214.

7. Bristow, *Alan Bristow*, 114.

8. Bristow, *Alan Bristow*, 115.

9. Bristow, *Alan Bristow*, 115.

10. Bristow, *Alan Bristow*, 115.

11. Bristow, *Alan Bristow*, 115.

12. Bristow, *Alan Bristow*, 115–16.

13. Bristow, *Alan Bristow*, 116.

14. Bristow, *Alan Bristow,* 116.

15. Bristow, *Alan Bristow*, 117.

CHAPTER 13

1. Michel Fleurence, *Rotors dans le ciel d'Indochine*, vol. 3, *Le livre d'or, 1950–1997* (Château de Vincennes, France: Service historique de la Défense, 2010), 327–42.

2. Fleurence, *Rotors dans le ciel d'Indochine*, 3:329.

3. 2e Groupe aérien d'observation d'artillerie.

4. Fleurence, *Rotors dans le ciel d'Indochine*, 3:332.

5. Fleurence, *Rotors dans le ciel d'Indochine*, 3:333.

6. Michel Fleurence, *Rotors dans le ciel d'Indochine*, vol. 1, *Les hommes, 1950–1997* (Château de Vincennes, France: Service historique de la Défense, 2003), 97.

CHAPTER 14

1. U.S. forces began using helicopters in Korea in late June 1950, when the Third Air Rescue Squadron was sent there from Japan. Mark Albertson, "The Korean War—the Helicopter," *Army Aviation Magazine*, n.d., www.armyaviationmagazine .com/index.php/history/not-so-current-2/1884-the-korean-war-the-helicopter.

2. Fredrik Logevall, *Embers of War* (New York: Random House, 2012), 219.

3. Andrew Barros and Martin Thomas, eds., *The Civilianization of War: The Changing Civil-Military Divide, 1914–2014* (New York: Cambridge University Press, 2018), 82.

4. Michel Fleurence, *Rotors dans le ciel d'Indochine*, vol. 3, *Le livre d'or, 1950–1997* (Château Vincennes, France: Service historique de la Défense, 2010), 334.

5. Philippe Boulay, "Raymond Fumat: Histoire d'un pilote oublié," Aerostories, 2002, aerostories.free.fr/giravia/personnages/boulay/fumat.

6. Michel Fleurence, *Rotors dans le ciel d'Indochine*, vol. 2, *Les opérations, 1950–1954* (Château Vincennes, France: Service historique de la Défense, 2006), 243.

7. Alain Vezin, "Un nuit dans la Plaine des Joncs," Histoires de aviateurs, 2009, http://aviateurs.e-monsite.com/pages/1946-et-annees-suivantes/une-nuit-dans-la -plaine-des-joncs.html.

8. Vezin, "Un nuit dans la Plaine des Joncs."

CHAPTER 15

1. Valérie Edmée André, *Madame le général* (Paris: Académique Perrin, 1988), 43.

2. André, *Madame le général*, 42.

3. André, *Madame le général*, 42–43.

4. André, *Madame le général*, 43.

5. André, *Madame le général*, 43.

6. André, *Madame le général*, 43.

7. André, *Madame le général*, 43.

8. André, *Madame le général*, 44.

9. "SNCAN (Nord) 1700 'Norelic' and 1710 Helicopters," Secret Projects, accessed March 13, 2022, http://www.secretprojects.co.uk/forum/index.php/topic ,15184.0/nowap.html?PHPSESSID=krrstdapiib3uns9i5pbb84mo1.

10. Blake Clark, "Mademoiselle Hélicoptère," *France illustration*, August 1953, 37.

11. Henri Boris, "En cinquante heures vous serez pilote d'hélicoptère" [In fifty hours you will be a helicopter pilot], *Paris illustration*, July 1950, 60.

12. André, *Madame le général*, 44.

13. André, *Madame le général*, 44.

14. Clark, "Mademoiselle Hélicoptère," 38.

15. André, *Madame le général*, 44.

16. André, *Madame le général*, 44.

17. Clark, "Mademoiselle Hélicoptère," 40.

18. André, *Madame le général*, 44.

19. André, *Madame le général*, 44.

20. André, *Madame le général*, 45.

CHAPTER 16

1. Valérie Edmée André, *Madame le général* (Paris: Académique Perrin, 1988), 46.

2. Jacques Dalloz, *The War in Indo-China 1945–1954* (Dublin, Ireland: Gill & McMillan, 1990), 125.

3. Valérie Edmée André, *Ici, Ventilateur!* (Paris: Calmann-Lévy, 1954), 12.

4. André, *Madame le général*, 46.

5. André, *Ici, Ventilateur!*, 12.

6. André, *Ici, Ventilateur!*, 12.

7. André, *Madame le général*, 46.

8. André, *Ici, Ventilateur!*, 13.

9. André, *Ici, Ventilateur!*, 13.

10. André, *Ici, Ventilateur!*, 13.

11. André, *Ici, Ventilateur!*, 13.

12. André, *Ici, Ventilateur!*, 14.

13. André, *Ici, Ventilateur!*, 14.

14. André, *Madame le général*, 47.

15. André, *Madame le général*, 47.

16. André, *Madame le général*, 48.

17. André, *Madame le général*, 48.

18. André, *Madame le général*, 48.

19. André, *Ici, Ventilateur!*, 19.

20. André, *Ici, Ventilateur!*, 20.

21. André, *Ici, Ventilateur!*, 20.

22. André, *Ici, Ventilateur!*, 21.

23. André, *Ici, Ventilateur!*, 21.

24. André, *Ici, Ventilateur!*, 21.

25. André, *Ici, Ventilateur!*, 22.

26. André, *Ici, Ventilateur!*, 20.

27. André, *Ici, Ventilateur!*, 22.

28. André, *Ici, Ventilateur!*, 22.

CHAPTER 17

1. Valérie Edmée André, *Madame le général* (Paris: Académique Perrin, 1988), 46.

2. André, *Madame le général*, 46.

3. André, *Madame le général*, 46.

4. Lucien Bodard, *The Quicksand War: Prelude to Vietnam* (Boston: Little, Brown, 1967), 323.

5. Jacques Dalloz, *The War in Indo-China 1945–1954* (Dublin, Ireland: Gill & McMillan, 1990), 123.

6. Pierre Pellissier, *De Lattre* (Paris: Librairie académique Perrin, 1998), 457.

7. Pellissier, *De Lattre*, 457.

8. Bodard, *The Quicksand War*, 351.

9. Bernard Fall, *Street without Joy* (Mechanicsburg, PA: Stackpole Books, 1961), 31.

10. Stanley Karnow, "Giap Remembers," *New York Times Magazine*, June 24, 1990, 122.

11. Dalloz, *The War in Indo-China 1945–1954*, 138.

CHAPTER 18

1. Valérie Edmée André, *Madame le général* (Paris: Académique Perrin, 1988), 53.

2. André, *Madame le général*, 53.

3. André, *Madame le général*, 53.

4. Robert H. Scales, *Firepower in Limited War* (Novato, CA: Presidio, 1997), 48.

5. Spencer C. Tucker, *Vietnam* (Louisville: University of Kentucky Press), 62.

6. Valérie Edmée André, *Ici, Ventilateur!* (Paris: Calmann-Lévy, 1954), 22.

7. André, *Ici, Ventilateur!*, 23.

8. André, *Ici, Ventilateur!*, 23.

9. André, *Ici, Ventilateur!*, 29.

10. André, *Ici, Ventilateur!*, 29.

11. André, *Ici, Ventilateur!*, 26; André, *Madame le général*, 52.

12. André, *Ici, Ventilateur!*, 27–28.

CHAPTER 19

1. Valérie Edmée André, *Ici, Ventilateur!* (Paris: Calmann-Lévy, 1954), 30.

2. Valérie Edmée André, *Madame le général* (Paris: Académique Perrin, 1988), 56.

3. André, *Ici, Ventilateur!*, 31.

4. Jacob Gold and Nguon Savan, "Turning Pepper into 'Black Gold,'" *Phnom Penh Post*, October 7, 2009.

5. André, *Ici, Ventilateur!*, 32.

6. André, *Ici, Ventilateur!*, 33.

7. André, *Ici, Ventilateur!*, 33.

8. André, *Ici, Ventilateur!*, 33.

9. André, *Ici, Ventilateur!*, 33.

10. André, *Madame le général*, 57.

11. André, *Ici, Ventilateur!*, 33.

12. André, *Ici, Ventilateur!*, 33.

13. André, *Madame le général*, 58.

14. André, *Ici, Ventilateur!*, 35.

15. André, *Madame le général*, 58.

CHAPTER 20

1. Valérie Edmée André, *Madame le général* (Paris: Académique Perrin, 1988), 53.

2. André, *Madame le général*, 58.

3. André, *Madame le général*, 58.

4. André, *Madame le général*, 59.

5. Lucien Bodard, *The Quicksand War: Prelude to Vietnam* (Boston: Little, Brown, 1967), 342.

6. The population of Vietnam is not composed of one homogenous race. In modern-day Vietnam, more than fifty ethnic minorities are officially recognized.

7. Valérie Edmée André, *Ici, Ventilateur!* (Paris: Calmann-Lévy, 1954), 37.

8. André, *Ici, Ventilateur!*, 38.

9. André, *Ici, Ventilateur!*, 37.

10. André, *Madame le général*, 59; André, *Ici, Ventilateur!*, 38.

11. André, *Madame le général*, 59.

12. André, *Madame le général*, 59.

13. André, *Ici, Ventilateur*, 18.

14. André, *Madame le général*, 60.

15. The Thais in Vietnam are an ethnic minority that number more than a million today in modern Vietnam and are directly related to the people of Thailand. Known colloquially as Tay Don or Tay Dam, the Thai settled mostly in northern Vietnam in proximity to the Laotian border.

16. André, *Ici, Ventilateur!*, 18.

17. André, *Ici, Ventilateur!*, 18.

18. Douglas Johnson, "Avis de décès: Général Maurice Redon," *Indépendant* (London), June 23, 2000.

19. André, *Ici, Ventilateur!*, 39.

20. André, *Ici, Ventilateur!*, 42.

21. André, *Ici, Ventilateur!*, 42; André, *Madame le général*, 61.

22. André, *Ici, Ventilateur!*, 43; André, *Madame le général*, 61.

23. André, *Madame le général*, 61.

24. André, *Madame le général*, 61–63.

25. André, *Madame le général*, 63. Note: Cardiotonics refers to the family of heart-related drugs that include digitalis.

26. André, *Madame le général*, 63.

27. André, *Madame le général*, 63.

28. André, *Ici, Ventilateur!*, 43.

29. André, *Madame le général*, 63.

30. André, *Madame le général*, 63.

31. André, *Madame le général*, 63.

32. André, *Madame le général*, 64.

33. André, *Ici, Ventilateur!*, 44.

34. André, *Ici, Ventilateur!*, 44; André, *Madame le général*, 64.

CHAPTER 21

1. The title for this chapter comes from Valérie André's own book, *Madame le général*, in the chapter there titled "La femme descendu du ciel." An alternative translation for this phrase can also be "the woman who came down from heaven."

2. General Valérie André, interview with the author [in French], November 23, 2016, Issy-les-Moulineaux, France.

3. André, *Madame le général* (Paris: Académique Perrin, 1988), 64.

4. André, interview.

5. André, *Ici, Ventilateur!* (Paris: Calmann-Lévy, 1954), 46.

6. André, *Madame le général*, 64.

7. André, *Ici, Ventilateur!*, 46.

8. André, *Ici, Ventilateur!*, 47.

9. André, *Ici, Ventilateur!*, 48.

10. André, *Ici, Ventilateur!*, 49.

11. André, *Ici, Ventilateur!*, 50.

12. André, *Ici, Ventilateur!*, 50.

13. André, *Ici, Ventilateur!*, 51.

14. André, *Ici, Ventilateur!*, 51.

15. André, *Madame le général*, 68.

16. André, *Ici, Ventilateur!*, 53.

17. André, *Madame le général*, 69; André, *Ici, Ventilateur!*, 53.

18. André, *Ici, Ventilateur!*, 54.

19. André, *Madame le général*, 69.

20. André, *Ici, Ventilateur!*, 54.

21. André, *Ici, Ventilateur!*, 55.

22. André, *Ici, Ventilateur!*, 55.

23. André, *Ici, Ventilateur!*, 56; André, *Madame le général*, 70.

24. André, *Ici, Ventilateur!*, 56.

25. André, *Ici, Ventilateur!*, 57.

26. André, *Ici, Ventilateur!*, 57.

27. André, *Ici, Ventilateur!*, 58.

28. André, *Ici, Ventilateur!*, 58; André, *Madame le général*, 71.

29. André, *Ici, Ventilateur!*, 58.

30. André, *Madame le général*, 71.

31. André, *Ici, Ventilateur!*, 58–59.

32. André, *Ici, Ventilateur!*, 59.

33. André, *Madame le général*, 78–79.

CHAPTER 22

1. CLAEO, or Corps de liaison administrative pour l'Extrême-Orient (Administrative Liaison Corps of the Far East).

2. Michel Fleurence, *Rotors dans le ciel d'Indochine*, vol. 2, *Les opérations, 1950–1954* (Château de Vincennes, France: Service historique de la Défense, 2006), 244–47.

3. Fleurence, *Rotors dans le ciel d'Indochine*, 2:285.

4. Groupements aeriens tactiques (Tactical Air Group).

5. Fleurence, *Rotors dans le ciel d'Indochine*, 2:235–36.

6. Fleurence, *Rotors dans le ciel d'Indochine*, 2:236.

CHAPTER 23

1. André, *Madame le général* (Paris: Académique Perrin, 1988), 71.

2. Valérie Edmée André, *Ici, Ventilateur!* (Paris: Calmann-Lévy, 1954), 61.

3. André, *Ici, Ventilateur!*, 62.

4. Henri Garric and Antoine Allibert, "Henri Bartier—ou le droit d'ingérence . . . sur le champ de bataille," Vétérans de Provence, 2009, http://www.veterans.fr /images/docs-site/Indochine/les-hommes/BARTIER-Henri.pdf.

5. Garric and Allibert, "Henri Bartier."

6. Garric and Allibert, "Henri Bartier."

7. Michel Fleurence, *Rotors dans le ciel d'Indochine*, vol. 2, *Les operations 1950–1954* (Château Vincennes, France: Service historique de la Défense, 2010), 492. Note: *Palmes* were symbols of additional merit added to the Croix de guerre. For the French air force, additional *palmes* were awarded for every twenty-five flights into a combat zone.

8. André, *Ici, Ventilateur!*, 62.

9. André, *Ici, Ventilateur!*, 62.

10. André, *Ici, Ventilateur!*, 62–63.

11. André, *Madame le général*, 71.

12. André, *Ici, Ventilateur!*, 63.

13. Bernard Fall, *Street without Joy* (Mechanicsburg, PA: Stackpole Books, 1961), 52.

14. Fall, *Street without Joy*, 52.

15. André, *Ici, Ventilateur!*, 64.

16. André, *Ici, Ventilateur!*, 64. Bernard Fall put the number of dead Viet Minh at closer to four hundred (Fall, *Street without Joy*, 53).

17. André, *Ici, Ventilateur!*, 64.

18. André, *Ici, Ventilateur!*, 65.

19. André, *Ici, Ventilateur!*, 65.

20. André, *Ici, Ventilateur!*, 66.

21. André, *Ici, Ventilateur!*, 66.

22. André, *Ici, Ventilateur!*, 69.

23. André, *Ici, Ventilateur!*, 69.

24. André, *Madame le général*, 75; André, *Ici, Ventilateur!*, 69.

25. André, *Madame le général*, 75.

26. André, *Ici, Ventilateur!*, 70.

27. André, *Madame le général*, 76.

28. André, *Ici, Ventilateur!*, 70; André, *Madame le général*, 75.

29. André, *Ici, Ventilateur!*, 71.

CHAPTER 24

1. Valérie Edmée André, *Ici, Ventilateur!* (Paris: Calmann-Lévy, 1954), 71.

2. André, *Ici, Ventilateur!*, 72.

3. André, *Ici, Ventilateur!*, 72.

4. André, *Ici, Ventilateur!*, 73.

5. André, *Ici, Ventilateur!*, 73.

6. André, *Ici, Ventilateur!*, 74.

7. André, *Ici, Ventilateur!*, 74.

8. André, *Ici, Ventilateur!*, 74; Valérie Edmée André, *Madame le général* (Paris: Académique Perrin, 1988), 77.

9. André, *Ici, Ventilateur!*, 74–75.

10. André, *Ici, Ventilateur!*, 75.

11. André, *Ici, Ventilateur!*, 76.

12. André, *Ici, Ventilateur!*, 76.

13. Bernard Fall, *Street without Joy* (Mechanicsburg, PA: Stackpole Books, 1961), 54–55.

14. André, *Ici, Ventilateur!*, 76; André, *Madame le général*, 78.

15. André, *Ici, Ventilateur!*, 77.

16. André, *Ici, Ventilateur!*, 77.

17. André, *Ici, Ventilateur!*, 77; André, *Madame le général*, 78.

CHAPTER 25

1. Anthony Clayton, *Three Marshals of France: Leadership after Trauma* (London: Brassey's, 1992), 163.

2. Valérie Edmée André, *Madame le général* (Paris: Académique Perrin, 1988), 149.

3. Valérie Edmée André, *Ici, Ventilateur!* (Paris: Calmann-Lévy, 1954), 79–80.

4. André, *Madame le général*, 80.

5. Daniel Marcelon, "Afin de defier, Francis Varcin: L'oubli, mort pour la France en Indochine," *Air ANSONA* 74, no. 3 (1998): 17–18.

6. André, *Madame le général*, 79.

7. Varcin's last leave was in 1949, according to the *Air ANSONA* article, when he returned to France for treatment of amoebic dysentery (Marcelon, "Afin de defier, Francis Varcin").

8. André, *Madame le général*, 79.

9. Marcelon, "Afin de defier, Francis Varcin," 18.

10. André, *Madame le général*, 80.

11. André, *Ici, Ventilateur!*, 89.

12. André, *Madame le général*, 80; André, *Ici, Ventilateur!*, 80.

13. Florent Bonnefoi, "Henri Bartier, ce héros oublié de la guerre d'Indochine," *La Provence*, June 17, 2018.

14. Anne-Gaelle Breton, e-mail to Charles Morgan Evans, May 26, 2022.

15. Michel Fleurence, *Rotors dans le ciel d'Indochine*, vol. 2, *Les opérations, 1950–1954* (Château Vincennes, France: Service historique de la Défense, 2006), 286.

16. Fleurence, *Rotors dans le ciel d'Indochine*, 2:286.

17. André, *Madame le général*, 80.

18. André, *Ici, Ventilateur!*, 81; André, *Madame le général*, 80.

19. André, *Ici, Ventilateur!*, 81.

20. André, *Ici, Ventilateur!*, 82.

21. André, *Ici, Ventilateur!*, 82.

22. André, *Ici, Ventilateur!*, 82; André, *Madame le général*, 81.

23. André, *Ici, Ventilateur!*, 84.

24. André, *Ici, Ventilateur!*, 83.

25. André, *Ici, Ventilateur!*, 83.

CHAPTER 26

1. André, *Ici, Ventilateur!* (Calmann-Lévy, 1954), 83.

2. André, *Ici, Ventilateur!*, 83.

3. André, *Madame le général* (Paris: Académique Perrin, 1988), 82.

4. André, *Ici, Ventilateur!*, 84.

5. André, *Ici, Ventilateur!*, 84.

6. André, *Ici, Ventilateur!*, 85.

7. André, *Ici, Ventilateur!*, 85.

8. André, *Ici, Ventilateur!*, 85.

9. André, *Ici, Ventilateur!*, 86.

10. André, *Ici, Ventilateur!*, 86; André, *Madame le général*, 83.

11. André, *Madame le général*, 83.

12. André, *Madame le général*, 83.

13. André, *Ici, Ventilateur!*, 87.

14. André, *Ici, Ventilateur!*, 89.

15. André, *Ici, Ventilateur!*, 87.

16. André, *Ici, Ventilateur!*, 88.

17. André, *Ici, Ventilateur!*, 88.

18. André, *Ici, Ventilateur!*, 88. The word for "fan," or ventilator, in the Vietnamese language is actually *quạt.* While *quetak* doesn't exactly translate into "ventilator lady" in Vietnamese, it is likely how Valerié André heard the phrase spoken.

CHAPTER 27

1. Valérie Edmée André, *Ici, Ventilateur!* (Paris: Calmann-Lévy, 1954), 89.

2. André, *Ici, Ventilateur!*, 89.

3. Michel Fleurence, *Rotors dans le ciel d'Indochine*, vol. 1, *Les hommes, 1950–1997* (Château Vincennes, France: Service historique de la Défense, 2003), 33.

4. André, *Ici, Ventilateur!*, 158.

5. André, *Ici, Ventilateur!*, 89.

6. André, *Ici, Ventilateur!*, 158. Valérie André only refers to this lieutenant by the first letter of his last name, "N."

7. André, *Ici, Ventilateur!*, 153, 158.

8. André, *Ici, Ventilateur!*, 92.

9. André, *Ici, Ventilateur!*, 92. Also refer to the online article "La cotonnière du Tonkin et l'usine de Nam Dinh," Belle Indochine, accessed March 13, 2022, http://belleindochine.free.fr/CotonniereDuTonkin.htm.

10. André, *Ici, Ventilateur!*, 93.

11. Fredrik Logevall, *Embers of War* (New York: Random House, 2012), 322.

12. André, *Ici, Ventilateur!*, 93.

13. André, *Ici, Ventilateur!*, 94.

14. Valérie Edmée André, *Madame le général* (Paris: Académique Perrin, 1988), 88.

15. André, *Ici, Ventilateur!*, 93; André, *Madame le général*, 87.

16. André, *Madame le général*, 88.

17. André, *Ici, Ventilateur!*, 94.

18. André, *Ici, Ventilateur!*, 95; André, *Madame le général*, 88.

19. André, *Ici, Ventilateur!*, 95.

20. André, *Ici, Ventilateur!*, 96.

21. André, *Madame le général*, 90.

22. André, *Ici, Ventilateur!*, 96.

23. André, *Ici, Ventilateur!*, 96.

24. André, *Ici, Ventilateur!*, 97.

25. André, *Ici, Ventilateur!*, 97.

26. André, *Ici, Ventilateur!*, 98.

27. André, *Ici, Ventilateur!*, 98.

28. André, *Ici, Ventilateur!*, 98.
29. André, *Ici, Ventilateur!*, 98.
30. André, *Ici, Ventilateur!*, 99.

CHAPTER 28

1. Valérie Edmée André, *Madame le général* (Paris: Académique Perrin, 1988), 92.

2. Michel Fleurence, *Rotors dans le ciel d'Indochine*, vol. 2, *Les opérations, 1950–1954* (Château Vincennes, France: Service historique de la Défense, 2006), 257.

3. Valérie Edmée André, *Ici, Ventilateur!* (Paris: Calmann-Lévy, 1954), 99.

4. André, *Ici, Ventilateur!*, 100.

5. André, *Ici, Ventilateur!*, 100.

6. André, *Ici, Ventilateur!*, 101.

7. André, *Ici, Ventilateur!*, 101.

8. André, *Ici, Ventilateur!*, 101; André, *Madame le général*, 92; Fleurence, *Rotors dans le ciel d'Indochine*, 2:257.

9. André, *Madame le général*, 93.

10. André, *Ici, Ventilateur!*, 101.

11. André, *Ici, Ventilateur!*, 102; André, *Madame le général*, 92.

12. André, *Ici, Ventilateur!*, 102.

13. André, *Ici, Ventilateur!*, 103.

14. André, *Ici, Ventilateur!*, 104.

15. André, *Ici, Ventilateur!*, 104.

16. André, *Ici, Ventilateur!*, 104.

17. André, *Ici, Ventilateur!*, 108.

18. André, *Ici, Ventilateur!*, 108.

19. Fleurence, *Rotor dans le ciel d'Indochine*, 2:263.

20. André, *Ici, Ventilateur!*, 109.

21. André, *Ici, Ventilateur!*, 109.

22. André, *Madame le général*, 95.

23. André, *Ici, Ventilateur!*, 109.

24. André, *Ici, Ventilateur!*, 110.

25. André, *Madame le général*, 95.

26. André, *Ici, Ventilateur!*, 111.

27. André, *Ici, Ventilateur!*, 112.

28. André, *Ici, Ventilateur!*, 112.

29. André, *Ici, Ventilateur!*, 112.

30. André, *Ici, Ventilateur!*, 112.

31. André, *Ici, Ventilateur!*, 113.

32. André, *Ici, Ventilateur!*, 113.

33. André, *Ici, Ventilateur!*, 113.

34. André, *Madame le général*, 97.

CHAPTER 29

1. Fredrik Logevall, *Embers of War* (New York: Random House, 2012), 321.

2. Michel Fleurence, *Rotors dans le ciel d'Indochine*, vol. 2, *Les opérations, 1950–1954* (Château Vincennes, France: Service historique de la Défense, 2006), 258–59.

3. Valérie Edmée André, *Ici, Ventilateur!* (Paris: Calmann-Lévy, 1954), 121.

4. André, *Ici, Ventilateur!*, 121.

5. André, *Ici, Ventilateur!*, 121.

6. André, *Ici, Ventilateur!*, 118.

7. André, *Ici, Ventilateur!*, 122–23; Valérie Edmée André, *Madame le général* (Paris: Académique Perrin, 1988), 99–100.

8. André, *Ici, Ventilateur!*, 153.

9. André, *Ici, Ventilateur!*, 153.

10. André, *Ici, Ventilateur!*, 153.

11. André, *Ici, Ventilateur!*, 150.

12. André, *Ici, Ventilateur!*, 149.

13. André, *Ici, Ventilateur!*, 150.

14. André, *Ici, Ventilateur!*, 150.

15. André, *Ici, Ventilateur!*, 158.

16. André, *Ici, Ventilateur!*, 126.

17. André, *Ici, Ventilateur!*, 126.

18. André, *Ici, Ventilateur!*, 126.

19. André, *Ici, Ventilateur!*, 126.

20. André, *Ici, Ventilateur!*, 127.

21. André, *Ici, Ventilateur!*, 127.

CHAPTER 30

1. Valérie Edmée André, *Ici, Ventilateur!* (Paris: Calmann-Lévy, 1954), 129.

2. André, *Ici, Ventilateur!*, 129.

3. Valérie Edmée André, *Madame le général* (Paris: Académique Perrin, 1988), 101.

4. André, *Madame le général*, 101.

5. André, *Ici, Ventilateur!*, 130; André, *Madame le général*, 101.

6. André, *Ici, Ventilateur!*, 130; André, *Madame le général*, 130.

7. André, *Madame le général*, 102.

8. André, *Ici, Ventilateur!*, 130.

9. André, *Ici, Ventilateur!*, 131.

10. André, *Ici, Ventilateur!*, 131.

11. André, *Ici, Ventilateur!*, 132; André, *Madame le général*, 102.

12. André, *Ici, Ventilateur!*, 131; André, *Madame le général*, 102.

13. André, *Ici, Ventilateur!*, 132.

14. André, *Ici, Ventilateur!*, 132.

15. André, *Ici, Ventilateur!*, 132.

16. André, *Ici, Ventilateur!*, 133.

17. André, *Ici, Ventilateur!*, 133.

18. André, *Ici, Ventilateur!*, 133; André, *Madame le général*, 103.

19. André, *Ici, Ventilateur!*, 134.

20. André, *Ici, Ventilateur!*, 134.

21. André, *Ici, Ventilateur!*, 134; André, *Madame le général*, 103.

22. André, *Ici, Ventilateur!*, 134.

23. André, *Ici, Ventilateur!*, 135.

24. André, *Ici, Ventilateur!*, 136.

25. André, *Ici, Ventilateur!*, 137.

26. André, *Ici, Ventilateur!*, 137.

27. André, *Ici, Ventilateur!*, 137; André, *Madame le général*, 104.

28. André, *Ici, Ventilateur!*, 138; André, *Madame le général*, 104.

29. André, *Ici, Ventilateur!*, 138.

30. André, *Madame le général*, 104.

31. Uremia is a condition related to kidney failure, where high amounts of urea are present in the bloodstream. André, *Ici, Ventilateur!*, 138; André, *Madame le général*, 104.

CHAPTER 31

1. Valérie Edmée André, *Madame le général* (Paris: Académique Perrin, 1988), 105.

2. Valérie Edmée André, *Ici, Ventilateur!* (Paris: Calmann-Lévy, 1954), 139.

3. André, *Ici, Ventilateur!*, 139.

4. André, *Ici, Ventilateur!*, 139.

5. André, *Ici, Ventilateur!*, 140.

6. André, *Ici, Ventilateur!*, 140.

7. André, *Ici, Ventilateur!*, 140.

8. André, *Ici, Ventilateur!*, 141; André, *Madame le général*, 106.

9. André, *Ici, Ventilateur!*, 141; André, *Madame le général*, 106.

10. André, *Ici, Ventilateur!*, 141; André, *Madame le général*, 106.

11. André, *Ici, Ventilateur!*, 141; André, *Madame le général*, 106.

12. André, *Ici, Ventilateur!*, 141; André, *Madame le général*, 106.

13. André, *Ici, Ventilateur!*, 142; André, *Madame le général*, 107.

14. André, *Ici, Ventilateur!*, 143; André, *Madame le général*, 107; Michel Fleurence, *Rotors dans le ciel d'Indochne*, vol. 2, *Les opérations, 1950–1954* (Château Vincennes, France: Service historique de la Défense, 2006), 287.

15. André, *Ici, Ventilateur!*, 143; André, *Madame le général*, 107.

16. André, *Ici, Ventilateur!*, 143.

17. André, *Ici, Ventilateur!*, 144.

18. André, *Ici, Ventilateur!*, 144; André, *Madame le général*, 107.

19. André, *Ici, Ventilateur!*, 145; André, *Madame le général*, 108.

20. André, *Ici, Ventilateur!*, 145.

21. André, *Ici, Ventilateur!*, 145.

22. André, *Ici, Ventilateur!*, 146.

23. André, *Ici, Ventilateur!*, 146.

CHAPTER 32

1. Michel Fleurence, *Rotors dans le ciel d'Indochine*, vol. 2, *Les opérations, 1950–1954* (Château Vincennes, France: Service historique de la Défense, 2006), 258–62.

2. Valérie Edmée André, *Ici, Ventilateur!* (Paris: Calmann-Lévy, 1954), 148.

3. Valérie Edmée André, *Madame le général* (Paris: Académique Perrin, 1988), 108.

4. Fleurence, *Rotors dans le ciel d'Indochine*, 2:492–93.

5. André, *Ici, Ventilateur!*, 148; André, *Madame le général*, 108; Fleurence, *Rotors dans le ciel d'Indochine*, 2:492–93. Valérie André believed that Henri Bartier received thirteen palms to his third Croix de guerre. In actuality, Bartier was awarded eight palms by July 1952. Overall, however, he was awarded fifteen palms over the course of his entire career.

6. André, *Madame le général*, 109.

7. Letter to Valérie André from General Lionel-Max Chassin, July 29, 1952; quoted in André, *Madame le général*, 109–10.

8. André, *Madame le général*, 110.

9. André, *Madame le général*, 110.

10. André, *Madame le général*, 110–11; Claude Guigues, "Valérie André," *Samedi soir*, September 13, 1952.

11. André, *Madame le général*, 111. See also H. Carrignon, *Caravelle*, 1952.

12. André, *Madame le général*, 111.

13. André, *Madame le général*, 111.

14. Blake Clark, "The Adventures of Mademoiselle Helicopter," *Reader's Digest*, September 1953, 111; Blake Clark, "Mademoiselle Hélicoptère," *France ilustration*, August 1953, 37.

15. Clark, "Mademoiselle Helicopter," 114.

16. Clark, "Mademoiselle Helicopter," 114; Clark, "Mademoiselle Hélicoptère," 38.

17. Peter Kalischer, "Pretty Doctor in a Copter," *Collier's*, June 6, 1953, 66.

18. Kalischer, "Pretty Doctor in a Copter," 66.

19. Kalischer, "Pretty Doctor in a Copter," 66.

20. Kalischer, "Pretty Doctor in a Copter," 68.

21. Kalischer, "Pretty Doctor in a Copter," 67.

22. Kalischer, "Pretty Doctor in a Copter," 68.

23. André, *Ici, Ventilateur!*, 170.

24. "Valérie André: Regards sur l'Indochine," YouTube, n.d., https://www.you tube.com/watch?v=xhzKD9EyhhU&t=24s. See also Hugues Tertrais, *Regards sur l'Indochine* (Paris: Coédition Gallimard, 2015).

25. André, *Ici, Ventilateur!*, 170.

CHAPTER 33

1. Valérie Edmée André, *Ici, Ventilateur!* (Paris: Calmann-Lévy, 1954), 164.

2. André, *Ici, Ventilateur!*, 165.

3. André, *Ici, Ventilateur!*, 165.

4. André, *Ici, Ventilateur!*, 165.

5. André, *Ici, Ventilateur!*, 165.

6. André, *Ici, Ventilateur!*, 166.

7. André, *Ici, Ventilateur!*, 166.

8. André, *Ici, Ventilateur!*, 166.

9. Escadrille de liaisons aériennes (ELA) 52 and 53 both consisted of a helicopter and fixed-wing division within each group. The operations and maintenance of the helicopters was a separate function from the fixed-wing aircraft within each unit.

10. Valérie Edmée André, *Madame le général* (Paris: Académique Perrin, 1988), 118.

11. André, *Ici, Ventilateur!*, 173.

12. André, *Ici, Ventilateur!*, 174.

13. Michel Fleurence, *Rotors dans le ciel d'Indochine*, vol. 2, *Les opérations, 1950–1954* (Château Vincennes, France: Service historique de la Défense, 2006), 306.

14. Fleurence, *Rotors dans le ciel d'Indochine*, 2:306–9.

15. André, *Ici, Ventilateur!*, 206.

16. André, *Ici, Ventilateur!*, 174.

17. André, *Ici, Ventilateur!*, 190.

18. Peter Kalischer, "Pretty Doctor in a Copter," *Collier's*, June 6, 1953, 68.

19. André, *Ici, Ventilateur!*, 206.

20. André, *Ici, Ventilateur!*, 194, 205.

21. André, *Ici, Ventilateur!*, 207.

22. André, *Ici, Ventilateur!*, 207.

23. André, *Ici, Ventilateur!*, 208.

24. André, *Ici, Ventilateur!*, 208.

25. André, *Ici, Ventilateur!*, 210.

26. André, *Ici, Ventilateur!*, 210.

27. André, *Ici, Ventilateur!*, 211.

28. André, *Ici, Ventilateur!*, 212.

29. André, *Ici, Ventilateur!*, 214–15.

30. André, *Ici, Ventilateur!*, 215.

31. André, *Ici, Ventilateur!*, 215.

32. André, *Ici, Ventilateur!*, 216.

33. André, *Ici, Ventilateur!*, 216.

34. André, *Ici, Ventilateur!*, 217.

35. André, *Ici, Ventilateur!*, 217.

36. André, *Ici, Ventilateur!*, 217.

37. André, *Ici, Ventilateur!*, 218.

38. André, *Ici, Ventilateur!*, 218.

39. André, *Ici, Ventilateur!*, 218.

40. André, *Ici, Ventilateur!*, 219.

CHAPTER 34

1. Valérie Edmée André, *Ici, Ventilateur!* (Paris: Calmann-Lévy, 1954), 221.

2. Valérie Edmée André, *Madame le général* (Paris: Académique Perrin, 1988), 221–22.

3. André, *Madame le général*, 138.

4. André, *Madame le général*, 138.

5. André, *Madame le général*, 138.

6. André, *Ici, Ventilateur!*, 223.

7. André, *Ici, Ventilateur!*, 223.

8. André, *Ici, Ventilateur!*, 225; André, *Madame le général*, 139.

CHAPTER 35

1. Paul Grauwin, *Doctor at Dien-Bien-Phu* (New York: John Day, 1955), 76.

2. Grauwin, *Doctor at Dien-Bien-Phu*, 84.

3. Grauwin, *Doctor at Dien-Bien-Phu*, 85–86.

4. "Chapitre III: Mourir à la guerre," Souvenir Français66 Mémorial, n.d., https://sites.google.com/site/souvenirfrancais66memorial/memorial-dedie-aux -morts-pour-la-france/chapitre-iii-mourir-a-la-guerre.

5. Grauwin, *Doctor at Dien-Bien-Phu*, 56–57.

6. Michel Fleurence, *Rotors dans le ciel d'Indochine*, vol. 1, *Les hommes, 1950–1997* (Château Vincennes, France: Service historique de la Défense, 2003), 47.

7. Michel Fleurence, *Rotors dans le ciel d'Indochine*, vol. 2, *Les opérations, 1950–1954* (Château Vincennes, France: Service historique de la Défense, 2006), 612.

8. Florent Bonnefoi, "Henri Bartier, ce héros oublié de la guerre d'Indochine," *La Provence*, June 17, 2018, https://www.laprovence.com/article/edition-aix-pays -daix/5024156/henri-bartier-ce-heros-oublie-de-la-guerre-dindochine.html.

9. Grauwin, *Doctor at Dien-Bien-Phu*, 110–11.

10. Fleurence, *Rotors dans le ciel d'Indochine*, 2:477.

11. Ted Morgan, *Valley of Death: The Tragedy at Dien Bien Phu That Led America into the Vietnam War* (New York: Random House, 2010), 141.

12. Grauwin, *Doctor at Dien-Bien-Phu*, 111.

13. Bonnefoi, "Henri Bartier."

14. Bonnefoi, "Henri Bartier."

15. Geoffrey Norman, "What the French Lost at Dien Bien Phu," *Military History*, June 2010.

16. Fredrik Logevall, *Embers of War* (New York: Random House, 2012), 535.

17. Pierre Vermeren, *Le choc des décolonisations: De la guerre d'Algérie aux printemps arabes* (Paris: Éditions Odile Jacob, 2015), 16.

18. Vietnamese government estimate. "Chuyên đề 4," Live.com, n.d., https:// view.officeapps.live.com/op/view.aspx?src=http%3A%2F%2Fdatafile.chinhsa chquandoi.gov.vn%2FQu%25E1%25BA%25A3n%2520l%25C3%25BD%2 520ch%25E1%25BB%2589%2520%25C4%2591%25E1%25BA%25A1o% 2FChuy%25C3%25AAn%2520%25C4%2591%25E1%25BB%2581%25204 .doc&wdOrigin=BROWSELINK.

19. World Peace Foundation, "Mass Atrocity Endings: Indochina: First Indochina War," Tufts, August 7, 2015, https://sites.tufts.edu/atrocityendings/2015/08/07/indo china-1st-indochina-war/#_ednref28.

20. World Peace Foundation, "Mass Atrocity Endings."

CHAPTER 36

1. Valérie Edmée André, *Madame le général* (Paris: Académique Perrin, 1988), 144.

2. André, *Madame le général*, 144.

3. André, *Madame le général*, 144.

4. André, *Madame le général*, 144.

5. André, *Madame le général*, 145.

6. André, *Madame le général*, 145.

7. André, *Madame le général*, 143.

8. Three of the wounded died en route to hospitals.

9. André, *Madame le général*, 145.

10. André, *Madame le général*, 145.

11. André, *Madame le général*, 145.

12. André, *Madame le général*, 146.

13. André, *Madame le général*, 145.

14. André, *Madame le général*, 146.

15. André, *Madame le général*, 147.

16. André, *Madame le général*, 147.

17. Fredrik Logevall, *Embers of War* (New York: Random House, 2012), 535.

18. Philippe Boulay, "Raymond Fumat: Histoire d'un pilote oublié," Aerostories, 2002, aerostories.free.fr/giravia/personages/boulay/fumat.

19. "Henri Bartier: L'Indochine fait partie de moi," Association hélicoptères air, accessed March 13, 2022, http://www.aha-helico-air.asso.fr/henri_bartier.htm.

20. Joël-François Dumont, "Interview with Gen. Michel Fleurence and Col. Betram Sansu," European Security, August 15, 2012, https://european--security-com. translate.goog/combattre-et-sauver-histoire-des-helicopteres-de-larmee-de-lair/?_x_tr_sl=fr&_x_tr_tl=en&_x_tr_hl=en&_x_tr_pto=sc.

21. Florent Bonnefoi, "Henri Bartier, ce hroes oublié de le guerre d'Indochine," *La Provence*, June 17, 2018, https://www.laprovence.com/article/edition-aix-pays-daix/5024156/henri-bartier-ce-heros-oublie-de-la-guerre-dindochine.html.

22. Jean Pierre Simon, *Les aviateurs dans l'guerre d'Indochine—1945–1957* (Paris: Éditions du Grenadier/Anovi, 2016), 189.

23. Dumont, "Interview with Gen. Michel Fleurence and Col. Betram Sansu."

24. "Ventilateurs: Helicopters in Indochina (1950–54)," Indo 1945–1954, n.d., http://indochine54.free.fr/cefeo/helicopt.html. The breakdown of all aircraft used in medical rescue included two Hiller UH-12/360s, seven Hiller H-23As, six Hiller H-23Bs, eleven Westland-Sikorsky WS-51s, and eighteen Sikorsky H-19As.

25. Michel Fleurence, *Rotors dans le ciel d'Indochine*, vol. 3, *Le livre d'or, 1950–1997* (Château Vincennes, France: Service historique de la Défense, 2010), 459–61.

26. As quoted in Marie-Catherine Villatoux, "Pilotes d'hélicoptères de l'armée de l'Air en guerre d'Algérie," Centre de recherche de l'école de l'air, October 2002, 6, https://crea.ecole-air-espace.fr/wp-content/uploads/2019/05/Pilotes_h%C3%A9 licopteres.pdf.

27. Villatoux, "Pilotes d'hélicoptères," 6.

28. André, *Madame le général*, 152.

29. André, *Madame le général*, 152.

30. Eric Vola, "Shipwrecked on Mont-Blanc: The Vincendon and Henry Tragedy," Summit Post, June 2017, https://www.summitpost.org/shipwrecked-on-mont -blanc-the-vincendon-and-henry-tragedy/1001404.

31. André, *Madame le général*, 152.

32. André, *Madame le général*, 154.

33. André, *Madame le général*, 154.

34. André, *Madame le général*, 154. Colonel Felix Brunet died from a heart attack on December 5, 1959, in Algeria. His career in the French air force totaled more than ten thousand hours of flight time, beginning as a pilot with the Free French Army during World War II—where he shot down two German aircraft—as well as service in Indochina and Algeria. He flew nearly twenty-three hundred combat missions, was wounded four times, and received twenty-six citations for his service.

35. André, *Madame le général*, 155.

36. André, *Madame le général*, 156.

37. André, *Madame le général*, 156.

CHAPTER 37

1. Valérie Edmée André, *Madame le général* (Paris: Académique Perrin, 1988), 154.

2. André, *Madame le général*, 157.

3. André, *Madame le général*, 158.

4. André, *Madame le général*, 158.

5. Gérard Finaltéri, "Le piège blanc" [The white trap], Association hélicoptères air, n.d., http://www.aha-helico-air.asso.fr/veh.htm.

6. Marie-Catherine Villatoux, "Pilotes d'hélicoptères de l'armée de l'air en guerre d'Algérie," Centre de recherche de l'école de l'air, October 2002, 9, https:// crea.ecole-air-espace.fr/wp-content/uploads/2019/05/Pilotes_h%C3%A9licopteres .pdf.

7. Villatoux, "Pilotes d'hélicoptères," 7.

8. André, *Madame le général*, 165.

9. André, *Madame le général*, 162.

10. André, *Madame le général*, 166.

11. André, *Madame le général*, 163.

12. André, *Madame le général*, 163.

13. André, *Madame le général*, 160.

14. Aviation légère de l'armée de terre (ALAT; Army Light Aviation).

15. André, *Madame le général*, 167–68.

16. André, *Madame le général*, 168.

17. André, *Madame le général*, 168.

18. André, *Madame le général*, 168.

19. Georges Agrissais (1927–2017). "Adieu Georges," Association nationale des officiers de reserve de l'armée de l'air, n.d., http://resair460.free.fr/adieu_georges _txt.pdf.

20. André, *Madame le général*, 177. Mission date: January 23, 1960.

21. André, *Madame le général*, 178.

22. André, *Madame le général*, 178.

23. André, *Madame le général*, 178.

24. André, *Madame le général*, 178.

25. André, *Madame le général*, 170.

26. André, *Madame le général*, 169.

27. André, *Madame le général*, 170.

28. André, *Madame le général*, 170.

29. André, *Madame le général*, 188–90.

30. General Maurice Challe, radio address, Algiers, April 22, 1961.

31. André, *Madame le général*, 189.

32. André, *Madame le général*, 189.

33. André, *Madame le général*, 190.

34. André, *Madame le général*, 158–59.

35. André, *Madame le général*, 187.

36. André, *Madame le général*, 190.

37. Charles de Gaulle, "Discours du président de la France à la suite du putsch de quatre généraux en Algerie," radio address, April 23, 1961, Perspective monde, June 7, 2022, https://perspective.usherbrooke.ca/bilan/servlet/BMDictionnaire?iddi ctionnaire=1766.

38. André, *Madame le général*, 191.

39. André, *Madame le général*, 191.

40. André, *Madame le général*, 191.

41. Jean-Louis Dufour, "Avril 1961: Le putsch d'Alger," *Historia*, no. 652 (January 4, 2001): 40–44; quoted in Miguel Andrés Cruz, "The Implications of ICT in Surviving a Coup d'État for a Popular Regime" (Honors thesis, Baylor University, May 2019), 22, https://baylor-ir.tdl.org/bitstream/handle/2104/10586/andres_cruz _honorsthesis.pdf?sequence=1.

42. André, *Madame le général*, 193.

43. André, *Madame le général*, 195.

44. André, *Madame le général*, 196.

EPILOGUE

1. André, *Madame le général* (Paris: Académique Perrin, 1988), 199.

2. André, *Madame le général*, 199.

3. André, *Madame le général*, 200.

4. Dominique Blanchard, "Colonel Santini," *Air actualités*, May 1994, 51.

5. Christine Garnier, "Valérie André: Le ciel d'abord" [Valérie André: The sky first], *Revue des deux mondes*, April 1, 1970, 177.

6. Jean-Marie Poutelle, "Issy-les-Moulineaux, l'héliport," Hélico-Fascination, August 27, 2008, http://www.helico-fascination.com/recits/jean-marie-potelle/article /issy-les-moulineaux-l-heliport.

7. Garnier, "Valérie André," 177.

8. André, *Madame le général*, 200.

9. André, *Madame le général*, 207.

10. CERMA: Centre d'enseignement et de recherche de médecine aéros.

11. André, *Madame le général*, 207.

12. André, *Madame le général*, 207.

13. André, *Madame le général*, 207.

14. André, *Madame le général*, 207.

15. André, *Madame le général*, 208.

16. André, *Madame le général*, 208.

17. André, *Madame le général*, 225.

18. André, *Madame le général*, 229.

19. André, *Madame le général*, 231.

20. André, *Madame le général*, 231–32.

21. André, *Madame le général*, 232.

22. Michel Fleurence, *Rotors dans le ciel d'Indochine*, vol. 3, *Le livre d'or, 1950–1997* (Château Vincennes, France: Service historique de la Défense, 2010), 253.

23. Centre d'instruction des équipages d'hélicoptères 341, Colonel Alexis Santini.

24. André, *Madame le général*, 236. Valérie André accumulated a total of thirty-two hundred flight hours in the course of her military career.

25. Garnier, "Valérie André," 174.

26. André, *Madame le général*, 237.

27. André, *Madame le général*, 237.

28. André, *Madame le général*, 237.

29. André, *Madame le général*, 238.

30. André, *Madame le général*, 239.

31. André, *Madame le général*, 240. Statistics provided were as of 1980.

32. "Summary of the National Reports of NATO Member and Partner Nations to the NATO Committee on Gender Perspectives," North Atlantic Treaty Organization, 2018, 149–55, https://www.nato.int/nato_static_fl2014/assets/pdf/2020/7/pdf/200713-2018-Summary-NR-to-NCGP.pdf. The breakdown of women serving in the French military as of 2018 is as follows: 11 percent in the army, 16 percent in the navy, 28 percent in the air force, and 58 percent in the medical corps.

33. André, *Madame le général*, 243.

34. Blanchard, "Colonel Santini," 51.

35. André, *Madame le général*, 206.

Bibliography

BOOKS

Ahnstrom, D. N. *The Complete Book of Helicopters*. New York: World, 1968.

André, Valérie Edmée. *Ici, Ventilateur!* Paris: Calmann-Lévy, 1954.

————. *Madame le général*. Paris: Académique Perrin, 1988.

————. *La pathologie du parachutisme*. Paris: R. Foulon, 1948.

Barros, Andrew, and Martin Thomas, eds. *The Civilianization of War: The Changing Civil-Military Divide, 1914–2014*. New York: Cambridge University Press, 2018.

Beevor, Anthony. *D-Day, the Battle for Normandy*. New York: Viking, 2009.

Bodard, Lucien. *The Quicksand War: Prelude to Vietnam*. Boston: Little, Brown, 1967.

Bristow, Alan, with Patrick Malone. *Alan Bristow: Helicopter Pioneer*. Barnsley, UK: Pen & Sword, 2010.

Cameron, Allan W., ed. *Viet-Nam Crisis: A Documentary History*. Vol. 1, *1940–1956*. Ithaca, NY: Cornell University Press, 1971.

Clayton, Anthony. *Three Marshals of France: Leadership after Trauma*. London: Brassey's, 1992.

Collins, Larry, and Dominique Lapierre. *Is Paris Burning?* New York: Simon & Schuster, 1965. Reprint, New York: Grand Central, 1991. Page references are to the 1991 edition.

Dalloz, Jacques. *Dictionnaire de la guerre d'Indochine, 1945–1954*. Paris: Armand Colin, 2001.

————. *The War in Indo-China 1945–1954*. Dublin, Ireland: Gill & McMillan, 1990.

Dunn, Peter M. *The First Vietnam War*. New York: St. Martin's, 1985.

Fall, Bernard. *Street without Joy*. Mechanicsburg, PA: Stackpole Books, 1961.

Fay, John. *The Helicopter: History, Piloting and How It Flies*. New York: Hippocrene Books, 1976.

Ferrari, Pierre, and Jacques M. Vernet. *Une guerre sans fin: Indochine 1945–1954.* Paris: Charles-Lavauzelle, 1984.

Ferry, Vital. *Croix de Lorraine et Croix du sud, 1940–1942.* Paris: Éditions du Gerfaut, 2005.

Fleurence, Michel. *Rotors dans le ciel d'Indochine.* Vol. 1, *Les hommes, 1950–1997.* Château Vincennes, France: Service historique de la Défense, 2003.

———. *Rotors dans le ciel d'Indochine.* Vol. 2, *Les opérations, 1950–1954.* Château Vincennes, France: Service historique de la Défense, 2006.

———. *Rotors dans le ciel d'Indochine.* Vol. 3, *Le livre d'or, 1950–1997.* Château Vincennes, France: Service historique de la Défense, 2010.

Gordon, Bertram M., ed. *Historical Dictionary of World War II France: The Occupation, Vichy, and the Resistance, 1938–1946.* Westport, CT: Greenwood, 1998.

Grauwin, Paul. *Doctor at Dien-Bien-Phu.* New York: John Day, 1955.

Irving, R. E. M. *The First Indochina War.* London: Croom Helm, 1975.

Karnow, Stanley. *Vietnam: A History.* New York: Viking, 1983.

Kedward, Rod. *France and the French: A Modern History.* New York: Overlook, 2005.

Lacouture, Jean. *De Gaulle, the Rebel 1890–1944.* New York: Norton, 1990.

Lartéguy, Jean. *Le guerre nue.* Paris: Stock, 1976.

Lattre, Simonne de. *Mon mari, 1926–1945.* Paris: Presses de la cité, 1972.

———. *Mon mari, 1945–1952.* Paris: Presses de la cité, 1972.

Lattre de Tassigny, Jean de. *The History of the French First Army.* Translated by Malcolm Barnes. London: Allen & Unwin, 1952.

Liebler, A. J., comp. *The Republic of Silence.* New York: Harcourt Brace, 1947.

Livet, Georges, and Francis Rapp, eds. *Histoire de Strasbourg des origines à nos jours.* Vol. 4. Strasbourg, France: Éditions des dernières nouvelles de Strasbourg, 1992.

Logevall, Fredrik. *Embers of War.* New York: Random House, 2012.

Morgan, Ted. *Valley of Death: The Tragedy at Dien Bien Phu That Led America into the Vietnam War.* New York: Random House, 2010.

Navarre, Henri. *Agonie de l'Indochine 1953–1954.* Paris: Librairie Plon, 1956.

Pellissier, Pierre. *De Lattre.* Paris: Librairie académique Perrin, 1998.

Renaud, Patrick-Charles. *Aviateurs en Indochine.* Paris: Éditions Grancher, 2003.

Roosevelt, Elliott. *As He Saw It.* New York: Duell, Sloan and Pearce, 1946.

Sainteny, Jean. *Ho Chi Minh and His Vietnam.* Chicago: Cowles, 1972.

Scales, Robert H. *Firepower in Limited War.* Novato, CA: Presidio, 1997.

Simon, Jean Pierre. *Les aviateurs dans l'guerre d'Indochine—1945–1957.* Paris: Éditions du Grenadier/Anovi, 2016.

Tertrais, Hugues. *Regards sur l'Indochine.* Paris: Coédition Gallimard, 2015.

Teston, Eugene, and Maurice Percheron. *L'Indochine moderne.* Paris: Librairie de France, 1932.

Tucker, Spencer C. *Vietnam*. Louisville: University of Kentucky Press, 1999.

Vaisse, Maurice. *L'armée française dans la guerre d'Indochine (1946–54)*. Château de Vincennes, France: Éditions complexe, 2000.

Vermeren, Pierre. *Le choc des décolonisations: De la guerre d'Algérie aux printemps arabes*. Paris: Éditions Odile Jacob, 2015.

Waddell, William McFall, II. "In the Year of the Tiger: The War for Cochinchina, 1945–1951." Dissertation, Ohio State University, 2014.

Whiting, Charles. *The Home Front: Germany*. New York: Time-Life, 1982.

Young, Arthur. *The Bell Notes: A Journey from Physics to Metaphysics*. New York: Delacorte, 1979.

Young, Warren. *The Helicopters*. Alexandria, VA: Time-Life, 1982.

PERIODICALS, NEWSPAPERS, AND JOURNALS

Aydin, Seckin, Baris Kucukyuruk, Bashar Abuzayed, Sabri Aydin, and Galip Zinhi Sanus. "Cranioplasty: Review of Materials and Techniques." *Journal of Neuroscience in Rural Practice* 2 (July–December 2011): 162–67.

Balasse, Jean Phillipe. "L'essor des rotors" [The rise of the rotors]. *Air actualités*, May 1994, 48–49.

Blanchard, Dominique. "Colonel Santini." *Air actualités*, May 1994, 50–51.

———. "General Valérie André." *Air actualités*, May 1994, 53–55.

Bonnefoi, Florent. "Henri Bartier, ce héros oublié de la guerre d'Indochine." *La Provence*, June 17, 2018. https://www.laprovence.com/article/edition-aix-pays-daix/5024156/henri-bartier-ce-heros-oublie-de-la-guerre-dindochine.html.

Boris, Henri. "En cinquante heures vous serez pilote d'hélicoptère" [In fifty hours you will be a helicopter pilot]. *Paris illustration*, July 1950, 59–62.

Clark, Blake. "The Adventures of Mademoiselle Helicopter." *Reader's Digest*, September 1953, 111–14.

———. "Mademoiselle Hélicoptère." *France illustration*, August 1953, 37–39.

Cunnier, Stephane. "Henri Bartier." *Air actualités*, May 1994, 56–58.

Garnier, Christine. "Valérie André: Le ciel d'abord" [Valérie André: The sky first]. *Revue des deux mondes*, April 1, 1970, 174–79.

Gold, Jacob, and Nguon Savan. "Turning Pepper into 'Black Gold.'" *Phnom Penh Post*, October 7, 2009.

Goscha, Christopher. "Colonial Hanoi and Saigon at War: Social Dynamics of the Viet Minh's Underground City, 1945–1954." *War in History*, April 2013, 222–50.

Guigues, Claude. "Valérie André." *Samedi soir*, September 13, 1952.

Johnson, Douglas. "Avis de décès: Général Maurice Redon." *Indépendant* (London), June 23, 2000.

Kalischer, Peter. "Pretty Doctor in a Copter." *Collier's*, June 6, 1953, 66–69.

Karnow, Stanley. "Giap Remembers." *New York Times Magazine*, June 24, 1990, sec. 6, 8.

Marcelon, Daniel. "Afin de defier, Francis Varcin: L'oubli, mort pour la France en Indochine." *Air ANSONA* 74, no. 3 (1998): 17–18.

Norman, Geoffrey. "What the French Lost at Dien Bien Phu." *Military History*, June 2010.

Wallace, Peter, and Arnold M. Meirowsky. "Repair of Dural Defect by Graft: An Analysis of 540 Penetrating Wounds Incurred in the Korean War." *Annals of Surgery*, February 15, 1960, 174–80.

WEB SOURCES

"Adieu Georges." Association nationale des officiers de reserve de l'armée de l'air, n.d. http://resair460.free.fr/adieu_georges_txt.pdf.

Albertson, Mark. "The Korean War—the Helicopter." *Army Aviation Magazine*, n.d. www.armyaviationmagazine.com/index.php/history/not-so-current-2/1884 -the-korean-war-the-helicopter.

Boulay, Philippe. "Raymond Fumat: Histoire d'un pilote oublié." Aerostories, 2002. aerostories.free.fr/giravia/personnages/boulay/fumat.

Bromberger, Jacqueline, et al. "October 1941—Resistance Starts in Clermont-Ferrand." In *The Strasbourg French University Is Transferred to Clermont-Ferrand*. Paris: Délégation à la mémoire et à l'information historique du Ministère des anciens combattants et victimes de guerre, 1993. http://mapage.noos.fr /jibro/resistance-universitaire/en/Chapitre_Premier_partie2.html.

"Chapitre III: Mourir à la guerre." Souvenir Français66 Mémorial, n.d. https://sites .google.com/site/souvenirfrancais66memorial/memorial-dedie-aux-morts-pour -la-france/chapitre-iii-mourir-a-la-guerre.

"Chuyên đề 4." Live.com, n.d. https://view.officeapps.live.com/op/view.aspx?src =http%3A%2F%2Fdatafile.chinhsachquandoi.gov.vn%2FQu%25E1%25BA%25 A3n%25201%25C3%25BD%2520ch%25E1%25BB%2589%2520%25C4%2591 %25E1%25BA%25A1o%2FChuy%25C3%25AAn%2520%25C4%2591%25E1 %25BB%2581%25204.doc&wdOrigin=BROWSELINK.

"Commemoration de la rafle de l'Université de Strasbourg repliée à Clermont-Ferrand (1943) 70e anniversaire, 1943–2013." Université de Strasbourg, 2013. https://www.unistra.fr.

"La cotonnière du Tonkin et l'usine de Nam Dinh." Belle Indochine, accessed March 13, 2022. http://belleindochine.free.fr/CotonniereDuTonkin.htm.

Cruz, Miguel Andrés. "The Implications of ICT in Surviving a Coup d'État for a Popular Regime." Honors thesis, Baylor University, May 2019. https://baylor-ir .tdl.org/bitstream/handle/2104/10586/andres_cruz_honorsthesis.pdf?sequence=1.

De Gaulle, Charles. "Discours du président de la France à la suite du putsch de quatre généraux en Algerie." Radio address, April 23, 1961. Perspective monde, June 7, 2022, https://perspective.usherbrooke.ca/bilan/servlet/BMDictionnaire?id dictionnaire=1766.

Dumont, Joël-François. "Interview with Gen. Michel Fleurence and Col. Betram Sansu." European Security, August 15, 2012. https://european--security -com.translate.goog/combattre-et-sauver-histoire-des-helicopteres-de-larmee-de -lair/?_x_tr_sl=fr&_x_tr_tl=en&_x_tr_hl=en&_x_tr_pto=sc.

Finaltéri, Gérard. "Le piège blanc" [The white trap]. Association hélicoptères air, n.d. http://www.aha-helico-air.asso.fr/veh.htm.

Garric, Henri, and Antoine Allibert. "Henri Bartier—ou le droit d'ingérence . . . sur le champ de bataille." Vétérans de Provence, 2009. http://www.veterans.fr /images/docs-site/Indochine/les-hommes/BARTIER-Henri.pdf.

"Henri Bartier: L'Indochine fait partie de moi." Association hélicoptères air, accessed March 13, 2022. http://www.aha-helico-air.asso.fr/henri_bartier.htm.

Landenburg, Thomas. "The French in Indochina." Digital History, 2007. http:// www.digitalhistory.uh.edu/teachers/lesson_plans/pdfs/unit12_1.pdf.

Panthou, Eric. "PRAT Henri, Albert, Eugène [pseudonyme dans la résistance: Sinfer 571]." Maitron, last updated February 20, 2022. https://maitron.fr/spip .php?article221611.

Poutelle, Jean-Marie. "Issy-les-Moulineaux, l'héliport." Hélico-Fascination, August 27, 2008. http://www.helico-fascination.com/recits/jean-marie-potelle/article /issy-les-moulineaux-l-heliport.

"Roosevelt and Churchill on Colonial Questions, August 10, 1941." Mount Holyoke College, n.d. Accessed June 6, 2022. https://www.mtholyoke.edu/acad/intrel /fdrwc.htm.

"SNCAN (Nord) 1700 'Norélik' and 1710 Helicopters." Secret Projects, accessed March 13, 2022. http://www.secretprojects.co.uk/forum/index.php/topic,15184.0 /nowap.html?PHPSESSID=krrstdapiib3uns9i5pbb84mo1.

"Summary of the National Reports of NATO Member and Partner Nations to the NATO Committee on Gender Perspectives." North Atlantic Treaty Organization, 2018. https://www.nato.int/nato_static_fl2014/assets/pdf/2020/7/pdf/200713 -2018-Summary-NR-to-NCGP.pdf.

Talbot, Gaélle. "Commemoration de la rafle du 25 novembre 1943: À l'Université de Strasbourg exilée à Clermont-Ferrand." Université de Strasbourg, November 25, 2014. https://www.unistra.fr/uploads/media/DP_comemoration _25nov1943_181114.pdf.

"Ventilateurs: Helicopters in Indochina (1950–54)." Indo 1945–1954, n.d. http:// indochine54.free.fr/cefeo/helicopt.html.

Vezin, Alain. "Un nuit dans la Plaine des Joncs." Histoires de aviateurs, 2009. http://aviateurs.e-monsite.com/pages/1946-et-annees-suivantes/une-nuit-dans-la -plaine-des-joncs.html.

Villatoux, Marie-Catherine. "Pilotes d'hélicoptères de l'armée de l'air en guerre d'Algérie." Centre de recherche de l'école de l'air, October 2002. https://crea.ecole -air-espace.fr/wp-content/uploads/2019/05/Pilotes_h%C3%A9licopteres.pdf.

Vola, Eric. "Shipwrecked on Mont-Blanc: The Vincendon and Henry Tragedy." Summit Post, June 2017. https://www.summitpost.org/shipwrecked-on-mont-blanc -the-vincendon-and-henry-tragedy/1001404.

World Peace Foundation. "Mass Atrocity Endings: Indochina: First Indochina War." Tufts, August 7, 2015. https://sites.tufts.edu/atrocityendings/2015/08/07 /indochina-1st-indochina-war/#_ednref28.

VIDEOS

"Valérie André: Regards sur l'Indochine." YouTube, n.d. https://www.youtube.com /watch?v=xhzKD9EyhhU&t=24s.

Index